Kidnapping and Violence

Stephen Morewitz

Kidnapping and Violence

New Research and Clinical Perspectives

Springer

Stephen Morewitz
California State University, East Bay
San Francisco, CA, USA

ISBN 978-1-4939-2116-4 ISBN 978-1-4939-2117-1 (eBook)
https://doi.org/10.1007/978-1-4939-2117-1

This Springer imprint is published by the registered company Springer Science+Business Media, LLC part of Springer Nature.
The registered company address is: 233 Spring Street, New York, NY 10013, U.S.A.

*To the loving memory of my mother,
Ruth August Morewitz, my father,
Burt M. Morewitz, and my uncle,
Dr. Harry A. Morewitz*

Preface

The practice of abducting individuals has existed since the dawn of civilization. For example, in ancient Rome and Greece, persons were captured during wars and then used as slaves. The term, kidnapping, comes from the word, kid, meaning child and nap (nab) meaning snatch (*Wikipedia*, Kidnapping, no date). This term dates back to 1673 and was originally employed to describe the practice of stealing children for use as servants or laborers in the American colonies. The term, abduction, has also been used to denote this phenomenon since 1768. In the nineteenth century, the term, shanghaiing was employed to show how men were kidnapped in order to serve as unwilling labor on board merchant ships, where the ship's captain was "king." At the same time, the term, "press ganging," was used to describe the conscription of civilians into the military, especially the British Navy, beginning in 1664 and continuing until the early nineteenth century (Wikipedia, Impressment, no date).

Kidnapping or abduction now refers to any illegal capture or detention of an individual or people against their will, regardless of age. It is frequently committed to obtain a ransom or to achieve other criminal goals, such as rape, slavery, and sex trafficking.

Since the "Lindbergh kidnapping" in 1932, highly publicized kidnappings and homicides have led to greater public recognition of the phenomenon as a social problem. Kidnapping has evolved into a number of different types, including infant and child abductions, political kidnappings, sex trafficking, bride abductions, and international and domestic parental (or family) kidnappings. In many instances, individuals are missing and are presumed to be the victims of foul play, including kidnapping and homicide.

With the increased public awareness of kidnapping as a social problem have come new laws and community/organizational responses to cope with this complex problem. For example, the Amber Alert system was initiated to improve the speed at which community residents and law enforcement personnel respond to kidnappings in the community.

This book analyzes kidnapping in three general ways. First, kidnapping, including the threat of kidnapping, reflects a breakdown in the mechanisms of social control in society. At the level of interpersonal relations, the weakening of social control processes allows kidnappers to function in different situations and for diverse motives. This book will address such questions as: What are the conditions under which kidnappers can evade social control by abducting or threatening to abduct another person? What factors trigger the response of social control mechanisms to kidnappers or attempted kidnappers? How effective are the institutional responses to abductions?

Second, governments and paramilitary and terrorist groups also employ kidnappings as part of their foreign and domestic policy. This analysis will evaluate why and under what conditions governments, paramilitary, and terrorist groups decide to abduct individuals and groups. Emphasis will be on how individuals, groups, and governments employ abductions to achieve their social, cultural, religious, and political objectives.

Third, certain cultural traditions foster abductions. This analysis will examine how cultural traditions in different societies emerge to foster behaviors such as bride abductions. Moreover, this book assesses the extent to which social change modifies these cultural patterns.

In several of the chapters, new research findings from the following five databases are used: (1) Stalking and Violence Project (SVP); (2) Missing Persons Project (MMP); (3) Ransom Kidnappings Project (RKP); (4) Aircraft Hijackings Project (AHP); and (5) Kidnapping Hoaxes Project (KHP). Results from these research projects are used to explore the characteristics of victims and suspects, the patterns of abductions, and the process of regulating suspects.

In Chap. 1, new patterns of partner kidnapping, a little known social phenomenon, are investigated.

Chapter 2 discusses bride abduction and focuses on the ways in which the cultural traditions of bride kidnapping become normative.

In Chap. 3, the risk factors for family abductions in the United States are presented. This chapter also analyzes legal responses to family abductions and their psychosocial impact on children and their families.

International family kidnappings are discussed in Chap. 4. This analysis focuses on the risk factors for international family abductions and legal responses to this form of abduction.

The remaining ten chapters include new research on different forms of kidnappings, including ransom kidnapping and aircraft hijacking. In addition, this book presents data on kidnapping hoaxes, a little known phenomenon.

San Francisco, CA, USA Stephen Morewitz

Acknowledgements I would like to thank Mrs. Myra Kalkin Morewitz and the late Dr. Harry A. Morewitz for their advice and editorial support. I also want to thank Sharon Panulla, Executive Psychology Editor at Springer, and Sylvana Ruggirello, Psychology Assistant Editor at Springer, who have been supportive as well as thorough and thoughtful.

Contents

About the Author

Dr. Stephen Morewitz is President of the consulting firm, Stephen Morewitz, Ph.D., and Associates, San Francisco and Tarzana, CA, which was founded in 1988. He is the Founder and President of the Forensic Social Sciences Association. He is a Lecturer in the Department of Justice Studies and Department of Sociology and Interdisciplinary Social Sciences, San Jose State University and is a Lecturer in the Department of Health Sciences, California State University, East Bay. Dr. Morewitz has been on the faculty or staffs of Michael Reese Hospital and Medical Center, University of Illinois at Chicago, College of Medicine and School of Public Health, DePaul University, and the California School of Podiatric Medicine. Dr. Morewitz, a triple-certified forensic social scientist, is the author of twelve books, one forthcoming book, and many other publications. His books include the award-winning *Handbook of Forensic Sociology and Psychology* (Co-Edited with Dr. Mark L. Goldstein) (New York: Springer, 2014), the award-winning *Death Threats. New Research and Clinical Perspectives* (New York: Springer Science+Business Media, LLC, 2008), the award-winning, *Domestic Violence and Maternal and Child Health* (New York: Kluwer Academic/Plenum Publishers/Springer Science+Business Media, LLC, 2004), the award-winning *Stalking and Violence. New Patterns of Trauma and Obsession* (New York: Kluwer Academic/Plenum Publishers/Springer Science+Business Media, LLC, 2003), and *Sexual Harassment and Social Change in American Society* (Bethesda, MD: Austin & Winfield, Rowman and Littlefield Publishing Group, 1996). In 2010, he was named San Jose State University Scholar Presenter for his book, *Death Threats. New Research and Clinical Perspectives* (New York: Springer Science+Business Media, LLC, 2008).

Chapter 1
Partner Abduction and Hostage-Taking

Persons may kidnap their ex-partner, partner, and family members, resulting frequently in police action (Booth et al. 2010; Lipsedge 2004; Fitzgerald and People 2006). In certain situations, ex-partner or partners may take their victim hostage. Hostage-taking in relationships can take the form of a hostage barricade incident in which individuals take hostages and the police besiege the location (Yokota et al. 2004; Bartol 2002). In another type of incident, known as the simple siege, the suspects barricade themselves without taking any hostages.

Perpetrators may abduct their former or current partners and wives and use them for other instrumental purposes, e.g., to force them to withdraw money from bank accounts. Offenders may carefully plan these instrumental kidnappings.

In contrast, in a hostage barricade crisis, suspects kidnap partners or ex-partners for expressive reasons. In these latter cases, the offenders are kidnapping their partners or ex-partners to express their frustration and anger (Van Hesselt et al. 2005; Fitzgerald and People 2006).

Barricaded crisis situations often take place during highly traumatic breakups of relationships, IPV, and DV. The victims and their children may be held hostage and these victims are at increased risk of being physically and psychologically injured.

Other forms of partner kidnappings may occur in the context of intimate partner violence (IPV) and domestic violence (DV).

Kidnappers and hostage-takers of partners and family members frequently fear and despair that their relationship with their partner is ending or has ended (Van Hasselt et al. 2005; Fitzgerald and People 2006). Offenders in these kidnapping and hostage-taking incidents use violence, including rape and physical abuse, and other controlling and abusive behaviors, such as stalking, death threats, sexual abuse, and physical abuse, as a way to control or regain control of their partners and family members (See Appendices A–C; Morewitz 2008). For example, Fitzgerald and People (2006), using data from 238 police-recorded abduction victims in New South Wales, described an ex-partner abduction case involving a male suspect and a 17-year-old girl who had been in a prior relationship with the suspect. After the girl had stayed with the suspect at his residence over a weekend, the suspect reportedly

S. Morewitz, *Kidnapping and Violence*,
https://doi.org/10.1007/978-1-4939-2117-1_1

threatened to smash her with an iron pole and stab her with a cricket stump when she began to exit his residence. The suspect allegedly hit the victim with a cricket stump, grabbed her hair, kneed her to the head multiple times, and pushed her into concrete. In another incident that evening, the suspect reportedly threatened to smash her, punched her in the head with a closed fist, pushed her to the ground, and began to knee her head.

Fitzgerald and People (2006) discussed another ex-partner abduction case involving a male perpetrator and 31-year-old woman who had been in a prior violent intimate relationship, and from that relationship, had three children younger than 10 years of age. The suspect reportedly entered the woman's home, grabbed her around her throat and arms, forced her into a lounge room, and physically and sexually assaulted her at that location. Then the suspect reportedly coerced the woman into her automobile and forced her to drive away. The alleged offender informed her that she must now reside with him and later threatened her with violence if she disobeyed him. The victim tried to get away, but the suspect found out and grabbed her by the throat and warned her that he would discipline her if she tried to escape.

Kidnapping and hostage-taking help the perpetrators to vent their frustration, anger, and fear over the break-up of relationships (Morewitz 2008; Fitzgerald and People 2006). These highly emotional situations are potentially lethal events for the perpetrators, victims, police, other emergency personnel, and bystanders.

Victims may report to the police that they were kidnapped and taken as hostages while they are seeking a restraining order against the suspect. One woman reported being kidnapped by her ex-boyfriend, while filing for a temporary restraining order against him (*The Star-Ledger* Continuous News Desk 2010). In other situations, friends, acquaintances, and strangers become aware of the incidents and then contact the police (Fitzgerald and People 2006).

Hostage-Taking in Different Settings

Analysts are studying different workplace settings in which partner abductions, hostage-taking, and related forms of violence occur (Turner 1988; Lightfoot 1998; Feldmann et al. 1997).

Male offenders will often force their way into the homes, workplaces, schools, or motor vehicles of their former or current girlfriends and partners. Booth et al. (2010) discovered that 55.4% of the cases occurred in a private residence.

Turner (1988) suggests that healthcare settings face the risk of hostage-taking incidents as individuals and groups attempt to express their powerlessness and suffering related to healthcare controversies such as abortion, genetic research, and animal testing.

Planned or Unplanned Kidnapping and Hostage-Taking Incidents

Kidnapping and hostage-taking incidents involving partners and family members may be planned or unplanned. In Booth et al's. (2010) report, 83.9% of the incidents were not planned.

Duration of Incidents

Kidnapping and hostage-taking incidents vary in their duration depending on the responses of the offenders, victims, police, special tactical units, and other situational factors (See Appendix C).

Victim Characteristics

Researchers are beginning to examine the characteristics of victims of DV-related kidnapping and hostage-taking incidents. Based on 56 captive-taking cases from the Hostage Barricade Database System (HOBAS) of the Federal Bureau of Investigation (FBI), Booth et al. (2010) discovered that females comprised 68.5% of the victims and Caucasians comprised the majority of the victims (61.8%).

Most of the victims in Booth et al. (2010)'s investigation were family members (44.9%); 12.4% had no relationship to the suspect. One victim was abducted and taken as a hostage in 71.4% of the cases.

The victims of hostage-taking incidents may be verbally, emotionally, physically, and sexually abused by the alleged hostage-taker (Gorner 2010; Pritchard 2009). Booth et al. (2010) discovered that 22.5% of the victims during the sieges had been both physically and verbally abused by the hostage-taker.

In instances of IPV and DV, the police and others can be taken as hostages. For example, a deputy was taken as a hostage while responding to an IPV incident involving a husband and his wife in a rural area (Hausner 2009).

Suspect Characteristics

Most kidnappers and hostage-takers in the context of DV are male (Booth et al. 2010; Taylor and Flight 2003). According to Butler and Wrightsman (1995), a majority of offenders who take children hostages are relatives.

Booth et al. (2010) reported that the suspects ranged in age from about 33–44 years. In media reports of IPV- and DV-related hostage-taking crises, some suspects have been in their twenties (Fujimoto 2009; Glod 2010).

Kidnappers and captive-takers in DV-related sieges vary in their racial and ethnic status. In Booth et al. (2010)'s analysis, Caucasians comprised most of the hostage-takers are Caucasian (63.4%).

Suspects in these incidents may be single, married, divorced, or living with a married partner. Many of the suspects have a relationship to their kidnapping and hostage victim. Booth et al. (2010) reported that 34.1% of the captive-takers were single and 29.3% were married.

Offenders and Weapons

Suspects frequently use weapons, such as firearms, knives, and blunt instruments to achieve their goals. Booth et al. (2010) showed that 31.7% used a handgun.

Suspects' Interpersonal and Mental Health Problems

Persons who are jealous, overly controlling, and obsessive are more likely to abduct their current or ex-partners and family members and hold them as hostages (See Appendix C). These offenders may believe that they "own" their partner and that no one else can "have" them. Batterers who feel that they have total right to their partners' services and obedience are especially at risk of committing homicide and/or suicide. These perpetrators are also likely to physically attack their partners whom they feel are cheating on them.

Kidnappers and hostage-takers may be suffering from acute depression and other serious mental disorders, and their mental health problems often contribute to the breakup of the relationships. Booth et al. (2010) discovered that 39% of the suspects had a history of mental health problems.

Homicides, suicides, and combined homicides-suicides frequently are a reaction to interpersonal conflict or loss (Haines et al. 2010). In one study, 12.2% of the suspects had made prior suicide attempts (Booth et al. 2010).

Saleva et al. (2007), using data from the National Suicide Prevention Project in Finland, found that the most typical homicide-suicide consisted of a man shooting a family member during the process of separation.

In an analysis of 44 cases of homicide-suicide in Tasmania, Australia, Haines et al. (2010) showed that offenders who perpetrated their acts were more likely to be angry and violent and more likely to act erratically prior to their demise. In these types of homicide-suicides, firearms (mostly handguns) frequently are used. In addition, the offender and victim often have been in an intimate or dating relationship.

Abductors may try to commit suicide by police action. A male suspect in one incident was arrested on suspicion of kidnapping and assaulting his girlfriend after he threatened to shoot police with an AK-47 (Mulick 2010). The suspect reportedly did not have a weapon.

Offenders who kidnap their partners may suffer from personality disorders. They frequently lack impulse control and empathy for their victims and have been abused and neglected as children. The offenders' acts of kidnapping often reflect a history of childhood abuse and neglect, other exposure to violence, and on-going personality disorders.

Criminal History and Antisocial Behavior

Persons with a criminal history, those involved in gangs, and individuals who exhibit antisocial behavior may be likely to become kidnappers and hostage-takers (See Appendix C-Cases). Males in gangs may be likely to abduct their former and current girlfriends, partners, and wives (Salazar 2010). These males frequently are antisocial and engage in a variety of criminal activities.

Booth et al. (2010) showed that 75.6% of the suspects involved in captive-taking situations had prior arrests. Almost 10% of the offenders had a prior restraining order against them.

Perpetrators Escalate Their Risk-Taking Behaviors

Persons who escalate their risk-taking behaviors may be more likely to act without considering the legal and social consequences of their actions. For example, after physically assaulting their current or ex-partners they may be more likely to escalate their risk-taking behaviors by abducting them and holding them as hostages.

Offenders May Stalk Their Victims

Before the kidnapping and hostage-taking incident, male perpetrators may stalk their victims by following them around, contacting them electronically, leaving them notes/letters, and pursuing them at their workplace (Morewitz 2003; See Appendices A–C).

Property Damage and Arson as Risk Factors

Men may vandalize the property of their former or current girlfriends and female partners as they take them as hostages (See Appendix C).

Alcohol and Other Drug Use

Just as alcohol and other drug use is associated with an increased likelihood of IPV and DV, being under the influence of alcohol and other/or other drugs and having a history of substance abuse increases the risk of kidnapping partners and family members and taking them as hostages (See Appendix C; Agar 2009).

Booth et al. (2010) found that 24.4% of the suspects had an alcohol abuse history. During the hostage-taking situations, 26.8% were using alcohol.

Offenders and Third Parties

Male offenders will also threaten or attack bystanders or family members who may try to intervene in hostage-taking situations (Gorner et al. 2010; See Appendix C).

Law Enforcement Responses to Hostage-Taking Incidents

The police typically respond to 911 calls related to IPV and DV. Neighbors and bystanders may have called 911or the victims and family members may have initiated the calls. When the police arrive at the scene of the disturbance, they must assess the situation and take appropriate action based on standard police policies and procedures (See Appendix C). The police will set up a perimeter to ensure public safety and will contact schools and other organizations to inform them of the incident.

Special Weapons and Tactics (SWAT) personnel may also participate in the kidnapping and captive-taking crisis (Mijares et al. 2000). SWAT officers are trained in making forced entries, extracting hostages, and containing or killing the perpetrator if necessary (Vecchi 2002). Law enforcement personnel will take positions in strategic locations to facilitate a resolution of the crisis.

The police typically set up a command post nearby and then coordinate hostage negotiation activities, including the use of different communication methods with the suspect to achieve a peaceful resolution of the crisis. In Booth et al. (2010) study, the police and negotiators used an existing phone service in 35.7% of incidents.

If the suspect has shot hostages, is noncompliant, or has refused to communicate with negotiators, the police may initiate tactical procedures. Authorities are faced with initiating tactical solutions when they have no clear-cut reason to take such potentially lethal action (Dalfonzo 2002). Law enforcement personnel may use pepper bombs to force the suspect out of an apartment (Wellner et al. 2009).

Law enforcement officers started communication with the suspect in 37.5% of the cases (Booth et al. 2010). Both police officers and negotiators started communication with the suspects in 46.4% of the incidents. Intermediaries are used in abduction and captive-taking incidents. Intermediaries were relied on in 25% of the cases. Law enforcement officials may rely on crisis negotiation teams, and mental health professionals can assist these teams (DeBernardo 2004).

Mental health professionals can determine whether the kidnapper and captive taker has a mental disorder and offer possible negotiation strategies (Rueth 1993). In an investigation of 300 U.S. law enforcement agencies that employ a negotiator in hostage incidents, Butler et al. (1993) reported that 39% of the organizations with a negotiator employed a mental health professional as a consultant to the negotiation team.

The New York City Police Department in 1973 was the first agency to use negotiation techniques in hostage, kidnapping, and other crisis incidents (Vecchi et al. 2005). The Attica prison riot in 1971 and the murder of Israeli athletes at the 1972 Olympic Games led authorities and mental health professionals to use negotiation strategies in different crisis situations.

Specialists have designed several types of negotiation strategies. One major approach is to use problem-solving methods to aid the police and negotiators to respond, manage, and resolve these crisis situations (McMain and Mullins 2001). However, various investigators have shown that the use of problem-solving techniques is only useful after the police and negotiators have minimized the offender's severe emotional state (Vecchi et al. 2005).

Negotiators seek to achieve four goals in resolving hostage incident successfully (Vecchi et al. 2005). First, negotiators attempt to establish communication and develop rapport with the subject. Second, authorities try to "buy time" since as time goes by, the subjects' emotional state can be minimized (Romano 2002). Third, negotiators attempt to defuse the offenders' intense emotions by carefully listening for the intense emotions underlying their statements and dealing with these emotions. Finally, negotiators gather information about the potential harm to hostages and others and the offender to assist them in negotiating the crisis peacefully.

The FBI Crisis Negotiation Unit designed the Behavioral Change Stairway Model (BCSM) that emphasizes building relationships between the perpetrator and the negotiator to achieve a peaceful resolution of the crisis (Flood 2003; Tucker et al. 2007). The BCSM has five sequential stages: (1) active listening; (2) empathy; (3) rapport; (4) influence, and (5) behavioral change.

Role playing is used to train and evaluate negotiators in crisis situations (Vecchi et al. 2005; Sharp 2000). Different scenarios are used to simulate crises involving family members, workers, and individuals who are suicidal (Vecchi et al. 2005).

Outcomes of Hostage-Taking Incidents

Victims, offenders, law enforcement personnel, negotiators, and bystanders may be injured or killed during a hostage incident. In Booth et al. (2010) investigation, a majority of the hostage victims (79.8%) and suspects (82.9%) were not injured.

To respond to injured law enforcement personnel, tactical emergency medical support may be deployed (Greenstone 1998). Jones et al. (1996) discovered that a civilian ambulance on standby at a predesignated location (69%) was the most commonly used form of medical support.

Since hostage-taking events threaten the offenders' need for security and safety, they can trigger a "fight or flight" reaction in them (Donohue et al. 1991). Professionals who successfully negotiate these crises are able to calm down the perpetrators, enhance the way decisions are made, and meet most of the offenders' needs (McMain and Mullins 2001).

The suspect's behavior during captive-taking situations may predict their future behaviors and outcomes of the hostage-taking incidents (Wilson 2000). According to the FBI, the risks to hostages are especially high if the offenders are threatening to injure the victims or if the victims have been injured and the perpetrators are not making real demands to third parties.

In hostage-taking crises, the perpetrators' possession of ordinance may increase the chances that the crisis ends violently (Friedland and Merari 1992). Competitive behavior between the captive takers and the negotiators increases the likelihood that law enforcement will use tactical strategies to resolve the hostage crisis (Taylor 2002)

In their investigation of hostage barricade cases in South Africa and Japan, Yokota et al. (2002) showed that the longer the duration of the incidents, the greater the chances that hostages were injured. In contrast, Vecchi et al. (2005) note that protracted negotiations may actually be an ally of the negotiators.

Criminal Justice System Responses

In one hostage incident, the suspect was held in jail on a $2 million bond (Wellner et al. 2009). Another suspect charged with hostage-taking and arson was ordered held in lieu of a $500,000 bail by the judge (Gorner et al. 2010).

Individuals who are convicted of kidnapping and related crimes often receive a prison sentence. In one kidnapping case, the hostage-taker was sentenced to 10 years in prison (Fujimoto 2009). In this court case, testimony was presented on behalf of both the reported victim and hostage-taker. The suspect in another hostage-taking incident was sentenced to five years on prison (Pritchard 2009).

References

Agar, J. (2009). Former girlfriends testify about Jenison man's alleged abuse, kidnapping. *The Grand Rapids Press*. October 14, 2009. http://www.mlive.com/news/grand-rapids/index.ssf/2009/10/former_girlfriends_testify_abo.html.

Bartol, C.R. (2002). Criminal behavior: A psychological approach. New Jersey: Prentice Hall.

Booth, B., Vecchi, G.M., & Angleman, A.J., et al. (2010). Captive-taking incidents in the context of domestic violence: A descriptive analysis. Vict & Offenders, 5 (2):183-198.

Butler, W.M., & Wrightsman, L.S. (1995). Child hostages. J Interpersonal Viol, 10 (3): 378-382.

Butler, W.M., Leitenberg, H., & Fuselier, G.D. (1993). The use of mental health professional consultants to police hostage negotiation teams. Behav Sci Law, 11 (2): 213-221.

Dalfonzo, V. (2002). National crisis negotiation course. Quantico, VA: FBI Academy.

DeBernardo, C.R. (2004). The psychologist's role in hostage negotiations. Int J Emerg Ment Health, 6 (1): 39-42.

Donohue, W., A., Ramesh, C., & Kaufmann, G., et al. (1991). Crisis bargaining in intense conflict situations. Int J Group Tensions, 21: 133-145.

Feldmann, T.B., Holt, J., & Hellard, S. (1997). Violence in medical facilities: A review of 40 incidents. J Ky Med Assoc, 95 (5): 183-189.

Fitzgerald, J., & People, J. (2006, July). Victims of abduction: Patterns and case studies. Crime & Justice Bull, 94, 1-14.

Flood, J.J. (2003). Hostage barricade database (HOBAS). Quantico, VA: FBI Academy.

Friedland, N., & Merari, A. (1992). Hostage events: Descriptive profile and analysis of outcome. J Applied Soc Psych, 22: 134-156.

Fujimoto, L. (2009). Man gets 10 years in kidnapping of girlfriend. *The Maui News*, Jun 27, 2009. http://www.mauinews.com/page/content.detail/id/520293/Man-gets-10-years-in-kidnapping-of-girlfriend.html.

Glod, M. (2010). Md. Man accused of kidnapping ex-girlfriend arrested, woman found. washingtonpost.com. April 20, 2010. http://voices.washingtonpost.com/crime-scene/montgomery/montgomery-police-search-for-k.html.

Gorner, J. (2010). Carpentersville man charged with kidnapping ex-girlfriend. http://articles.chicagobreakingnews.com/2010-04-06/news/28508442_1_carpentersville-man-girlfriend-cell-phone.

Gorner, J., Hoffman, H., & Ford, L. (2010). Hostage, cop hurt in shootings before West Side fire. http://articles.chicagobreakingnews.com/2010-01-10/news/28528019_1_hostage-situation-swat-officers-chicago-police-officer.

Greenstone, J.L. (1998). The role of tactical emergency medical support in hostage and crisis negotiations. Prehosp Disaster Med, 13 (2-4): 55-57.

Haines, J., Williams, C.L., & Lester, D. (2010). Murder-suicide: A reaction to interpersonal crises. Foren Sci Int, 202 (1-3): 93-96.

Hausner, T. (2009). An officer's worst nightmare. Lessons learned from being taken hostage. FBI Law Enforce Bull, July, 14-19.

Jones, J.S., Reese, K., & Kenepp, G., et al. (1996). Into the fray: Integration of emergency medical services and special weapons and tactics (SWAT) teams. Prehosp Disaster Med, 11 (3): 202-206.

Lightfoot, S. (1998). Workplace violence: Hostage situations in the healthcare setting. J Healthc Prot Manage, 14 (2): 32-44.

Lipsedge, M. (2004). Hostage-taking and domestic sieges. Psychiatry, 3 (8): 24-26.

McMain, M.J., & Mullins, W.C. (2001). Crisis negotiations: Managing critical incidents and hostage situations in law enforcement and corrections (2nd ed.). Cincinnati, OH: Anderson Publishing.

Mijares, T.C., McCarthy, R.M., & Perkins, D.B. (2000). The management of police specialized tactical units. Springfield, IL: Charles C. Thomas.

Morewitz, S.J. (2003). Stalking and violence. New patterns of trauma and obsession. New York: Kluwer Academic/Plenum Publishers.
Morewitz, S.J. (2008). Death threats and violence. New York: Springer Science + Business Media, LLC.
Mulick, S. (2010). Man faces charges of assaulting girlfriend. The Olympian.com. http://www.theolympian.com.
Pritchard, D. (2009). Man jailed for violent hostage-taking. Sun Media, The Winnipeg Sun. http://cnews.canoe.ca/CNEWS/Crime/2009/11/02/11602671-sun.html.
Romano, S.J. (2002). Personal communication. Crisis Negotiation Unit, Critical Incident Response Group. Quantico, VA: FBI Academy.
Rueth, T.W. (1993). Onsite psychological evaluation of a hostage taker. Psychol Rep, 73 (2): 659-664.
Salazar, D. (2010). Gangster wanted in ex-girlfriend's kidnapping. April 7, 2010. http://www.ocregister.com.
Saleva, O., Putkonen, H., & Kiviruusu, O., et al. (2007). Homicide-suicide—An event hard to prevent and separate from homicide or suicide. Forensic Sci Int, 166, 204-208.
Sharp, A.G. (2000). The importance of role-playing in training. Law and Order: The Magazine for Police Management, 48: 97-100.
Taylor, P.J. (2002). A partial order scalogram analysis of communication behavior in crisis negotiation with prediction of outcome. Int J Conflict Managem, 13: 4-37.
Taylor, K., & Flight, J. (2003). Hostage-taking incidents involving women inmates: A profile & exploratory investigation. Ottawa, Canada: Correctional Service of Canada, Research Branch.
The Star-Ledger Continuous News Desk (2010). Jersey City man is accused of kidnapping, sexual assault of ex-girlfriend. September 16, 2010. http://www.nj.com/news.
Tucker, A.S., Spaulding, T., & Henry, J., et al. (2007). Critical incident stress management in a mid-sized police department: A case illustration. Int J Emerg Ment Health, 9 (4): 299-303.
Turner, J.T. (1988). Hostage-takers in health care setting. Psychiatr Clin North Am, 11 (4): 649-664.
Van Hasselt, V.B., Flood, J.J., & Romano, S.J., et al. (2005). Hostage-taking in the context of of domestic violence: Some case examples. J Family Viol, 20 (1): 21-27.
Vecchi, G.M. (2002). Hostage/barricade management: A hidden conflict within law enforcement. FBI Law Enforce Bull, 71: 1-6.
Vecchi, G.M., Van Hasselt, V.B., & Romano, S.J. (2005). Crisis (hostage) negotiation: current strategies and issues in high-risk conflict resolution. Aggression Viol Behav, 10: 533-551.
Wellner, B., Lemmon, D., & Brown, C., et al. (2009). Geneseo standoff suspect has history of domestic violence, authorities say. http://qctimes.com/news/local/articles_5e45d6c-e6d5-11de-b96b-001cc4c002e0.html.
Wilson, M.A. (2000). Toward a model of terrorist behavior in hostage taking incidents. J Conflict Resolution, 44: 403-424.
Yokota, K., Watanabe, S., & Canter, D., et al. (2002). Descriptive characteristics of hostage barricade incidents and their outcomes. International comparisons between Japan and South Africa. Acta Criminol Japanese, 68: 119-128.
Yokota, K., Iwami, H., & Watanabe, K., et al. (2004). J Investig Psych Offender Profiling, 1: 139-151.

Chapter 2
Bride Abduction

Bride abduction (BA), also known as bride capture or marriage by abduction, is a type of forced marriage that is practiced in some traditional patriarchal and agricultural-based cultures (*Academic Dictionaries and Encyclopedias* no date; Ouattara et al. 1998). BA is practiced in Central Asia, the Caucasus area, regions of Africa, Southeast Asia, Mexico, and Europe. Some forms of the practice are on a continuum between forced marriage and arranged marriage (Werner 2009; Kleinbach and Salimjanova 2007; *Academic Dictionaries and Encyclopedias* no date). The women who are abducted, raped, and forced to consent to marriage are similar to victims of human trafficking (HT) and in some cases, may become HT victims (Americans for UNFPA, no date).

The History of BA and Rape

In ancient times, BAs and rapes took place in the Mediterranean region. The *Book of Judges* in the *Bible* discusses the practice in reference to the tribe of Benjamin (http://www.usccb.org/nab/bible/judges/judges21.htm). Marriage by capture was also depicted in Greek history. The Trojan War was started when the Greek hero, Paris, stole Helen of Troy from her husband, Menelaus. Marriage by capture was also portrayed in the *Rape of Sabine Women* by the founder of Rome, Romulus. In addition, in ancient Sparta, BA was prevalent.

Laws were enacted to prevent marriage by capture. For example, Emperor Constantine passed a law in 326 A.D. that made the ritual illegal. According to the edict, the practice was made a public crime. A kidnapped bride could even be punished if she agreed to marry the abductor (Evans-Grubbs 1989).

Throughout history, suitors who were rejected by the women might kidnap them as a way of restoring their honor (Evans-Grubbs 1989). In the eleventh century, East Slavic tribes followed the custom of marriage by capture. The Russian monk, Nestor, in his *Chronicles*, noted that the *Drevlian* tribe kidnapped their wives

S. Morewitz, *Kidnapping and Violence*,
https://doi.org/10.1007/978-1-4939-2117-1_2

(Kowalewsky 1890). In contrast, the *Radimich, Viatich*, and *Severian* tribes would reach an agreement with their prospective brides before they "abducted" them. Church leaders may have helped to reduce the frequency of this custom (MacDermott 1998).

In Croatia, the 1605 Croatian legal code, *Politza*, refers to the custom (Kowalewsky 1890; Kovalesky 1891). Vuk Karadzic, a scholar and folk chronicler of Serbian traditions, described how a man would put on clothes for "battle" before abducting the woman. The man would often use physical force to carry out the bride capture (Kovalesky 1891).

In Kenya, the Turkana tribe has followed the custom of *akomari* (BA). The man kidnaps the prospective bride before a marriage is arranged with the family of the bride. If the man is successful, his status in the community will increase, and he will then be able to obtain a lower bride price with his bride's family. However, if the man is not successful, he must pay the bride price to the bride's family, offer other gifts and payments, and have an *akota* (arranged marriage) (Emley 1927).

In China, *Qiangqin* (marriage by kidnapping) took place in different areas until the 1940s (McLaren 2001). This ritual could have emerged so that the groom would not have to pay a bride price. Other experts believe the custom was based on an agreement between the bride's parents and the groom to avoid the bride's agreement to marry.

Experts believe that the bridal lament developed in China in response to wife capture. A new bride in imperial China reportedly would sing, chant, and sob in public two to three times daily to express her problems and complaints (McLaren and Qinjian 2000).

The history of *kyz ala kachuu* (bride capture) in Kyrgyzstan is controversial. Kleinbach and Salimjanova (2007) dispute the widely held notion that the ritual was prevalent and socially approved in ancient times.

Portrayal of BA in Film, Documentaries, Radio/Television, and Literature

The custom of BA has been depicted in film, television, and literature. The fictional character, Borat, in the 2006 parody of Kazakhstan, Borat, tries to abduct Pamela Anderson, a Canadian actress, using a "wedding sack" (Wiltenburg 2005). Pietro Germi directed a dark comedy about the Sicilian custom of BA in his film, *Sedotta e abbandonata* (*Seduced and Abandoned*). Various documentaries have examined the controversial nature of bride capture (PBS no date). Radio and television have portrayed the custom in their programs (BBC no date). Bride capture has also been a topic in literature.

Modern BA

The process of BAs in modern times has varied depending on the laws, views of the political leadership, economic conditions, and patriarchal values and beliefs of a given region or country. In Kyrgyzstan, *kyz ala kachuu* generally involves one man, the intended groom, and his friends and relatives kidnapping a woman, usually a young woman, by force or through deception for the purpose of obtaining a wife for the intended groom (*Academic Dictionaries and Encyclopedias* no date; Americans for UNFPA no date). The abducted woman may be taken to the intended groom's residence, where relatives of the intended groom use physical force or psychological coercion in order to compel the kidnapped woman to "agree" to marry the intended groom. The woman signifies her agreement by having a *jooluk* (wedding scarf) placed on her head. However, if the kidnapped victim opposes the abduction and proposed marriage, the process of physical and psychological intimidation could last a short time more or even days longer. The primary kidnapper often rapes the woman, and their rapes frequently take place before the victims agree to the coerced marriages. The abductor rapes the woman in order to shame her into remaining at his residence instead of going back to her home in disgrace.

Young girls are the victims of BA in different areas. In Ethiopia, 11-year-old girls have been abducted for the goal of marriage (U.N. Office for the Coordination of Humanitarian Affairs no date). In an investigation of *telefa* (marriage by abduction) in northwest Ethiopia, Getahun (2001) discovered that the median age of the BA victims (at their first marriage) was 13 years, with a range of 7–20 years of age.

In Kenya, girls aged ten years and older are forced to marry men who are more than twenty years older than them (United States State Department 2008a). In traditional Romani (gypsy) culture, adolescent boys abduct girls as young as 12 years old for marriage (McDonald 2007). Turkish gypsies may get married by buying, exchanging, or kidnapping girls, aged 13–17 years old (Ozkan 2006).

The abductor may be in a dating relationship with the girl or woman. For example, in *Karakalpakstan*, BA originated among couples in dating relationships (Aminova 2005). BA also may be carried out by multiple abductors. In the variation of the ritual, the family of the BA victim in Caucasus may try to convince her to remain with her kidnapper because of the stigma associated with the presumed consummation of the marriage (Kiryashova 2005).

In other cases, the bride abductor and victim are both strangers (Human Rights Watch 2006).

As part of *qicnquin* (marriage by abduction) in certain areas of China, the kidnapper might come to the woman's residence with about twenty friends. The prospective groom would try to cut off the woman's pants with scissors as his friends carried the victim away (McLaren 2001).

The groom in some modern cultures participates in a ritual or symbolic abduction of the bride (*Academic Dictionaries and Encyclopedias* no date).

A couple that has already agreed to marry may participate in this symbolic kidnapping to honor the practice, which may be part of their cultural tradition.

Some experts view the honeymoon period as a surviving tradition of marriage by capture (Walsh 1897). The honeymoon comes from the ritual in which the husband goes into hiding with his wife to escape retaliations from his wife's relatives. According to this tradition, the wife is supposed to be pregnant at the end of one month. However, Westermarck (1922) denies the association between honeymoon and marriage by capture.

The motivations for BA differ among regions and countries (*Academic Dictionaries and Encyclopedias* no date). Marriage by capture occurs in patriarchal societies that do not allow premarital interactions (*Academic Dictionaries and Encyclopedias* no date).

Men who engage in BA often have low socioeconomic status (SES) and other undesirable social characteristics (Stross 1974). The men's low SES and decreased attractiveness may be due to different factors such as their criminal history and health problems. In traditional *Hmong* culture, men who carried out bride capture had to pay an increased bride price because of the abduction (Scott 1986).

Men may be blocked from obtaining a wife legitimately because of a bride price (Stross 1974). However, in her cross-cultural analysis, Ayres (1974) did not discover any association between BA and differences in status, bride price, or beliefs about premarital virginity.

Some experts suggest that *kyz ala kachuu* in Kyrgzstan enables men to assert their masculinity in their culture (Handrahan 2004). Women in Kyrgzstan who challenge *kyz ala kachuu* are stigmatized because they are viewed as rejecting the country's culture. Other writers criticize the practice as barbaric and as a way to keep women in subordinate roles in society where they must endure domestic violence (DV), intimate partner violence (IPV), and exploitation.

BA is most prevalent in agricultural and patriarchal societies where children work within the family unit (*Academic Dictionaries and Encyclopedias* no date). When a woman marries, she often leaves her biological family's residence and also no longer works for them. Instead, the bride becomes a member of the groom's family. The daughter's family does not want her to marry young because they will lose her vital labor. Therefore, they demand a bride price (economic compensation) when their daughters get married.

The interests of the bride's family conflict with the interests of the groom's family (*Academic Dictionaries and Encyclopedias* no date). Instead of trying to delay marriage, the groom wants to have an early marriage since the marriage will bring him increased social status. The groom's family will profit from the marriage since they will obtain the wife's labor to assist the family farm or business (Human Rights Watch 2006).

The victim of marriage by capture paradoxically may benefit from the practice. Victims of BAs are precluded from selecting a husband on their own, and in the process, may be protected from being disowned or murdered by her husband (*Academic Dictionaries and Encyclopedias* no date). BA may offer the only socially desirable method for the woman to become a mother, which is very desirable for women in these societies.

BA can be especially lucrative when women are the victims of HT. Researchers have reported instances in which abducted brides have been transported to other countries or imprisoned as slaves at home (Kiryashova 2005). Saida Gojamanli, from the Human Rights and Legislation Protection Bureau, reported that kidnapped girls have been used as housekeepers. In regions of China, men abduct women and sell them to men in financially disadvantaged areas of the country or to other countries, such as Mongolia (Insight News TV no date).

BA can be influenced by changes in laws, policies, and social institutions (United States State Department 2007). The fall of the Soviet Union may have led to a revival of the practice in Central Asian nations. Russia and later the USSR had criminalized the ritual. However, after the fall of the Soviet Union, BA may have been revived as a way to promote cultural identity (Human Rights Watch 2006).

Coercion, Deception, and Fraud

The kidnapped women are victims of physical and psychological coercion, deception, and fraud. For example, in areas of Ethiopia, the kidnapper may use his friends to carry out the bride capture and use a horse to assist in the escape (BBC 1999). The abductor will then keep his bride hidden and rape her until she becomes pregnant. He can now claim the woman as his wife since he is the father of her child.

In Azerbaijan, a young woman is transported to the residence of the kidnapper's parents by deception or coercion (Kiryashova 2005). Bride kidnappers in Kazakhstan, may offer a woman a ride home as a pretense (Werner 2004).

BA, Rape, and Stigma

The practice is influenced by patriarchal values regarding the extreme stigma against sex or pregnancy outside of marriage, illegitimate births, and rape (Kiryashova 2005; Kokhodze and Uchidze 2006; *Academic Dictionaries and Encyclopedias* no date). Kiryashova (2005) found that *Azeri* BA victims who spend a night away from their house bring great shame on themselves. Kokhodze and Uchidze (2006) showed that the suspicion of lost virginity is linked to significant social stigma. Even if the woman is not raped, the woman feels coerced to marry the perpetrator because she has few cultural alternatives.

Similarly, in Kenya, men in the *Kisii* ethnic group will abduct their prospective bride and rape her in order to get her pregnant (Immigration and Refugee Board of Canada no date). Because of the severe stigma of pregnancy and rape, the woman is forced to marry her kidnapper.

Girls and women have challenged their kidnappers (Werner 2009). Sometimes a kidnapped bride is rescued by her parents. In other instances, the groom's parents free the abducted bride. However, the abducted brides face substantial shame when they resist the custom. Girls and women who oppose this ritual may be perceived as traitors to their ethnic traditions.

Health Effects of BA, Rape, and Sexual Assault

BA victims are at increased risk of rape, sexual assault, and other injuries and health problems. In a cross-sectional study of *telefa* (marriage through abduction) in a rural district of North West Ethiopia, Getahun (2001) found that the kidnapped brides had an increased likelihood of being raped.

BA victims and other women who are raped or sexually assaulted can suffer postcoital injuries (Drocton et al. 2008; Palmer et al. 2004). Muleta and Williams (1999) examined 91 young Ethiopian women who developed total fecal incontinence from postcoital injuries and were treated at the Addis Ababa Fistula Hospital between 1991 and 1997. Seventy-eight of the 91 women in the sample had been reportedly abused sexually "under the cover" of marriage. Victims may be at increased risk of other health problems. Chowdhary and Patel (2008) showed that IPV against married women was linked to gynecological problems and low body mass index (BMI).

Victims who remain married to their kidnappers are at increased risk of suffering persistent IPV. Getahun (2001) showed that the BA victims had an increased risk of being an IPV victim.

Physical, sexual, and emotional forms of IPV can injure girls and women in a variety of ways. Using a cross-sectional survey of physical violence against married women in southern Ethiopia, Deyessa et al. (1998) showed that 46% reported having physical violence-related minor lacerations or scars and 7% had suffered a fracture or dislocation.

These victims are at increased risk of developing IPV-related sexually transmitted infections (STIs), including HIV infection (UN Office for the Coordination of Humanitarian Affairs no date; Silverman et al. 2008).

BA victims who are raped and sexually assaulted face an increased risk of IPV before, during and after pregnancy (Morewitz 2004). Victims and other girls and women who suffer IPV are more likely to have negative reproductive health and pregnancy outcomes (Morewitz 2004; Sarkar 2008). Getahun (2001) found that BA victims were more likely to have had an abortion.

Sarkar (2008) found that IPV against pregnant women is associated with an increased risk of preterm delivery, low birth weight infants, and neonatal death. IPV also adversely affects postpartum breastfeeding. Ouattara et al. (1998) discovered that nonconsensual child marriages were associated with increased rates of infant mortality.

Girls and women who are kidnapped and raped for marriage and other IPV victims can suffer severe social, emotional, and mental problems (Sarkar 2008). Victims can suffer from the rape trauma syndrome, also known as the rape crisis syndrome (Giannelli 1997).

Like other kidnapped victims, BA victims may be at increased risk of suffering the Stockholm syndrome, depending on the duration and severity of their abduction. For example, in Kyrgyzstan, some families will keep the kidnapped bride hostage for several days to force her to agree to the marriage. The families may even threaten to curse her if she tries to leave. Threatening to curse the kidnapped bride can be effective since residents there are often superstitious (Smith 2005).

Female victims of IPV also often experience reduced sexual autonomy. In addition, the BA victims may be forced into slavery by the groom's family and can be severely traumatized by this forced servitude (Kiryashova 2005).

Victims may become anxious, depressed, and suicidal. Pusurmankulova (2004) reported that BA victims may refuse to marry their kidnappers and may even kill themselves. Based on a population-based cohort study of 1,750 married women in Goa, India, Chowdhary and Patel (2008) discovered that IPV was associated with a depressive disorder and an increased risk of suicide attempts.

Using population-based survey data in rural and urban Bangladesh, Naved and Akhtar (2008) found that both physical and emotional IPV was associated with an increased rate of suicidal ideation. For example, women in rural areas who were the victims of severe physical IPV during the last 12 months and women in urban areas were two times more likely to have suicidal ideation than women who had not suffered IPV.

The age of the kidnapped and raped brides can affect the severity of the psychosocial and physical damage. In a study of child marriage in West Africa, girls who get married before they are 15 years old are more likely to be bride price or dowry brides have a higher rate of infant mortality and are at increased risk of sexual violence (Ouattara et al. 1998). Children who marry before the age of 15 are especially vulnerable because they lack information about sexuality and are more likely to be illiterate. In addition, girls can be especially traumatized by the BA and rape since they do not have the same level of emotional maturity as adults.

The children born to the bride capture victims may themselves be at increased risk of physical and emotional abuse as children and later as adults. Using a population-based telephone survey, Bensley et al. (2003) demonstrated that women who reported physical abuse during childhood or observing violence between parents were four to six time more likely to suffer physical IPV.

Childhood DV is also associated with an increased risk of poor physical and mental health in adulthood. For example, in Bensley et al. (2003)'s investigation, women who were physically abused during childhood had an increased risk of poor physical health. In addition, women who suffered any form of childhood DV had an increased chance of frequent mental distress.

Social and SES Implications of BAs

Because of the severe stigma associated with premarital sex, rape, and pregnancy outside of marriage in traditional patriarchal cultures, the kidnapped bride is often treated as a social outcast if she resists the practice. The presumption of consummation of the marriage generally means that the bride has had sex with the groom and is impure. Therefore, generally she cannot go back to her family of origin because going back would bring great shame on her and her family.

The abducted brides who resist the practice may suffer severe social rejection because they are threatening an ethnic group's cultural identity as well as norms and values about masculinity (Handrahan 2004; https://eurasianet.org).

Because the prospective grooms frequently do not have the financial resources to obtain a bride legally, the abducted brides lack upward mobility and in fact may suffer lower SES. Moreover, the captured brides face significantly diminished social status because, as noted earlier, the prospective grooms frequently have a criminal history, character problems, and/or abuse alcohol and other drugs.

Like other bride price girls and women, victims of BA may have reduced decision-making roles in the family, reduced independence, and unequal gender roles. In Uganda, based on focus group discussions and in-depth interview, Kaye et al. (2005) discovered that research participants felt that bride price payments meant that the woman was "bought" into the groom's family. As a result, they felt that the bride price payments weakened the bride's decision-making authority, reduced their independence, and fostered persistent gender role inequality.

BA victims may have unstable marriages, and this marital instability may be due to their increased risk of IPV. Getahun (2001) demonstrated that in northwest Ethiopia, *telefa* was linked to marital instability and girls and women having more than one marriage in their lifetime.

Some victims may not be officially married, causing them to become social outcasts. For example, in Rwanda, some abductors decide not to have an official marriage; instead they choose to keep their bride as a concubine (Ruremesha 2003).

Victims may have fewer educational and occupational opportunities (Positive Deviance no date, http://www.positivedeviance.org). Girls who fear being abducted are more likely to not attend school. Ouattara et al. (1998) reported that children in forced child marriages have an increased rate of illiteracy.

Restitution for the Family of the Abducted Brides

The ritual of BA can provide for restitution for the family of the abducted bride. Restitution can occur in instances in which the abducted girl or woman resists the kidnapping. In Kazakhstan, the groom and his family may offer an apology to the bride's family if she resists his kidnapping (Werner 2004).

Police and Court Responses to BAs

Despite the fact that young girls and women are kidnapped and often raped as part of this cultural practice, and some of them even may become HT victims, the response of the police and the courts to these activities has been minimal (Kleinbach and Salimjanova 2007; Werner 2009; United States State Department 2008b). In imperial China, *qiangqin* was institutionalized even though it was illegal (McLaren 2001). The problem of BA is exacerbated in Chechnya because it is practiced widely, and the police do not take any against the custom (United States State Department 2006a, b, c).

According to Russian law, an abductor who fails to free his kidnapped bride could receive a prison sentence of eight to ten years (Isayev 2007). However, if the man frees the woman or marries her with her permission then will not be prosecuted.

In Kyrgyzstan, the pluralistic nature of its legal system may inhibit the prosecution of men who commit BA. Prosecutors may be reluctant to respond to BAs because councils of elders and *aqsaqal* courts decide on BA issues (Human Rights Watch 2006).

According to the Human Rights Watch, prosecutors in the Georgian justice system frequently will not bring charges against the bride abductor. Instead, they encourage the woman to make up with her assailant (Human Rights Watch 2006). The justice system's failure to investigate and prosecute BA is similar to their failure to respond to DV and sexual violence in this country (United States State Department no date; Amnesty International 2006).

In some regions and countries, the police, courts, and government leaders may consider the ritual to be a useful practice and not a major crime (Americans for UNFPA no date). For example, the one-child policy in China may necessitate BA to help overcome the low birth rate of girls in the population. In certain geographical areas, the courts do not take into account the woman's consent in determining the validity of a marriage.

Laws restricting or forbidding bride capture are enacted in various countries. However, members of the population often do not comply with these new laws. For example, in Ethiopia, the practice has been made illegal and increased the age of marriage to 18. This law has not been implemented effectively and the custom continues to be practiced (UN Office for the Coordination of Humanitarian Affairs no date).

Marriage by capture has become a legal problem when individuals immigrate to a country and practice the custom in their new homeland illegally. In lawsuits, the male defendant may be able to use a cultural defense (Yang 2004; Rimonte 1991).

Media, Organizational, and Community Responses to BA

The media, organizations, and community groups have publicized the plight of the victims of BAs, forced marriages, HT, slavery, and other related practices. Scholars, staff from nonprofit organizations, and human rights and women's rights advocates have written articles, books, and have used the Internet and film documentaries and movies to shed light on these practices (Ruremesha 2003).

One website, the Americans for UNFPA, for the Health and Dignity of Women Everywhere, calls for greater knowledge about the practice, its cultural meanings and effects on the reproductive health and civil rights of women (Americans for UNFPA no date). The organization recommends more attempts to alert political, legal, law enforcement, and religious leaders about the ritual's harmful impact. They also seek changes in legislation and law enforcement procedures to apprehend and punish offenders.

References

Academic Dictionaries and Encyclopedias (no date). Bride kidnapping. http://en.academic.ru/dic.nsf/enwiki/1057109.

Aminova, A. (2005). Only a few are aware that bride kidnapping is a criminal offense. CaucAsia: Traditions and Gender, 5. http://www.wcg.org.ge.

Amnesty International (2006). Georgia—Thousands suffering in silence: Violence against women. AI Index: EUR 56/009/2006, Sept. 2006, at 11.

Ayres, B. (1974). Bride theft and raiding for wives in cross-cultural perspective. Anthro Quarterly, 47 (3), 245.

BBC (1999). Ethiopia: Revenge of the abducted bride. http://news.bbc.co.uk/2/hi/africa/371944.stm, June 18, 1999.

BBC (no date). League of gentlemen. http://www.bbc.co.uk.

Bensley, L., Van Eenwyk, J., & Wynkoop Simmons, K. (2003). Childhood family violence history and women's risk for intimate partner violence and poor health. Am J Prev Med, 25 (1): 38–44.

Chowdhary, N., & Patel, V. (2008). The effect of spousal violence on women's health: Findings from the Stree Arogya Shodh in Goa, India. J Postgrad Med, 54 (4): 306–312.

Deyessa, N., Kassaye, M., & Demeke, B., et al. (1998). Magnitude, type and outcomes of physical violence against married women in Butajira, southern Ethiopia. Ethiop Med J, 36 (2): 83–92.

Drocton, P., Sachs, C., Chu, L., & Wheeler, M. (2008). Validation set categories of anogenital injury after sexual assault. Acad Emerg Med, 15 (3): 231–238.

Emley, E.D. (1927). The Turkana of Kolosia District. J Royal Anthro Instit of Great Brit and Ireland, 57: 157–201.

Evans-Grubbs, J. (1989). Abduction marriage in antiquity: A law of Constantine (Cth IX. 24. I) and its social context. J Roman Stud, 79: 59–83.

Getahun, H. (2001). Marriage through abduction ('*telefa*') in rural north west Ethiopia. Ethiop Med J, 39 (2): 105–112.

Giannelli, P. (1997). Rape trauma syndrome. Crim Law Bull, 33: 270–279.

Handrahan, L. (2004). Hunting for women: Bride-kidnapping in Kyrgyzstan. Int Feminist J Politics, 6 (2): 207–233.

Human Rights Watch (2006). Georgia: Human rights developments. http://www.hrw.org/wr2k2/europe9.html.

Immigration and Refugee Board of Canada (no date). Kenya: Information on Kisii marriage customs and whether women are, at times, abducted and coerced into marriage. http://www.unhcr.org/refworld.

Insight News TV (no date). China, Mongolia: Kidnapped wives. http://www.insightnewstv.com/d08/.

Isayev, R. (2007). In Chechnya, attempts to eradicate bride abduction. Prague Watchdog, Nov. 16, 2007. http://www.watchdog.cz/?show=000000-000015-000006-000024&lang=1.

Kaye, D.K., Mirembe, F., & Ekstrom, A.M., et al. (2005). Implications of bride price on domestic violence and reproductive health in Wakiso District, Uganda. Afr Health Sci, 5 (4): 300–303.

Kiryashova, S. (2005). Azeri bride kidnappers risk heavy sentences. Institute of War and Peace Reporting, November 17, 2005. http://www.iwpr.net/?p=wpr&s=f&o=258105&apc_state=henpwpr.

Kleinbach, R., & Salimjanova, L. (2007). *Kyz ala kachuu* and *adat*: Kidnapping and tradition in Kyrgyzstan. Central Asian Survey, 26 (2): 217–233.

Kokhodze, G., & Uchidze, T. (2006). Bride theft rampant in Southern Georgia. http://www.iwpr.net/?p=crs&s=f&o=321627&apc_state=henh.

Kovalesky, M. (1891). Modern customs and ancient laws of Russia. London: David, Nutt, & Strand.

Kowalewsky, M. (1890). Marriage among the early Slavs. Folklore, 1 (4): 463–480.

MacDermott, M. (1998). Bulgarian folk customs.

McDonald, H. (2007). Gardai hunt gang accused of seizing Roma child bride. http://www.guardian.co.uk/world/2007/sep/23/ireland, Guardian, U.K., Sept. 3, 2007.

McLaren, A.E. (2001). Marriage by abduction in twentieth century China. Modern Asian Studies, 35 (4): 953–984.

McLaren, A.E., & Qinjian, C. (2000). The oral and ritual culture of Chinese women. Bridal lamentations of Nanhui. Asian Folklore Studies, 59 (2): 205–238.

Morewitz, S.J. (2004). Domestic violence and maternal and child health. New York: Kluwer Academic/Plenum Publishers.

Muleta, M., & Williams, G. (1999). Postcoital injuries treated at the Addis Ababa Fistula Hospital, 1991-1997. Lancet, 354 (9195): 2051–2052.

Naved, R.T., & Akhtar, N. (2008). Spousal violence against women and suicidal ideation in Bangladesh. Womens Health Issues, 18 (6): 442–452.

Ouattara, M., Sen, P., & Thomson, M. (1998). Forced marriage, forced sex: the perils of childhood for girls. Gend Dev, 6 (3): 27–33.

Ozkan, A.R. (2006). Marriage among the gypsies of Turkey. Soc Sci J, 43 (3): 461–470.

Palmer, C.M., McNulty, A.M., D'Este, C. & Donovan, B. (2004). Sex Health, 1 (1): 55-59.

PBS, Public Broadcasting System. (no date). Bride kidnapping. http://www.pbs.org/frontlineworld/stories/kyrgyzstan/thestory.html.

PBS, Public Broadcasting System. (no date). The Mann Act. Retrieved from http://www.pbs.org.

Positive Deviance. (no date). Save the children, learning from children, families and communities to increase girls' participation in primary school. http://www.positivedeviance.org/projects/ethopedu/Ethiopia_girls_ed.pdf.

Pusurmankulova, B. (2004, June 15). Bride kidnapping: Benigh or savage tradition? Voice of Freedom Initiative of the Human Rights Working Group. Retrieved from en.wikipedia.org/wiki/Ala_kachuu.

Rimonte, N. (1991). A question of culture: Cultural approval of violence against women in the Pacific-Asian community and cultural defense. Stanford Law Rev, 43 (6): 1311–1326.

Ruremesha, J. (2003). Rights-Rwanda: Marriage by abduction worries women's groups. http://www.aegis.com/default.asp?req=http://www.aegis.com/news/ips/2003/IP031005.html. Inter Press Service, Oct. 7, 2003.

Sarkar, N.N. (2008). The impact of intimate partner violence on women's reproductive health and pregnancy outcome. J Obstet Gynaecol, 28 (3): 266–271.

Scott, G. (1986). The migrants without mountains: The sociocultural adjustment among the Lao Hmong refugees in San Diego. Ann Arbor, MI: A Bell and Howell Co.

Silverman, J.G., Decker, M.R., & Saggurti, N., et al. (2008). Intimate partner violence and HIV infection among married Indian women. JAMA, 300 (6): 703–710.
Smith, C.S. (2005). Abduction, often violent, a Kyrgyz wedding rite. New York Times, April 30, 2005.
Stross, B. (1974). Tzeltal marriage by capture. Anthro Quarterly, 47 (3): 328–346.
United States Department of State (no date). Family abduction. http://travel.state.gov/family/abduction.htm.
United States Department of State (2006a). Azerbaijan: Country reports on human rights practices – 2007. http://www.state.gov/g/drl/rls/hrrpt/2006/78801.htm.
United States Department of State (2006b). Georgia: Country reports on human rights practices – 2006. March 6, 2007. http://www.state.gov/g/drl/rls/hrrpt/2006/78813.htm.
United States Department of State (2006c). Russia: Country reports on human rights practices – 2007. March 6, 2007. http://www.state.gov/g/drl/rls/hrrpt/2006/78835.htm.
United States Department of State (2007). China: Country reports on human rights practices – 2007. March 11, 2008. http://www.state.gov/g/drl/rls/hrrpt/2007/100518.htm.
United States Department of State (2008a). Kenya: Country reports on human rights practices – 2007. March 11, 2008. http://www.state.gov/g/drl/rls/hrrpt/2007/100487.htm.
United States Department of State. (2008b). The U.S. Country Report on Human Rights Practices for Mexico 2008 noted that "kidnapping remained a serious problem for persons of all socioeconomic levels." U.S. Dep't of State, 2008 Human Rights Report: Mex. (Feb. 25, 2009).
Walsh, W.S. (1897). Curiosities of popular customs and of rites, ceremonies, observances, and miscellaneous antiquities. New York: Lippincott Co.
Werner, C. (2004). The rise of nonconsensual bride kidnapping in post-Soviet Kazakhstan. In: Pauline Jones Luong (Ed.), The transformation of Central Asia: States and societies from Soviet rule to independence. Ithaca, NY: Cornell University Press.
Werner, C. (2009). Bride abduction in post-Soviet Central Asia: marking a shift towards patriarchy through local discourses of shame and tradition. J Royal Anthro Instit, 15 (2):314–331.
Westermarck, E. (1922). The history of human marriage. New York: Allerton Book Co.
Wiltenburg, M. (2005). Backstory: The most unwanted man in Kazhakhstan. Christian Science Monitor, Nov. 30, 2005.
Yang, J.A. (2004). Marriage by capture in the Hmong culture: The legal issue of cultural rights versus women's rights. Law Soc Rev at UCSB, 3: 38–49.

Chapter 3
Family Abduction in the United States

In recent decades, the problem of children who are kidnapped by family members has been a major social problem in society. The abducted child may be missing, or the child's location may be known (Hammer et al. 2002).

The National Incidence Studies of Missing, Abducted, Runaway, and Thrownaway Children (NISMART-2) surveyed family abductions (FAs) and included several definitional elements in developing a national database of FA cases (Hammer et al. 2002). In FAs, a family member takes or keeps a child in violation of a custody order, decree, or other official custodial rights (Hammer et al. 2002). The abductor may conceal the taking or location of the child. The family member who kidnaps the child may transport the child out of state or out of the country to make recovery of the child difficult.

In these instances, the child is under 18 years of age. For children who are 15 years of age and older, NISMART-2 requires evidence that the kidnapper used some type of coercion (Hammer et al. 2002). In their database, a family member is defined as a biological, adoptive, or foster family member. A family member also may be someone acting on behalf of such a family member. In addition, a family member may be a family member's romantic partner.

According to NISMART-2, in 1999,203,900 children were abducted by a family member (Hammer et al. 2002). Among the victims of FAs in this investigation, 117,200 were kidnapped from their caretakers. Of the total number of children kidnapped by a family member, an estimated 56,500 (28%) were reported to law enforcement officials for help in locating and returning these kidnapped children.

In NISMART-2, most of the respondents were mainly female caretakers of children (Hammer et al. 2002). In addition, caretakers who had their child abducted typically provided all information about custodial rights and other characteristics of the kidnappings. Parties in these incidents often dispute the accuracy and legitimacy of these issues, and NISMART-2 investigators did not try to assess the veracity of their answers.

In the Stalking and Violence Project (SVP), 57 out of 519 or 11% of the sample of individuals filing restraining orders related to intimate partner violence (IPV) and

S. Morewitz, *Kidnapping and Violence*,
https://doi.org/10.1007/978-1-4939-2117-1_3

domestic violence (DV) indicated that their children had been threatened with FA or their children had been actually kidnapped by a family member (see Appendices A and B, Tables B.1–B.9).

Investigators have difficulty determining the true prevalence and incidence of FAs. One problem is that the legal definition ranges from instances in which a family member abducts a child for a short time period to cases in which the family member kidnaps and keeps the child permanently (Hegar and Greif 1994).

Another major problem is that left-behind family members may not report FA episodes (Plass et al. 1997).

Problems in Determining Risk Factors

Investigators encounter obstacles in ascertaining the risk factors of FAs. One problem is that researchers have not used control groups of children to compare with FA victims (Plass et al. 1997).

Another obstacle is that some investigators have relied on cases of FAs that are drawn from court records, missing children's organization, or other official sources (Plass et al. 1997; Janvier et al. 1990). Cases obtained from these official sources tend to involve the most serious or stereotypical FAs in which family members kidnap their children for long periods of time or permanently. However, FAs involve a wide spectrum of episodes from permanent abductions to much milder cases involving less serious, temporary FAs. Combining stereotypical cases with less serious ones may limit the usefulness of determining the risk factors.

Researchers also have problems in assessing risk factors for FAs because the reporting of FAs to the police may influence these conditions (Plass et al. 1997). Episodes of FAs reported to the police may represent merely the "tip of the iceberg" and, therefore, may be unreliable. Data from the NISMART studies help to overcome this problem because the investigations use a national, representative sample of parents who are interviewed directly about FA episodes.

Characteristics of the Children and Family Members

NISMART-2 indicated that the racial/ethnic characteristics of these children were similar to children in the general population (Hammer et al. 2002).

Other researchers discovered that FAs occurred more frequently among white families than among minority families (Greif and Hegar 1993). These results may be due to the fact that whites are more likely to report FAs to official agencies than African Americans (Plass et al. 1997). In addition, these findings may be biased because the studies failed to use control groups.

Most investigations have shown that children who are younger than age 5 or 6 are more likely to be kidnapped by a family member (Hammer et al. 2002). Young children may be more likely to be abducted by a family member because they are less able to decide about which parent they want to be with, and they are more easily concealed than older children (Plass et al. 1997).

The use of official records, however, may be misleading because parents may be more likely to report young children as kidnapped by a family member (Plass et al. 1997). Parents may be more likely to report their young children as kidnapped by a family member because they view the abduction of young children as more threatening than that of older children.

The results of the NISMART-2 survey in 1999 did not find any gender differences among children kidnapped by family members (Hammer et al. 2002).

Hegar and Greif (1994) found that high rates of FAs occurred in cross-cultural or international marriages.

Some investigators assume that FAs may be more likely to occur among family with high socioeconomic status (SES) (Plass et al. 1997). High-SES family members can afford to kidnap a child and take them in hiding for long periods of time. However, Plass et al. (1997) point out that these SES differences, like the racial/ethnic differences, may result from differences in reporting patterns. Members of high-SES families may be more likely to report FAs than low-SES family members.

Another possibility is that high-SES family members are more likely to kidnap their children for longer periods of time than low-SES family members (Plass et al. 1997). Researchers in the past have focused on these long-term FAs. Low-SES family members may be more likely than members of high-SES families to kidnap their children for shorter time periods, which might not result in contact with official agencies. Johnston (1994) and Sagatun-Edwards (1996) discovered that family kidnappers tended to have low SES and some were unemployed.

According to NISMART-2 survey, children were more likely to be kidnapped by family members in families where the children were not residing with both parents, and this situation provided a motivation for the abduction (Hammer et al. 2002).

Research on marital status as a risk factor for FA is mixed (Plass et al. 1997). FAs may be less prevalent among parents who were never married legally because fewer opportunities may exist for conflict over child custody issues among never married parents. In the SVP, only 8.8% of those persons who were in dating relationships or who were engaged reported that they were threatened with FAs or that their children were actually abducted (see Tables B.3 and B.4).

Investigations that have been based on clinical samples have demonstrated that FAs frequently involve the kidnapping of one child from the family (Plass et al. 1997; Greif and Hegar 1993). Experts assume that family members will tend to kidnap one child because they are better able to conceal one child.

Moreover, family members may be more likely to abduct only one child from the family because they lack the financial resources to abduct more children from the family. However, Plass et al. (1997) believe that family members may be just as likely or even more likely to kidnap a number of children from larger size families for shorter periods of time. However, these short-term abductions of multiple children by family members may be less likely to be included in official data sources.

Children living in families who experience persistent parental conflict such as litigation over child custody, physical or verbal aggression have a higher likelihood of being kidnapped by a family member. According to the SVP results, individuals who were in child custody disputes (80.4%) were more likely to be the victims of threatened or actual FAs than those who were not (5.6%) (see Table B.6).

Moreover, the risk of FAs increases when parent–child alliances are established that exclude the other parent. FAs can occur even though the parents have joint custody of the children or frequent parental visitation.

The prevalence of FAs may increase during the time between separation and divorce and before a divorce and soon thereafter since these time periods are often characterized by high levels of conflict.

Research has shown that DV and IPV were reported in more than 50% of the FA cases (Greif and Hegar 1993). In one investigation, 75% of the male family kidnappers had been violent in the past and 25% of the female family kidnappers had been violent in the past (Greif and Hegar 1993).

Mothers may take their children away from the home and reside in a DV shelter because they are fearful that their abusive partners will physically, sexually, mentally, and emotionally abuse their children (Johnston 1994). Janvier et al. (1990) showed that child abuse allegations were made against the family abductor in 66% of cases involving FAs in the U.S.

Despite the high rates of DV and IPV in cases involving FAs, some investigations reveal that DV and IPV may not predict FAs (Johnston 1994). In the SVP, only one type of violence, making death threats, was linked to threatened or actual FAs and only among African Americans.

Suspects' Demographic Characteristics

NISMART-2 data revealed a higher frequency of male suspects (66%) than female suspects (34%) (Hammer et al. 2002).

In the SVP, suspects who allegedly threatened or actually kidnapped their partners' children were more likely to be Hispanic (46.4%) and African American (39.3%) than White (12.5%) and Asian and other ethnic/racial groups (1.8%) (see Table B.4).

Numbers of Suspects Involved

According to the NISMART-2 investigation, one suspect carried out the abduction in 61% of the FAs (Hammer et al. 2002).

Suspects' Relationship to the Family-Kidnapped Child

In the NISMART-2 survey, biological fathers were suspects in 53% of the cases of the family kidnappings, followed by biological mothers (25%) (Hammer et al. 2002). According to the SVP, 98.3% of the suspects who threatened or actually kidnapped their partners' children were parents of at least one child, compared to 60.8% of suspects who did not reportedly do so.

Suspects' Criminal Background

Sagatun-Edwards (1996) found that many of the family kidnappers had a criminal history.

Suspects' Ties to a Geographic Area

Family members who do not have financial, emotional, and social ties to their place of residence may have an increased probability of kidnapping a child (Sagatun-Edwards 1996).

Offenders who have financial and emotional ties to another country, especially the offender's native country, have an increased probability of carrying out a FA (Sagatun-Edwards 1996).

Researchers have analyzed the characteristics of the FA incidents such as the location, season, duration and severity of the episodes.

Location

NISMART-2 survey results indicated that family members frequently abduct a child from the family in someone else's home or yard (37%) or in their own home or yard (36%) (Hammer et al. 2002).

Season

The results of NISMART-2 revealed some seasonal patterns of FAs (Hammer et al. 2002). In 35% of the cases, a family member kidnapped the child during the summer. These findings suggest that children are at increased risk of FAs because they frequently are with the noncustodial parents during this time period.

Duration

According to the NISMART-2 survey findings, 91% of the kidnapped children had been returned to the family by the time of the survey interview (Hammer et al. 2002). Forty-six percent of the victims had been returned to the family in less than one week and 23% had been abducted for less than one day.

FA Suspects' Behaviors During the Incidents

In NISMART-2, the family kidnappers reportedly engaged in threatening behaviors in 4% of the FAs (Hammer et al. 2002). The suspect allegedly used force in carrying out the abduction in 7% of the cases.

Seventeen percent of the alleged perpetrators in NISMART-2 took the child out of state in order to make recovery of the child more difficult (Hammer et al. 2002).

Left-Behind Parents Seek Assistance Regarding FA

Local, state, and federal law enforcement organizations investigate FAs, and the courts respond to FAs (Girdner 1994a). Law enforcement personnel investigate incidents, search for the kidnappers and the children, and file criminal charges against the suspects.

Left-behind parents and other family members frequently notify law enforcement agencies first when their child has been abducted from the family. As noted earlier, parents reported the abduction to the police in 56,500 FA cases or 28% of the cases in NISMART-2 (Hammer et al. 2002).

Hatcher et al. (1993) showed that left-behind parents called the police first in 90% of the episodes. In 62% of the incidents, left-behind parents contacted law enforcement within 24 h of their first awareness and concern about the abduction. In their report, left-behind family members also indicated that they had notified the National Center for Missing and Exploited Children (NCMEC) in 41% of the incidents. In 21% of the episodes, families also asked the relatives of the suspect for help.

Law enforcement professionals will investigate FA episodes if they view them as serious, e.g., if the child is transported out of state (Girdner 1994b). If a court order for custody has been issued in the state where the kidnapping occurred, the police will be more likely to respond the incident. If a restraining order has been filed, police will be more likely to search for the kidnapped child (Girdner 1994b).

The police and other law enforcement agencies will investigate FA cases if there is a history of abuse in the family and if the child is in danger of sexual abuse or other forms of abuse and neglect. The police also will respond to FA incidents if the abducted child requires medications or has other medical needs (Collins et al. 1993).

One investigation surveyed parents to assess how the police responded to reports of kidnappings by parents (Plass et al. 1995). In the survey, 58% of the police officers interviewed the parent. Fifty-four percent of the parents indicated that a police officer came to the crime scene.

In the survey, 36% of the parents reported that law enforcement professionals referred the kidnapping case to another agency (Plass et al. 1995). Law enforcement personnel may refer the cases to family courts, social service organizations, and prosecutors (Collins et al. 1993).

Plass et al. (1995) also revealed that parents frequently did not view the police procedures as adequate. Sixty-three percent of the parents were somewhat or very dissatisfied with the way law enforcement professionals responded to the kidnapping episodes.

Researchers also have evaluated how judges handle request for orders of protection in cases involving allegations of threatened or actual FAs. In the SVP, petitioners who reportedly were threatened with FAs or who had their children kidnapped were more likely to request that the court protect their dependents (72.7%) than petitioners who had not been victimized in these ways (40.7%) (see Table B.8). The courts were more likely to approve requests for protection of dependents in cases involving threatened or actual FAs (65.2%) than in incidents not involving these allegations (42.9%).

Girdner (1994c) notes that the public does not view FAs as harmful to the abducted children since they are being cared for by the parent/abductor. In addition, even law enforcement professionals may perceive FAs as a civil matter and a private family issue and, therefore, should be handled outside the criminal justice system.

When law enforcement officials take the matter seriously, they indicate that they encounter various difficulties in responding to FA incidents (Collins et al. 1993). Left-behind family members and the abductors may offer false and inconsistent information about the kidnapping episode.

Law enforcement personnel may have difficulty corroborating custody orders. For example, the custody orders may be documented insufficiently. In addition, the custody orders may have different interpretations.

Kidnapping laws and statutes may be vague, and law enforcement personnel may have trouble understanding them. Law enforcement personnel must be familiar with both civil and criminal laws. Civil laws were passed to deal with the difficulties associated with interstate and international FAs: (1) The Uniform Child Custody Jurisdiction Act (UCCJA) (www.uniformlaws.org/shared/docs/child_custody_jurisdiction/uccja68.pdf) seeks to eliminate jurisdictional conflicts between states in making and changing custody awards; (2) The Parental Kidnapping Prevention Act of 1980 (PKPA) attempts to offer stability for the families who were experiencing custodial disputes; and The 1980 Hague Convention on the Civil Aspects of International Child Abduction seeks to provide prompt return of children under the age of 16 to the country of their "habitual residence" if they have been wrongfully removed or retained (Slota 2009; Shetty and Edleson 2005). The U.S. Congress passed the International Child Abduction Remedies Act, which is mainly concerned with requests for the return of children from the U.S.

In regard to criminal laws, the Missing Children Act of 1982 was passed by the U.S. Congress to help law enforcement agencies locate missing children. In 1984, the Missing Children's Assistance Act of 1984 was passed by U.S. Congress (Pollet 1993). The National Child Search Assistance Act of 1990 was passed by Congress to prohibit law enforcement organizations from requiring waiting periods before a child was declared missing.

States also have passed various criminal parental child abduction (PCA) statues that are known as criminal custodial interference laws (Pollet 1993). Some of these statues treat PCAs as a misdemeanor, while others classify it as a felony.

In different jurisdictions, the police and other agents also may face difficulty in delineating the different roles of the police and prosecutors. In enforcing civil custody orders, law enforcement agencies must deal with uncooperative judges.

Pollet (1993) offers recommendations to help the courts prevent PCAs. One recommendation is that the courts should require mediation in disputed custody cases unless DV or child abuse has taken place. Another recommendation is that the courts should consider evidence of DV in deciding child custody. The courts should consider parenting behaviors of the pre-divorce family in determining the least detrimental custody arrangements in disputed custody cases. The courts also should participate in systems that make the tracking of kidnapped children easier.

Another problem involves the police reporting missing children (Chiancone no date). Whether the police make an NCIC entry is sometimes based on the left-behind parent's marital and custodial status because of the nature of certain custodial interference laws in different states (Girdner 1994b). If a custody order had been filed, the number of states with an NCIC entry on the child was almost two or three times more likely compared to states in which a custody order had not been filed.

State Missing Children Clearinghouses Respond to FA Children

State missing children clearinghouses help the police and other law enforcement organizations in investigating and recovering children who have been kidnapped by family members (Chiancone no date). These clearinghouses, which are located in every state, offer education and information to the public and provide communication and coordination with parents, police, and others involved in investigating and retrieving kidnapped children.

Based on an investigation of state missing children clearinghouses, Girdner (1994b) discovered that about 50% of the organizations had responded to more than

200 FA episodes. The survey revealed that in particular abduction cases, almost 75% of the clearinghouses offered technical assistance and maintained a central file of cases.

Federal Bureau of Investigation

The Federal Bureau of Investigation (FBI) is authorized by the Parental Kidnapping Prevention Act of 1980 to investigate incidents in which children have been kidnapped by parents or their agents across state lines or abroad (Chiancone no date). In their analysis of FA incidents, Hatcher et al. (1993) discovered that the FBI did not provide assistance in 73.1% of the episodes. Their findings revealed that more than 39% of the left-behind parents who did not receive FBI assistance indicated that their child would have been retrieved faster if the FBI had participated in the investigation. About 26% of these left-behind parents felt that based on information available to them, their incidents qualified for FBI involvement.

Prosecutors and Criminal Courts

State and federal criminal laws now provide for enforcement of FAs, especially in cases where a parent abducts and transports a child out of state and obtains a custody order there (Chiancone no date). Before the Uniform Child Custody Jurisdiction Act (UCCJA) (www.uniformlaws.org/shared/docs/child_custody_jurisdiction/uccja68.pdf) and Parental Kidnapping Prevention Act (PKPA) of 1980 (28 U.S.C. 1738(a)), left-behind parents might have been unable to recover their child if their partner had transported the child to another state and obtained a custody order there. Another difficulty is that in the past the civil courts had rarely imposed their authority in these cases even when they had the authority to do so (Blomquist 1992).

Another problem is that personnel in the criminal justice system in different jurisdictions may not have extensive experience in handling FA episodes (Chiancone no date). A number of factors may explain why many FA cases are screened out of the criminal justice system (Girdner 1994a). First, some state statues categorize parental child stealing as a misdemeanor and others as a felony. Second, agencies in many states use inconsistent procedures or fail to use procedures in investigating the cases. For example, agencies may not consistently use school and birth records to aid them in investigating the cases. Third, because of chronic underfunding, the police and missing children clearinghouses do not give priority to FAs compared to other crimes. Finally, prosecutors and the police may be inexperienced or are unfamiliar with state and federal laws and procedures for investigating these cases.

One national survey that was conducted by the American Prosecutors Research Institute revealed that 78% of the prosecutors' offices dealt with only 1 to 5 cases of FAs each year (Klain 1995). The survey found that 90% of the prosecutors' offices prosecuted between 1 and 20 cases annually.

Using 43 FA cases from a family court services agency in California, between 1983 and 1987, Sagatun-Edwards and Barrett (1990) discovered that in 58% of the cases, criminal prosecution was initiated. The mother was the suspect in 67% of these kidnappings, and the father was the suspect in 33% of these cases. A warrant was issued in 52 of the cases. Suspects were arrested in 69% of the cases in which a warrant was issued.

In the SVP, suspects in threatened or actual FAs reportedly were more likely to be arrested for any reason (20.0%) than suspects who were not involved in threatened or actual FAs (9.3%). However, the percentage of suspects in the SVP who reportedly went to jail or prison for any reason did not vary between those who allegedly threatened or actually carried out a FA (12.5%) and those who did not (7.5%) (see Table B.9).

Girdner (1994b), based on a survey of state missing children clearinghouses, discovered that more than in criminal cases of FAs, 40% of the clearinghouses reported that prosecutors' offices assisted in the case. Most of the time, their involvement consisted of obtaining warrants.

Impact of FAs on the Kidnapped Children

Parental–child stealing can be very traumatic for both the abducted children and their left-behind family members. FA can be especially traumatic when the child is abducted by force, concealed, or the child is held for a lengthy time period.

Using findings from the NISMART survey, Plass et al. (1996) found that abducted children who were 5 years or older and those who had been abducted for longer time periods had a higher probability of suffering trauma-related problems. In their study, disruption of the children's routine, increased conflict among parents, and the children's awareness of the abduction increased the risk of trauma.

Children who are abducted on a long-term basis may become traumatized by the abduction. The kidnapped children may be deceived by the abducting parent and relocated frequently to avoid detection. This nomadic lifestyle makes it very difficult for the children to attend school and have friends.

Very young children who are separated from the left-behind parent may not remember that parent very well and, therefore, will have difficulties adjusting when they are reunited. Recovered children may experience grief and rage toward their left-behind parent. The kidnapping parent may have indoctrinated them, and these children may be showing symptoms of mental indoctrination. Recovered children frequently suffered from eating problems, sleep problems, aggressive behavior, and fearfulness.

In a longitudinal investigation of victim parents, Greif (1998a, b) discovered that for the most part, the recovered children were doing well. However, those who were doing the most poorly in terms of their functioning had been kidnapped for a longer time period, had been reunited with their left-behind family for a shorter time period, and had no contact with their kidnapping parent.

Impact on the Left-Behind Parents

Based on a survey of left-behind parents, Greif and Hegar (1991) showed that they may develop feelings of loss and rage and have sleep disturbances. Some of these left-behind parents reported feeling depressed, lonely, and fearful. To help them deal with their difficulties, 50% of this group sought assistance from a professional.

The parents' psychosocial functioning may vary depending on the stage of the family kidnapping (Chiancone no date).

In other instances, many of the parents reported that their level of psychosocial stress was higher after the child had been recovered than it had been before the kidnapping. Their increased psychological disturbance may have been due to their concern about the kidnapper re-offending and the stresses related to the reunification process. Hatcher et al. (1993) showed that 73.1% of left-behind parents in the survey reported that they were fearful that their child would be kidnapped again.

FAs can lead to substantial financial expenses for the left-behind parents, worsening their psychosocial distress. One study showed that the average cost of looking for a kidnapped child in domestic cases was more than $8,000 and more than $27,000 in international cases (Janvier et al. 1990).

References

Blomquist, M.E. (1992). Prosecutors' response to parental child stealing: A state-wide study. Final report to the U.S. Department of Justice. Sacramentao, CA: Office of the California Attorney General.

Chiancone, J. (no date). Parental abduction: A review of the literature. Washington, DC: U.S. Department of Justice, Office of Justice Programs, Office of Juvenile Justice and Delinquency Prevention.

Collins, J., Powers, L.L., & McCalla, M.E., et al. (1993). Law enforcement policies and practices regarding missing children and homeless youth. Research Summary. Washington, DC: U.S. Department of Justice, Office of Justice Programs, Office of Juvenile Justice and Delinquency Prevention.

Girdner, L. (1994a). Key laws relating to parental abductions and obstacles to their effectiveness. In L. Girdner & P. Hoff. (Eds.), Obstacles to the recovery and return of parentally abducted children. Final Report. Washington, DC: U.S. Department of Justice, Office of Justice Programs, Office of Juvenile Justice and Delinquency Prevention.

Girdner, L. (1994b). The view from state missing children clearinghouses. In Obstacles to the recovery and return of parentally abducted children, Final Report. L. Girdner & P. Hoff (Eds.), Washington, DC: U.S. Department of Justice, Office of Justice Programs, Office of Juvenile Justice and Delinquency Prevention.

Girdner, L. (1994c). Executive summary. In L. Girdner & P. Hoff (Eds.), Obstacles to the recovery and return of parentally abducted children, Final Report. Washington, DC: U.S. Department of Justice, Office of Justice Programs, Office of Juvenile Justice and Delinquency Prevention.

Greif, G.L. (1998a). The long-term impact of parental abduction on children: Implications for treatment. J Psychiatry Law, 26: 45–60.

Greif, G.L. (1998b). Many years after the parental abduction: Some consequences of relevance to the court system. Family and Conciliation Courts Rev, 36 (1): 32–40.

Greif, G.L., & Hegar, R.L. (1991). Parents whose children are abducted by the other parent: Implications for treatment. Am J Fam Therapy, 19 (3): 215–225.

Greif, G.L., & Hegar, R.L. (1993). When parents kidnap: The families behind the headlines. New York: Free Press.

Hammer, H., Finkelhor, D., & Sedlak, A.J. (2002). Children abducted by family members: National estimates and characteristics. NISMART. National incidence studies of missing, abducted, runaway, and thrown away children. Washington, DC: U.S. Department of Justice, Office of Juvenile Justice and Delinquency Prevention.

Hatcher, C., Barton, C., & Brooks, L. (1993). Reunification of missing children: Training manual. Washington, DC: U.S. Department of Justice.

Hegar, R.L., & Greif, G.L. (1994). Parental abduction from interracial and cross-cultural marriages. J Compar Family Studies, 25 (1): 135–146.

Janvier, R.F., McCormick, K., & Donaldson, R. (1990). Parental kidnapping: A survey of left-behind parents. Juven Fam Court J, 41: 1–8.

Johnston, J.R. (1994). Final report of stage 1, part B: Identification of risk factors—The interview study. In: L. Girdner & J. Johnston (Eds.). Prevention of parent or family abduction through early identification of risk factors. Report to the Office of Juvenile Justice and Delinquency Prevention. Washington, DC: American Bar Association Center on Children and the Law.

Klain, E.J. (1995). Parental kidnapping, domestic violence and child abuse: Changing legal responses to related violence. Arlington, VA: American Prosecutors Research Institute.

Missing Children Act of 1982 (28 U.S.C. 534).

Parental Kidnapping Prevention Act (PKPA) (28 U.S.C. 1738(a)).

Plass, P.S., Finkelhor, D., & Hotaling, G.T. (1995). Police response to family abduction episodes. Crime Delinq, 41 (2): 205–217.

Plass, P.S., Finkelhor, D., & Hotaling, G.T. (1996). Family abduction outcomes: Factors associated with duration and emotional trauma to children. Youth and Society, 38 (1): 109–130.

Plass, P.S., Finkelhor, D., & Hotaling, G.T. (1997). Risk factors for family abduction: Demographic and family interaction characteristics. J Family Viol, 12 (3): 333–348.

Pollet, S.L. (1993). Parental kidnapping: Can laws stem the tide? J Psychiatry Law, Winter, 417–445.

Sagatun-Edwards, I.J. (1996). Final report of stage 1, part A: A documentary study. In: Prevention of parent or family abduction through early identification of risk factors. Report to the Office of Juvenile Justice and Delinquency Prevention. L. Girdner & J. Johnston (Eds.), Washington, DC: American Bar Association Center on Children and the Law.

Sagatun-Edwards, I.J., & Barrett, L. (1990). Parental child abduction: The law, family dynamics, and legal system responses. J Crim Justice, 18: 433–442.

Shetty, S., & Edleson, J.L. (2005). Adult domestic violence in cases of international parental child abduction. Viol Against Women, 11 (1): 115–138.

Slota, H.J. (2009). Preventing and responding to international child abduction. Amer J Family Law, 23 (2): 73–78.

Chapter 4
International Family Abduction

International family abduction (IFA) is a significant problem in the U.S. and in other countries, and the problem has received substantial media attention. One investigation found that 350,000 children are abducted annually in the U.S. (Rigler and Wieder no date; Slota 2009). Ten thousand of these children are kidnapped and held in another country by a parent who has a different nationality (National Report —International Child Custody for the Common Law Judicial Conference on International Child Custody no date).

Since the late 1970s, 16,000 cases of child abductions into and out of the United States have come to the attention of the U.S. Department of State's Office of Children's Issues (Shetty and Edleson 2005; U.S. Department of State no date). The Office of Children's Issues manages cases children abducted from the United States and taken to other countries. The U.S. Department of State (2003) reported to Congress that parents in the U.S. filed 904 international kidnapping applications in 2003. The largest number of these outgoing cases involved transportation of abducted children to Mexico (154), followed by other countries, including Germany (41), Jordan (34), and Japan (33).

According to the *Boston Globe*, the courts in the U.S. between 1995 and 2002 handled 2,688 cases under the Hague Convention on the Civil Aspects of International Child Abduction (Cambanis 2002). Left-behind parents in IFAs may also contact nonprofit organizations for assistance in getting their children returned (Shetty and Edleson 2005). The National Center for Missing and Exploited Children (NCMEC) is a U.S. nongovernmental organization that is officially designated to help left-behind parents in foreign countries find and return their children who were abducted into the U.S. In 2002, the NCME reported that they received 445 IFA applications from left-behind parents in foreign countries. The number of applications had increased from 241 in 1998 (Subcommittee on International Child Abduction of the Federal Agency Task Force on Missing and Exploited Children and the Policy Group on International Parental Kidnapping 1999). Left-behind parents who filed applications came mostly from Europe and Eurasia (169), Mexico

S. Morewitz, *Kidnapping and Violence*,
https://doi.org/10.1007/978-1-4939-2117-1_4

(129), and Central and South America (69). Shetty and Edleson (2005) believe that many more IFAs are not reported to either the U.S. State Department or NCMEC.

Parents may kidnap their children without warning (Slota 2009). However, various conditions may increase the likelihood that they will abduct their children and take them across international borders.

Contested Child Custody

A risk factor for IFAs is parents who are in conflict over child custody issues or who are undergoing divorce, separation, or family conflict (Jaffee et al. 2003; Girdner and Johnston 1994). Noncustodial parents may abduct their children and take their children across international borders. In Missing Persons Project (MPP) Case YYY1, a 4-year-old girl was reportedly kidnapped by her noncustodial mother on November 11, 1998, from Auburn, Washington (see Appendix D). The noncustodial mother and her abducted daughter are thought to be from Costa Rica.

Children during parent–child visits are especially at risk for IFAs.

Domestic Violence (DV) and Intimate Partner Violence (IPV)

Domestic violence (DV) and intimate partner violence (IPV) increase the risk of IFAs (Shetty and Edleson 2005). Research has revealed that almost 50% of families suffering adult family violence also exhibit signs of child mistreatment (Dunford-Jackson 2004).

Abused mothers may abduct and transport their children across international borders because of their deep concern for their children's safety (Humphreys 1995; Shetty and Edleson 2005). Fathers who batter their wives and children may kidnap their children and take them across international borders as part of their harassment of their battered partner during child custody fights.

Parents in bicultural families are more likely to commit IFAs than those not in bicultural families.

Individuals, who are fluent in English and their native language, may be better able to kidnap their children and transport them to their native country than kidnapping parents who are not bilingual. Bilingual parents will be better able to adjust to living in their native countries than non-bilingual parents.

Being an immigrant increases a parent's risk of committing an international child kidnapping (Slota 2009). Likewise, parents who live in another country may be more likely to kidnap their children. Parents may threaten their partner with both deportation and IFA.

Parents in states that border Mexico may be likely to abduct their children and take their children across the border.

Individuals who are knowledgeable about international child abduction laws may be more likely to kidnap their children and transport them to countries and jurisdictions where they believe that the courts will grant them child custody. These parents will engage in so-called "forum shopping" (Kiedrowski et al. 1994).

Parents who have close ties to their country of origin or another country are more likely that they will abduct their children and take them across international borders (Slota 2009). Those parents who have family and friends in another country are at increased risk of carrying out an IFA.

Parents who have financial resources to travel abroad and remain there may be at increased risk of abducting their children and crossing international borders.

The parents' type of occupation may increase their chances of carrying out international child abduction. The abducting father in MPP XXX4 worked usually as an unskilled laborer, which allowed him to move easily across borders and take available work as needed.

Certain behaviors such as quitting a job, obtaining passports, and buying airline tickets are signals of an impending IFA (Slota 2009).

Impact of IFA

Children who have been kidnapped and transported across international borders by their parents and other family members can suffer a range of psychosocial problems and impairments.

Responding to IFAs

The 1980 Hague Convention on the Civil Aspects of International Child Abduction provides for the prompt return of children under the age of 16 to the country of their "habitual residence" if they have been wrongfully removed or retained (Slota 2009; Lamont 2009). Slota (2009) noted that unless a divorce judgment has a provision to the contrary, parents are allowed to transport their children across international borders during their placement without the permission of the other parent as long as the visit is less than 90 days.

If a child from the U.S. is kidnapped and taken to another country, then that country's laws and policies will influence whether and how the child is returned (Slota 2009). Left-behind parents may not be able to recover their children if they have been kidnapped and taken to a country that is not a signatory to the Hague Convention on the Civil Aspects of International Child Abduction. Trying to recover a kidnapped child may be very costly. Parents may have to spend as much as $100,000 in litigating a Hague Convention case in a court of a foreign country.

In 1988, the U.S. Congress recognized the global nature of kidnapped and missing children and ratified the Hague Convention on missing children by enacting the International Child Remedies Act (42 U.S.C. 11601–11610). This act authorized the U.S. State Department to respond to noncustodial parental kidnappings in situations under which the kidnapping parent takes the child outside the U.S.

In 1993, the U.S. Congress passed the International Parental Child Kidnapping Act (IPCKA) (18 U.S.C. 1204). This act made it a felony for an individual to remove a child from the U.S. in order to interfere with custody orders (Allender 2007).

Data from the MPP reveal that law enforcement agencies are handling a number of the IFA cases under the terms of the Hague Convention on the Civil Aspects of International Child Abduction and the IPCKA.

Preventing IFAs

Slota (2009) offers advice to family law attorneys who suspect that a kidnapping is possible. Attorneys should consider having their clients take photographs of their children, having their children fingerprinted, notifying schools and other organizations about their concerns. Parents should also contact the airlines and ask them to notify them if reservations are made or tickets issued in their children's names.

References

Allender, D.M. (2007, July). Child abductions: Nightmares in progress. FBI Law Enforcm Bulletin, 76 (7): 1–7.

Cambanis, T. (2002, April 16). Advocates say children put at risk. *Boston Globe*, B1. http://www.boston.com.

Dunford-Jackson, B.L. (2004). The role of family courts in domestic violence. The U.S. experience. In P.G. Jaffe, et al. (Eds.), Protecting children from domestic violence: Strategies for community intervention. New York: Guilford.

Girdner, L., & Johnston, J. (Eds.). (1994). Prevention of parent or family abduction through early identification of risk factors. Report to the Office of Juvenile Justice and Delinquency Prevention. Washington, DC: American Bar Association Center on Children and the Law.

Humphreys, J.C. (1995). Dependent-care by battered women: Protecting their children. Hlth Care for Women Intl, 16: 9–20.

International Child Remedies Act (42 U.S.C. 11601–11610).

International Parental Child Kidnapping Act (IPCKA) (18 U.S.C. 1204).

Jaffe, P.G., Lemon, N., & Poisson, S. (2003). Child custody and domestic violence: A call for safety and accountability. Thousand Oaks, CA: Sage.

Kiedrowski, J., Jayewardene, C.H.S., & Dalley, M. (1994). The police and parental abduction: An overview for police direction. Ottawa: Royal Canadian Mounted Police.

Lamont, R. (2009). Re M and beyond: Managing return when a child has settled following abduction. J Soc Welfare Family Law, 31 (1): 73–81.

National Report—International Child Custody for the Common Law Judicial Conference (no date). http://travel.state.gov/family/abduction/resources/resources_543.html.

Rigler, Hon. W.R., & Wieder, H.L. (no date). The epidemic of parental child-snatching: An overview. http://travel.state.gov/family/abduction/resources/resources_545.html.

Shetty, S., & Edleson, J.L. (2005). Adult domestic violence in cases of international parental child abduction. Viol Against Women, 11 (1): 115–138.

Slota, H.J. (2009). Preventing and responding to international child abduction. Amer J Family Law, 23 (2): 73–78.

Subcommittee on International Child Abduction of the Federal Agency Task Force on Missing and Exploited Children and the Policy Group on International Parental Kidnapping. (1999). A report to the attorney general on international parental Kidnapping. Washington, DC: U.S. Department of Justice. http://www.ncjrs.org/html/ojjdp/ojjdp_report_ip_kidnapping/RptParentalKidnap.pdf.

United States Department of State (no date). Family abduction. http://travel.state.gov/family/abduction.htm.

United States Department of State. (2003). Report to Congress on international child abductions in response to the statement of managers accompanying F-103 Omnibus Appropriations Bill P.L. 108-7. http://travel.state.gov/family/abduction_hague_05.html.

Chapter 5
Nonfamily Juvenile Abduction

Nonfamily juvenile abduction (NFJA) is infrequent even though the incidents are often sensationalized and exaggerated by the media, which often portray child abduction as an epidemic (Miller et al. 2008; Beyer and Beasley 2003; Shutt et al. 2004; Moscowitz and Duvall 2011). The media devotes a great deal of attention to child abductions, including high-profile cases, such as the Elizabeth Smart, Jaycee Dugard, and Danielle van Dam kidnappings, creating fear and anger in parents and members of the public (Miller et al. 2008). For example, Eichelberger et al. (1990) discovered that parents in their survey were more concerned about the risk that their children would be kidnapped and abuse drugs than suffering from physical injury in childhood.

These media depictions of NFJAs reaffirm cultural traditions, such as the Little Red Riding Hood fairy tale. Many of these fairy tales and media accounts focus on the vulnerability of children and instances in which parents fail to fulfill their obligations to protect children from predators.

Parents may be influenced by media coverage of child kidnappings to such an extent that they will initiate communication with their children about strategies to respond to these risks (Martin and Wilson 2011).

Media depiction of child abductions may not be uniform. For example, the media's coverage of child abductions may differ depending on the type of abduction allegedly committed (Taylor et al. 2013). Based on an analysis of newspaper accounts and results from NISMART-2 (Hammer et al. 2002), Taylor et al. (2013) demonstrated that in newspaper coverage of abductions involving children 11 years of age and under, the newspapers provided more accounts of girls than boys who had been kidnapped by individuals who were not family members. In contrast, Taylor et al. (2013) discovered that the newspapers provided a factual description of the demographic characteristics of children who were the victims of other types of kidnappings.

However, the cultural traditions and media coverage of JAs may mislead the public legislators by neglecting the complexities of this phenomenon (Best and Thibodeau 1997; Miller et al. 2008; Moscowitz and Duvall 2011; Shutt et al. 2004).

S. Morewitz, *Kidnapping and Violence*,
https://doi.org/10.1007/978-1-4939-2117-1_5

As a result, criminal justice system responses may be affected by inaccurate and sensationalized media coverage of JAs.

In their study of U.S. newspaper accounts of child kidnappings from 2000 to 2003, Moscowitz and Duvall (2011) discovered that newspapers focused on young, middle and upper SES white girls who had been kidnapped from their residence by male strangers even though these crimes were rare.

High-profile cases of JAs that are reported in the media often do not reflect the actual risk of juvenile abductions by strangers or slight acquaintances (Finkelhor et al. 2002; Shutt et al. 2004; Finkelhor and Ormrod 2000). Juvenile kidnappings by strangers take place less often than family abductions (FAs) (Shutt et al. 2004). According to the National Incidence Studies of Missing, Abducted, Runaway, and Thrownaway Children (NISMART-2), about 12,100 NFJAs occurred in 1999 (Finkelhor et al. 2002). However, the estimate is based on an extremely small sample size, making its precision and confidence interval unreliable.

The risks of stereotypical stranger kidnappings are rarer (Shutt et al. 2004). According to the definition of stereotypical kidnapping in NISMART-2, the offender, a stranger or slight acquaintance, detains the juvenile overnight, transports her or him at least 50 miles, holds the juvenile for ransom, and kidnaps the juvenile in order to keep him or her permanently, or murders the juvenile (Finkelhor et al. 2002).

A stranger is defined as an offender of unknown identity (Finkelhor et al. 2002). A slight acquaintance is a nonfamily offender and the juvenile or family members do not know the perpetrator's name before the kidnapping. The juvenile or family may not know the perpetrator well enough to speak to this person or the juvenile or family has known the abductor for less than 6 months. The kidnapper may be someone who the juvenile or family has known for more than 6 months but has seen less than once a month.

In 1999, NISMART-2 reported only 115 stereotypical abductions, which is 0.00016% of the child population (Finkelhor et al. 2002). Hanfland et al. (1997) found that in 48% of the cases the child abductors knew their victims. The perpetrator–victim relationship varies depending on such factors as the age of the victim. Strangers and acquaintances are more likely to kidnap children of school age, whereas family members are more likely to abduct infants and toddlers (Boudreaux et al. 2000).

The National Incident-Based Recording System (NIBRS) in 1997 recorded 1,214 kidnappings involving victims ages 17 and younger from jurisdictions in 12 states. The NIBRS revealed that 49% of these JAs were by family members. In addition, juveniles were more likely to be kidnapped by an acquaintance (27%) than by a stranger (24%). These results refute the cultural myths and media emphasis on JAs by strangers.

In addition, the chances of stereotypical stranger kidnappings that lead to homicide are very rare (Shutt et al. 2004). Offenders, who are often strangers, may commit sexual murders of children, and they may abduct their victims (Heide et al. 2009). According to Heide et al. (2009), sexual murders of children share common characteristics; the offenders are similar to perpetrators who are classified as sadistic. These sadistic offenders are different from those who commit sexual murders of adult women.

Definition and Measurement of JAs

JA is difficult to define because experts do not agree on a single definition (Boudreaux et al. 2000). For example, the legal definitions of the terms "child" and "abduction" can differ from one jurisdiction to another.

One definition can refer to moving and detaining a person by force for a short time period, while other legal definitions refer to coercive movement and imprisonment for a long-term basis (Boudreaux et al. 2000). In California, moving an individual 22 feet has been viewed as kidnapping.

The 1932 Lindbergh kidnapping significantly influenced federal law regarding kidnappings (Forst and Blomquist 1991; Boudreaux et al. 2000). Federal law originally did not involve the prosecution of parents. Federal law also permitted the use of the death penalty. However, the courts would not impose the death penalty if the victim was freed unharmed. Federal law also assumed that after 7 days, interstate transport of the victim had occurred. This law later was changed to 24 h. According to federal law, kidnapping occurs if the offender takes and/or confines the victim and holds for ransom, reward, or the perpetrator uses ruse, lure, or trickery or uses force to take and confine the victim.

Another factor that may complicate the definition of JAs is that both children and adolescents are included as victims. Traditionally, the term child kidnapping or child abduction has been used in research. However, the use of the term, child abduction, may exclude adolescents from the studies, leading to an undercount of JA victims.

Moreover, another measurement problem is that researchers traditionally have lumped acquaintance abduction (AA) and stranger abduction (SA) into one category of NFJA. Finkelhor and Ormrod (2000) suggest that AAs have unique features and therefore should be viewed as separate from SAs.

Motivational Factors

Different motivations among kidnappers will affect the nature and outcome of the crime. However, Boudreaux et al. (2000) point out that the perpetrators' motivations and behaviors often are unclear.

Researchers have found that kidnappers will abduct a juvenile because of the maternal desire to have a child. Women typically will kidnap an infant from a hospital nursery or other setting because of their pathological need for a baby.

A substantial minority of NFJAs may involve child sexual abuse. Gallagher et al. (2008) analyzed attempted and completed incidents of stranger-perpetrated child sexual abuse and JA based on a sample of 161 children who had reported that the last incident had been committed by a stranger. The investigators identified four types of incidents: (1) indecent exposure, (2) touching, (3) kidnapping, and (4) combined behaviors.

Offenders will abduct a child because of their desire to obtain money. Abduction laws in the U.S. were enacted to deal with kidnapping for profit (Finkelhor et al. 1991; Boudreaux et al. 2000).

NFJAs may occur as part of human trafficking (HT).

In other instances, perpetrators abduct juveniles because of a desire to kill. Fortunately, kidnappings that result in homicide are less common than JAs that result in the child being returned alive. According to NISMART-2, of the 115 stereotypical child abductions that took place, 46 were murdered by their offender, representing 0.000066% of the child population (Finkelhor et al. 2002).

Other Child Kidnapper Characteristics in NFJA Cases

The majority of the perpetrators are male. Boudreaux et al. (1999) discovered that offenders in NFJAs tended to be male, white, and often abducted children of their own race.

Finkelhor and Ormrod (2000) suggest that AA should not be combined with SA. A higher percentage of juveniles tend to commit AAs. In addition, perpetrators are more likely to sexually assault or physically assault their victims in AAs. The researchers found that AAs are more likely to occur in residences.

In contrast, in Finkelhor and Ormrod's (2000) analysis, offenders in SAs have a higher probability of committing the offense in outdoor locations. SA is the form of abduction mostly likely to be associated with the use of a gun.

The patterns of behavior of offenders may be based on the perpetrator's gender, motive for the kidnapping, and relationship to the victim (Miller et al. 2008).

Researchers have evaluated child kidnappers' patterns of prior offending. Based on a sample of 750 child abductors, Beasley et al. (2009) demonstrated that perpetrators had committed an average of seven prior crimes based on the National Crime Information Center (NCIC) criminal history for each perpetrator. The abductor's prior offenses took place over an average of 12 years. Child abductors with a criminal history were more likely to have been arrested for assault (41%), larceny (40%), burglary/breaking and entering (35%), forcible sex crimes (33%), drug crimes (25%).

Children's Risk

The likelihood that children will be kidnapped may vary depending on the type of abduction, the victims' age, and other factors. Finkelhor and Ormrod (2000) showed that in family kidnappings, children under age 6 are more likely to be abducted. In their study, children of both sexes had an equal chance of being kidnapped in family abductions.

In Finkelhor and Ormrod's (2000) analysis of AAs, victims were more likely to be female and adolescents. AAs involved the highest proportion of injured victims. Victims in this type of kidnapping are more likely to be the victims of other crimes, especially sexual and physical assault.

In SAs, Finkelhor and Ormrod (2000) demonstrated that females had a higher probability of being victimized than males. In terms of age, both adolescents and school-age children had the same chances of being kidnapped. The investigators also discovered that in SAs, female victims had a greater likelihood of being sexually assaulted, while in some instances male victims were more likely to be robbed. Victims of this type of kidnapping are more likely to have a firearm used against them.

Boudreaux et al. (1999) demonstrated that overall although females had a higher probability of being kidnapped than males, males, aged birth to three, were more likely to be kidnapped than females. From preschool through high school (aged 3–18 years), the investigators discovered that females were at least three times more likely to be abducted than males.

Risks of victimization may vary depending on the type of crimes committed. Boudreaux et al. (1999) revealed that profit-motivated kidnappings involving extortion, robbery, drugs, and other criminal activities were more likely to have older victims such as high school students.

Location of NFJAs

Children may be abducted despite the fact that parents closely watch their children (Beck and Miltenberger 2009). In 1999, 77% of the NFJAs occurred in the streets and parks of the community where the victim lived. Twenty-three percent of the NFJAs occurred in the victim's home or yard (Finkelhor et al. 2002).

References

Beasley, J.O., Hayne, A.S., & Beyer, K., et al. (2009). Patterns of prior offending of child abductors: A comparison of fatal and non-fatal outcomes. Intl J Law Psychiatry, 32, 273–280.

Beck, K.V., & Miltenberger, R.G. (2009). Evaluation of a commercially available program and in-situ training by parents to teach abduction-prevention skills. J Appl Behav Anal, Winter, 42 (4): 761–772.

Best, J., & Thibodeau, T.M. (1997). Measuring the scope of social problems. Apparent inconsistencies across estimates of family abductions. Just Quarterly, 14: 719–736.

Beyer, K.R., & Beasley, J.O. (2003). Nonfamily child abductors who murder their victims. Offender demographics from interviews with incarcerated offenders. J Interpers Viol, 18 (10): 1167–1188.

Boudreaux, M.C., Lord, W.D., & Dutra, R.L. (1999). Child abduction: Age-based analyses of offender, victim, and offense characteristics in 550 cases of alleged child disappearance. J Forensic Sci, 44: 539–553.

Boudreaux, M.C., Lord, W.D., & Etter, S.E. (2000). Child abduction: An overview of current and historical perspectives. Child Mistreatment, 5 (1): 63–71.

Eichelberger, M.R., Gotschall, C.S., Feely, H.B., et al. (1990). Parental attitudes and knowledge of child safety. A national survey. Am J Dis Child, June; 144(6): 714–720.

Finkelhor, D., & Ormrod, R. (2000). Kidnapping of juveniles: Patterns from NIBRS. Office of Juvenile Justice Delinquency Prevention, Juvenile Justice Bull, 1–7.

Finkelhor, D., Hotaling, G.T., & Sedlak, A. (1991). Children abducted by family members: National household survey of incidence and episode characteristics. J Marr Family, 53, 805–817.

Finkelhor, D., Hammer, H., & Sedlak, A.J. (2002). Nonfamily abducted children: National estimates and characteristics. Washington, DC: U.S. Department of Justice.

Forst, M.L., & Blomquist, M.E. (1991). Missing children: Rhetoric and reality. Lexington, MA: Lexington Books.

Gallagher, B., Bradford, M., & Pease, K. (2008). Attempted and completed incidents of stranger-perpetrated child sexual abuse and abduction. Child Abuse & Neglect, 32: 517–528.

Hammer, H., Finkelhor, D., & Sedlak, A.J. (2002). Children abducted by family members: National estimates and characteristics. NISMART. National incidence studies of missing, abducted, runaway, and thrownaway children. Washington, DC: U.S. Department of Justice, Office of Juvenile Justice and Delinquency Prevention.

Hanfland, K.A., Keppel, R.D., & Weis, J.G. (1997). Case management for missing children homicide investigation. Olympia, WA: Attorney General of Washington.

Heide, K.M., Beauregard, E., Myers, W.C. (2009). Sexually motivated child abduction murders: Synthesis of the literature and case illustrations. Victims & offenders: An Intl J Evidence-Based Res Policy Pract, 4(1): 58–75.

Martin, N., & Wilson, B.J. (2011). Parental communication about kidnapping stories in the US news. J Children Media, 5(2): 132–146.

Miller, J.M., Kurlycheck, M., & Hansen, J.A., et al. (2008). Examining child abduction by offender type patterns. Just Quarterly, 25 (3): 523–543.

Moscowitz, L., & Duvall, S.-S. (2011). Every parent's worst nightmare. Myths of child abductions in US news. J Children Media, 5(2): 147–163.

Shutt, J.E., Miller, J.M., Schreck, C.J., et al. (2004). Reconsidering the leading myths of stranger abduction. Crim Just Studies: A Crit J Crime, Law Soc, 17(1): 127–134.

Taylor, J., Bolsvert, D., Sims, B., & Garver, C. (2013). An examination of gender and age in print media accounts of child abductions. Crim Just Stud: A Crit J Crime Law Soc, 26(2): 151–167.

Chapter 6
Responses to Abducted Children

In the United States, since the 1930s, laws, policies, organizations, and treatment programs have been established to improve responses to the problems of abducted and missing children (Karmen 2010; Beck and Miltenberger 2009; Griffin 2010; Jones 2003; Office of Juvenile Justice and Delinquency Prevention 2008). Individuals and local communities also may develop strategies to prevent abductions and react to incidents that occur.

For Zgoba (2004a), moral panic develops from the media's coverage of child abduction. People may hear about a few sensational child abduction cases and then incorrectly perceive the problem of child kidnappings as a pervasive and intense threat to society. Their false social constructions of the social problems outweigh the true nature of the problem. These crime myths may become embedded in our consciousness and lead policy-makers to develop laws and policies that are not based on reliable research (Kappeler and Potter 2005; Zgoba 2004a).

Prior to 1932 in the U.S., no federal agency had any jurisdiction in responding to kidnapping cases (Allender 2007). These incidents were considered local problems that were best resolved by local law enforcement agencies.

However, the Charles A. Lindbergh, Jr., kidnapping changed this situation. On March 1, 1932, Charles A. Lindbergh, Jr., the 20-month-old son of the famous aviator, Charles Lindbergh, was kidnapped from his home in Hopewell, New Jersey, and killed by Bruno Richard Hauptmann, a paroled German convict who had entered the U.S. illegally (Allender 2007; World Almanac and Book of Facts 2009).

Members of the public were very upset that the extensive resources of the U.S. government could not be immediately used to resolve this important kidnapping (Allender 2007). Later during 1932, the U.S. Congress responded to the public outrage over the Lindberg kidnapping by enacting the Federal Kidnapping Act (FKA) (18 U.S.C. 1201(a)(1). This Act enabled federal agencies to provide law enforcement assistance in kidnapping incidents.

S. Morewitz, *Kidnapping and Violence*,
https://doi.org/10.1007/978-1-4939-2117-1_6

In 1955, the National Child Safety Council (NCSC) was established (www.nationalchildsafetycouncil.org). The NCSC was the first private and voluntary organization of its kind.

Between 1932 and 1968, little had changed in how law enforcement agencies investigated missing children (Allender 2007). Meanwhile, divorce became more prevalent and child custody issues became salient for many American families. One problem has been that a parent during divorce proceedings could go out of state and get a judge to issue a custody order that conflicted with the original order. The parent could then remain out of state and keep custody of her or his children.

The U.S. Congress in 1968 addressed this child custody problem by passing the Uniform Child Custody Jurisdiction Act (UCCJA) (19 U.S.C. Chap. 16; (www.uniformlaws.org/shared/docs/child_custody_jurisdiction/uccja68.pdf)) (Allender 2007). The UCCJA prohibited a parent from going to another state in order to change custody. However, even after the act was enacted, judges still issued conflicting orders. As a consequence, when parents reported their children missing, law enforcement agencies were confused about which custody order to enforce. Authorities had to resolve each controversy using a cumbersome case-by-case approach.

The U.S. Congress passed the Juvenile Justice and Delinquency Prevention Act (JJDPA) (Pub. L. No. 93-415, 42 U.S.C. 5601 et seq., www.ojjdp.gov/about/legislation.html) in 1974. The JJDPA required that runaway youth receive shelter but not be arrested and incarcerated.

In 1977, the state of California became the first state to make violations of child custody agreements a felony.

The dilemma of missing children was an important social problem in the 1980s, and a number of policy innovations occurred during this period (Allender 2007). In 1980, the U.S. Congress amended the JJDPA to allow law enforcement departments to hold chronic runaway youth under court order until they came home.

In 1980, the U.S. Congress enacted the Parental Kidnapping Prevention Act (PKPA) (28 U.S.C. 1738(a)) to enhance the UCCJA (Allender 2007). The PKPA also created a locator service that enabled states to use social security numbers and address information to find fugitive parents who had kidnapped their children. The PKPA also provided for the use of the Fugitive Felon Act (FFA) (18 U.S.C. 1073) against these fugitive parents.

One year later, a U.S. Senate subcommittee held the first hearings on the issue of missing children. In 1981, child safety groups established a Child Tragedies Coalition (Karmen 2010).

Authorities in that same year solved the mysteries surrounding the disappearances of 28 children in Atlanta, Georgia, over a period of 2 years. A young man was arrested and convicted of homicide (Karmen 2010).

Prior to 1982, many children kidnapped by a noncustodial parent could not be entered into the National Crime Information Center (NCIC) (Allender 2007). The U.S. Congress enacted the Missing Children Act of 1982 (28 U.S.C. 534), which authorized the entry of these kidnapped and missing children into the NCIC system, even though the noncustodial parents would not be subject to criminal prosecution.

To increase public recognition of the problem of missing and abducted children, the U.S. Congress in 1982 designated May 25 as National Missing Children's Day.

One year later, an estimated 55 million people viewed a television docudrama about the kidnapping and murder of a boy named Adam (Karmen 2010).

The Missing Children's Assistance Act (MCAA) (42 U.S.C. 5771) was passed in 1984. The MCAA established the National Center for Missing and Exploited Children (NCMEC) to offer assistance to those seeking help for their abducted and missing children. The NCMEC also created an advisory board to assist government agencies in responding to the problems of abducted and missing children.

After the broadcast of a television documentary in 1985, President Ronald Reagan asked members of the public to help authorities locate missing children. Sixty photographs were broadcasted, resulting in the quick reunions of three children with their families (Karmen 2010).

The first annual National Conference on Missing and Exploited Children was held in 1986 (Karmen 2010).

One year later, The National Association of Missing Child Organization (NAMCO) is established (Karmen 2010). NAMCO shares information about missing children and maintains standards for professionals.

The U.S. Congress in 1988 amended the MCAA to allocate funds for creating and maintaining state-level clearinghouses (Karmen 2010). These clearinghouses help coordinate local police agencies, social service organizations, and educational efforts.

As noted in Chap. 5, the U.S. Congress in 1988 ratified the Hague Convention on missing children by enacting the International Child Remedies Act (42 U.S.C. 11601-11610). This act authorized the U.S. State Department to handle noncustodial parental kidnappings in situations under which the kidnapping parent takes the child outside the U.S.

In the decade of the 1990s, more laws were enacted. In 1990, the U.S. Congress established the National Child Search Assistance Act (NCSAA) (42 U.S.C. 5779). This act mandated the police officers immediately enter information about missing children, including all reported runaway youth, into the NCIC system (Allender 2007). In addition, the NCSAA expanded the participation of the NCMEC in law enforcement activities.

In 1993, the U.S. Congress passed the International Parental Child Kidnapping Act (IPCKA) (18 U.S.C. 1204), making it a felony for an individual to remove a child from the U.S. in order to interfere with custody orders (Allender 2007).

State and federal legislators in 1993 passed "three strikes and you're out" laws to lock up three-time felons for life in response to the kidnapping and murder of a 12-year-old girl, Polly Klaas, in California, by a parolee, Richard Allen Davis (Karmen 2010).

In 1994, the U.S. Congress enacted the Jacob Wetterling Crimes Against Children and Sexually Violent Offender Registration Act (42 U.S.C. 14701) (Allender 2007). This Act provides information on the number of sex offenders and authorized the development of a database that law enforcement agencies can access in case a child is kidnapped or goes missing. The database provides information on possible suspects.

Later, Megan's Law (community notification) authorized law enforcement agencies to offer information on registered sex offenders to the public (Jacob Wetterling Crimes Against Children and Sexually Violent Offender Registration Act; 42 U.S.C. 14701)

As a consequence of these changes, websites were implemented to offer this information to the public. In 2006, the U.S. Congress provided federal sanctions for sex offenders who failed to register.

The U.S. Department of Justice in 1996 established the Victim Reunification Travel Program (VRTP) (U.S. Department of Justice 1996, Victim Reunification Travel Program, www.missingkids.com/Reunification). This program assists parents whose children have been illegally kidnapped and transported abroad by family members.

Organizational and policy developments continue in the twenty-first century to deal with the problems of abducted and missing children. In 2001, the NCMEC established a cold case unit to investigate incidents of abducted and missing children that date back to 1947.

In 2003, the U.S. Congress enacted the Prosecutorial Remedies and Other Tools to End the Exploitation of Children Today Act (PROTECT Act) (18 U.S.C. 2252), a bill that helps states create a national abduction "AMBER Alert" broadcasting system. The AMBER Alert broadcasting system was named after a 9-year-old girl, Amber Hagerman, who in 1996 was kidnapped from her bicycle in broad daylight in Arlington, Texas, and murdered by a sex offender (Allender 2007).

In 2007, MySpace reported that it had installed an AMBER Alert system to its Internet social network. As a result, the system reaches 108 million more persons (Bright 2007). The staff of MySpace noted that with the implementation of the AMBER Alert system, they hope that its services will be safer for its younger users.

The AMBER Alert broadcasting system involves the public in finding a kidnapped child by quickly giving the public descriptions of the abductor, the child, and vehicle that the abductor may be using (Allender 2007). The system is a partnership among law enforcement organizations, other government entities, and the news media, which is designed to create public service announcements about kidnapped and missing children.

The AMBER Alert systems are based on several social values (Zgoba 2004b). The system is designed to rescue kidnapped and missing children. According to the NCMEC (2003), 113 children had been rescued from their kidnappers. Quick responses to the kidnapping report are essential to rescue the missing children.

Another social value underlying the AMBER Alert systems is the belief in promoting community participation in responding to system alerts and maintaining social control in local communities (Zgoba 2004b). Law enforcement can be enhanced with the sharing of information by community residents.

Fostering collaboration among and within law enforcement organizations is another social value embedded in the AMBER Alert programs (Zgoba 2004b). For example, local and state police departments have to contact their local transportation departments and emergency broadcasting systems to activate AMBER Alert messages.

The news media cannot participate in the search and rescue of every missing child case because of the volume of cases would be too high (Allender 2007). To maintain the salience of the AMBER Alerts, authorities try to use the system carefully. Initially, the system was designed to inform the public about stranger kidnappers. Additional evaluation showed that children were more likely to be abducted by noncustodial parents or other family members than strangers. As a result, the AMBER Alert system was changed to notify the public about abductions by family members.

Since every kidnapped child cannot receive the same coverage, how can the AMBER Alert system effectively respond to needs of these victims? The organizing organization, the U.S. Department of Justice, suggests that law enforcement uses the AMBER Alert system under specific circumstances. First, law enforcement personnel should reasonably believe that a kidnapping has taken place. Second, law enforcement professionals should feel that the child is in imminent danger of substantial injury or death. Third, law enforcement should have an adequate description of the kidnapped or missing child and the kidnapping incident. Fourth, law enforcement should know that the victim is 17 years or younger. Finally, law enforcement personnel should have entered the child's name and other relevant information into the NCIC system, indicating that it is a child abduction case.

Law enforcement personnel are expected to follow other procedures when using the AMBER Alert system (Allender 2007). A law enforcement agency should request the alert. Law enforcement must file a police report, which is a prerequisite for entering data into the NCIC system. The police should provide a recent picture of the victim and description of what the child was wearing when kidnapped, but this information is not mandatory. The police should use the AMBER Alert system if the kidnapping has occurred within 5 h, but as long as 24 h ago. Law enforcement has no required waiting period for entering missing person data into the NCIC system. The police should use the AMBER Alert system along with other law enforcement strategies that they would use for potentially dangerous violent suspects.

Effectiveness of AMBER Alert Broadcast System

Technical difficulties have occurred in implementing AMBER Alert messages (Zgoba 2004b). Many message signs have not posted the same message in different regions. Programs have had limited placement of changeable message signs. In addition, systems have been limited by the fact that most signs are just placed near urban freeways.

Another limitation has been that transportation department staffing has been restricted during off hours.

Based on an analysis of 333 publicized AMBER Alert successful cases, Griffin (2010) found that AMBER Alert was successful in recovering the kidnapped and missing children. However, in most of these successful cases, the AMBER Alert did not lead to a rescue of the child in the 3-hour time period that is considered essential in most child-kidnapping murders. The child was not in a life-threatening situation in most of the successful cases that were studied.

Other investigations have demonstrated mixed results. Using a sample of 227 AMBER Alerts issued in 2007, the NCMEC (2003) discovered that 39 AMBER Alerts were kidnapping hoaxes (KHs) or were not kidnappings. The NCMEC (2003) found that only 48 of the cases were resolved because of the alert. In addition, the findings revealed children were rarely rescued within the critical 3-hour time period for resolving cases.

An analysis of AMBER Alert cases by the Scripps–Howard news service showed that 50% of the 233 AMBER Alerts in 2004 involved less serious family abductions associated with custody disputes and other issues (Hargrove 2005). In addition, 20% of the alerts were KHs or were issued because of simple errors such as misunderstandings.

Griffin and Miller (2008) demonstrated that AMBER Alerts were helpful in recovering almost a third of the cases. However, the system was most effective in cases such as parent–child abductions rather than cases where the offender had sinister intentions. Nevertheless, even in these successful cases, the AMBER Alerts were rarely effective within the critical 3-hour time period. The system was least effective in recovering children where the perpetrator had evil intentions.

Griffin and Miller (2008) suggest that law enforcement faces substantial difficulties in rescuing children with the use of the AMBER Alert systems. In order to rescue kidnapped and missing children, the police need to have immediate information that the event has taken place. They should have an accurate and comprehensive description of the offender and child, and timely tips from local residents. Unfortunately, these conditions are rarely met.

Another weakness with the system is when authorities decide to issue an AMBER Alert (Griffin and Miller 2008). These alerts are frequent problems when the incident is a KH or when it involves a less serious family kidnapping.

Griffin and Miller (2008) argue that another problem with the system is that the system is based on a false premise. The underlying assumption of the system implies that response time is more critical than the offender's nature and motivation. The system's slow response time does not necessarily result in the child's death; rather, the perpetrator's intention to murder the child quickly will mean any system response is too slow.

Another difficulty with the AMBER Alert system is that citizens have trouble remembering the details of AMBER Alerts and the incidents that triggered these alerts (Miller et al. 2009). People have trouble with cognitive processes, including acquisition, retention, and retrieval of information, making it difficult for individuals to assist in AMBER Alerts.

The helping behaviors of individuals in the community also may be problematic (Miller et al. 2009). Researchers do not know the extent to which people are willing to report AMBER Alerts to law enforcement. Rather, most research focuses on the willingness of persons to report their own criminal victimization. Such factors as social influence, e.g., advice from significant others and peer pressure, the characteristics of witnesses and individuals' perception of the incident may help to determine a person's involvement in an AMBER Alert incident.

The possible impact of the AMBER Alert on the perpetrators is another area of concern (Miller et al. 2009). The alerts may not have a deterrent effect on offenders since these individuals often suffer impairment in cognitive and emotional functioning.

In fact, the alerts may cause the perpetrator to quickly complete the crime, e.g., murder the child to avoid being apprehended.

The Feeney Amendment

With the publicized successes of the AMBER Alert programs in different states, the U.S. Congress decided to evaluate the existing AMBER Alert legislation (Zgoba 2004b). Congress then passed a bill that supported the AMBER Alert systems and also included the Feeney Amendment, which was designed to reduce judges' sentencing power and discretion. The Feeney Amendment eliminated the power of judges to depart from sentencing guidelines for crimes against children and sex crimes, preventing them from giving offenders reduced sentences. The Feeney Amendment also has a number of provisions such as life imprisonment for child sex offenders who are convicted two times, denying pretrial release to defendants charged with crimes against children, eliminating the statute of limitation of 5 years for the prosecution of sex crimes against children, and broadening the National Sex Offender Registry to include convicted child pornographers.

Advocates of the Feeney Amendment believe that to fight child predators, efforts should be made to prevent recidivism by keeping a watch on child predators, and increasing their punishment (Zgoba 2004b). Promoters of the Feeney Amendment also favor the increased predictability of sentencing of child predators. The advocates suggest that sentencing standardization creates a balanced criminal justice system. Promoters of the amendment believe that both sentencing standardization and eliminating the downward departures from sentencing guidelines will lead to longer sentences for offenders.

However, the Feeney Amendment faces difficulties (Zgoba 2004b). For example, the mandate for life imprisonment for two-time convicted child sex offenders puts a huge strain on state and federal prisons. Without expansion of the prison systems and additional funding and correctional officer training, the life imprisonment mandate will be very difficult, if not impossible, to implement.

Another problem with implementing the Feeney Amendment is that judges may not be able to pass just sentences due to their loss of discretion and authority (Zgoba 2004b). The amendment takes away the experiences of judges, which can limit their ability to pass responsible sentences.

Code Adam Responses

Code Adam responses have been implemented in stores, shopping malls, and other commercial establishments to help rescue kidnapped and missing children (National Center for Missing and Exploited Children, NCMEC, no date, Code Adam. www.missingkids.com/CodeAdam; Karmen 2010). These responses involve procedures such as locking exits and checking all individuals leaving the establishment to immediately rescue the child after the Code Adam response has been activated.

Use of Child Security Devices

Residents in various communities can use child security devices to help prevent child abductions. For example, parents can use child electronic security devices (Dixon and Pasnak 1997). In a small questionnaire study, Dixon and Pasnak (1997) discovered that respondents felt that child electronic security devices were needed. Respondents also felt that parents who used these devices were more responsible than parents who do not use such devices.

Sex Offender Registration

The U.S., United Kingdom, and Canada use sex offender registration to enable authorities to monitor the residence and activities of sex offenders. In the U.S., authorities make sex offender registry information available to the public using a website or other procedure. In some localities, the public does not receive a complete list of sex offenders. Sex offenders who are on parole or probation may face restrictions that other parolees or probationers do not face. For example, sex offenders may be restricted in being near minors, living close to a school, or using the Internet.

Under the Sexual Offences Act of 2003 in the United Kingdom, the records of sex offenders are included in the Violent and Sex Offender Register (ViSOR) (ViSor, Violent and Sex Offender Register, no date, www.psni.police.uk/service_procedure_30-09_amended_28-6-12_-redacted_version.pdf), which is managed by the National Policing Improvement Agency of the Home Office (legislation.gov.uk, no date, Sexual Offences Act of 2003. 2003c. 42 Table of Contents www.legislation.gov.ukpga/2003/42/contents).

Offenders who have been incarcerated for more than 12 months for violent crimes and individuals who are considered at risk of committing a crime are required to register with the police. The police, National Probation Service, and HM Prison service staff can access this database.

In Australia, the web-based Australian National Child Offender Register (ANCOR) allows authorities to keep track of individuals convicted of child sex crimes and other offenses after they have been released (CRIMTRAC (no date), www.crimtrac.gov.au/our_services/ChildProtectionServices.html).

The National Sex Offender Registry (NSOR) was established in Canada in 2004, with the enactment of the Sex Offender Information Registration Act (SOIR Act) (Royal Canadian Mounted Police (no date, www.rcmp-grc.gc.ca/tops-opst/bs-sc/nsor-rnds/index-eng.htm).

In the U.S., California was the first state to implement a sex offender registry in 1947 (California Department of Justice, no date). Sex offender registration has been for individuals who commit crimes other than sex offenses. For example, drug offenders in California must register in a similar way as sex offenders.

The previously mentioned federal statute, Jacob Wetterling Crimes Against Children and Sexually Violent Offender Registration Act (42 U.S.C. 14701) (Jacob Wetterling Act), in 1994, required that all states enact legislation mandating registration of all sex offenders with state sex offender registries (Allender 2007).

In 2007, the Adam Walsh Child Protection and Safety Act (Adam Walsh Act) (AWA) (the Sex Offender Registration and Notification Act (SORNA), under 42 U.S.C. 1691 *et seq.*) was enacted to ensure new uniform requirements for sex offenders in different states. The AWA provides for new and enhanced criminal offenses for sex offenders, a new national sex offender registry, and standardized requirements for registering sex offenders in different states. As a result of the AWA, all states have enacted laws mandating that sex offenders register with the police. The Act requires that sex offenders report their residence after leaving prison or being convicted of any offense.

The AWA has sparked considerable controversy because it provides much stiffer punishment of sex offenders. Several sex predators were prosecuted under the Act before any state had adopted it. One individual received a life sentence for failing to register (Dewan 2007). This sex offender had been homeless and was not able to register a physical address.

In California, the voters in 2006 passed Proposition 83, which provides for lifetime tracking of convicted sex offenders and the establishment of sex-predator-free zones. Proposition 83 was challenged on the grounds that it applied retroactively. However, a federal court rules that Proposition 83 did not apply *ex post facto*.

Various individuals have criticized sex predator registration laws in the U.S. For example, the mother of Jacob Wetterling, Patty Wetterling, feels that the laws since the enactment of the Jacob Wetterling Act have applied to too many crimes. She also believes that the enhanced criminal offenses make it hard for professionals to rehabilitate these sex offenders (Wetterling 2007).

The U.S. Supreme Court has upheld the constitutionality of sex offender registration laws with regard to two challenges: *ex post facto* and due process. The U.S. Supreme Court ruled that the sex offender registration law in Alaska was constitutional in *Smith v. Doe*, 538 U.S. 84 (2003). The High Court ruled by a 6–3 margin that the law is not an unconstitutional *ex post facto* law because the sex offender registration statute deals with civil laws and does not constitute punishment.

The U.S. Supreme Court also upheld the constitutionality of the sex offender registration law in Connecticut in *Connecticut Dept. of Public Safety v. Doe*, 538 U. S. 1 (2003). The High Court held that the law did not violate procedural due process of sex offenders. However, the U.S. Supreme Court did not rule on whether the statute violates substantive due process principles.

In two states, Hawaii and Missouri, two challenges to the state sex offender registration laws have been successful. The Hawaii State Supreme Court ruled in *State v. Bani*, 36 P.3d 1255 (Haw. 2001) that the state's sex offender registration law violated the due process clause of the state's Constitution. The Hawaii State Supreme Court held that the registration statute authorized public notification of a potential registrant's status without providing notice, a chance for the potential registrant to have his views heard, or without any preliminary assessment of whether this individual poses a threat.

Many individuals have successfully challenged the sex offender registration law in Missouri because the Missouri Constitution prohibits laws that are retroactive in their operation (Missouri Constitution, no date). The Missouri Supreme Court in *Doe v. Phillips*, 194 S.W.3d 837 (Mo. Banc 2006) ruled that the state constitution did not permit anyone from being entered into a registry if they had been convicted or pleaded guilty to a sex offense before the registration statute was enacted. However, the Missouri Supreme Court in 2009 ruled that the Missouri law prohibiting laws retrospective in operation no longer exempts persons from registering if they are subject to SORNA (Title I of the Adam Walsh Child Protection and Safety Act, the Sex Offender Registration and Notification Act (SORNA), under 42 U.S.C. 1691 *et seq*.)

To what extent are sex offender policies effective in controlling recidivism among sex predators? Based on study of 261 sexual abuse professionals, Levenson et al. (2010) discovered that few of the professionals think that Megan's Law is very useful in reducing the prevalence of sex offenses (Jacob Wetterling Crimes Against Children and Sexually Violent Offender Registration Act (42 U.S.C. 14701)). The investigators found that about 25% of the respondents asserted that sex offenders should not be permitted to reside in their community areas. However, majority of the sexual abuse professionals surveyed think that restricting the residential locations of sex offenders does not reduce rates of re-offenses. The investigators discovered that criminal justice professionals were more likely to support sex offender notification policies than mental health professionals. In their investigation, Levenson et al. (2010) showed that professionals who were conservative supported more restrictive policies than more liberal professionals.

Levenson et al. (2007) evaluated the impact of Megan's Law on the reentry of sex offenders into the community (Levenson et al. 2007; Jacob Wetterling Crimes Against Children and Sexually Violent Offender Registration Act (42 U.S.C. 14701)). The investigators discovered a number of adverse consequences of the community notification law. After community notification, sex offenders frequently reported loss of housing, physical violence, property damage, threats, harassment, and their family members experienced problems. The authors found that the sex offenders surveyed also reported psychosocial difficulties, including depression, feelings of hopelessness, and shame. These findings suggest that Megan's Law may limit the reentry of sex offenders into the community and lead to recidivism because of the obstacles that face sex offenders after incarceration.

Treatment of Sex Offenders

Maladaptive beliefs and distorted thinking may promote or justify crimes by sex offenders (Ward et al. 1997). Maladaptive beliefs and distorted thinking can lead to the initiation, maintenance, and justification of sexual offenses.

Levenson et al. (2010) reported that a majority of the sexual abuse professionals feel that sex offender treatment is useful even though scientific data to support their implementation are not available.

Clinicians have used different treatments such as cognitive behavioral therapy (CBT), pharmacological, and surgical approaches to treat individuals with sexual disorders (Codispoti 2008; Guay 2009; Briken et al. 2003). A meta-analysis, involving controlled outcomes assessments of 22,000 sex offenders, showed that the mean recidivism rate for sex offenders in the treated groups was lower (19%) than for those in the control groups (27%) (Codispoti 2008). However, other investigators have demonstrated lower recidivism rates for treated sex offenders.

In a literature review, Codispoti (2008) found that most of the therapy for sex predators involved CBT (64%); only 7.5% of the studies used pharmacological interventions. The treatment studies were conducted in different settings including outpatient settings (36%) and prisons (31%). In the treatment investigations, 65% of the subjects were adult men and 17.5% were adolescents. Sex offenders in these investigations had committed a variety of offenses, including child molestation (74%) and incest (48%).

Because of the methodological weaknesses in many studies, researchers have great difficulty in determining which treatment best reduced recidivism (Codispoti 2008). However, Codispoti (2008) found that CBT and hormonal approaches have the highest potential for the future. The author demonstrated that voluntary treatment was more effective than mandatory therapy.

Multisystemic therapy (MST) may be helpful in treating juvenile sex offenders (Letourneau et al. 2009). MST is an intensive, home-based treatment for families of youth with social, emotional, and behavioral problems. In MST interventions, masters-level therapists have worked with family members to identify and alter individual, family, and environmental factors that are promoting the adolescents' dysfunctional behaviors (Littell et al. 2005).

Drug treatment of sex offenders is based on the assumption that drug therapy can help control paraphilias, which refer to recurrent, intense, sexually arousing fantasies, urges, or behaviors over a period of 6 months or longer (Guay 2009). Paraphilias involve nonhuman objects, suffering, or humiliation of the offenders or their partners, or children, or other persons who do not consent to such behaviors. In vitro and in vivo research has demonstrated that serotonin and prolactin inhibit sexual arousal (Guay 2009).

Guay (2009) suggests that for all sex offenders, CBT should be used. CBT should be implemented with drug treatment at the same time for those who are at highest risk of recidivism because this approach has been found to be more effective than either treatment alone. For offenders who exhibit violent or nonphysical paraphilias and for those who have a low probability of recidivism, serotoninergic monotherapies (selective serotonin reuptake inhibitors (SSRIs)) or tricyclic antidepressants may be helpful.

Civil Commitment of Sex Offenders

Civil commitment statutes have been introduced in states in response to the belief that sex offenders will re-offend after being released from prison and that civil commitment is the best approach to ensuring public safety. Levenson (2003) noted that civil commitment statutes have been introduced in 16 states that enable convicted sex offenders to be assessed for involuntary and indefinite commitment in a psychiatric hospital after they have been released from prison.

Levenson and Morin (2006) analyzed factors that may predict the selection of sexually violent predators for civil commitment under Florida's Jimmy Ryce Act ("Ryce Act"), Fla. Stat. ch. 394.910, *et seq.* (2001). Using a sample of 450 sex offenders, the investigators demonstrated that the diagnoses of pedophilia and paraphilia not otherwise specified, a psychopathological disorder, actuarial risk evaluation, the younger age of the victim, and nonminority status of the offender predicted civil commitment recommendations in 90% of the cases. The investigators found that sex predators who were recommended for civil commitment consistently met the criteria established in the U.S. Supreme Court case, *Kansas v. Hendricks,* 521 US 346, 117 S. Ct. 2072, 138 L. Ed. 2d 501.

Effectiveness of Child Abduction Prevention Training

Experts have designed programs to teach abduction-prevention knowledge and skills to children (Johnson et al. 2006; Beck and Miltenberger 2009; Boyle and Lutzker 2005). Behavioral skills training (BST) has been employed in teaching children abduction prevention knowledge and skills (Johnson et al. 2006).

Children in these programs are taught in either naturalistic or simulated settings to respond to a stranger's lure by saying "no," running away, and telling an adult about the offender. Typical lures include simple lures, authority lures, incentive lures, and assistance lures. A kidnapper may use a simple lure, such as asking the child if he or she would like to go for a walk. An abductor also may use an authority lure, such as telling the targets their mother told him to pick them up from school. Kidnappers may use incentive lures such as telling the potential victims that they have candy in their automobile and asking them if they would like to go there to get the candy. Abductors may use the assistance lure such as telling the potential victims that they lost their puppy and asking them to help him find the lost puppy.

In BST, trainers typically model the effective responses to these lures and the children then rehearse the appropriate responses in a variety of role-playing vignettes (Johnson et al. 2006). During these situations, the trainer gives the child praise when she or he behaves correctly and offers instruction if the children do not correctly respond to the kidnapper's lures.

Specialists may evaluate the children's performance in BST programs using in situ assessments, e.g., determining if the children could respond effectively to the kidnapper's lures in a realistic kidnapping situation without knowing that they were being evaluated. Evaluators often do follow-up evaluations to determine the degree to which children are able to maintain their abduction prevention skills over time.

Studies have demonstrated that children in BST programs tend to increase their child abduction prevention skills. However, Marchand-Martella et al. (1996) discovered that children did not maintain their abduction-prevention skills.

Researchers have assessed the use of group-training procedures in BST programs (Olsen-Woods et al. 1998). These investigations reveal that some but not all children learn child-kidnapping prevention skills in BST programs that use group-training procedures.

The use of an in situ component may enhance the students' acquisition of knowledge and skills to prevent child-kidnapping lures. In in situ assessments, specialists assess the degree to which children respond correctly to abduction lures in realistic situations without knowing that they are being evaluated (Johnson et al. 2006). In in situ training, the trainer enters the situation and changes the evaluation into a training component. Johnson et al. (2005) showed that the use of in situ training with BST helped children acquire the necessary child-kidnapping prevention skills.

Parents' Responses to the Risks of Child Abductions

Parents can respond to the risks of child kidnappings in different ways. Parents can try to restrict their children's access to their neighborhoods and other public settings (Blakely 1994). Based on their assessment of the potential kidnapping risks in the social and physical settings, parents may attempt to restrict their children's access.

Martin and Wilson (2011) assessed parents' communication about kidnapping accounts in the U.S. media using a telephone survey of 182 parents. Their findings showed that parents in the survey reported three approaches. First, based on the U.S. media depictions of child abductions, parents may warn their children, suggesting that these child abductions have a probability of taking place. Second, parents may respond to the media reports by reassuring their children and indicate that these abductions are rare. A third strategy followed by parents in response to media accounts of child kidnappings is that they warn their children about the risks of these crimes. These parents will offer specific approaches to respond to the threat of child abductions. They also will recommend that their children stay vigilant.

References

Adam Walsh Child Protection and Safety Act (Adam Walsh Act) (AWA), the Sex Offender Registration and Notification Act (SORNA), Title I under 42 U.S.C. 1691 *et seq.*

Allender, D.M. (2007, July). Child abductions: Nightmares in progress. FBI Law Enforcm Bulletin, 76 (7): 1–7.

Beck, K.V., & Miltenberger, R.G. (2009). Evaluation of a commercially available program and in-situ training by parents to teach abduction-prevention skills. J Appl Behav Anal, Winter, 42 (4): 761–772.

Blakely, K.S. (1994). Parents' conceptions of social dangers to children in the urban environment. Children's Environments, 11(1): 16–25.

Boyle, C.L., & Lutzker, J.R. (2005). Teaching young children to discriminate abusive from nonabusive situations using multiple exemplars in a modified discrete trial teaching format. J Family Viol, 20 (2): 55–69.

Bright, P. (2007, January 23). MySpace activates Amber Alert System, new instant messaging system. http://www.associatedcontent.com/article/132309/myspace_activates.

Briken, P., Hill, A., & Berner, W. (2003). Pharmacotherapy of paraphilias with long-acting agonists of hormone-releasing hormone: A systematic review. J Clin Psychiatry, 64 (8): 890–897.

California Department of Justice. (no date). California Megan's Law. California Department of Justice, Office of the Attorney General. http://www.meganslaw.ca.gov/Sexreg.aspx?lang=ENGLISH.

Codispoti, V.L. (2008). Pharmacology of sexually compulsive behavior. Psychiatr Clin North Am, 31 (4): 671–679.

Dewan, S. (2007). Homelessness could mean life in prison for offender. The New York Times, August 3, 2007. http://www.nytimes.com/2007/08/03/us/03homeless.html?ex=1343793600&en=c2844b3791a25a5ae&ei=5088&partner=rssnyt&emc=rss.

Dixon, R.M., & Pasnak, R. (1997). Perceptions of the risk of child abduction or loss and the utility of child electronic security devices. Child Care Health Dev, 23 (5): 415–421.

Doe v. Phillips, 194 S.W.3d 837 (Mo. Banc 2006).

Federal Kidnapping Act (FKA). Also known as the Lindbergh Kidnapping Act; 18 U.S.C. 1201(a) (1).

Fugitive Felon Act (FFA) (18 U.S.C. 1073).

Griffin, T. (2010). An empirical examination of AMBER Alert successes. J Crim Just, 38 (5): 1053–1062.

Griffin, T., & Miller, M.K. (2008). Child abduction, AMBER Alert, and crime control theatre. Crim Just Rev, 33 (2), 159–176.

Guay, D.R. (2009). Drug treatment of paraphilic and nonparaphilic sexual disorders. Clin Ther, 31 (1): 1–31.

Hargrove, T. (2005). False alarms endangering future of AMBER Alert System. New York: Scripps Howard News Service.

International Child Remedies Act (42 U.S.C. 11601–11610).

International Parental Child Kidnapping Act (IPCKA) (18 U.S.C. 1204).

Jacob Wetterling Crimes Against Children and Sexually Violent Offender Registration Act (42 U.S.C. 14701).

Jimmy Ryce Act ("Ryce Act"), Fla. Stat. ch. 394.910, *et seq.* (2001).
Johnson, B.M., Miltenberger, R.G., & Egemo-Helm, K., et al. (2005). Evaluation of behavioral skills training for teaching abduction-prevention skills to young children. J Appl Behav Analysis, 38: 67-78.
Johnson, B.M., Miltenberger, R.G., & Knudson, P., et al. (2006). A preliminary evaluation of two behavioral skills training procedures for teaching abduction-prevention skills to school children. J Appl Behav Analysis, 39 (1): 25–35.
Jones, M. (2003, May-June). Amber alert system saves children's lives. The Crime Victims Report, 7 (2): 20, 28.
Juvenile Justice and Delinquency Prevention Act (JJDPA) (1974). (Pub. L. No. 93-415, 42 U.S.C. 5601 et seq., www.ojjdp.gov/about/legislation.html).
Kansas v. Hendricks, 521 US 346, 117 S. Ct. 2072, 138 L. Ed. 2d 501.
Kappeler, V.E., & Potter, G.W. (2005). The mythology of crime and criminal justice. Long Grove, IL: Waveland Press.
Karmen, A. (2010). Crime victims. An introduction to victimology. Belmont, CA: Wadsworth Cengage Learning.
Legislation.gov.uk (no date). Sexual Offences Act of 2003. 2003c.42 Table of Contents www.legislation.gov.ukpga/2003/42/contents.
Letourneau, E.J., Henggeler, S.W., & Borduin, C.M., et al. (2009). Multisystemic therapy forjuvenile sexual offenders: 1-year results from a randomized effectiveness trial. J FamPsychol, 23 (1): 89–102.
Levenson, J.S. (2003). Policy interventions designed to combat sexual violence: Community notification and civil commitment. J Child Sex Abuse, 12 (3-4): 17–52.
Levenson, J.S., & Morin, J.W. (2006). Factors predicting selection of sexually violent predatorsfor civil commitment. Int J Offender Ther Comp Criminol, 50 (6): 609–629.
Levenson, J.S., D'Amora, D.A., & Hern, A.L. (2007). Megan's Law and its impact on community re-entry for sex offenders. Behav Sci Law, 25 (4): 587–602.
Levenson, J.S., Fortney, T., & Baker, J.N. (2010). Views of sexual abuse professionals about sex offender notification policies. Int J Offender Ther Comp Criminol, 54 (2): 150–168.
Littell, J.H., Popa, M., & Forsythe, B. (2005). Multisystemic therapy for social, emotional, and behavioral problems in youth aged 10-17. Cochrane Database Syst Rev, Jul 20; (3): CD004797.
Marchand-Martella, N., Huber, G., & Martella, R., et al. (1996). Teaching preschoolers to avoid abduction by strangers: Evaluation of maintenance strategies. Educ & Treatment of Children, 19: 55–59.
Martin, N., & Wilson, B.J. (2011). Parental communication about kidnapping stories in the US news. J Children Media, 5(2): 132–146.
Miller, M.K., Griffin, T., & Clinkinbeard, S.S., et al. (2009). The psychology of AMBER Alert: Unresolved issues and implications. Soc Sci J, 46 (1): 111–123.
Missing Children Act of 1982 (28 U.S.C. 534).
Missouri Constitution. (no date). Missouri Constitution. http://www.moga.mp.gov/const/A01013.HTM.
Missing Children's Assistance Act (MCAA) (42 U.S.C. 5771).
National Center for Missing and Exploited Children (NCMEC). (2003). Amber Plan. Washington, DC: National Center for Missing and Exploited Children. www.missingkids.com.
National Child Search Assistance Act (NCSAA) (42 U.S.C. 5779).
National Center for Missing & Exploited Children, NCMEC, no date, Code Adam. http://www.missingkids.com/CodeAdam.
Office of Juvenile Justice and Delinquency Prevention (OJJDP). (2008, Winter). The front line. Newsletter. http://www.missingkids.org.
Olsen-Woods, L.A., Miltenberger, R.G., & Foreman, G. (1998). Effects of correspondence in an abduction prevention training program. Child & Family Behav Ther, 20: 15–34.
Parental Kidnapping Prevention Act (PKPA) (28 U.S.C. 1738(a)).

Prosecutorial Remedies and Other Tools to End the Exploitation of Children Today Act (PROTECT Act) (18 U.S.C. 2252).

Royal Canadian Mounted Police. (no date). National Sex Offender Registry. http://www.rcmp-grc.gc.ca/tops-opst/bs-sc/nsor-rnds/index-eng.htm).

United States Department of Justice (1996). Victim Reunification Travel Program (VRTP). www.missingkids.com/Reunification.

ViSOR, Violent and Sex Offender Register (no date). http://www.psni.police.uk/service_procedure_30-09_amended_28-6-12_-redacted_version.pdf).

Ward, T., Hudson, S.M., & Johnston, L., et al. (1997). Cognitive distortions in sex offenders: An integrative review. Clin Psychol Rev, 17 (5): 479–507.

Wetterling, P. (2007). Patty Wetterling: The harm in sex-offender laws. The Sacramento Bee, September 14, 2007. http://www.sacbee.com/110/story/377462.html.

World Almanac & Book of Facts. (2009). Notable U.S. kidnappings since 1924. World Almanac & Book of Facts, 462.

Zgoba, K. (2004a). Spin doctors and moral crusaders: The moral panic behind child safety legislation. Crim Just Stud: A Crit Crim Law Soc, 17(4): 385–404.

Zgoba, K. (2004b). The Amber Alert: The appropriate solution to preventing child abduction? J Psychiatry Law, 32, 71–88.

Chapter 7
Infant Abduction

Most of the research on infant abduction (IA) has focused on nonfamily IAs. In nonfamily abduction cases in which infants are abducted from healthcare facilities, the abductor may impersonate a nurse or other healthcare personnel (Missing Person Project/MPP Case # 13; see Appendix D). Criminals may kidnap infants during the commission of different crimes. During carjackings, the offender may intentionally or unintentionally kidnap the infants.

Several Cases of IAs

One prevalent type of IA is nonfamily abductions in which a stranger, acquaintance, or friend intentionally kidnaps an infant. In nonfamily abduction cases in which infants are abducted from healthcare facilities, the abductor may impersonate a nurse or other healthcare personnel (Missing Person Project/MPP Case # 13; see Appendix D).

Parents also may kidnap their own infants. In MPP Case # 252, a mother reportedly abducted and concealed her newborn son, from Fairfield, California, on November 3, 2005 (see Appendix D). One month later a warrant was issued for the suspect.

Criminals may kidnap infants during the commission of crimes. During carjackings, the offender may intentionally or unintentionally kidnap the infants. For example, after robbing two stores, a male suspect allegedly carjacked an automobile occupied by a father and mother with their infant son, who was sitting in the back (*The People, Plaintiff and Respondent, v. Jesse Raul Duran, Jr., Defendant and Appellant*, No. G024274, 88 Call App. 4th 1371; 106 *Cal Rptr.* 2d 812; 2001 Cal. App. LEXUS 354; 2001 Cal. Daily Op. Services 3892).

Another form of abduction is kidnapping by cesarean section (Burgess et al. 2002).

During times of war and conflict infants are kidnapped by individuals, groups, and governments for strategic, political, and social/cultural goals.

S. Morewitz, *Kidnapping and Violence*,
https://doi.org/10.1007/978-1-4939-2117-1_7

Prevalence

In 1983, the first year that the National Center for Missing and Exploited Children (NCMEC) began collecting data on nonfamily IAs, five infants were kidnapped from hospitals, residences, and other settings (Burgess et al. 2008). In 1987, the annual incidence of nonfamily IAs rose to 18, and in 1989, the incidence was 17. The NCMEC reported an 82% reduction in IAs from healthcare settings between 1991 and 1995 (Hospital Security Safety Management 1997).

Rabun (2002) reported on the nonfamily IAs that occurred between 1983 and February 2002, using data from the NCMEC, International Association for Healthcare Security and Safety, and Federal Bureau of Investigation (FBI)-National Center for the Analysis of Violent Crime (NCAVC). During this period, nonfamily members kidnapped 215 infants (ranging in age from birth to 6 months) from a healthcare organization, residence, or other location.

In Canada, five infants had been abducted from hospitals between 1990 and 2002 (Shogan 2002).

Characteristics of the Infants Who Were Abducted

Burgess et al. (2008) analyzed 247 nonfamily IA incidents documented by the NCMEC (121 incidents from 1983 through 1992 and 126 from 1993 through 2006). Using the entire sample, they discovered that about an equal number of infant boys (N = 121) and girls (N = 121) were kidnapped. One hundred and three (43%) of the kidnapped infants were African-American, 75 (30%) were white, 61 (25%) were Hispanic, and in 8 incidents (3%), the race/ethnicity was not documented.

Most of the kidnapped infants (235 or 95%) were recovered (Burgess et al. 2008). Twelve or 5% of the abducted infants are still missing.

Burgess et al. (2008) compared IAs between 1983 and 1992 with those between 1993 and 2006 to ascertain possible differences in abduction patterns from the earlier to the later period. They discovered that the percentage of Hispanics infants who were kidnapped increased from 17 to 23%. In contrast, the proportion of abducted white infants decreased from 40 to 21%. The percentage of abducted African-American infants did not change significantly (41% and 43%, respectively).

The investigators discovered that the percentage of infants who were kidnapped before they were one day old increased from 7% in 1983–1992 to 11% in 1993–2006 (Burgess et al. 2008). This increase occurred at the same time that the number of fetal abductions increased from 1 to 6%.

Characteristics of Abductors and Their Partners

Researchers have analyzed the characteristics of nonfamily infant kidnappers. Burgess et al. (2008) showed that most of the nonfamily infant kidnappers are women (237 of 247 or 96%). Ninety-one or 41% of the kidnappers are African-American, 93 or 39% White, and 47 or 20% Hispanic.

Ninety or 36% were in their twenties, 64 or 26% were in their 30s, 49 or 20% were teenagers, and 24 or 10% were in their 40s (Burgess et al. 2008).

In terms of marital status, the percentage of abductors who were married went down from 28% between 1983 and 1992 to 19% between 1993 and 2006 (Burgess et al. 2008). In contrast, the percentage of suspects who were not married increased from 32% between 1983 and 1992 period to 52% in the later period.

In Burgess and Lanning's (2003) investigation, staff from healthcare settings reported that the kidnapper was a friend or recent acquaintance of the victim parents in 22% of the cases. According to the healthcare staff, the victim parents did not know the kidnapper in 78% of the incidents.

Data on the obstetrical history and parental status of the offenders were available for 156 cases (Burgess et al. 2008). Sixty-nine (44%) of the suspects had living biological children. Twenty-seven (17%) had a miscarriage or a stillbirth and 11 (7%) had both living children and had reported having a prior miscarriage.

Burgess et al. (2008) analyzed the extent to which cohabiting or married partners knew that their partners had kidnapped an infant. Partner awareness that their partner had abducted an infant decreased from 17% in the 1983–1992 period to 10% in the 1993–2006 period. The percentage of partners who were not aware increased from 40 to 47%.

Kidnappers' Motivation

Experts view IAs as nontraditional because they are not primarily motivated by typical criminal goals such as ransom, sexual gratification, revenge, or the desire for power (Burgess and Lanning 2003).

Offenders may kidnap infants because of their pathological obsession and need for a baby (Burgess et al. 1995). They may be having difficulties getting pregnant themselves or be unable to get pregnant. Women may face significant societal pressure to fulfill their role as mothers in society and will abduct an infant to help them fulfill this societal role. The perpetrators may have suffered a significant loss, such as a miscarriage or stillborn, and kidnap an infant in response to this devastating social loss. For example, one female suspect, age 25, was charged with kidnapping a week-old baby boy after she had reportedly miscarried four months earlier (Ross 2009).

Female offenders frequently feign pregnancy (Burgess and Lanning 2003). They let people know that they are pregnant and over time they alter their appearance to trick people into believing that they are pregnant.

Individuals may commit these crimes because of their desire to "cement" or maintain a relationship with a significant other (Baker et al. 2002; Burgess et al. 1995). Burgess et al. (1995) described a case in which a young woman did not want to disappoint her boyfriend after she had a stillborn delivery.

Kidnappers of infants may have various idiosyncratic reasons for abducting infants (Baker et al. 2002). They tend to be driven by self-interest and self-absorption. Their actions are not logical, and they are the only ones who believe that their actions are rational or logical.

The perpetrators often have extreme resolve to carry out their crimes and their extreme resolve is reflected in the fact that they may commit suicide after being caught (Baker et al. 2002).

Infant abductors may also murder or abandon the infants after they kidnap them (Main 2000; Ross 2009). For example, a 2-week old infant was reportedly kidnapped from a nursery at Loyola University Medical Center in Maywood, IL, and the next morning was found dead in a laundry hamper in an apartment (Main 2000).

Kidnappers' Mental Disorders

Experts have developed diagnostic typologies to explain infant and child abductors. Yutzy et al. (1993) recommends classifying kidnappers based on their diagnosis instead of their motive. Kidnappers can be classified based on whether they have mild mental impairment, schizophrenia, psychopathic personalities, and personality disorders.

Abductors' Methods

Baker et al. (2002) found that perpetrators used planning and premeditation in carrying out violent IAs.

Burgess et al. (2008) discovered that in 157 (75%) of 210 IA cases, the suspects visited the kidnapping site prior to the abduction. The perpetrators were more likely to visit the site before committing the offense in the 1993–2006 period (80%) than in the 1983–1992 period (69%).

The perpetrator may have a prior meeting with the victim before committing the offense (Baker et al. 2002). The meeting may take place with the victim mother days to weeks and months before the kidnapping.

Suspects will frequently use a confidence-style approach in carrying out the offenses (Baker et al. 2002). For example, the offenders will pretend that they need assistance, such as the need to use the bathroom or get a drink of water.

Suspects sometimes wear disguises during the offense, and these disguises might include wearing a hospital uniform. In their study, Burgess et al. (2008) found that during the offense, 110 offenders (45%) impersonated a healthcare staff member. Kidnappers used disguises more frequently in healthcare settings (41%) between 1983 and 1992 than between 1993 and 2006 (11%). Similarly, the percentage of suspects who impersonated a healthcare staff member went down from 60% between 1993 and 1992 to 29% between 1993 and 2006.

According to Burgess and Lanning (2003), members of healthcare settings indicated that in 76% of the abduction episodes, the kidnappers' appearance or behavior before the episode was not considered suspicious.

In Burgess et al.'s (2008) analysis, 33 kidnappers (13%) had made an abduction attempt previously.

Perpetrators may have others involved in carrying out the kidnapping (Baker et al. 2002).

Burgess et al. (2008) found that 44 perpetrators (18%) employed violence while carrying out the offense. The suspects used violence in nine (8%) of the kidnappings in healthcare settings and in 35 (27%) of the 131 kidnappings in non-healthcare settings. The researchers discovered that the suspects' use of a weapon increased from 11% between 1983 and 1992 to 20% between 1993 and 2006.

Investigative Strategies and Outcomes

Law enforcement personnel use a variety of strategies in responding to IAs. The NCMEC provides a checklist to guide law enforcement personnel in responding effectively to reports of kidnapped infants and children (Steidel 2000). The NCMEC provides guidelines for personnel involved in intake and dispatching officers to the scene and broadcasting known details about the abduction, first responders, investigative officers, and personnel with supervisory responsibility.

Law enforcement personnel should make effective use of available technology in responding to IAs. In one case, investigators were able to track the female suspect, age 39, through her automobile, which was seen on a video camera (Genova 2009).

Researchers have evaluated the amount of time involved in recovering kidnapped infants. In Burgess et al.'s (2008) investigation, the time to recover the abducted infants went down significantly from the 1983–1992 period to the 1993–2006 period. The percentage of infants who were recovered within 12 h increased from 20 to 27%. The percentage of infants who were recovered within 12–24 h increased from 30 to 36%.

Recovery time was faster for infants who were kidnapped from healthcare settings (Burgess et al. 2008). Fifty-seven percent of the infants abducted in the 1983–1992 period were kidnapped from healthcare organizations and recovered within 24 h and the percentage increased to 85% in the later period.

Tips to law enforcement can significantly help in the recovery of kidnapped infants (Burgess and Lanning 2003). Researchers in one investigation found that telephone tips to local police agencies were the leading reason why offenders were arrested (Burgess and Lanning 2003). Burgess et al. (2008) discovered that the percentage of tips to law enforcement by family members increased from 12% between 1983 and 1992 to 17% in the 1993–2006 period.

In Burgess and Lanning's (2003) analysis, members of healthcare organizations indicated that media coverage of the kidnapping aided in the recovery of the baby in 67% of the incidents. The staff of healthcare facilities felt that media coverage of the kidnappings were not helpful in 31% of the cases.

Burgess et al. (2008) found that the percentage of instances in which media reports led to tips from the public to police agencies increased from 20% in the 1983–1992 period to 30% in the later period.

The percentage of suspects arrested increased from 88% between 1983 and 1992 to 94% between 1993 and 2006 (Burgess et al. 2008).

Burgess and Lanning (2003) discovered that in 57 cases, 35 kidnappers entered guilty pleas and no criminal trial was held. In 22 criminal trials, 19 defendants were found guilty and three were acquitted.

Healthcare organizations that suffer IAs face potential civil litigation because of their failure to maintain the safety and health of infants under their care as well as the safety and health of parents of the abducted infants and others during the abductions.

In one IA case, the parents of a 2-week-old baby filed two negligence suits against Loyola University Medical Center (*Chicago Sun-Times* 2000). In this case, the baby had died after being abducted. The medical center subsequently settled the two negligence cases and the terms of the settlement were not disclosed. The medical center released a statement, noting that no dollar amount could compensate the family for their losses.

Healthcare Institution Security and the Joint Commission on Accreditation for Healthcare Organizations

Accredited healthcare organizations must follow Joint Commission on Accreditation for Healthcare Organizations (JCAHO) standards for ensuring the security of infants (Burns 2003). For years, JCAHO viewed perinatal facilities to be a security priority. The agency added IA and the problem of infants who are discharged to the wrong family to the list of Sentinel Event Procedures on April 1, 1998. The agency wants healthcare organizations that might have such an incident to rigorously assess the root causes identified by healthcare facilities that have had IAs and infant discharges to wrong families to initiate policies and procedures to minimize these risks.

Twenty-three cases of IAs or infants who were discharged to the wrong family were reported to JCAHO between January 1995 and March 13, 2002 (Rabun 2002; Burns 2003). These cases constituted 1.4% of all sentinel events reported to JCAHO during this period. In their Sentinel Event Alert of April 9, 1999, the agency reviewed all 8 cases of IAs that had been reported since 1996. JCAHO found that all of these kidnappings had occurred in hospitals that had more than 400 beds (Joint Commission on Accreditation for Healthcare Organizations 1999; Burns 2003). Five of the kidnappings took place in the mother's room, two occurred in the newborn nursery, and one occurred in the neonatal intensive care unit (NICU). Within a few hours of the kidnapping, 7 of the infants had been recovered unharmed and without harm to the mother. However, one abducted baby remained missing.

Female suspects allegedly had kidnapped the infants in every case (Joint Commission on Accreditation for Healthcare Organizations; Burns 2003). A woman pretended to be a nurse or aide in 3 cases. A woman posed as a physician, infant's mother, or volunteer in other incidents. In one case, the biological mother kidnapped the infant in the custody of the state in the NICU.

JCAHO requires a healthcare institution to perform a root cause analysis when a sentinel event takes place (Burns 2003; Joint Commission on Accreditation for Healthcare Organizations no date). This root cause analysis is designed to help the healthcare institution find out why the incident took place and ways to prevent a reoccurrence.

Previous case studies reveal that infants are kidnapped when they are transported for testing, while they are being taken back to the nursery, when they are in the nursery and not monitored, or while in the mother's room when the mother is sleeping or taking a shower (Burns 2003). Three of the 8 hospitals had reported failed IA attempts in the period before the kidnapping had taken place. Four IAs took place during the day shift, which tends to be the busiest time for hospitals. In 2 cases, the IA occurred during the evening shift and 2 took place during the night shift.

The root causes of the IAs included: unmonitored stairwell access and elevators, equipment malfunction, education deficits, lack of public information, and the reluctance of the hospital staff to question unidentified persons in the hospital (Joint Commission on Accreditation for Healthcare Organizations no date; Burns 2003).

JCAHO requires that hospitals conduct at least 1 annual proactive risk assessment of a high-risk process as a component of its Patient Safety Initiative (Joint Commission on Accreditation for Healthcare Organizations 2002; Burns 2003). Burns (2003) reported that Metropolitan Methodist Hospital, San Antonio, Texas, and another Methodist healthcare organization chose to review its infant security program and make subsequent changes to its program. After completing a Failure Mode Cause and Effect Review, the hospital identified several impaired processes that could cause an infant kidnapping. The hospital staff found incomplete or incorrect data entry concerning the location of mother and baby, accidental or intentional removal of the infants' security sensors, the failure of staff and physicians to wear unique identification badges, misaligned doors preventing the operation of magnetic doors, and staff's failure to question the identification of visitors' identification.

Self-assessment

The NCMEC published healthcare professional guidelines on preventing and responding to IAs. These guidelines include a Self-assessment for Healthcare Facilities to help these organizations improve their processes and policies and procedures to prevent IAs (Rabun 2002; Burns 2003). Four areas are included in the self-assessment: (1) general topics; (2) proactive procedures; (3) physical-security safeguards; and (4) critical incident-response plan.

In the self-assessment, general topics cover issues such as procedures for handling individuals who may be potential abductors and reporting requirements when kidnappings take place (Rabun 2002; Burns 2003). Healthcare facilities must have proactive procedures, such as having a prevention plan, taking color photograph of infants in addition to foot printing them before transporting them from the birthing room, storing the infants' cord blood until one day after their discharge, having unique color identification badges for staff working with the infants. In addition, proactive procedures involve not divulging the infants' home address and avoiding birth announcements.

Healthcare facilities should have physical-security safeguards to reduce the risk of IAs (Rabun 2002; Burns 2003). Organizations should have a written evaluation of the potential for infant abduction at their facilities. They should install alarms on all stairwell and exit doors on the perimeter of the perinatal and pediatric areas. The facilities should install security cameras so that the faces of all individuals using the perinatal and pediatric areas are visible.

According to the self-assessment, healthcare organizations should have a critical incident response plan that includes a written plan about what procedures should be taken in the event of a kidnapping (Burns 2003). The critical incident response plan should describe how the institution's security staff should notify law enforcement and secure the crime scene until local law enforcement arrives at the scene. The plan should provide information about how law enforcement should enter the infant's name and description in the FBI Center's Missing Person File and how law enforcement should request NCMEC to assist technical support, network with other organizations, and obtain help with disseminating details about the abduction.

In addition, the critical incident response plan should detail how parents of the abducted infant are moved to a private room with the same nurse who has been providing care for the mother and her infant (Rabun 2002; Burns 2003). In addition, the critical incident plan should provide information about how the medical records of the mother and infant are secured and how the facility's laboratory should be notified, and the infant's cord blood placed on a hold. The plans also should detail how the organization should notify NCMEC to obtain technical support in managing the crisis.

Abduction Prevention Technology

Public concern over completed and attempted IAs and the availability of technological knowledge, materials, and other resources led to the development of new abduction prevention technology. For example, the VeriChip Corporation, a subsidiary of Applied Digital, sells the Hugs Infant Protection System (*Business Wire* 2005). The Hugs infant protection system uses radiofrequency identification deployment (RFID) technology. In 2005, about 900 hospitals in the U.S. had installed the Hugs RFID system. Infants using this system wear a very small radio transmitter their ankle or wrist that is designed to prevent IAs. With this system, the staff is able to monitor electronically exits in the healthcare institution to identify IAs.

The Hugs RFID system is also designed to prevent accidental discharge of infants to the wrong families (*Business Wire* 2005). According to one report, infant mismatching incidents occur 20,000 times each year.

In addition to healthcare organizations, communities need to be alerted quickly and effectively to IAs to assist law enforcement efforts. Forty-one hospitals in Maine established a statewide security system for responding to abductions, bomb threats, and other security problems (*Modern Healthcare* 1997).

Healthcare Facilities' Use of IA Prevention Strategies

The NCMEC reported that 7 infants were kidnapped from healthcare facilities by nonfamily members between May 1997 and March 2002 (Nahirny 2002; Burns 2003). In one of the incidents, the prevention system would not allow the kidnapper to open a stairwell door and eventually the infant was returned to the mother. In another case, the system initially blocked the abductor, but the offender then discovered and removed the infant's security tag. The abductor, in another incident, removed the infant's tag while in a bathroom on the maternity area and then walked down the stairwell to the first floor. The abductor in another incident cut off the infant's security tag and then left the institution.

Burns (2003) evaluated the experiences of healthcare facilities that had suffered infant abductions. One hospital was very dismayed with its IA prevention system at the time of the kidnapping. At this hospital, the infant's sensor tag could be easily taken off and the alarm did not work. This hospital now has a new system that includes having an infant's sensor tag that can be monitored on an electronic screen with a blueprint of the surroundings. An alarm will go off if the infant is within two feet of an exit or if the infant's sensor band is loose or cut.

A second hospital had used a sensor system at the time of the kidnapping and replaced it with another sensor system that uses electronic sensors and a system for tracking the infants (Burns 2003). The hospital staff found two problems with their current system. They noted that the sensor will produce an alarm if the sensors are not put on the infants correctly. In addition, the staff reported that the system produces an alarm if the sensors are shielded, and this occurs most often when the infants are being fed.

A third hospital had blocked a kidnapping because the offender could not exit through the locked stairwell door (Burns 2003). At the time of the kidnapping attempt, the hospital did not have a tracking system is contemplating buying a system that includes the capacity to track infants. The staff reported that their current system is plagued by frequency interference, which is most often caused by pagers.

Other Preventative Policies and Procedures

Health personnel should implement a variety of other policies and procedures to prevent IAs in healthcare facilities. Burgess et al. (2008) recommend parent education, media participation, staff education, collaboration among nursing organizations, prevention policy, and research for achieving this goal.

In terms of parent education, health professionals should provide expectant mothers and new parents information about their procedures such as visitation and security (Burgess et al. 2008). Expectant mothers and new parents should be warned about individuals who they do not know or who show an unusual interest in their pregnancy or baby.

Health professionals should involve the media, including news reports and public service announcements (Burgess et al. 2008). Collaboration between the media and police agencies can be effective in recovering abducted children. According to the Bureau of Justice Statistics, America's Missing: Broadcast Emergency Response (AMBER) Alerts have helped rescue 400 children (Office of Justice Programs 2008).

Staff education is essential in preventing IAs in healthcare settings (Burgess et al. 2008). Staff education, including educational programs such as Safeguard Their Tomorrows can help reduce the incidence of successful IAs from healthcare facilities.

Collaboration among the NCMEC and nursing organizations, such as the Association of Women's Health, Obstetric, and Neonatal Nurses, and National Association of Neonatal Nurses, has led to the development of Safeguard Their Tomorrows and other educational programs (Burgess et al. 2008).

The development of evidence-based guidelines by the NCMEC provides a basis for healthcare settings to reduce the likelihood of successful IAs (Burgess et al. 2008).

Research should help lay the foundation for future policies and procedures. Research into the area of perpetrator motivation, personality, and cognitive functioning could result in more effective policies and procedures to reduce the incidence of successful IAs (Burgess et al. 2008).

Policies and Procedures in Other Settings

Families can take precautions to minimize the risk that their newborn will be kidnapped. For example, families should avoid publishing birth notices in the media (Vincent 2009).

Impact of IAs

Parents and other family members can suffer severe stress related to an IA. When they realize that their infant has been stolen, parents can experience terror, disbelief, and shock (Burgess and Lanning 2003). In these instances, the bonding between the parents and their infant becomes "frozen."

Parents must cope with their anxiety and fear about their abducted infant as they work with law enforcement authorities in attempting to recover their kidnapped infant (Burgess and Lanning 2003). Parents must provide information to strangers about their infant's kidnapping and the nature of the interview questions may make parents feel that they were somehow responsible for their infant's abduction.

Once their infant is recovered, parents and other family members are significantly relieved (Burgess and Lanning 2003). The parents now re-bond with their infant, but this bonding tends to be limited because the parents are fearful that their infant may be stolen again. Parents may become extremely vigilant about their infant. In addition, because of their original bonding with their infant had become frozen, they may need to re-bond with their baby over time. This re-bonding may require a long period of time, depending on the duration of the abduction and the parents' fears about their infant's victimization experience.

During criminal and civil court litigation, the parents may become traumatized again (Burgess and Lanning 2003). Family members suffer stress, anger, fear, and anxiety as they must re-live their infant's kidnapping during litigation-related depositions and trials. These events may challenge their sense of justice. Parents may become especially traumatized if they do not feel protected from the kidnapper and if the litigation is unsuccessful.

Parents may become very anxious and angry when the suspect receives a light sentence or when the perpetrator is released from prison (Burgess and Lanning 2003).

In one case, the abductor insisted that the baby that she had kidnapped was her baby, and the parents of this kidnapped infant would be very fearful the offender would try to kidnap their infant again after getting out of prison.

In the initial years after their infant is recovered, the parents may limit their normal activities in response to the kidnapping. They may live in fear episodically and are extremely vigilant over a long period of time. Parents of recovered infants may develop post traumatic stress disorder (PTSD).

Parents may suffer from an increased startle response, have difficulty concentrating, experience sleep problems, including nightmares related to their infant's abduction and general nightmares as well (Burgess and Lanning 2003). Parents often are anxious that a stranger will kidnap their infant. Over time, parents, may fantasize their child will be in danger when no one is around.

Some infants who are recovered quickly are thought not to sustain negative social and health consequences (Burgess and Lanning 2003). However, parents report that their recovered infants may still suffer from a variety of problems.

Burgess and Lanning (2003) found that some infants are physically injured or have serious health problems after being recovered. In one case, a parent described how her recovered baby girl developed a severe gastrointestinal problem at the age of 2 and ½ years.

A number of parents indicate that their recovered infants suffer from psychosocial difficulties (Burgess and Lanning 2003). Recovered children may have difficulties in sleeping and have abduction-related night terror reactions and nightmares. In other instances, parents note that their recovered child is fearful and has flashbacks. According to one parent, her recovered baby girl becomes terrified when she hears a car backfire or similar noise.

The severity of the recovered infants' symptoms may vary depending on factors such as whether the offenders used violence in carrying out the abduction.

In Burgess and Lanning's (2003) analysis, some parents were apprehensive their abducted babies had been sexually abused by the abductors or others in their family. In three cases, the infants had been kidnapped by perpetrators who had a criminal record for sexually abusing children. However, there were no indications that they had been sexually abused.

When abducted infants are murdered or remain missing, parents and other family members often are devastated by their tragic loss. The loss of a sibling at a young age can be especially traumatic for the surviving siblings (Greif and Bowers 2007). The effects may be particularly severe when the sibling is young and is abducted by a nonfamily member.

IAs can be extremely traumatic for health personnel who are working at the site of the abduction. In Burgess and Lanning's (2003) study, the news about an IA came as a shock to nurses regardless if they were on duty at the time of the incident. During the period in which the abducted infant is missing, some nurses developed feelings of powerlessness, guilt, and failure.

Some nurses suffered distress even after the infant had been recovered (Burgess and Lanning 2003). Nurses, who had responsibility for the kidnapped infant, showed symptoms of PTSD. During interviews, nurses indicated that every time they hear about another kidnapping incident, they immediately recall the IA at their facility. Nurses also stated that they can never forget the IA at their healthcare organization. Regardless of whether support services were offered, the nurses had these types of PTSD symptoms.

Burgess and Lanning (2003) found that administrators indicated that they took measures to protect the organization. For example, administrators reported that they reprimanded a nurse and pressed charges against her for giving the baby to the kidnapper.

Psychosocial Support for Victims and Health Personnel

Support services can be effective in helping parents and other family members cope with the trauma associated with an IA. In Burgess and Lanning's (2003) analysis, 77% of the healthcare organizations provided support in the form of some combination of social services, spiritual counseling, and psychiatric/psychological assessment and counseling. Twenty-three percent of the healthcare facilities did not provide such services.

Burgess and Lanning (2003) found that during or after an IA, 59% of the healthcare organizations had support services for healthcare personnel. Staff members were more likely to receive support services from a clinical nurse, followed by social services staff, or the organization's chaplain.

References

Baker, T.B., Burgess, A.W., & Rabun, J.B. (2002). Abductor violence in nonfamily infant kidnapping. J Interpers Violence, 17 (11): 1218–1233.

Burgess, A.W., & Lanning, K.V. (eds.). (2003). An analysis of infant abductions (2nd Edit). Alexandria, VA: National Center for Missing & Exploited Children.

Burgess, A.W., Burgess, A.G., & Dowdell, E.B., et al. (1995). Infant abductors. J Psychosoc Nurs, 33 (9): 30–37.

Burgess, A.W., Baker, T., & Nahirny, C., et al. (2002). Newborn kidnapping by cesarean section. J Forensic Sci, 47 (4): 827–30.

Burgess, A.W., Carr, K. E., & Nahirny, C., et al. (2008). Nonfamily infant abductions, 1983–2006. Amer J Nurs, 108 (9): 32–38.

Burns, A.L. (2003). Protecting infants in healthcare facilities from abduction. A facility's search for a sound infant security system. J Perinat Neonat Nurs, 17 (2): 139–147.

Business Wire. (2005). VeriChip Corporation's RFID technology prevents infant abduction at North Carolina Hospital. *Business Wire*, July 18, 2005. http://www.thefreelibrary.com/VeriChip+Corporation%27s+RFID+Te.

Chicago Sun Times. (2000). Loyola settles lawsuits in infant's abduction. Chicago Sun-Times, August 18, 2000. http://www.highbeam.com/doc/1P2-4549759.html.

Genova, W. (2009). Kidnapped Tennessee baby recovered in Alabama. AHN All Headline News, October 3, 2009.

Greif, G.L., & Bowers, D.T. (2007). Unresolved loss: Issues in working with adults whose siblings were kidnapped years ago. Amer J Family Therapy, 35 (3): 203–219.

Hospital Security Safety Management. (1997). Special report. Infant kidnapping update: Electronic security, officer training, parent alertness help foil abductors in 1996. Hosp Secur Saf Manage, 17 (10): 5–10.

Joint Commission on Accreditation of Healthcare Organizations. (1999). Sentinel Event Alert. April 9, 1999: 1–2.

Joint Commission on Accreditation of Healthcare Organizations. (no date). Sentinel Event Statistics-January 1995 through March 13, 2002. http://www.jcaho.org/sentinel/se_stats.html. Accessed April 15, 2002.

Joint Commission on Accreditation for Healthcare Organizations. (2002). Comprehensive Accreditation Manual for Hospitals. Oakbrook Terrace, IL: Joint Commission on Accreditation of Healthcare Organizations; Update May 2002, LD.5.2:LD40-LD41.

Main, F. (2000). Stolen baby's parents sue Loyola hospital. Chicago Sun-Times, May 13, 2000.

Modern Healthcare. (1997). Baby APB. Modern Healthcare, 27 (45): 1. http://web.ebscohost.com.proxylib.csueastbay.edu/ehost/detail?vid=&&.

Nahirny, C. (2002). Infants abducted from hospitals with security tagging systems. Alexandria, VA: National Center for Missing & Exploited Children.

Office of Justice Programs. (2008). U.S. Department of Justice. AMBER alert. America's missing: Broadcast emergency response. Frequently asked questions. http://www.amberalert.gov/faqs.htm.

Rabun, J.R., Jr. (2002). Newborn/infant abductions. Alexandria, VA: National Center for Missing & Exploited Children.

Ross, E. (2009). Suspect in infant abduction says she needed to find a baby. KWTX.com, September 22, 2009. http://www.kwtx.com/home/headlines/60020647.html.

Shogan, M.G. (2002). Emergency management plan for newborn abduction. J Obstet Gynecol Neonatal Nurs, 31 (3): 340–346.

Steidel, S.E. (Ed.). (2000). Missing and abducted children: A law-enforcement guide to case investigation and program management. Alexandria, VA: NCMEC.

The People, Plaintiff and Respondent, v. Jesse Raul Duran, Jr., Defendant and Appellant, No. G024274, 88 Call App. 4th 1371; 106 *Cal Rptr*. 2d 812; 2001 Cal. App. LEXUS 354; 2001 Cal. Daily Op. Services 3892).

Vincent, J.L. (2009). Infant hospital abduction: Security measures to aid in prevention. MCN Am J Matern Child Nurs, 34 (3): 179–83.

Yutzy, S.H., Wolfson, J.K., & Resnick, P.J. (1993). Child stealing by cesarean section: A psychiatric case report and review of child stealing literature. J Forensic Sci, 38: 1926.

Chapter 8
Kidnapping by Cesarean Section and State-Sponsored Abduction of Newborns

Individuals may kidnap a pregnant mother and steal her baby by performing a cesarean section (CS) (Geberth 2006; Burgess et al. 2002). Just like offenders who steal a baby from a newborn nursery or other setting, perpetrators who commit fetal kidnapping may be motivated to strengthen or "cement" a relationship with a partner (Burgess et al. 2002; Geberth 2006). Female offenders may seek to fulfill a childbearing and delivery fantasy (Geberth 2006). These female kidnappers become a mother by proxy by acting out a fantasy in which they deliver a baby. Offenders also may commit fetal kidnapping for financial motives.

In other instances, fetal and newborn kidnapping may be perpetrated for political reasons (Avery 2004). Regimes may seek to erase the biological identities of the pregnant mothers and their children. In addition, those in power may want to profit from the illegal sale of these newborn babies to couples and families.

Nonpolitical Fetal Kidnappings

Investigators have classified non-political forms of fetal kidnapping by type of crime (Burgess et al. 2002). In their 2002 report on 6 cases of kidnapping by CS, Burgess et al. (2002) classified four of the six cases as: "personal cause homicide, subtype CS homicide." One of the remaining cases was classified as "personal cause, subtype domestic homicide," and the other case was classified as "criminal enterprise homicide."

In Burgess et al.'s (2002) study, case 4 is an example of the personal cause homicide, subtype CS homicide. In this case, Felecia Scott, age 29, contacted her former friend, a 17-year-old adolescent, who was 9-months pregnant. Scott met the victim on the pretense of going to dinner. Scott wanted to have a baby to enhance her relationship with her common-law partner. She told him and family that she was

S. Morewitz, *Kidnapping and Violence*,
https://doi.org/10.1007/978-1-4939-2117-1_8

pregnant even though in 1994, she had a documented hysterectomy. Scott reportedly had shot the victim repeatedly in the head and had opened the mother's abdomen with a knife.

Case 3 in Burgess et al.'s (2002) report illustrates the personal cause, subtype domestic homicide by CS. In case 3, the pregnant mother previously had filed a protective order against her ex-boyfriend, who was one of the offenders who carried out a crude CS of the victim after she had been shot.

In Burgess et al.'s (2002) analysis, case 2 represents the criminal enterprise homicide, in which the pregnant mother, age 25, allegedly was befriended by two suspects who were sisters (Burgess et al. 2002; The PK Papers, Cesarean Kidnapping, Checklist no date). These two sisters told the pregnant victim that her visit to a physician at a clinic in Matamoros, Mexico, would be their gift. When the pregnant victim arrived at the clinic, a physician reportedly gave her an injection that caused her to go unconscious. The physician then reportedly performed a CS and gave the baby to the two sisters.

Offenders who use the kidnapping by CS approach often use a confidence style method to commit their crimes. The perpetrators may be acquainted or friends with the pregnant woman and then use that relationship to facilitate the crime. The perpetrator often uses a pretense to get in close proximity to the victims to carry out the kidnapping by CS.

As part of a female kidnapper's crime plan, she may fake her pregnancy prior to carrying out the crime so by the time of the crime, she will be able to claim the kidnapped newborn is her own (Geberth 2006).

The suspect will want to get the pregnant woman in a private residence or other secluded area to carry out the crime without detection.

The offenders plan their crime and obtain surgical instruments, knives, weapons, surgical manuals, and other resources to carry out the crime. In other cases, the perpetrator had just a kitchen knife (Bobbie Jo Stinnett case) or a box cutter (VO case) (The PK Papers, Cesarean Kidnapping, Checklist no date).

In Kittanning, Pennsylvania, in 2005, the alleged perpetrator reportedly knocked her neighbor unconscious and later performed a CS over the victim's old scars from an earlier CS (The PK Papers, Cesarean Kidnapping, Checklist no date).

The kidnapper may kill the pregnant mother by using a knife, blunt instrument, and gun or by strangulation. They may also tie up their victims.

Individuals who are present at the crime scene such as the pregnant victim's children may also be killed or removed from the scene prior to the fetal kidnapping.

The pregnant mother occasionally survives this crime. For example, in Fullerton, California, in 2002, the pregnant mother reportedly survived a stabbing by the suspect and escaped before the CS incision was made (The PK Papers, Cesarean Kidnapping, Checklist no date). In 2005, the victim reportedly survived by killing her perpetrator before the CS incision was made.

The newborn may not survive these horrific crimes. If the newborn dies, the offenders may dispose of the body.

The suspect may take the newborn to a health care facility, alleging that she delivered the baby. The kidnapper also may try to obtain false birth records for the abducted newborn. In the LL case, birth records were falsified, and the baby boy was kidnapped for two years before the child was recovered (The PK Papers, Cesarean Kidnapping, Checklist no date).

Offender Characteristics

In terms of demographic characteristics, Geberth (2006) found that most of the perpetrators are female in the 19–40 years-old age group.

Offenders frequently preselect and stalk their victims (Geberth 2006; Morewitz 2003).

Offenders often have a criminal history involving theft and deception (Burgess et al. 2002).

Perpetrators may suffer from severe psychopathology that their disorders help to explain their motives and crime methods (Burgess et al. 2002).

More than one individual may work together to plan and carry out the kidnapping by cesarean section. These perpetrators may contribute different skills to planning and carrying out the crime, while others may have access to potential targets. Some of the offenders may have health training sufficient to perform the CS. In Burgess et al.'s (2002) research, Case 3 involved three suspects and one primary abductor, and case 2 involved multiple suspects.

Responses to the Crime

Individuals who are passing by may become suspicious of the activities surrounding the fetal kidnapping. For example, in Pennsylvania, in 2005, an adolescent male saw the suspect performing a CS on a woman in a wooded area (The PK Papers, Cesarean Kidnapping, Checklist no date). He became suspicious even though the perpetrator had told him that everything was normal and notified the police.

If the kidnapping suspect comes to the healthcare facilities with the newborn, healthcare professionals may become suspicious of this person. They may decide to order tests to determine if the woman delivered the baby. Offenders who bring premature newborns who are dead are especially likely to raise suspicions among the hospital personnel. The police may also become suspicious and obtain testing to determine if the suspect delivered a baby recently.

The police should immediately notify detectives and initiate an America's Missing: Broadcast Emergency Response (AMBER) Alert of the victim's description when they first receive a report of a missing pregnant woman (Geberth 2006). After an abduction, speed of apprehension is critical because often the perpetrators will kill the pregnant woman and try to deliver the fetus within about two hours of the kidnapping. Law enforcement should also canvas the area where the kidnapping most likely occurred to ascertain if the pregnant victim was seen with suspects. A female in the company of the pregnant victim may appear pregnant. Canvassing individuals at this location may result in information about the suspects, automobile license plates and other vehicle information, and other identifying information.

The police will use crime investigative methods, such as an analysis of videos, cell phone text messages, emails, and voicemail, to reconstruct the history of the relationships between the suspects and the victims. In addition, law enforcement personnel will examine sales records of purchases of surgical instruments, surgical manuals, rope, and other related items. In the BJS case, law enforcement investigators traced email messages to the suspect (The PK Papers, Cesarean Kidnapping, Checklist no date).

Criminal Justice Outcomes

Individuals arrested for committing CS kidnappings are prosecuted and face a variety of outcomes depending on the seriousness of the crime and other factors (The PK Papers, Cesarean Kidnapping, Checklist no date). Criminal defendants may be acquitted as insane (The PK Papers, Cesarean Kidnapping, Checklist no date). In a case involving two murders, the defendant, age 37, was viewed as incompetent and was not tried (The PK Papers, Cesarean Kidnapping, Checklist no date).

In other incidents, the criminal defendant may be sentenced to life imprisonment. For example, in one case, the perpetrator, age 19, was sentenced to life imprisonment after being convicted of strangling the victim, age 23, and using a car key to remove her baby (The PK Papers, Cesarean Kidnapping, Checklist no date).

In a case involving three murders, the three defendants each were sentenced to death, but the Illinois governor granted them clemency in 2002 (The PK Papers, Cesarean Kidnapping, Checklist no date).

Perpetrators may be sentenced to life imprisonment for premeditated attempted murder.

After being arrested, the kidnapper may commit suicide. In a case involving two murders, the defendant hanged herself before the sentencing hearing (The PK Papers, Cesarean Kidnapping, Checklist no date).

State-Sponsored Fetal Kidnappings

Illegal Adoptions, and Child Trafficking

Newborn abduction and abduction by CS is not a new crime and is not limited to individual cases. Between 1976 and 1983, in Argentina, fetal and newborn abduction was perpetrated systematically on a widespread basis against pregnant women who were abducted and later murdered by the Argentine junta (Avery 2004). The military junta that overthrew the Peron government initiated a so-called "Dirty War" that consisted of systematic kidnapping, torture, and forced disappearances (murder) of thousands of people (Avery 2004). The junta carried out these crimes in a way similar to Hitler's *Nacht und Nebel Erlass* (Night and Fog Decree). In the name of national security, up to 30,000 people disappeared under the command of the Argentine junta. The *Comision Nacional sobre la Desparicion de Personas* (CONADEP) verified 8,960 cases of forced disappearance. The junta did not have to account to the public or courts and had no reason to keep the victims alive.

As in the case of Hilter's *Nacht und Nebel Erlass,* the Argentine junta made citizens "disappear" without a trace (Avery 2004). Thousands of innocent men, women, and children from all socioeconomic status backgrounds were kidnapped and never seen again. As a result of these state-sponsored kidnappings and forced disappearances, a new term, *desaparecidos* (the disappeareds), was used to describe these victims. The junta employed the word, *desaparecido,* to deny that they had abducted, tortured, and murdered thousands of individuals.

The *desaparecidos* included ordinary citizens and prominent attorneys, journalists, and trade union members (Avery 2004). Only a few of the thousands of the *desaparecidos* were directly associated with left-wing activities, while others had only minimal associations with the leftist terrorists. For example, they may have been just acquaintances of left-wing terrorists.

Many *desaparecidos* were kidnapped and taken to one of the regime's secret detention centers, where they were tortured and eventually killed (Avery 2004). Thirteen hundred victims were imprisoned in more than 340 detention centers or concentration camps before they permanently disappeared. By September 1976, the junta reportedly kidnapped an average of 30 citizens daily. Only one percent of the victims' location could be verified. Members of the Argentine Anti-Communist Alliance (Triple A) death squads would drive around in their Black Ford Falcons, and these automobiles became the symbol of the kidnappings and forced disappearances.

The courts in Argentina did not oppose the junta's atrocities (Avery 2004). They denied about 80,000 writs of habeas corpus. In fact, many of the attorneys preparing the writs also disappeared and were never seen again.

The widespread abduction and murder of pregnant mothers and the kidnapping of their newborns by cesarean section and use of serums were one of the most heinous aspects of the junta's reign of terror and genocide (Avery 2004). The junta would systematically kidnap pregnant women and imprison them until they were ready to give birth. Members of the junta would then steal their babies to sell as part of a system of illegal adoptions and child trafficking.

One of the leaders of the Argentine junta, Admiral Emilio Eduardo Massera, set up the junta's largest concentration camp, known as *Escuela Mecanica de la Armada* (ESMA), at the Navy Mechanics School (Avery 2004). The camp was viewed as the "Argentine Auschwitz." At this concentration camp, pregnant women were among the people abducted and later murdered.

The regime established crude maternity wards at ESMA and at the Campo de Mayo Hospital (Avery 2004). At these two concentration camps, staff members administered serums or performed CSs on these kidnapped pregnant mothers to speed up the birth of their babies. Staff at these two locations would blind-fold the pregnant mothers and tie their hands and feet to beds to perform the CSs. In other instances, the staff would induce the inmate's labor in the middle of the night to minimize the number of witnesses to the births.

Few pregnant mothers survived their imprisonment at the concentration camps (Avery 2004). Military officers who participated in the killings testified that after abducted mothers gave birth, they would be taken to the Campo de Mayo hangar, flown in military planes, and then thrown into the sea. The junta also killed the abducted pregnant mothers by shooting them in the head execution style.

Members of the junta would forge illegal birth records and then sell their stolen babies to families, such as military couples, who were politically connected to the regime. Members of the regime forged birth records to ensure erasure of the original identities of both the mothers and their newborns.

The junta had established a well-organized system that was very lucrative for the regime since prospective adoptive parents with political connections, e.g., military couples, could afford to pay significant fees for the stolen babies whose family identities had been erased (Avery 2004). Some prospective adoptive parents even could choose their babies based on the appearances and educational background of the kidnapped pregnant mothers.

Increasingly, the junta found itself under attack by human rights organizations (Avery 2004). Despite the pervasive fear in Argentine society created by the junta, two small groups of women, the mothers (*Madres de Plaza de Mayo*) and the grandmothers (*Abuelas de Plaza de Mayo*) of the *desaparecidos* started to protest the plight of their relatives and sought to reunite their biological families who had been torn apart by the regime. These two groups initiated a campaign to protest the regime's atrocities.

The first group, the *Madres de Plaza de Mayo* to be established, campaigned to secure information about their missing children (Avery 2004). Members of the group refused to accept the junta's self-described ignorance about their fate. On April 30, 1977, 14 women held a silent protest in the main square of Buenos Aires and the group held many more silent protests afterwards. The police did not allow public assembly so the group began a ritual circling of the square. The *Madres* walked counterclockwise as a sign of their defiance of the junta. The *Madres* were harassed by mounted police, had machine guns pointed at them from the rooftop of buildings in the square and were ridiculed as "*las locas de la Plaza de Mayo*."

The *Madres* demanded the return of their missing children and punishment for their kidnappers (Avery 2004). In October 1977, the *Abuelas* joined the *Madres* in trying to locate the missing children (Avery 2004). In contrast to the *Madres*, the *Abuelas* emphasized finding *los desaparecidos con vida* (the living disappeared), who were the newborns abducted from the *Abuelas*' murdered daughters and sons. They wanted to find out if their grandchildren were alive and well. The *Abuelas* discovered that more than 500 babies born in the junta's detention centers/concentration camps were illegally adopted. In their search for their grandchildren, the *Abuelas* were both advocates for human rights and detectives (Avery 2004).

The junta attempted to hide its participation in genocide using a policy of denial and "willful" ignorance (Avery 2004). However, some abducted victims did survive the state-sponsored torture, and they publicized their victimization. Despite the survivors' reports of torture, the work of the *Madres* and the *Abuelas*, and public knowledge about the *desaparecidos,* the junta denied the existence of the detention centers/concentration camps. Members of regime asserted that the *desaparecido* wanted to live secretly to engage in subversive activity against the state. In other instances, the junta claimed that left-wing organizations murdered the *desaparecido* because they were traitors.

In the early 1980s, the junta was weakened because the Argentine economy had deteriorated significantly, and the junta was greedy, corrupt, and divisive (Avery 2004). The regime tried to change public attention away from these problems by getting involved in the Falkland Islands War in April 1982. As a result of their ill-advised involvement in this war, the United States and Great Britain terminated economic and diplomatic relations with the Argentine government, and the junta subsequently collapsed.

The junta distributed the *Documento Final* (*Final Report*) as the regime was getting ready to relinquish power in April 1983 (Avery 2004). In this report, the regime claimed that they had defeated the opposition. The document provided an excuse for the activities of the junta leaders who carried out the Dirty War. The report indicated that certain individuals would be gone permanently and that no more information would be provided.

National elections were held in late 1983 and Dr. Raul Alfonsin was elected president (Avery 2004). The president established the *Comision Nacional sobre la Desaparicion de Personas* (CONADEP) to research and disseminate information on the atrocities. In its report titled, *Nunca Mas* (Never Again), CONADEP provided detailed descriptions of the abductions, torture, and murder of the *desaparecidos* based on more than 50,000 pages of documented testimonies. *Nunca Mas* established that a majority of the victims were not connected with those involved in subversive activities.

The president had the junta leaders charged and tried for their crimes using the results of the CONADEP (Avery 2004). Five of the generals charged were found guilty and received sentences ranging from four and a half years to life. However, the remaining four generals were found not guilty. Moreover, all nine generals were found not guilty of kidnapping newborns and creating false identities for these kidnapped babies.

Members of the military pushed for a pardon since they claimed that their responses to the opposition were essential to ensure national security (Avery 2004). In contrast, human rights advocates were appalled by the sentences; they felt that the light sentences would promote a "culture of impunity."

Hundreds of new court cases alleging human rights violations during the Dirty War were filed after the trials of the junta's generals (Avery 2004). The military held several revolts against these court cases because they were afraid that the court proceedings would lead to guilty verdicts against 200 or more mid-level officers. Alfonsin met the military's demands by establishing the first of two amnesty laws known as the Full Stop or Final Point law. This act substantially restricted the number of human rights violation cases that could be filed in Argentine court. The Full Stop law established a 60-day statute of limitations for all trials associated with the Dirty War, and the status of limitation expired on February 23, 1987. In response to this law, human rights advocates filed many claims before the statue of limitations expired, but hundreds of suspects were not prosecuted because of this statute.

The military held another revolt because of the Dirty War court cases and Alfonsin responded by passing a second amnesty law known as the Law of Due Obedience, which restricted the scope of prosecutions in the Dirty War cases (Avery 2004). The act assumed that suspects varied in their culpability depending if they gave the orders, followed the orders, or were excessive in their illegal actions. The law presumed that those members of the military who were following the orders of superior officers were least culpable and had the presumption of innocence.

Alfonsin resigned several months before the end of his presidency, and Carlos Saul Menem became President (Avery 2004). The new president pardoned all the senior-level military officers who were not protected by the amnesty laws. Twelve months later, he pardoned all junta leaders who had been convicted in the early trials. As a result, the leaders of the junta serve only limited time in prison.

The *Abuelas* Continue Their Search for Missing Children

The *Abuelas* relied on traditional investigative strategies to identify missing children and reunify families. For example, one nine-month-old infant, Carlita Artes, was reportedly abducted from her mother, Graciela Artes, by the junta. Later, Carlia Artes recognized herself when she saw a woman on television holding a poster with her picture and the words: "Carlita, nine months of age, disappeared."

The *Abuelas*' efforts to find their missing loved ones also led scientists to apply innovative DNA techniques to prove the identities of many disappeared individuals (Avery 2004). Laboratory analysis of genetic markers in the blood enabled scientists to calculate an "index of grandpaternity" (Penchaszadeh 1997; Di Lonardo et al. 1984). The index of grandpaternity quantifies the chance that a child shares genes with a specified set of grandparents because she or he is their grandchild compared to the probability that only by chance does she or he share similar genes.

Scientists later used nuclear DNA typing and mitochondrial DNA sequencing for genetic identification (Penchaszadeh 1997). A 1997 report reported that 56 children had been discovered and identified using methods of genetic identification (Penchaszadeh 1997). Thirty of these children were reunited with their biological families, 13 stayed with families who had adopted them in good faith, 6 remain in custody litigation in the courts, and 7 had died.

In one case, the court ordered genetic testing to prove the identity of Paula Eva Loagares, who was kidnapped with her biological parents in Uruguay in 1977 (Avery 2004). Paula was discovered living with an ex-police chief who kidnapped her from the junta's detention center where Paula's parents were last seen alive before they became *desaparecidos*. The genetic testing proved Paula's identity beyond any doubt, and she was reunited with her grandmother.

Forensic anthropologists and other scientists assisted used other methods to identify conclusively victims of the junta (Avery 2004; Kirschner and Hannibal 1994). Encouraged by the success of forensic identification of the victims of the Dirty War, the *Abuelas* lobbied successfully President Alfonsin to establish the National Bank of Genetic Data (Avery 2004). The bank, which was the first in the world, provided the latest scientific identification services to the relatives of disappeared children and to any person whose identity was controversial.

Eventually, Alfonsin met some of the *Abuelas*' demands to help reunite the *desaparecidos*' children with their biological families (Avery 2004). For example, the president agreed to rally the support of the Argentine people in these activities. In 1992, the government established the National Commission on the Right to Identity (CONADI) to help search for the missing children and return them to their rightful families.

The *Abuelas* challenged Argentina's adoption laws that they thought help to protect the abductors and hid the true identity of the abducted children (Avery 2004). They opposed the nation's closed system of adoption that fostered illegal adoptions and child trafficking. The *Abuelas* rejected the notion that their stolen children's best interest would be to stay with their illegal adoptive parents. Instead, they felt that the biological families offer the best home environments.

Argentine judges recognized the systematic kidnappings of the *desaparecidos*' infants and attempt to kill the babies' identity and impose a new identity on them (Avery 2004). Judge Adolfo Bagnasco found that the junta organized the baby-stealing scheme in two phases. In the first phase, during the first three years of the regime, junta leaders who went to the detention/centers/concentration camps were likely to know about the kidnappings. In the second phase, members of the junta tried to cover up these abductions. The second phase often involved "second disappearances," in which couples who illegally adopted the abducted babies escaped from Argentina when their children's identities became publicized. Judge Bagnasco ordered the arrest of eight charged military leaders for the kidnappings.

International human rights organizations identified the crimes of the Argentine junta as violations of human rights (Avery 2004). For example, the United Nations and Organization of American States (OAS) declared that the systematic forced disappearances of people were crimes against humanity. Article 18 of the U.N. Declaration on the Protection of All Persons from Enforced Disappearance states that suspected offenders shall not be exempt from any amnesty laws or other measures that exempt them from criminal prosecution. The identification of the second disappearances by the *Abuelas* encouraged the OAS to broaden the Pan American Convention of Human Rights to expand protection for the disappeared children and to require the extradition of suspected abductors under the Montevideo Treaty.

References

Avery, L. (2004). A return to life: The right to identity and the right to identify Argentina's 'living disappeared.' Section c babies born in captivity. Harvard J Law Gender, November 15, 2004, p. 241.

Burgess, A.W., Baker, T., & Nahirny, C., et al. (2002). Newborn kidnapping by cesarean section. J Forensic Sci, 47 (4): 827–30.

Di Lonardo, A.M., Darlu, P., & Baur, M., et al. (1984). Human genetics and human rights. Identifying the families of kidnapped children. Am J Forensic Med Pathol, 5 (4): 339–347.

Geberth, V. (2006). Homicides involving the theft of a fetus. Law & Order, 54 (3): 40–42, 44–46.

Kirschner, R.H., & Hannibal, K.E. (1994). The application of the forensic sciences to human rights investigations. Med Law, 13 (5–6): 451–460.

Morewitz, S.J. (2003). Stalking and violence. New patterns of trauma and obsession. New York: Kluwer Academic/Plenum Publishers.

Penchaszadeh, V.B. (1997). Genetic identification of children of the disappeared in Argentina. J Am Med Womens Assoc, 52 (1): 16–21, 27.

The PK Papers, Cesarean Kidnapping, Checklist. (no date). http://thepkpapers.com/cesarean-kidnapping-checklist/.

Chapter 9
Human Trafficking

Definition of Human Trafficking (HT)

The most widely cited definition of HT is in the UN *Protocol to Prevent, Suppress and Punish Trafficking in Persons*, which came into force in 2003 (WHO 2012). The UN Protocol defines HT "… as the recruitment, transportation, transfer, harbouring or receipt of persons, by means of the threat or use of force or other forms of coercion, of abduction, of fraud, of deception, of the abuse of power or of a position of vulnerability or of the giving or receiving of payments or benefits to achieve the consent of a person having control over another person, for the purpose of exploitation. Exploitation shall include, at a minimum, the exploitation of the prostitution of others or other forms of sexual exploitation, forced labour or services, slavery or practices similar to slavery, servitude or the removal of organs" (UNODC).

The UN protocol definition of HT does not require the movement of persons from one site to another. This is similar to the definition used in the U.S. Trafficking Victims Protection Act of 2000 (TVPA) which states that an individual under 18 years of age is classified as a HT victim even if no movement is involved (Anon., May 2009).

All countries do not agree on one universal legal definition of HT. Definitions of HT that are based on the requirement for the use of deception and force may be subjected to different interpretations (Aronowitz 2001). Drawn by the expectations of earning a higher income, some migrants sign up to be transported abroad to work in the sex trade, at hard labor, as domestics, etc. Countries that require a definition of deception and coercion may not define these illegal migrants as victims of HT. The Sexual Offenses Act (SOA), 2003 in the United Kingdom, applies to any individual who enters the United Kingdom to participate in sex work even if they have consented to being trafficked (UK-SOA 2003). Prostitution, often considered a form of violence and abuse against women, is viewed as exploitative or de facto

S. Morewitz, *Kidnapping and Violence*,
https://doi.org/10.1007/978-1-4939-2117-1_9

slavery in Sweden, Norway, and Iceland. Both Sweden and the United States have diplomatic offices aimed specifically at curbing human trafficking (Alli 2013).

HT may also be confused with migrant smuggling, which like HT, is a type of irregular migration (Aronowitz 2001). Both HT and smuggling victims frequently leave their country voluntarily and thus become illegal aliens in their destination country and are ripe for exploitation.

Prevalence of HT

Although HT is illegal, yet in many countries corrupt government officials participate in or facilitate HT, and as a result, researchers have had difficulty in accurately determining its prevalence (Laczko and Gramengra 2003; Tyldum and Brunovskis 2005). Many HT victims do not self-identify as such because they fear retaliation or prosecution. They also may feel stigmatized and shamed (Stolz 2010).

In 2004, the U.S. Department of State estimated that internationally between 600,000 and 800,000 persons are victims of HT, and that between 14,500 and 17,500 victims are trafficked into the U.S. each year (Miko 2004; U.S. Department of Justice 2004a; U.S. Department of Justice 2005). The U.S. Government General Accountability Office (GAO) has questioned the accuracy of these estimates because specific "country data are not available, reliable or comparable" (Mellto 2006).

In 2008, the United Nations (UN) reported that almost 2.5 million individuals from 127 countries were victims of HT worldwide (UN, February 6, 2008).

A UN report on HT for 2006, which aggregated the data from 61 countries, showed that 66% of the victims were women, 13% were girls, 12% were men, and 9% were boys (UNODC/UN.GIFT, February 2009).

A UN report on HT victims detected over the period 2003–2006 showed that 67% of the victims were women, 13% were girls, 13% were men, and 7% were boys (UNODC 2007).

Of the approximately 43,000 worldwide HT victims detected over the period 2007–2010, 59% were women, 17% were girls, 14% were men, and 10% were boys (UNODC 2012).

In 2012, as a result of using aggregated data from 118 countries and a "more sophisticated methodology", the ILO revised upward their previous estimate of worldwide victims of forced labor to 20.9 million. Of this group, 4.5 million were victims of forced sexual exploitation, 14.2 million were victims of forced labor exploitation in the private economy, and 2.2 million were in state-imposed forms of force labor. "9.1 million victims (44%) have moved internally or internationally. The majority, 11.8 million (56%) are subjected to forced labor in their place of origin or residence" (ILO 2012a; ILO 2014).

Multiplying the ILO 2012 forced labor estimate of 20.0 million victims by the ratio of forced labor to trafficking from the ILO 2005 study, yields a revised estimate of 4.1 million persons who were trafficked.

However, of this estimated 4.1 million HT global victims in 2012, only 46,570 victims were actually identified, and of these 7,705 cases were prosecuted, and 4,746 convicted (USDS. p. 46, 2013a, b). "… part of the enforcement problems is that many victims lack official identities—230 million children do not have birth certificates, which makes them virtually impossible to trace" (Gladstone 2014).

The various reports, even from the same organizations, cannot be directly compared to one and another because of different data sources, data quality, and methodology. Regardless of the conflicting figures cited, it is obvious that HT is a serious problem.

Also, according to the UN *Global Report on Trafficking in Persons 2012*, "at least 136 different nationalities were trafficked and detected in 118 different countries."

Children are especially vulnerable to HT. Children of both sexes between the ages of 5 and 17 are often forced into debt bondage; recruited as child soldiers; brainwashed into becoming terrorists; forced or sold into prostitution; exploited by pornographers; used to carry out illegal drug sales; involved at low levels in the illicit arms trade; and engaged in other illegal activities worldwide.

Revenues from HT

In 2004, the ILO estimated human trafficking gross earnings were in the neighborhood of $31.6 billion for the approximately 2.5 million forced laborers who were trafficked, or $12,640 per victim (Belser 2005).

In 2014, the ILO estimated that gross earnings from global forced labor were $150 billion, with $99 billion ($21,800 per victim) of this being generated by commercial sexual exploitation (CSE). Approximately 4.5 million persons are employed in CSE, which largely consists of HT victims. Most of the profits from FL were generated in Asia, with 67% of these profits originating from CSE (UNODC, 2014).

Laws usually divide HT into two subcategories: forced labor (FL) and sex trafficking (ST) (Belser, 2005).

Forced Labor (FL)

Forced labor (FL) has been part of society since ancient times. Its victims (men, women, and children) have been called slaves, indentured servants, impressed seamen, peons, serfs, etc. These victims have lost their basic freedom and must cope with an existence where they are continuously beset by oppressive demands and subject to the arbitrary whims of a master.

FL is a major form of HT (Smartt 2003). FL can involve trafficking children and adults within countries and/or to other countries and then coercing the victims into a variety of labor activities (USDS 2010). These jobs may include nannies and maids/housekeepers forced into domestic servitude; waiters, cooks, bus boys, etc., employed in restaurants; manicurists working in salons; magazine and candy or flowers sales crews; both unskilled and skilled workers hired by small construction companies, and industrial cleaning companies. FL workers have also been found working in large scale factories, and agricultural settings.

In the twenty-first century, FL is still alive, well, and flourishing, primarily because poverty is still opening the doors to economic exploitation. FL becomes profitable whenever businesses look for the cheapest labor supply, (Wheaton et al. 2010). Political, social, ethnic/racial, and historical factors, such as armed conflict, low socioeconomic status (SES), natural disasters, and government corruption and ineffectiveness also increase the risk of FL (Avery 2004).

FL primarily is a gender-based criminal activity (WHO 2012; de Sousa e Silva and Urani, December 2002). Women and girls have a higher probability of being trafficked into the sex industry and domestic servitude (USDS 2011). In contrast, men and boys are often trafficked into the labor market depending on the labor needs of the country, or the regional area and the individual employer (UNODC 2008).

In some nations, local social systems promote FL. For example, in the Middle East, the *kafala* system, which "requires all unskilled migrant workers to have an in-country sponsor, usually their employer, who is responsible for their visa and legal status" (Wikipedia 2014d). This system has been used to traffic migrant construction and domestic workers (Jureidini 2010). There are 8 million foreign workers in Saudi Arabia, of whom 1.5 million are women domestic workers. Majority of complaints were made by domestic workers regarding abuses by their employers. There are documented cases of trafficking, forced labor, or slavery-like conditions (HRW 2008). Bahrain modified its version of the *kafala* system in 2009, but little changed, since the law is minimally enforced (MRO 2009). In 2014, after an international outcry over the mistreatment of migrant workers working on facilities for the 2022 World Cup, Qatar also promised to replace its *kafala* sponsorship system (Black et al. 2014). Recently, New York University came under censure for allowing the abuse of 6,000 workers who were employed by private contractors to build its new campus in Abu Dhabi (Kaminer 2014).

FL often involves menial labor for which the victims, contrary to their expectations, receive little, if any, money. Often the victims are required to sign contracts that restrict their freedom of movement, and/or prevent them from contacting their friends and family. For all intents and purposes, they have been kidnapped and must live in forced confinement. In addition, they and their families are threatened with deportation, violence, and even death by traffickers and so-called "enforcers" should they resist or try to escape (WHO 2012; Morewitz 2008). To make matters worse, traffickers often confiscate the HT victims' passports and other legal documents and may substitute false documents (USDS 2010; WHO 2012; Aronowitz 2001; Olaniyi 2003; Morewitz 2008).

Men are at increased risk of being forced into unskilled work. The International Labour Organization (ILO) reported that around the world $31 billion is generated yearly by this form of unskilled labor (ILO, May 11, 2005). These victims are engaged in activities such as domestic servitude, agricultural work, sweatshop factory work, janitorial labor, food service, and begging (USHHS 2012).

(a) **Child Labor**

In the year 2000, an estimated 245.5 million children (16% of the world's children) in the 5–17-year-old age group participated in child labor throughout the world, and 170.5 million of these children were engaged in hazardous work (ILO 2002). By 2012, the total number had been reduced to 168 million children (10.6% of the global child population) and 85 million of these children still performed hazardous work. "The largest absolute number of child labour is found in Asia and the Pacific region but Sub-Saharan Africa continues to be the region with the highest incidence of child labour, even though there has been a decline there" (ILO 2013).

Children may work either at home with their family members or in nonfamily settings. Child labor is especially problematic in third world countries that are characterized by underdeveloped economic, educational, political, and family institutions. In these countries, poverty increases the likelihood that children will participate in the labor market. Many low-income families either include their children in family employment activities or send them to work outside the family. Both rural and urban areas of Afghanistan, where many low-SES children are engaged in child labor, are examples of this pattern (Hunte 2009, June).

Multiple resolutions of the 1989 United Nations Convention on the Rights of the Child (CRC) may be violated when a child's labor limits his/her education, and/or is harmful to the child's physical health, and social, spiritual, and moral well-being (UNCRC 1989).

(b) **Bonded Labor**

Bonded labor or debt bondage is widely used to force individuals into slavery (WHO 2012; USHHS no date; USDS 2010). "Victims become bonded laborers when their labor is demanded as a means of repayment for a loan or service in which its terms and conditions have not been defined or in which the value of their services as reasonably assessed is not applied toward the liquidation of the debt." The value of their work is a greater than the original sum of money 'borrowed' (USHHS no date).

Afghan men who work in the fields of construction and agriculture have been engaged in forced labor or debt bondage in countries such as Iran, Pakistan, and Greece (USDS 2010). Indigenous Tharu farming families, who live along the Nepal–Indian border, sell their daughters into servitude, for a year at a time, as part of the traditional *kamlari* system of bonded labor (BBC News 2007). There is lax enforcement of laws against bonded labor in India, where only 866 bonded laborers in the whole country were identified and freed in 2004–2005 (Grammaticas 2007; Finn 2007).

(c) **Forced Begging (FB)**

Forced begging (FB) is another example of forced labor (Smartt 2003; Delap 2009). FB is prevalent in low-SES countries in Europe such as Bulgaria, where criminal gangs kidnap men and women and force them to beg in urban areas, and then take their proceeds (Gloria and Samuel 2012). Such gangs threaten to kill the forced beggars or their family members if they resist or try to escape (Morewitz 2008).

In Azerbaijan, children are trafficked internally for FB and other types of HT. In Afghanistan, Mafia groups run begging rings which are reported to be expanding. In Albania, traffickers exploit children for begging and other types of forced labor activities. Albania is considered a source country for this form of forced labor (USDS 2010).

FB also takes place in prosperous countries such as Austria, where both Roma children and children from Eastern Europe are trafficked for FB (USDS 2010).

Criminal gangs often teach beggars how to invoke the most sympathy from people on the street (Al Hetal and Kabir 2013). These tutors insist that their students develop the mannerisms and machinations that will help them develop into profitable beggars. Beggars may use posters or other written materials related to nonexistent and/or extinct charitable organizations or companies in their effort to prove themselves legitimate. In Nigeria, beggars display photographs of "relatives" with terminal illnesses to evoke sympathy.

FB in Bangladesh is especially prevalent. It is estimated that Bangladesh has 700,000 beggars, and that the city of Daka alone has about 40,000. A large percentage of beggars in Bangladesh initially were kidnapped, maimed, and disabled by a so-called "beggar mafia", who amputated limbs or otherwise mutilated the victims. The victims were plied with alcohol and drugs, but given little food or water, and incarcerated in large containers for long periods of time (Al Hetal and Kabir 2013). The "mafia" have also killed children and dumped their bodies into rivers (CNN 2011). The "beggar mafia" often traffic destitute children and individuals with disabilities, such as those who are visually impaired, deaf, or crippled, in order to increase the mafia's begging groups (Hara 2012). Beggar women often rent infants for use as props, in order to increase their earnings.

Advocates believe that the "beggar mafia" has kidnapped at least 5,000 children in Bangladesh. The "mafia" uses taxis and private vehicles to transport the infants and children to prime locations near traffic stops; mosques; bus stands; railway stations; markets; etc. The Bangladesh mafia syndicate may have joined together with a similar Indian "beggar mafia" to facilitate cross-border trafficking of kidnapped and maimed child beggars. The children who have been abducted from their villages are transported to urban areas, where they are used as street beggars. The mafia takes a large portion of the beggar's earnings and manages to gross millions of dollars to support their activities and lifestyles (Al Hetal and Kabir 2013).

According to one report, beggars in the urban areas of Bangladesh make an average of 100 taka or $1.50 each day (Yusuf 2012).

Sex Trafficking (ST)

ST, especially the trafficking of women and children, is one of the most prevalent forms of HT (Guevarra 2004; Barrows and Finger 2008; Kristof and WuDunn 2009).

ST can involve kidnapping and captivity, resulting in social isolation, physical violence, threats of violence, and debt bondage for the victims (USDS 2010; Kristof and WuDunn 2009). They may also be made submissive and dependent through the forced use of drugs and alcohol, thus increasing the profits for their abusers (WHO 2012; Kristof and WuDunn 2009). On the other hand, ST victims may voluntarily use alcohol and drugs as a means of coping with an unbearable situation (WHO 2012). The resulting addiction may be severe. Kristof and WuDunn (2009) describe how one ST victim was so addicted to methamphetamines that she returned to her brothel life to obtain more drugs.

Traffickers may threaten the ST victims with deportation if they resist (USDS 2010). In Antigua and Barbuda brothel managers have been known to confiscate the ST victims' passports and threaten them with deportation until they repay both their supposed travel expenses and other so-called living "expenses".

ST takes place in different settings. Women and children are trafficked to work as hostesses in bar/club operations such as Eastern European/Russian stripping or exotic dancing parlors, Latino cantina bars, Asian room salons, and karaoke clubs. (In instances in which sexual services are not provided at these entertainment settings, this type of participation is classified under LT.)

Pimp controlled prostitution is a highly prevalent type of ST which can take place in brothels: homes, apartments, trailer parks, on the street, truck stops, hotels, bars and/or private parties, and many other settings.

Escort services and massage parlors are often used as fronts for prostitution. Escort services arrange contacts between interested parties. These services typically advertise on the Internet, newspapers, magazines, and on phone chat lines (Wikipedia 2014b). Some massage parlors are legitimate, but worldwide many also serve as a public face for brothels (Wikipedia 2014c; Gold 2014).

ST on the Internet

Prostitutes, pimps, and others in sex-oriented businesses have long used online classified ads such as those posted on Craigslist's popular "Erotic Services" listings. In November 2008, Craigslist reached an agreement with the attorney generals of 40 states to curb ST ads by requiring potential advertisers to provide a phone number and credit card for identification (Stone 2008). In March 2009, the sheriff of Cook County, Illinois sued Craigslist saying that Craigslist was "the single largest source of prostitution in the nation." Although the case was dismissed, Craigslist shut down its Adult Services category in September 2010 (Grady 2009, October).

However, escort advertisements can still be found in other Craigslist categories. When Craigslist closed its Adult Services category, new escort postings rose on Backpage, its main competitor (Kolker 2010). Backpage, owned by Village Voice Media, now accounts for about 70% of all prostitution ads found on the five leading ST web sites. In 2012, the attorney generals of 48 states sent a joint letter to Village Voice Media, demanding they discontinue profiting from the sex trade. Backpage.com, reportedly earned more than 22 million dollars a year from prostitution ads alone. (Kristof 2012, March).

ST Internet sites, such as those on Backpage, have been used not only by pimps, but also by consenting adult prostitutes, as well as by law enforcement agents (Kristof 2012, January). As a result of the law enforcement activity, many ST advertisers now use restricted Internet sites.

Child Prostitution

Child prostitution is prevalent around the world and is facilitated by cultural practices which differ from country to country. In Africa and the Middle East, more than 2/3 of the detected trafficking victims were children, of whom 58% were sexually exploited (Gladstone 2014).

In the U.S., children are the most vulnerable group for becoming victims of ST. It has been estimated that in the United States there were at least 100,000 children who were ST victims. (The accuracy of this estimate has been questioned, both because of the hidden nature of ST, and because of the use of questionable methodologies.) Most U.S. prostitutes started out when they were minors (Kotria 2010).

In the United States the reported rate of child sexual abuse declined 62% from 1992 to 2012. However, this rate increased 2% from 2011 to 2012. 62,700 cases of child sexual abuse were reported in 2012. Over the same period, the reported rate of physical abuse of children decreased 54% and the rate of child neglect declined 14% (Finkelhor et al. 2014).

In Azerbaijan, children are trafficked internally for child prostitution (USDS 2010).

In Belize, low-SES families may send their daughters to provide sexual services to upper-SES, older men. In exchange, these wealthy older men, who are known as "sugar daddies", pay the girls' school fees and provide gifts and additional money. This so-called "sugar daddy" practice also occurs in other Caribbean countries. In these countries, law enforcement personnel and the public may not recognize this custom as a type of ST (USDS 2010).

In Barbados, ST can involve "transactional sex" in which a third party, such as a family member, allows a child to be commercially sexually exploited in return for a benefit. Child prostitution also takes place in family settings where some stepfathers, force their children to have sex with them (USDS 2010).

In those Southeast Asian countries where enforcement of laws against both child prostitution and child pornography is weak, international child sex tourism is prevalent. Annually, thousands of men from Western Europe, the U.S., Australia, and other countries travel to Southeast Asia to have sex with male and female child prostitutes. This practice contributes to a financially rewarding child prostitution and pornography business. International child sex tourists look for young children under the age of 12 or even 10 years of age. Some patrons believe that having sex with young children will help them live longer. A persistent rumor claims that that having sex with young children can decrease the risk of acquiring HIV/AIDS (Berkman 1996). There is also an ancient myth that having sex with a child can cure venereal diseases.

Children who are trafficked as minors may be at risk for longer periods of prostitution and other forms of HT. Silverman et al. (2006) found that girls who were trafficked as minors in Mumbai, India, were confined for 18.5 months in brothels compare to 9.6 months for those who were first trafficked at older ages.

Investigators have analyzed ST in countries of origin, transit, and destination. Societal acceptance of women as sex objects fosters international ST (Adelman 2003–2004). According to Guevarra (2004), traditional gender stereotypes in the Philippines promote women and girls as sex objects and these stereotypes encourage their participation in pornography and other sexual work in destination countries. Other factors such as poverty and declining traditional family structure foster the participation of Filipina women and girls in the pornography industry.

Women and girls are also trafficked for work in the sexually oriented entertainment industry (Guevarra 2004). Still today, women and young girls are trafficked to destination countries where they work as strippers and prostitutes. These jobs are often promoted as entertainment jobs.

In Japan, women are trafficked for the entertainment industry and sexually exploitative work (Cameron and Newman 2008). For example, corporations pay for young women to pour alcoholic drinks and light cigarettes for male customers and make pleasing conversation to foster bonding among company workers.

The ST victims are recruited into the sex industry in various ways (Barrows and Finger 2008; MacKinnon 2004–2005). Perpetrators may first force the victims into debt bondage, and then physically coerce or trick them into prostitution. Other ST victims may have been kidnapped and then forced into prostitution, pornography, and/or associated activities. Sometimes, potential ST victims are promised employment as domestic or service workers and then taken to brothels or other sexual settings where their passports and other identification documents are confiscated. The victims may be then beaten and imprisoned in order to force them to conform to their "masters'" demands (Moens et al. 2001).

Two countries that are considered to have the worst records for child ST are Thailand and Brazil (Anon. 2012).

Based on a sample of 160 ST victims, Silverman et al. (2007) showed that most of the victims were originally trafficked as minors by persons who they knew.

In this study, 55% of the victims were reportedly lured by promises of financial opportunities, and 26.3% of the victims had been abducted through drug use or coercion.

Pornography

Commercial pornography was for many years a highly lucrative industry for the ST of women, men, and children (MacKinnon 2004–2005). To produce pornographic materials, such as films, videos, etc., women, men, and children were rented and forced to commit sex acts. The pornographic items were then sold to buyers for the purpose of sexual stimulation. In 2005, according to Paul Fishbein, the founding president of Adult Video News (AVN), about 800 million adult videos were rented in the U.S., resulting in a revenue of about $20 billion per year, and $57 billion per year worldwide (Corliss 2005, March). However, in 2007, AVN's Fishbein estimated that in the United States, pornographic video rental and sales steadily increased from $1.6 billion in 1992 to $4.2 billion in 1997 and then roughly leveled off from 1997 to 2005. In 2006 this income declined 15% from 2005. The industry's online revenue was $2.8 billion in 2006, compared to $2.5 billion in 2005, but was not growing quickly enough to compensate for the decline in video sales and rentals (Richtel 2007). By 2013, "more people were watching porn for free over the internet instead of purchasing it." One retired adult porn performer noted that "80% of the companies that were around five years ago either don't exist or are hanging by a thread" (Moye 2013).

Little technical knowledge is required to obtain and trade internet child pornography content (Lowrey 2014; Dank et al. 2014). However, there is still a demand for commercial child pornography. In 2006 a web site named "Illegal CP" was discovered by federal agents who developed evidence that led to the convictions of 560 individuals in 47 states (Wikipedia 2014a). Maksym Shynkarenko, the chief conspirator, was sentenced to 30 years in federal prison (Associated Press 2014a).

In 2014, the Royal Canadian Mounted Police rescued 5 children who were pictured in online porn. Hundreds of computers containing more than 2 million images or videos were seized. Some of the pictures involved infants and toddlers. Police filed 343 criminal charges against 150 people. The charges included: sexual assault, and the possession and distribution of child pornography (Associated Press 2014b).

In June 2014, the FBI conducted a week-long operation in 106 U.S. cities and rescued 168 children from the sex trade. During the same period 281 pimps were arrested on state and federal charges. Many of the child victims had never been reported missing. This operation was the eighth such FBI operation. All eight FBI operations have rescued a total of nearly 3,600 children (Tucker 2014).

Mail Order Brides (MOBs)

The demand for MOBs is substantial (Guevarra 2004; Smartt 2003; Lloyd 2000; Stone 2004; Chun 1996). MOB agencies advertise on the Internet and elsewhere. They promote prospective brides, from areas such as Asia, South America, and Eastern Europe to men in developed countries. The number of MOB agencies in the United States increased from more than 200 in 1997 to more than 500 in 2008 (Tahirih 2008).

The number of MOBs imported to the United States has increased from year to year. In 1997, out of 40,000 to 50,000 annual marriages of foreign women to U.S. citizens, 4,000 to 5,000 were MOB's (Scholes 1997). Scholes (1999) estimated that 4,000 to 6,000 foreign MOBs married U.S. citizens annually. Based on INS statistics for foreign fiancés admitted to the U.S. in 2007, estimates of foreign MOBs in the U.S. had increased to 11,000 to 16,500 per year, plus thousands more admitted annually as foreign spouses (Tahirih 2008). Sarker et al. (2013) estimated that each year there are 16,500 MOB marriages in the U.S.

Guevarra (2004) noted that Filipino women seek to marry men in other countries in order to improve their financial opportunities. In the early 1990s, more than 700,000 Filipino women became fiancées and then married men from Germany, Great Britain, Australia, and Taiwan.

In 2006, 23,532 Filipino women were married to Australian men who were generally older (55 years old and up) compared to the women (20–34 years old). Although domestic violence is common in Australia, Filipinas are six times more likely to be victims of homicide than other Australian women. In Australia, between 1980 and 2007, 23 Filipina women were murdered by their husband or partner (CPCA 2011).

MOBs may be at increased risk for abuse in their country of destination. One report described the various types of abuse that Russian-speaking MOBs may face, including being isolated and having limited finances (Crandall et al. 2005). "Abuse rates in marriages between U.S. citizens and foreign women are approximately several times higher than in the general U.S. population (Haas et al. 2006). In 1998 less than 2,5000 foreign women used the *Violence Against Women Act*, a resource for abused women, to apply for permanent U.S. residence, without their husbands' agreement. In fiscal year 2006, 9,500 women applied, (Porter 2006).

In March 2006, *The International Marriage Broker Regulation Act* went into effect. This U.S. law requires dating agencies to provide information about a man's criminal record and marital history to the woman, and then get her permission prior to disclosing her contact information (Porter 2006).

MOBs from certain countries may feel stigmatized in their destination country (Kelaher et al. 2001). The social process of adjustment for these MOBs is more problematic because they may look different from local residents.

Forced Marriage (FM)

FM, another type of HT, involves one or both parties getting married against their will (Smartt 2003; Razack 2004). Other terms for the FM are forced conjugal association and conjugal slavery. FM can be divided into four categories: marriage by rape, marriage by sale, marriage by kidnapping, and child marriage (Gladstone 2014). Some writers suggest that the term, FM, erroneously legitimizes the arrangement of marriage when in fact the arrangement is illegitimate and coercive (Anonymous 2014).

Although FMs are outlawed in many countries, including Afghanistan, Austria, Belgium, Cyprus, Canada, Denmark, Ethiopia, Ghana, Germany, Malta, Turkey, U. K., and Zimbabwe, FMs still take place in those countries and all over the world (Anon. 2012; Rubin 2012; Anon. 2014). Obviously, laws are not enough to stop FMs, which are especially prevalent in Africa, East Asia, and South Asia. "Globally, between 2004 and 2014, 10 million girls were forced to marry or are expected to be forced to marry before their 18th birthday" (Anon. 2013).

Culture and poverty are the main driving forces which lead to FMs. In those cultures where girls are treated as commodities, such as Somalia, the father receives a bride price in 90% of marriages. In rural Afghanistan, plagued by war and drought, many fathers sell their daughters into marriage. Because of the AIDS pandemic in Sub-Saharan Africa, there are millions of orphans who are subject to both child trafficking and forced marriages (Ryerson-Cruz et al. 2008).

Throughout history, FMs have been used to integrate a slave or prisoner of war into her or his local community and accept his or her life situation. FMs were thought to reconcile the captive to accept her or his fate as a member of the captor's community. A captive might also be given the choice of forced marriage or death.

One form of FM is the "shotgun wedding", which occurs because of an unplanned pregnancy and the need to avoid an out-of-wedlock birth. In some cultures, marriage is required because out-of-wedlock births are considered sinful, illegal, and/or stigmatized. In the U.S. in the eighteenth and nineteenth centuries, violent coercion was commonly employed in shotgun weddings. However, such violent coercion is now illegal in the United States (Anon. 2014).

FMs can force individuals, especially young girls and women, into a cycle of poverty and subjugation. FMs can also be used to promote political goals. For example, in Cambodia, FMs took place during the Khmer Rouge regime (1975–1979) to expand the population size and promote the revolution (Anderson 2010).

A Ugandan rebel group, the "Lord's Resistance Army", has forced girls to serve as "wives" of commanders (Okeowo 2013). In 2014, *Boku Haram*, a Nigerian terrorist group, kidnapped 276 girls and threatened to sell them (Gladstone 2014). Both the "Lord's Resistance Army", and *Boku Haram* are listed as terrorist groups by the U.S. Government (USDS 2014).

In parts of Pakistan and Afghanistan, the compensation marriage (also known as *vanni*, *swara*, and *sang chatti*) takes place. This form of FM is used to coerce young girls and women into marriages to settle tribal disputes. According to one report, hundreds of Pakistani girls who were living in the New York area have been transported to Pakistan to participate in FMs. Those who resisted such FMs were reportedly threatened and forced to acquiesce (Katz 2007).

Intercountry Adoptions (ICAs)

Infant and child trafficking for the primary purpose of adoption, also known as child laundering, is another type of HT (Smolin 2010; Smartt 2003; Yemm 2010; Rasor et al. 2010/2011). Infants and children are especially at risk for becoming trafficked on the black market for international adoptions, also known as intercountry adoptions (ICAs). Illegal financial transactions, subterfuge, and/or coercion have been used to obtain infants and children who are then trafficked for foreign adoption. Some of these children may be forced into child labor.

In the U.S., more than 250,000 foreign children were adopted between 1960 and 2010 (Yemm 2010; Gildersleeve-Neumann et al. 2012–2013). In the U.S., the annual number of ICAs peaked at 22,884 in 2004 and declined to 8,668 by 2012. Worldwide the number of ICAs peaked at 34,785 in 2004 and went down to 23,609 in 2011 (Voigt and Brown 2013). Multiple factors have led to this decline, both in the U.S. and worldwide. *The Hague Convention on the Protection of Children and Co-operation in Respect of Inter-country Adoption* established standards of practice to safeguard intercountry adoptions. It entered into force in the U.S. in 2008 (Anon. 2014; Navarro 2008). Recently, many countries have enforced new rules concerning foreign adoptions. As of January 1, 2013, Russia, which had been a major source of child adoptees in the U.S., banned all adoptions by U.S. citizens. China's new rules have reduced the total number of ICAs to 4,418 in 2011 from 13,415 in 2004, while the number of children in Chinese orphanages has doubled to 92,000 (Voigt and Brown 2013).

Economic, social, family, political, legal, cultural, and technological conditions influence ICAs. In the 1920s, the highly restrictive immigration policies in the U.S. limited immigration, including ICAs (Yemm 2010). However, after World War II, Americans' sympathy for the plight of European children led to the enactment of the Displaced Persons Act, which permitted the entry and adoption of European orphans. During this period, the reduced pool of American orphans increased the desire for international adoptions.

Other armed conflicts increased ICAs. For example, after the Korean War, international adoptions increased as U.S. troops stationed in South Korea became aware of the problems of South Korean orphans (Yemm 2010). More than 38,000 children from South Korea were adopted by U.S. parents during the period, 1953–1981. Many of these adopted children were fathered by U.S. military personnel (Wallace 2003; Yemm 2010).

Major natural disasters, such as earthquakes and typhoons that destroy communities result in orphans, who are forced to live in institutional settings or on the streets. Parents, who are unable to care for their children following a natural disaster, may give them up for adoption.

In addition to international conflicts and natural disasters, varying social trends since the 1950s have affected the supply and demand for adoptable children (Yemm 2010). In the first world countries, the increasing use of contraceptives and abortion, and the declining stigma associated with single parenthood, has resulted in a reduction in the availability of adoptable children in the U.S. Individuals in prosperous nations often seek to adopt children for humanitarian reasons (Carlson 1988; Yemm 2010). Even though federal immigration policy in the U.S. has promoted ICAs, the process of ICAs is expensive and cumbersome for the prospective parents (Banks 2004; Voigt and Brown 2013).

ICAs are a controversial topic between adoptive parents, civil rights leaders, advocates of children's rights, and nationalists in countries with large numbers of excess orphans (Yemm 2010; Smolin 2010). One of the central questions is what is in the best interests of the orphans living in impersonal institutional care, dire poverty, and disorganized communities. Advocates for ICAs argue that adoption is in the best interest of these children even though illicit procedures may have been used in carrying out the adoption. Advocates believe that prosperous and highly motivated individuals can provide the best socialization for these adoptable children. In contrast, opponents of ICAs argue that ICAs uproot children from their home countries, exploit the resources of these countries and are frequently achieved through abusive and illegal procedures, including coercion and fraud. In some cases, biological parents have been misled into believing that their children died during childbirth or that they will maintain contact with their children after they are adopted. In one case, an American couple adopted two children from India. The couple later discovered that the children had been kidnapped from their mother (Voigt and Brown 2013).

An analysis of ICAs in different countries periods reveal the historical, ethical, environmental, social, political, legal, and cultural factors that impact this controversial process. The issue of ICAs was drawn to public attention in Haiti after the major earthquake in Port-au-Prince. A group of U.S. Christian missionaries were charged with kidnapping after they attempted to transport 33 children from the devastated area to the Dominican Republic (Rasor et al. 2010/2011). The missionaries stated that they were rescuing the children out of humanitarian concern for these children whom they thought had been orphaned after the earthquake. Other reports claimed that the missionaries had tried to purchase the children from their living parents. Some reports indicated that the missionaries misinformed the parents by promising them that their children would be educated and that they could see them any time (Rasor et al. 2010/2011; Penhaul 2010). The Haitian court convicted the missionary group leader of "organization of irregular trips", which is a lesser offense than kidnapping (CBS News.com, April 27 2010).

In Romania, during the period, 1966–1989, Nicolae Ceausescu, the Communist dictator, substantially influenced the demand for ICAs by banning birth control and abortion, and thus increased the number of children living in institutions (Yemm 2010).

In Guatemala, the traditional use of private, non-centralized adoptions enabled the country to be a leader in exporting ICAs (Yemm 2010). However, in January of 2008, the Guatemalan government closed its ICA program amid evidence of child trafficking. Although initially, 4,000 pending adoptions were held up, this number was reduced to 150 pending adoptions by 2012 (Swarns 2012).

Private adoptions are unregulated in Greece. As a result, ICA is thriving, driven by a low native birthrate. Most of the babies originate in Roma settlements in Bulgaria, and are sold for an average of $4,000, and as much as $33,000 (Kitsantonis and Brunwasser 2006).

Drug Trafficking

Drug trafficking is another form of HT (Smartt 2003; ILO 2002). While the exact number of children participating in the drug trade is unknown, this activity is widespread. Children play different roles in illicit drug trafficking. They are often used in drug trafficking activities in various countries, including Columbia, Cambodia, United States, U.K., Russia, Italy, Brazil, Pakistan, and Iran (ILO 2002).

In Brazil, children are used in the retail area of drug trafficking (ILO 2002). In Afghanistan, boys are trafficked to participate in forced labor in the drug smuggling industry in Pakistan and Iran (USDS 2010). In London, children as young as 11 years of age have been used to transport drugs into the surrounding countryside (Topping 2014). Between 2008 and 2013, in the San Diego area, 978 minors were charged with drug trafficking (McIntyre 2014). In Foggia, Italy, a drug ring used 10 and 11-year-old children as couriers (Anon. 2013b).

Child Soldiers

Both children and adults have been trafficked for use as soldiers and terrorists in armed conflicts (USDS 2010; Derluyn et al. 2004; Klasen et al. 2011). Around the world, more than 250,000 children have been conscripted as child solders. In many instances these children have been kidnapped (Derluyn et al. 2004; Klasen et al. 2011). According to Klasen et al. (2011), almost 50% of the children and adolescents used as soldiers are in Africa.

Armed groups reportedly exploit the child soldiers sexually (USDS 2010). Groups of insurgents make false promises to trick the children into becoming child soldiers. In Afghanistan, the insurgents promised boys that they would be able to enter Islamic schools in Pakistan and Iran; instead, these boys were taken to training camps for paramilitary operations. In Syria, according to *Human Rights Watch,* militant groups have recruited children as young as 15 years old. They were promised a free education, but were instead sent into battle (Reuters 2014).

In terms of other terrorist activities, children have been trafficked and coerced into becoming suicide bombers (USDS 2010). In Afghanistan, the Taliban reportedly has used children in the 12–16 age group as suicide bombers. Some of these children may have been coerced or tricked into these activities. However, other adolescents view soldiering as the best economic option, or join up because of ideology (ILO 2002).

In an investigation of 330 former Ugandan child soldiers, Klasen et al. (2011) found that they ranged in age between 11 and 17 and 48.5% were female. They had been kidnapped and used as child soldiers at the average age of 10.75 years and continued for an average of 19.81 months. The former child soldiers reported observing killings (86.4%), being the victim of death threats (87.9%) and being forced to kill another individual (52.6%). Almost 26% of the former child soldiers reported being raped.

According to the United Nations, children have been found working for the Afghan National Police (ANP) (USDS 2010). The Afghan government claims that it is trying to improve the ways in which individuals' ages are verified prior to employment in the ANP.

The Lord's Resistance Army, which has been active in Uganda, abducted at least 66,000 children between 1986 and 2006. Some of these children were forced to become child soldiers or sex slaves (USDS 2012b).

Organ Trafficking

There is a worldwide shortage of human organs available for transplantation. In the U.S. there are currently 123,084 people awaiting an organ transplant, each day 79 people receive transplants and 18 people die waiting for an organ (Woerner 2014; USHHS 2014). The number of candidates waiting for transplants continues to dwarf the number of donor organs available (USHHS 2014). This has led to the development of an international marketplace where organs are even advertised online (Anon. 2007). Although this latter activity is illegal in all countries except Iran, it is tolerated in many countries.

Individuals are trafficked for removal of their organs and other biological materials (Scheper-Hughes 2004; Budiani-Saberi and Delmonico 2008; Jafar 2009). Organ trafficking involves recruiting, transporting, or receipt of individuals through various forms of exploitation, including fraud, deceit, violence, kidnapping and/or threats of violence. In many cases, the trafficked individuals receive payments or other benefits for "donation" of their organs or other biological materials (Budiani-Saberi and Delmonico 2008). Worldwide networks of organ brokers, surgical technicians, physicians, and hospital facilities participate in the market of trafficked organs (Jafar 2009). The act of organ donations is commendable in many societies, but the process may have been taken over by illicit organizations (Jafar 2009). Unethical physicians may exacerbate the covert nature of this illicit activity by concealing and disguising their participation through the use of medical confidentiality (OSCE, 2013). Transplant tourism in which transplant recipients or donors go across national borders may or may not involve illicit organ trafficking (Budiani-Saberi and Delmonico 2008).

Financial incentives for organ trafficking substantially increase the probability that networks of physicians, brokers, and hospitals will participate in the trafficking of organs around the world (Jafar 2009). The price per kidney has ranged from US $1,000 to $5,000 and package deals for kidney transplant tourism ranged from US $35,000 to $150,000. Low-SES persons in developing countries without strong legal safeguards and moral–ethical standards are especially vulnerable to selling their organs or working as brokers in the illicit organ market.

The increasing incidence and prevalence of cardiometabolic disease has resulted in a substantial need for organ transplantation (Jafar 2009). For example, during the 1990 period in the U.S., the number of patients with end-stage kidney failure (ESKF) almost doubled. Advances in human transplantation have made kidney transplantation the best approach to achieving survival, making it the treatment of choice for many ESKF patients. Moreover, the public has increasingly accepted organ donations as a socially and legally appropriate treatment. Likewise, the types and conditions for organ donations have expanded. Between 1988 and June 2014, there were 129,462 kidney transplants in the U.S. In 2013, approximately 6,000 living people donated one of their kidneys. However, more than 100,000 Americans are on waiting lists, and most will wait for at least five years before a kidney from a deceased donor is available (Healy 2014; OPTN 2014). The number of transplants in the U.S. and other developed nations still does not meet the demand.

In an undercover ethnography of illicit organ trafficking, Scheper-Hughes (2004) found examples of persons who were lured and coerced into donating a kidney. One young man was 18 years old when he was lured from Mingir, a village, to the city of Chisenau in Moldova, and then to Istanbul. The young man reportedly had been told that he would be employed at a dry-cleaning store. Instead, he was told that he would be selling a kidney.

Scheper-Hughes (2004) found that traffickers may use weapons to make death threats against individuals who refuse to sell a kidney. For example, one victim from Chisenau allegedly was threatened with a knife and firearm after he refused to sell his kidney.

Individuals in the above instances who illicitly sold a kidney faced severe stigma, social ostracism, and discrimination (Scheper-Hughes 2004). These persons often felt that they were a disgrace to themselves, their family, community, and country. In the above organ trafficking case involving the 18-year-old man from Mingir, his father was so upset with him over the organ trafficking that at the time his relationship with his father was severely impaired. Organ trafficking victims also face employment discrimination since employers and coworkers do not want to have a "one-kidney" in the workplace. To cope with their stigma and discrimination, kidney sellers will cover up their scars and keep the operation a secret.

Data on the prevalence and incidence of organ trafficking are limited because this activity is secret and illicit. According to one report, organ trafficking makes up five to 10 percent of kidney transplants that take place globally each year (Budiani-Saberi and Delmonico 2008). Increasingly, patients in rich countries travel abroad and buy human organs. As of 2006, foreigners received two-thirds of the kidney transplants performed each year in Pakistan (ISTTOT 2008). *The Declaration of Istanbul* seeks to fight transplant commercialism and organ trafficking. Various European transplant organizations reportedly are working closely to deal with this issue.

Worldwide Risk Factors for HT

Worldwide, a number of factors at the individual, community, and national level increase the risk of HT. The process of globalization, the growth of transnational economies, the growth of the worldwide Internet, and social trends such as the rise of sex tourism, are some of those factors (Orchard 2007).

While poverty and the lack of education are the primary trafficking vulnerability factors, but this is not necessarily the case. In a study of the Greater Mekong Subregion, the *United Nations Inter-agency Project on Human Trafficking* (UNIAP), found that: people with means are more likely to migrate, rather than the poorest, and that adventurous young people along with the more educated young people, want to leave their villages to seek urban jobs, and thus are at risk for HT (UNIAP 2007).

Social and economic injustices increase the probability that HT will occur in failed and failing countries. Since these countries are unable to maintain the rule of law, and have many corrupt officials, they lack legitimacy even among their own citizens. Extreme poverty, unemployment, and severe income inequality exists among the various socioeconomic status (SES) groups in such countries (Bailliet 2010).

Significant Income Inequality, Homelessness, and Associated Problems

Around the world, HT victims and their families are often in dire financial situations (Ribando Seelke 2011; Studnicka 2010; May 2009). Source countries with the greatest income inequality may be more likely to foster HT (World Bank 2013).

In an investigation of ST and health care in Metro Manila, Williams et al. (2010) found that environmental deterioration had led to a disruption of traditional types of labor. The displaced workers suffered from low SES, increasing their risk of becoming HT victims. The extreme poverty that parents faced forced some of them to sell their children in order to survive (May 2009; Van Hook et al. 2006; Bales 2005).

Poverty is a risk factor for ST in Nepal. Traffickers have transported thousands of Nepali girls into brothels in Kolkata (formerly Calcutta), India (Kristof and WuDunn 2009).

In Nepal, extremely low SES, indigenous *Tharu* farming families may rent their daughters for $75 per annum, an amount that is a third of their yearly income (May 2009).

Family Loss, Violence, and Other Family Dysfunction

HT victims' vulnerability to victimization is increased by their experiences of low SES, and the gender-based mistreatment of girls and women (Williams et al. 2010). Adult women may be divorced, abandoned, or suffer domestic violence (DV) prior to their victimization (Silverman et al. 2007).

Individuals who suffered abuse during childhood are at increased risk of becoming an HT victim (Williams et al. 2010). In addition, orphaned, abandoned, or runaway children and adolescents are vulnerable to HT. Minors traveling alone also may be a risk group for HT (Derluyn et al. 2010).

Natural catastrophes may increase the risk for HT and slavery (CdeBaca 2010). For example, after the devastating 2010 earthquake in Haiti, one U.S. organization reportedly attempted to transport orphans out of the country without the proper documentation (Rasor et al. 2010/2011).

HT is Financially Rewarding for Criminal Groups and Networks

Worldwide, organized crime groups use force and the threat of force, monopoly control, and the corruption of government officials to participate in ST, drug trafficking, HT, and other activities that arise from a huge public demand for illicit services (Albanese 2004).

HT is very lucrative for criminals worldwide. According to the UNECE, total annual revenue for HT ranges from $5 billion and $9 billion (UNECE 2004). The Council of Europe estimates that the annual market for HT worldwide is $42.5 billion (Requena 2006).

Transnational organized crime networks earn considerable profits from the trafficking of women (Hughes et al. 2007; Reynolds and McKee 2010). Criminal earnings from the trafficking of women rank third after drugs and arms trafficking. The ST of women produces high profits and is a low-risk venture which needs a minimum of investment capital.

The trafficking of children also generates substantial profits and is a low-risk criminal enterprise (Hansen 2001). Child trafficking does not need extensive capital or other commodities such as drugs or arms.

Official Corruption, Ineffectiveness, and Indifference

HT flourishes in many countries because governments often are unable or do not try to control the criminal enterprises (Studnicka 2010; Hansen 2001; Van Hook et al. 2006; Albanese 2004). Many investigations have found that corrupt government authorities are often associated with HT (Studnicka 2010; Bales 2005; CPMI 2004). However, there is a large amount of HT even in some countries that are otherwise governed well, because HT victims are not recognized as such (CdeBaca 2014).

Bales (2005) found that corruption of government officials in a source country is a significant factor in HT. Using both data on corruption incidents plus other data sources in Brazil, Studnicka (2010) found that Brazilian law enforcement agents believe that document preparation and victim control are crucial areas in increasing the risk of official corruption-related domestic HT. Some border control officers, who are involved in the screening and processing of individuals entering Brazil, participate in HT. A Brazilian government investigation evaluated 89 HT cases out of 561 sexual crime cases that occurred between 1994 and 2003 and showed that 63 (71%) of these cases were associated with official corruption (CPMI 2004).

Frequently, government authorities either may be indifferent to the problem of HT, or they may actually support and facilitate HT. There also seems to be some correlation between government instability and HT, but HT also occurs even in countries with stable governments, such as the U.S. In the fight against HT, no country is doing a perfect job (CdeBaca 2014).

During World War II, an estimated 200,000 women were forced into ST by the Japanese military and their agents (Yoshimi 2002). These "comfort women" were from various countries, including Korea, China, Japan, and the Philippines. In the early stages of the war, Japanese officials recruited prostitutes using conventional methods. Many women were promised legitimate employment opportunities such as work in factories and health care, but instead were incarcerated in "comfort stations" in various countries to provide sexual services for Japanese military personnel. The situation for local residents in areas controlled by the Japanese military became worse as the war progressed (Yoshimi 2002). When the Japanese military rated local women as hostile, they were indiscriminately kidnapped from their residences and raped. The Japanese military forced many of these women into this system of prostitution. Private agents managed the comfort stations under the supervision of the Japanese military.

In modern times, traffickers have set up similar systems of prostitution near U.S. military bases in South Korea (Hughes et al. 2007).

Cross-Border Migration

The migration of individuals across international borders increases the risk of HT (Molland 2010; Kristof and WuDunn 2009). Molland (2010) describes the migration of Lao sex workers across the Lao-Thai border. Similarly, the border between Nepal and India is used for the trafficking of girls for ST (Kristof and WuDunn 2009). Nearly 7,000 women and girls are trafficked annually from Nepal to India, and approximately 200,000 are working in Indian brothels (Orlinsky 2013).

A study of repatriated ST Nepalese girls and women found that they had a high prevalence of HIV infection. Those who had been trafficked before the age of 15 had an increased risk for HIV infection. Being trafficked to Mumbai, India, and a longer duration of coerced prostitution also increased the risk of HIV infection (Silverman et al. 2007).

Cultural and Societal Ideologies and Practices

Cultural and societal ideologies and norms facilitate HT and slavery. For example, in various countries, destitute parents sell their children to strangers, relatives, and friends (Hansen 2001). In these societies, HT is facilitated by deeply ingrained cultural practices (May 2009).

Individuals in many societies believe that prostitution has existed since ancient times, is ingrained in society and therefore concerted regulation will be ineffective. Cultural beliefs such as the desire to have sex with virgins and light-skinned young women foster ST (Kristof and WuDunn 2009). The myth still persists that having sex with a virgin can cure HIV/AIDS. This is a modern variation on the sixteenth-century European folk myth of a cure for syphilis, gonorrhea, and other sexually transmitted diseases (Groce and Trasi 2004).

In a number of countries, people treat children, especially girls, as property that can be sold to eliminate a family debt (Hansen 2001). In rural south India, the belief in the *Devadasi* (servant/slave of the God) tradition, promotes child prostitution, which has long been part of the region's political economy (Orchard 2007).

Although it is forbidden by China's adoption laws, the buying and selling of babies is a long-standing and lucrative business, which has increased following the development of the Internet (Tatlow 2014).

History of Sexual and Physical Violence

Societies that condone domestic violence (DV) and other forms of sexual and physical violence tend to foster ST (Zimmerman et al. 2008; Van Hook et al. 2006; Silverman et al. 2007). DV perpetuates feelings of powerlessness that tends to increase the victims' risk for HT.

War, Armed Conflict, and Militarism

Around the world, during periods of war and armed conflict, women are frequently abducted and raped as part of a larger pattern of human rights abuses. In northern Uganda, since the late 1980s, members of the Lord's Resistance Army (LRA) kidnapped between 52,000 and 75,000 people and forced them to become soldiers, sex slaves for their commanders, and porters (Pham et al. 2009). One cross-sectional study of 2,875 victims of crimes allegedly perpetrated by the LRA revealed that 33% reported being kidnapped. A survey of 991 internally displaced women in Sierra Leone, showed that many had experienced or known of war-related human rights abuses that included murder, kidnappings, and rape (Amowitz et al. 2002).

Beyrer (2001) evaluated how persistent conflict in the Shan States of Burma was a factor in facilitating the ST of Shan girls and women into the prostitution industry in Southeast Asia.

During periods of armed conflict, sex workers and widows increasingly must seek self-determination and become responsible for earning income and managing their households despite communities which resist their efforts because they contradict the long-standing customs of the area (Tambiah 2004). Sex workers who gain new political and economic rights during periods of armed conflict and postwar reconstruction period have better chances of determining their own sexual and reproductive activities.

Health and Psychosocial Effects of HT

The World Health Organization (2012) notes that limited research has been done on the social, psychological, and physical impact of HT in large part because of the secret and illegal nature of these activities. HT victims are at increased risk of suffering a variety of physical and psychosocial problems, depending in part on the victims' age, gender, and type of HT (WHO 2012).

Trafficked females suffer multiple post-trafficking physical and mental health problems according to a survey of 192 women entering post-trafficking assistance services in Europe (Zimmerman et al. 2008). As noted earlier, 95% of the women and adolescent girls in this investigation reported sexual violence or physical abuse during trafficking; 59% of the victims reported similar abuse prior to trafficking. Their most common and reported symptoms included: headaches (82%), feeling easily tired (81%), dizzy spells (70%), back pain (69%), memory difficulty (62%), stomach pain (61%), pelvic pain (59%), and gynecological infections (58%). Zimmerman et al. (2008) showed that women entering post-trafficking assistance services were also more likely to exhibit symptoms of depression, anxiety, and hostility compared to a baseline study of the mental health of adult women in the general U.S. population (Derogatis 1993).

ST victims face violence from customers, other criminals, and law enforcement personnel (Jayasree 2004). The ST victims' problems are worsened by the fact that they often have no access to health care and have high rates of HIV/AIDS. HT victims also suffer because they frequently lack shelter and childcare support (WHO 2012).

In Thailand, the growth of the HIV/AIDS epidemic has been enhanced by the rise of the commercial sex industry there, as well as the social inequalities between men and women which have existed throughout the country's history (Nyamathi et al. 2007). Likewise, the ST of *Shan* girls and women into the sex industry in Southeast Asia has led to a high prevalence of HIV/AIDS among them (Beyrer 2001).

Despite the health risks, ST victims often have difficulty avoiding high-risk behaviors, i.e., they continued to have multiple sex partners, and many avoided the use of condoms, because of their need to survive financially (Ntozi et al. 2003).

HT victims can be stigmatized when their activities become known to their communities. Even though Vietnamese women may enter ST to pay off a family obligation, they still face substantial stigma and dishonor when they return to normal life, and tend to disguise the fact that they had been prostitutes (Vijeyarasa 2010).

MOBs face cultural marginality and the stigma of being perceived as foreigners with questionable motives (Kelaher et al. 2001; Crandall et al. 2005). As a result, MOBs may encounter discrimination and social isolation, resulting in impairment in social and psychological functioning and associated physical health complaints.

As noted previously, HT victims are more likely to be forced into abusing alcohol and drugs or use alcohol and other drugs as a coping mechanism. As a result, HT victims face health problems associated with substance abuse. Many of them often are forced to use illicit drugs to keep them passive. HT victims, including children who live on the street, also abuse drugs as a coping mechanism (Sherman et al. 2005). Street children often will exchange sex for drugs (Chettiar et al. 2010).

Victims of HT, including labor migrants, are at increased risk of suffering a variety of health problems, including depression, anxiety, and posttraumatic stress disorder (PTSD) (Zimmerman et al. 2008; Lindert et al. 2009).

Child soldiers, child terrorists, and child police, because of their severe victimization, are at increased risk of substantial psychosocial and physical health problems. Betancourt et al. (2011) studied 273 former child soldiers (29% females) from Sierra Leone. These children had observed and committed violence at similar rates. Those who had injured or killed others, tended to have higher levels of depression, anxiety, and hostility. Those male victims, who had survived rape, were likely to have greater anxiety and hostility.

A study of 142 former child soldiers in Nepal by Kohrt et al. (2010) showed that children who had greater exposure to trauma, especially torture, had lower levels of psychosocial adjustment. Children with higher education attainment had better psychosocial outcomes.

In their analysis of 330 former Uganda child soldiers, Klasen et al. (2011) found that 33% of the children met the diagnostic criteria for PTSD. Children with PTSD were more likely to have higher guilt cognitions.

Because of their participation in war, many former child soldiers face significant stigma and associated psychosocial adjustment difficulties when they return to their communities (Betancourt et al. 2010). Former child soldiers, who were accepted by their communities, were more likely to develop adaptive attitudes and behaviors, than those who lacked community acceptance.

Based on an investigation of 39 captured or escaped Mozambique child soldiers, Boothby et al. (2006) found that rehabilitation services can help former child soldiers become productive individuals in the community. (Those services that taught the victims skills in coping with trauma and grief, gave them a sense of social responsibility; those services that focused more on self-control than on security were helpful.)

Other individuals who have been conscripted into armed conflict also face severe trauma. In their investigation of persons who reported being kidnapped by the LRA in northern Uganda, Pham et al. (2009) discovered that more than two-thirds of these persons met the criteria for PTSD. Multivariate analysis revealed that the risks of PTSD were increased if the individual was: female; a member of the *Acholi* ethnic group; a participant or observer a number of trauma-related events and had social readjustment problems after returning to his/her community.

Pham et al. (2009) also evaluated conditions that increased the risk of depression in persons who reported having been abducted by the LRA. Victims who were older at the time of their participation in violence, and those who had subsequent difficulties in social readjustment, were at increased risk of depression.

Social, Legal, Policy, and Organizational Responses to HT

Persistent differences in political views toward ST and prostitution lead to inadequate cooperation in fighting these activities in many countries. The modern abolition movement is weakened by the divisiveness between political groups (Kristof and WuDunn 2009). However, occasionally groups are able to pass anti-ST legislation despite their political differences. For example, substantial differences between Republicans and Democrats in the U.S. were overcome enough to enable the enactment of the TVPA. Nevertheless, political differences remain regarding ways to fight prostitution and ST. For example, liberals differ from conservatives in how they view prostitution. Liberals often describe ST participants using the nonjudgmental phrase, "sex workers". In contrast, conservatives as well as some feminists refer to these individuals, who are seen as engaging in a demeaning activity, as "prostitutes" or "prostituted women".

Laws Against HT

A variety of laws and policies have been developed in the U.S. to combat ST and prostitution. In the U.S., on June 25, 1910, the White-Slave Traffic Act (WSTA) (ch. 395, 36 Stat. 825), also known as the *Mann Act*, was enacted (PBS no date) (Anon. 1911) (Langum 1994). The WSTA was codified as amended at 18 U.S.C. 2421 (Anon. 2011). The WSTA originally made white slavery illegal. (White slavery refers to the slavery of Caucasians.) The act also prohibited the interstate trafficking of females for purposes of an immoral nature.

The WSTA had ambiguous language and as a result, individuals were selectively prosecuted using the law (WETA 2005a; Langum 1994). The act was later amended to prohibit only trafficking for the purpose of prostitution or illegal sexual activity. The WSTA was frequently used to prosecute men for having sexual intercourse with underage girls and others who angered authorities for engaging in immoral activities. The U.S. Congress in 1978 updated the definition of "transportation" in the WSTA and provided protections for minors who were the victims of sexual exploitation for profit (WETA 2005b; Langum 1994). In 1986, an amendment was added to provide additional protections to minors and also provided protection for adult males. The 1986 amendment replaced ambiguous language, such as the term, "debauchery", with the specific phrase: "any sexual activity for which any person can be charged with a criminal offense". The 1986 amendment also made the law gender neutral.

The passage of the WSTA led to a number of legal controversies (Langum 1994). For example, in *Hoke v. United States*, 227 U.S. 308, the U.S. Supreme Court held that the U.S. Congress could not regulate prostitution per se since the states regulated prostitution. However, Congress could regulate interstate travel for prostitution or other immoral activities (JUSTIA no date, a). The U.S. Supreme Court in *Athanasaw v. United States*, 227 U.S. 326, ruled that the WSTA was not restricted to prostitution; the law also applied to debauchery (JUSTIA no date, b).

The U.S. currently has laws against HT at both the state and federal levels. More than 50% of the states have laws the prohibit HT. However, state laws are not as severe as federal laws. Federal and state authorities seek to regulate sex tourism and international marriage brokers. Potential brides may be able to obtain criminal background checks on their prospective husbands, and information on support services.

The New York State Anti-Human Trafficking Act of 2007 was passed to give assistance on how to handle HT victims and how to remove them from hazardous situations. However, over the next two years, there were only 18 arrests and one conviction for trafficking, with 3 cases still pending by the end of 2009 (Berger 2009).

The Trafficking Victims Protection Act of 1991 (TVPA) was passed by the U.S. Congress to improve existing criminal penalties for HT, offer new protections to victims of HT, and provide some benefits and services for victims who have suffered severely from trafficking-related activities (106th United States Congress, October 28, 2000). The TVPA established a federal interagency task force at the Cabinet level and set up a federal program to offer services to HT victims. TVPA allows potential MOBs to obtain criminal background checks on their prospective husbands, and information on support services.

The TVPA was designed to prevent HT by fostering public recognition of the problem. The act also facilitates consultations with nongovernmental organizations (NGOs) to develop strategies to promote public awareness of HT. Finally, the TVPA was enacted to reduce poverty to decrease the risk of HT victimization. Economic programs include job skill training and counseling and promoting programs that help keep children in school (McClain 2007).

The TVPA was reauthorized as the *Trafficking Victims Protection Reauthorization Act* (TVPRA) in 2003 and again in 2005, 2008, and 2013 (USDS 2013a, b). In order to protect transnational HT victims and prevent smuggling, the TVPRA added border interdiction laws. The law provides for shelters for transnational HT victims and offers training for border guards. In addition, the TVPRA promotes the use of international media to increase the awareness of both potential victims and the public. The act also introduced international media in HT source countries.

The TVPRA also created a private right of action for individuals who are trafficked to the U.S. (Kim and Hreshchyshyn 2004–2005). Advocates for this modification in the law realized the difficulties in implementing a prosecution-oriented strategy for combating HT. Using a civil law approach can be a useful way to compensate HT victims.

However, the TVPRA has caused a serious unintended consequence: the immigration courts are overwhelmed. This problem was the result of a huge surge of young children from Central America seeking to escape gang violence. From October 1, 2013 until June 15, 2014, 52,193 unaccompanied minors were caught at southern U.S. borders (Hulse 2014; Blow 2014). In 2008 there were approximately 280,000 immigration cases pending in the U.S., and since then, there has been a yearly increase in pending cases. By July 2014 the number of cases reached 366,758. In 2014 there were only 243 immigration judges. The average case takes 578 days before resolution, and some cases take as long as 5 years (Becerra 2014).

Laws Against Worldwide HT

In terms of worldwide HT, international legislation has been enacted to combat HT and associated abuses. The *ILO Forced Labour Convention,* ILO (1930) *(No. 29)* (ILO 2012b), the *ILO Abolition of Forced Labour* Convention, 1957 (No. 105) (ILO 2012c), *the ILO Minimum Age Convention, 1973 (No. 138)* (ILO 2012d), and the *ILO Worst Forms of Child Labour Convention, 1999 (No. 182)* (ILO 2012e) are examples of this international legislation.

In 2000, in Palermo, Italy, the UN adopted the *Convention against Transnational Organized Crime* (also called the Palermo Convention) and two so-called Palermo protocols: (1) the *Protocol to Prevent, Suppress and Punish Trafficking in Persons, especially Women and Children* (known as the Trafficking Protocol), and (2) the *Protocol against the Smuggling of Migrants by Land, Sea, and Air* (UNODC no date). This legislation reflects current international law to combat HT. On December 23, 2003, the Trafficking Protocol went into force and 117 countries and 137 parties had ratified the instrument by June 2010 (UNODC no date).

The UN Trafficking Protocol is reportedly the first binding agreement worldwide to fight HT in over 50 years (UNODC no date). The instrument is the only one that established an agreed upon definition of trafficking. The UN Trafficking Protocol is designed to foster international cooperation in fighting HT.

To fight HT worldwide, the UNODC helps many NGOs. The UNODC responded to the armed conflict in Lebanon in 2006 by working with NGO Caritas Migrant to raise awareness about the plight of HT victims. The UNODC supported the Community Vigilance project to assist victims in the area bordering India and Nepal. To further HT prevention activities in Bosnia, Croatia, and Herzegovina, the organization also provided financial support to other groups combating HT (UNODC no date).

Based on international agreements made at the UN and a grant made on behalf of the United Arab Emirates, UNODC initiated the *UN Global Initiative to Fight Human Trafficking* (UN.GIFT). The UN Children's Fund and other organizations manage UN.GIFT. The initiative assumes that governments alone cannot tackle HT; instead, HT is a global problem that requires multiple stakeholders to formulate national strategies on a worldwide basis.

The Council of Europe (COE) *Convention on Action against Trafficking in Human Beings* is another effort to combat HT globally (COE 2005). The COE created a *Group of Experts on Action against Trafficking in Human Beings* (GRETA) to help evaluate the Convention's activities. Protection for HT victims is also achieved through the *COE Convention on the Protection of Children against Sexual Exploitation and Sexual Abuse*.

The Organization for Security and Corruption in Europe (OSCE) seeks to raise public recognition of HT and encourage participating states to fight HT. The Office of the Special Representative for Combating the Traffic of Human Beings coordinates the OSCE's activities (OSCE, 2013, July).

Various anti-HT programs and policy recommendations have been established around the world to combat different forms of HT. These efforts continue to face barriers. For example, the Afghanistan government is reportedly trying to combat HT by referring identified HT victims to care organizations (USDS 2010). Despite these activities, the Afghanistan government is not increasing its efforts and they did not use a 2008 law to prosecute or convict individuals who are convicted of HT. In addition, ST victims were incarcerated and convicted of adultery or prostitution.

Laws and Policies Against Specific Forms of HT

Laws and policies have been established to provide ethical and effective systems for organ donations such as the *U.S. Uniform Anatomical Gift Act in 1968* (Jafar 2009). In 1991, the 44th World Health Assembly approved the World Health Organization's *Guiding Principles on Organ Transplantation WHA44.25* (WHO 1991).

New international and national legislation have been created to stop ICAs (Yemm 2010). These laws were designed to foster the best interests of orphans and abandoned children and were consistent with the goals of the *Hague Convention on Protection of Children and Co-operation in Respect of Inter-country Adoption* (HCCH 1993).

Research on the incidence, prevalence, and risk factors of diverse forms of HT has been a major component of anti-HT efforts. The United Nations, World Health Organization, and the United States Department of State have implemented research programs in these topical areas.

Despite the legal, policy, research, training, and organizational responses to combat HT, the problem is widely prevalent throughout the world. A major difficulty is that many law enforcement agencies do not investigate incidents of HT. Based on a survey of 3,189 municipal, county, and state law enforcement organizations in the U.S., Farrell et al. (2010) found fewer than 10% of the agencies investigated HT between 2000 and 2006. However, this problem is gradually improving. Worldwide in 2008 there were: 30,961 identified HT victims; 5,212 prosecutions; and 2,983 convictions for HT. Worldwide in 2011 there were: 42,291 identified HT victims; 7,909 prosecutions; and 3,969 convictions for HT (USDS 2014b).

Stolz (2010) has suggested that policy efforts should focus on four areas. First, more law enforcement officers should be trained to identify and enforce HT. Second, protocols should be designed to help the police identify HT and respond to the problem. Third, efforts should be undertaken to collect and report on investigations of HT. Finally, HT law enforcement activities should be better integrated into local law enforcement responses.

Other policy recommendations involve assisting in HT law enforcement at countries' borders and at other ports of entry (Gozdziak 2010). More anti-HT resources should be provided to law enforcement to assist in their control of points of entry into countries. Comprehensive training should be provided to both immigration authorities and local police. The staff of the U.S. Office of Refugee Resettlement (ORR) facilities for undocumented children should be trained in HT problems. In addition, the children in ORR facilities should be screened to determine if they are victims of HT. Governments should give high priority to identifying child victims of HT. Immigration officials also should share information about potentially trafficked children with the staff of other governmental and NGO organizations.

More social services and mental health programs and services need to be established for child victims of HT. Unfortunately, few programs and services exist to meet the needs of these children. Fong and Berger Cardoso (2010) noted that while most research and programs have emphasized adult victims of HT, there is an increased prevalence of child HT victims.

Social services and mental health professionals need specialized training in understanding HT victimization, in order to be able to respond adequately to the needs of these victims. Vijeyarasa (2010) has suggested that government officials and social service providers should avoid imposing their own moral judgments on Vietnamese HT victims as they help them readjust to normal life in their communities.

Berman (2010) found that *Article 18 of Italian Law 40 (1998)* has been successful in increasing cooperation in prosecuting traffickers because the law assumes that the victims themselves should have a say in what they want to do to with their lives.

Another important area of policy concern is the need for training health care professionals in the most effective techniques to use in response to HT victims needs (Wong et al. 2011). Health care professionals, including sexual outreach workers, physicians and nurses, have an essential role in identifying HT victims and assessing and treating their physical and psychosocial problems (World Health Organization, 2012; Barrows and Finger 2008; Sabella 2011). These professionals should be alert to the risks of HT, including ST; be able to identify those who are victims; and then deliver comprehensive care and referrals as part of a system of post-HT treatment (World Health Organization 2012). However, the topic of HT may not be covered in the curricula of many medical schools. Wong et al. (2011) surveyed 262 first- and second-year medical students at a major medical school in Canada, and found that 48.5% of the students had inadequate knowledge about HT. Although, 76% of the students considered that HT was an important curricular topic in medical school, especially learning how to identify HT victims and their health needs, but almost 89% of the students were unable to identify the signs and symptoms of HT victimization.

Williams et al. (2010). suggests that policy developments should focus on ways to assist local health care systems in assisting the victims of HT. Health care systems can deal with HT victims through primary, secondary, and tertiary prevention strategies. Increasing the awareness of the wide range of severe physical and psychosocial effects of HT can inform both policy makers and health and social service professionals of the importance in funding and implementing programs and services for HT victims (World Health Organization 2012; Zimmerman et al. 2009).

Moreover, health professionals should become aware of the barriers that HT victims face in accessing health, social, and occupational training and employment opportunities (World Health Organization 2012). These barriers include language difficulties, differences in cultural traditions, low SES, and fear among HT victims.

Finally, programs that reduce poverty, low SES, family dysfunction, government corruption, and other underlying risk factors for HT should be implemented, because these are the conditions that facilitate HT worldwide.

References

18 U.S.C.A., 924 (c). 106th United States Congress (2000, Oct., 28). PUBLIC LAW 106–386—Victims of Trafficking and Violence Protection Act of 2000. http://www.state.gov/documents/organization/10492.pdf,%2011 4%20Stat.%201464,%20Public%20Law%20106-386,%20Oct.%2028,%202000 108 Stat. 1796. Anti-Corruption Act of 1993.

Adelman, M.R. (2003–2004). International sex trafficking: Dismantling the demand. S Cal Law & Women's Stud, 13, 387.

Al Helal, A., & Kabir, K.S. (2013). Exploring cruel business of begging: The Case of Bangladesh. Asian J Business & Econo, 3 (1): 1–14.

Albanese, J.S. (2004). North American organized crime. Global Crime, 6 (1): 8–18.

Alli, R. (2013, November). The psychology behind trafficking laws: The paternalistic/sexist undertones that lie beneath the laws. International Journal of Law in the New Century, 1(2). http://www.google.com/url?sa=t&rct=j&q=&esrc=s&source=web&cd=4&ved=0CD0QFjAD&url=http%3A%2F%2Fwww.lawjournal.ir%2Findex.php%2Flj%2Farticle%2Fview%2F23%2F10&ei=mS6BU4PxOZG6oQTX14CIDQ&usg=AFQjCNHkZV_utNKpjRb47CMpq450AicxSw&sig2=njUAxXutDPWFugW2xMVzzg.

Amowitz, L.L., Reis, C., & Lyons, K.H. (2002). Prevalence of war-related sexual violence and other human rights abuses among internally displaced persons in Sierra Leone. JAMA, 287 (4): 513–521.

Anderson, N. (2010). Charging forced marriage as a crime against humanity. Documentation Center of Cambodia, Rutgers School of Law-Newark, NJ. http://www.d.dccam.org/Abouts/Intern/Natalae_Forced_marriage.pdf.

Anonymous. (1911). The statues at large of the United States of America from March, 1909 to March, 1911. Vol. XXXVI, Part 1 - Public Acts and Resolutions. Pages 825 – 827 Government Printing Office, Washington, D.C., 1911. http://books.google.com/books?id=EEkFAAAAYAAJ&pg=PA825.

Anonymous. (2009, May). The national report on domestic minor sex trafficking: America's prostituted children. Shared Hope International, Arlington, VA. http://sharedhope.org/wp-content/uploads/2012/09/SHI_National_Report_on_DMST_2009without_cover.pdf.

Anonymous. (2011). U.S. Code 2011, Title 18 – Crimes and Criminal Procedure, Chapter 17 Transportation for Illegal Sexual Activity and Related Crimes, Page 558. http://www.gpo.gov/fdsys/pkg/USCODE-2011-title18/pdf/USCODE-2011-title18-partI-chap117.pdf.

Anonymous. (2012). The crisis of child sexual exploitation in Brazil. LibertadLatina.org. http://www.libertadlatina.org/LA_Brazils_Child_Prostitution_Crisis.htm.

Anonymous. (2013a, September). Baird co-hosts signature event at UN on early and forced marriage. Media Relations Office, Foreign Affairs, Trade and Development Canada. http://www.international.gc.ca/media/aff/news-communiques/2013/09/25b.aspx?lang=eng.

Anonymous. (2013b, December). Kids as young as 10 used as drug couriers in crime ring. Gazzetta del Mezzogiorno.it, December, 02, 2013. http://www.lagazzettadelmezzogiorno.it/english/kids-as-young-as-10-used-as-drug-couriers-in-crime-ring-no674591/.

Anonymous. (2014). Understanding the Hague Convention. Intercountry adoption, Bureau of Consular Affairs, U.S. Department of State. http://adoption.state.gov/hague_convention/overview.php.

Anonymous. (2007). Experts warn against organ trade. BBC News. 2007-01-08. http://news.bbc.co.uk/2/hi/health/6240307.stm.

Aronowitz, A.A. (2001). Smuggling and trafficking in human beings: The phenomenon, The markets that drive it and the organizations that promote it. Europ J Crim Policy & Res, 9: 163–195.

Associated Press. (2014a). Founder of child porn site gets 30 years in prison. http://www.nytimes.com/aponline/2014/06/17/us/ap-us-child-porn-website-operator.html?ref=news.

Associated Press. (2014b). Canadian police rescue 5 children from online porn. http://www.nytimes.com/aponline/2014/06/19/world/ap-cn-canada-online-child-porn-sweep.html?ref=news&_r=0.

Avery, L. (2004). A return to life: The right to identity and the right to identify Argentina's 'living disappeared.' Section c babies born in captivity. Harvard J Law Gender, November 15, 2004, p. 241.

Bailliet, C.M. (2010). Towards holistic transnational protection: An overview of international public law approaches to kidnapping. Denver J Internat Law & Policy, 38 (4): 581–622.

Bales, K. (2005). Understanding global slavery. Berkeley, CA: University of California Press.

Banks, J. (2004). Note, the U.S. market for Guatemalan children: Suggestions for slowing the rapid growth of illegal practices plaguing international child adoptions. Suffolk Transnatl Law Rev, 28: 31, 35.

Barrows, J., & Finger, R. (2008). Human trafficking and the healthcare professional. South Med J, 101 (5): 521–524.

BBC News, (2007). Desperate plight of Napal 'slave girls', BBC News, March 2, 2007. http://news.bbc.co.uk/2/hi/south_asia/6405373.stm.

Becerra, H. (2014). Immigration court backlog adds to border crisis. Los Angeles Times, July 9, 2014. http://www.latimes.com/nation/la-na-immigration-court-20140710-story.html#page=1.

Belser, P. (2005). Forced labor and human trafficking: Estimating the profits, WP-42, International Labour Office, Geneva. http://www.gao.gov/assets/260/250812.pdf.

Berger, J. (2009). Despite law, few trafficking arrests. New York Times, December 3, 2009. http://www.nytimes.com/2009/12/04/nyregion/04trafficking.html?module=Search&mabReward=relbias%3Aw%2C[%22RI%3A8%22%2C%22RI%3A14%22.

Berkman, E.T. (1996). Responses to the international child sex tourism trade. BC Int & Comp Law Rev, 19: 397.

Berman, J. (2010). Biopolitical management, economic calculation and 'trafficked women.' Int Migr, 48 (4): 84–113.

Betancourt, T.S., Agnew-Blais, J., & Gilman, S.E., et al. (2010). Past horrors, present struggles: the role of stigma in the association between war experiences and psychosocial adjustment among former child soldiers in Sierra Leone. Soc Sci Med, 70 (1): 17–26.

Betancourt, T.S., Borisisova, II, & de la Soudiere, M., et al. (2011). J Adolesc Health, 49 (1): 21–28.

Beyrer, C. (2001). Shan women and girls and the sex industry in Southeast Asia; political causes and human rights implications. Soc Sci Med, 53 (4): 543–550.

Black, I., Gibson, O., & Booth, R., (2014). Qatar promises to reform labour laws after outcry over 'World Cup slaves'. The Guardian, May 14, 2014. http://www.theguardian.com/world/2014/may/14/qatar-reform-labout-laws-outcry-world-cup-slaves.

Blow, C.M. (2014). The crisis of children at the border. New York Times, July 9, 2014. http://www.nytimes.com/2014/07/10/opinion/charles-blow-the-crisis-of-children-at-the-border.html?hp&action=click&pgtype=Homepage&module=c-column-top-span-region&region=c-column-top-span-region&WT.nav=c-column-top-span-region.

Boothby, N., Crawford, J., & Halperin, J. (2006). Mozambique child soldier life outcome study: Lessons learned in rehabilitation and reintegration efforts. Glob Public Health, 1 (1): 87–107.

Budiani-Saberi, D.A., & Delmonico, F.L. (2008). Organ trafficking and transplant tourism: Commentary on the global realities. Amer J Transplantation, 8 (5): 925–929.

Cameron, S., & Newman, E. (2008). Trafficking in humans: Social, cultural and political dimensions. United Nations, Harvard University Press, New York. http://isites.harvard.edu/fs/docs/icb.topic1382728.files/Cameron_ch4.pdf.

Carlson, R.R. (1988). Transnational adoption of children. Tulsa Law Journal, 23: 317, 323.

CBSNews.com. (2010, April 27). Haiti nixes kidnapping charges against Americans. CBS News.com. http://www.cbsnews.com/news/haiti-nixes-kidnapping-charge-against-americans/.

CdeBaca, L. (2010). Best practices: Human trafficking in disaster zones. Office to Monitor and Combat Trafficking in Persons, U.S. Department of State, May 24, 2010. http://www.state.gov/j/tip/rls/rm/2010/142160.htm.

CdeBaca, L. (2014). Briefing on the trafficking in persons report 2014. U.S. Office to Monitor and Combat Trafficking in Persons, Department of State, June 20, 2014. http://www.state.gov/j/tip/rls/rm/2014/228067.htm.

Chettiar, J., Shannon, K., & Wood, E., et al. (2010). Survival sex work involvement among street-involved youth who use drugs in a Canadian setting. J Public Health (Oxf), 32 (3): 322–327.

Chun, C.S.Y. (1996). The mail-order bride industry: The perpetuation of transnational economic Inequalities and stereotypes. U Pa J Intl Econ Law, 17: 1155.

CNN. (2011). Gang profit from maimed child beggars. http://thecnnfreedomproject.blogs.cnn.com/2011/05/04/gang-profits-from-maimed-child-beggars.

COE. (2005). Council of Europe Convention on Action against Trafficking in Human Beings (CETS No. 197). http://conventions.coe.int/Treaties/Html/197.htm.

Corliss, R. (2005, March). That old feeling: When porno was chic, Time Magazine, March 29, 2005. http://content.time.com/time/arts/article/0,8599,1043267,00.html.

CPCA. (2011). Violent deaths and disappearances of Filopina women and children in Australia since 1980. Center for Philippine Concerns – Australia, August 6, 2011. http://cpcabrisbane.org/CPCA/Deaths.htm.

CPMI [Comissao Parlamentar Mista de Inquerito – Joint Parliamentary Commission of Inquiry]. (2004). Camara dos deputados e senado federal no Brazil internal report.

Crandall, M., Senturia, K., & Sullivan, M., et al. (2005). 'No way out': Russian-speaking women's experiences with domestic violence. J Interpers Violence, 20 (8): 941–958.

Dank, M., Khan, B., Downey, P.M., et al. (2014, March 12). Estimating the size and structure of the underground commercial sex economy in eight major US cities. The Urban Institute. http://www.urban.org/UploadedPDF/413047-Underground-Commercial-Sex-Economy.pdf.

de Sousa e Silva, J. & Urani, A. (December, 2002). Investigating the worst forms of child labour No. 20, Brazil, Children in Drug Trafficking: A Rapid Assessment. International Labour Organization, International Programme on the Elimination of Child Labour (IPEC), ISBN: 92-2-112977-2. http://www.ilo.org/ipecinfo/product/download.do?type=document&id=384.

Delap, E. (2009). Begging for change, anti-slavery international. http://www.antislavery.org/includes/documents/cm_docs/2009/b/beggingforchange09.pdf.

Derluyn, I., Lippens, V., & Verachtert, T., et al. (2010). Minors travelling alone: A risk group for human trafficking. Int Migr, 48 (4), 164–85.

Derluyn, I., Broekaert, E., & Schuyten, G., et al. (2004). Post-traumatic stress in former Ugandan child soldiers. Lancet, 363 (9412): 861–863.

Derogatis, L. (1993). BSI Brief Symptom Inventory. Administration, Scoring and Procedures Manual. NCS Pearson, Minneapolis, Minn.

Farrell, A., McDevitt, J., & Fahy, S. (2010). Where are all the victims? Understanding the determinants of official identification of human trafficking incidents. Criminology & Public Policy, 9 (2): 201–233.

Finkelhor, D., Jones, L., Shattuck, A., & Saito, K. (2014). Updated trends in child maltreatment (Revised 2-20-2014). Crimes Against Children Research Center, University of New Hampshire, Durham, NH. http://www.unh.edu/ccrc/pdf/CV203_Updated%20trends%202012_Revised_2_20_14.pdf.

Finn, D. (2007). Bonded labor in India. Topical Research Digest: Human Rights and Contemporary Slavery. https://www.du.edu/korbel/hrhw/researchdigest/slavery/india.pdf.

Fong, R., & Berger Cardoso, J. (2010). Child human trafficking victims: Challenges for the child welfare system. Eval Program Plann, 33 (3): 311–316.

Gladstone, R. (2014). Real threat in a known market for children. New York Times, May 7, 2014. http://www.nytimes.com/2014/05/08/world/africa/real-threat-in-a-known-market-for-children.html.

Gloria, O.E. & Samuel, A. (2012). The prevalence of street begging in Nigeria and the counseling intervention strategies. Rev Europ Studies, 4 (4): 77–83.

Gold, S. (2014). Cities are trying to get the upper hand on illicit massage parlors. Los Angeles Times, June 17, 2014. http://www.latimes.com/search/dispatcher.front?Query=massage+parlors&target=all&isSearch=true.

Gozdziak, E.M. (2010). Identifying child victims of trafficking: Toward solutions and resolutions. Crim Public Policy, 9 (2): 245–255.

Grady, J.F. (2009, October 20). *Dart vs CraigsList, Inc.* Case No. 09C1385, US District Court, Northern District of Illinois. http://pub.bna.com/eclr/dartvcraigslist.pdf.

Grammaticas, D. (2007). Bonded to the sari loom. BBC News, March 29, 2007. http://newsvote.bbc.co.uk/mpapps/pagetools/print/news.bbc.co.uk/2/hi/south_asia/6505961.stm.

Groce, N.E. & Trasi, R. (2004). Rape of individuals with disability: AIDS and the folk belief of virgin cleansing. The Lancet, May 22; 363(9422): 1663–1664.

Guevarra, N.H. (2004). Trafficking in women and children and smuggling of migrants. Pages 125–136 in: UNAFEI Resource Material Series, No. 62. http://www.unafei.or.jp/english/pdf/PDF_rms_all/no62.pdf.

Hansen, B. (2001, August 31). Children in crisis. CQ Researcher, 11 (29): 657–688.

Hara, M.S. (2012). Stopping the numbers of infants in begging. The Financial Express, February 7, 2012.

Hass, G.A., Ammar, N., & Orloff, L. (2006, April). Battered immigrants and U.S. citizen spouses. Legal Momentum, April 24, 2006. http://niwaplibrary.wcl.american.edu/reference/additional-materials/research-reports-and-data/research-US-VAIW/copy_of_BB_RSRCH_ImmVictims_Battered_Imm.pdf.

HCCH, Hague Conference on Private International Law. (1993, May 29). Convention on Protection of Children and Co-operation in Respect of Intercountry Adoption. http://www.hcch.net/upload/conventions/txt33en.pd.

Healy, M. (2014). Is there a cost to kidney donation? Yes, but … says study. Los Angeles Times, February 12, 2014. http://www.latimes.com/science/sciencenow/la-sci-sn-kidney-donation-health-costs-20140211-story.html.

HRW, Human Rights Watch. (2008). "As if I am not human." Human Rights Watch. July 8, 2008. http://www.hrw.org/node/62143/section/2 http://www.azleg.state.az.us/FormatDocument.asp?inDoc=/ars/13/00419.htm&Title=13&DocType=ARS http://www.nytimes.com/1997/08/17/us/louisiana-law-allows-force-on.

Hughes, D.M., Chon, K.Y., & Ellerman, D.P. (2007). Modern-day comfort women: The U.S. military, transnational crime, and the trafficking of women. Viol Against Women, 13 (9): 901–22; discussion, 923–926.

Hulse, C. (2014) Immigrant surge rooted in law to curb child trafficking. New York Times, July 7, 2014. http://www.nytimes.com/2014/07/08/us/immigrant-surge-rooted-in-law-to-curb-child-trafficking.html?module=Search&mabReward=relbias%3Ar%2C{%221%22%3A%22RI%3A10%22}&_r=0.

Hunte, P. (2009, June). Beyond poverty. Factors influencing decisions to use child labour in rural and urban Afghanistan. Afghanistan Research and Evaluation Unit Synthesis Paper Series. http://www.areu.org.af/editiondetails.aspx?EditionId=440&Content=7&ParentId=7&Lang=en-us.

ILO. (2000) International Labour Organization, Minimum Age Convention, 1973 (No. 138). http://www.ilo.org/ilolex/cgi-lex/convde.pl?C138).

ILO. (2002). A future without child labour. ISBN 92-2-112416-9, International Programme on the Elimination of Child Labor International Labour Office, Geneva http://www.ilo.org/wcmsp5/groups/public/—dgreports/—dcomm/—publ/documents/publication/wcms_publ_9221124169_en.pdf.

ILO, International Labour Organization, Forced Labour Convention. (1930). (No. 29). http://www.ilo.org/ilolex/cgi-lex/convde.pl?C029.

ILO, International Labour Organization, International Programme on the Education of Child Labor (IPEC). (February 2002). Investigating the worst forms of child labour No. 20. Brazil. Children in drug trafficking: A rapid assessment.

ILO, International Labour Organization. (May 11, 2005). A global alliance against forced labour. ILO, May 11, 2005.

ILO, International Labour Organization. (2012b). Forced Labour Convention, 1930 (No. 29), International Labour Office, Geneva, Switzerland. http://www.ilo.org/dyn/normlex/en/f?p=NORMLEXPUB:12100:0::NO::P12100_ILO_CODE:C029.

ILO, International Labour Organization. (2012c). ILO Abolition of Forced Labour Convention, 1957 (No. 105). http://www.ilo.org/dyn/normlex/en/f?p=NORMLEXPUB:12100:0::NO::P12100_ILO_CODE:C105.

ILO, International Labour Organization. (2012d). ILO Minimum Age Convention, 1973 (No. 138). http://www.ilo.org/dyn/normlex/en/f?p=NORMLEXPUB:12100:0::NO:12100:P12100_ILO_CODE:C138.

ILO, International Labour Organization. (2012e). ILO Worst Forms of Child Labour Convention, 1999 (No. 182). http://www.ilo.org/dyn/normlex/en/f?p=NORMLEXPUB:12100:0::NO:12100:P12100_ILO_CODE:C182.

ILO, International Labour Organization. (2012a). 21 million people are now victims of forced labour, ILO says, International Labour Organization, Geneva. http://www.ilo.org/global/about-the-ilo/newsroom/news/WCMS_181961/lang–en/index.htm.

ILO, International Labour Organization. (2013). Marking progress against child labour: Global estimates and trends 2000–2012. International Programme on the Elimination of Child Labour, International Labour Office, Geneva, Switzerland. http://www.ilo.org/wcmsp5/groups/public/—ed_norm/—ipec/documents/publication/wcms_221513.pdf.

ILO. (2014). Profits and poverty: The economics of forced labour. Special Action programme to Combat Forced Labour (SAP-FL), Fundamental Principles and Rights at Work Branch, International Labour Office, Geneva, Switzerland http://www.ilo.org/wcmsp5/groups/public/ed_norm/declaration/documents/publication/wcms_243027.pdf.

International Summit on Transplant Tourism and Organ Trafficking. (2008). The Declaration of Istanbul on Organ Trafficking and Transplant Tourism. Clin J Am Soc Nephrol, 3 (5): 1227–1231.

Jafar, T.H. (2009). Organ trafficking: Global solutions for a global problem. Amer J Kidney Dis, 54 (6): 1145–1157.

Jayasree, A.K. (2004). Searching for justice for body and self in a coercive environment: Sex work in Kerala, India. Reprod Health Matters, 12 (23): 58–67.

Jureidini, R. (2010). Trafficking and contract migrant workers in the Middle East. Int Migr, 48 (4): 142–63.

JUSTIA. (no date, a). *Hoke v. United States* –227U.S. 38 (1913). http://supreme.justia.com/cases/federal/us/227/308/case.html.

JUSTIA. (no date, b). *Athanasaw & Sampson v. United States* – 227 U.S. 326 (1913). http://supreme.justia.com/cases/federal/us/227/326/case.html.

Kaminer, A., (2014). Vigilance urged for N.Y.U. after abuses in Abu Dhabi. New York Times, May 21, 2014. http://www.nytimes.com/2014/05/22/nyregion/vigilance-urged-for-nyu-after-abuses-in-abu-dhabi.html?module=Search&mabReward=relbias%3Ar.

Katz N.L. (2007). Parents force daughters to fly home to Pakistan for arranged marriages. NY daily News November 24, 2007. http://www.nydailynews.com/news/parents-force-daughters-fly-home-pakistan-arranged-marriages-article-1.256915#ixzz320FM5TGj.

Kelaher, M., Potts, H., & Manderson, L. (2001). Health issues among Filipino women in remote Queensland. Aust J Rural Health, 9 (4): 150–157.

Kim, K., & Hreshchyshyn, K. (2004–2005). Human trafficking private right of action: Civil rights for trafficked persons in the United States. Hastings Women's Law J, 16: 1.

Kitsantonis, N., & Brunwasser, M. (2006). Baby trafficking is thriving in Greece. New York Times, December 18, 2006.

Klasen, F., Schrage, J., & Post, M., et al. (2011). Guiltless guilty—Trauma-related guilt and posttraumatic stress disorder in former Ugandan child soldiers. Prax Kinderpsychol Kinderpsychiatr, 60 (2): 125–142.

Kohrt, B.A., Jordans, M.J., & Tol, W.A., et al. (2010). Social ecology of child soldiers: Child, family, and community determinants of mental health, psychosocial well-being, and reintegration in Nepal. Transcult Psychiatry, 47 (5): 727–753.

Kolker, R. (2010). The new prostitutes. Opionator Blog, New York Times, June 29, 2010. http://opinionator.blogs.nytimes.com/2013/06/29/the-new-prostitutes/?action=click&module=Search&region=searchResults&mabReward=relbias%3Ar%2C[%22RI%3A9%22%2C%22RI%3A13%22]&url = http%3A%2F%2Fquery.nytimes.com%2Fsearch%2Fsitesearch%2F%23%2FCraigslist%2Bprostitution%2F.

Kotrla, K. (2010). Domestic minor sex trafficking in the United States. Soc Work, 55 (2): 181–7.

Kristof, N.D. (2012, March 31). Financiers and sex trafficking. The New York Times, March 31, 2012. http://www.nytimes.com/2012/04/01/opinion/sunday/kristof-financers-and-sex-trafficking.html?action=click&module=Search&region=searchResults&mabReward=relbias%3Ar%2C[%22RI%3A10%22%2C%22RI%3A15%22]&url=http%3A%2F%2Fquery.nytimes.com%2Fsearch%2Fsitesearch%2F%3Faction%3Dclick%26region%3DMasthead%26pgtype%3DSectionFront%26module%3DSearchSubmit%26contentCollection%3Daponline%26t%3Dqry48%23%2FWhere%2520Pimps%2520Peddle&pagewanted=print.

Kristof, N.D., & WuDunn, S. (2009). Half the sky. Turning oppression into opportunity for women worldwide. New York: Vintage Books, Random House, Inc.

Laczko, F., & Gramengna, M. (2003). Developing better indicators of human trafficking. Brown J World Aff, 10: 179.

Langum, D.J. (1994). Crossing over the line. Legislating morality and the Mann Act. Chicago: University of Chicago Press.

Lindert, J., Ehrenstein, O.S., & Priebe, S., et al. (2009). Depression and anxiety in labor migrants—A systematic review and meta-analysis. Soc Sci Med, 69 (2): 246–257.

Lloyd, K.A. (2000). Wives for sale: The modern international mail-order bride industry. Northwestern J Intl Law & Bus, 20: 341.

Lowrey, A. (2014). In-depth report details economics of sex trade. New York Times, March 12, 2014. http://www.nytimes.com/2014/03/12/us/in-depth-report-details-economics-of-sex-trade.html.

MacKinnon, C.A. (2004–2005). Pornography as trafficking. Mich J Intl Law, 26: 993.

May, M. (2009, February 8). Domestic slavery. A special report. Saving Nepal's indentured girls. San Francisco Chronicle, February 8, A1, A16-A17.

May, M. (2009, February 8). Olga's girls. Pulitzer Center on Crisis Reporting. http://pulitzercenter.org/articles/olgas-girls.

McClain, T. R. (2007). An ounce of prevention: improving the preventative measures of the Trafficking Victims Protection Act. Vanderbilt University, School of Law. http://www.thefreelibrary.com/An+ounce+of+prevention%3A+improving+the+preventative+measures+of+the…-a0166185443.

McIntyre, E.S. (2014). Teenage drug mules: Cartels are tapping minors to smuggle meth, coke. Aljazeera America, February, 18, 2014. http://america.aljazeera.com/articles/2014/2/18/teenage-drug-mulescartelsaretappingtheyoungesttosmugglemethcoke.htm.

Mellto, T. (2006). Human trafficking: Better data, strategy, and reporting needed to enhance U.S. anti-trafficking efforts abroad, GAO-06-825. http://www.gao.gov/assets/260/250812.pdf.

Miko, F.T. (2004). Trafficking in persons: The U.S. and international response. Washington, DC: Congressional Research Service for Congress.

Moens. B., Orfano, I. Hopkins, R. et al., (2001). Research based on case studies of victims of trafficking in human beings in 3 EU Member States i.e Belgium, Italy and The Netherlands, Commission of the European Communities DG Justice & Home Affairs Hippokrates JAI/2001/HIP/023. http://ec.europa.eu/justice_home/daphnetoolkit/files/projects/2001_010/int_trafficking_case_studies_be_it_nl_hippokrates.pdf.

Molland, S. (2010). "The perfect business": Human trafficking and Lao-Thai cross-border migration. Dev Change, 41 (5): 831–855.

Morewitz, S.J. (2008). Death threats and violence. New York: Springer Science + Business Media, LLC.

Moye, D. (2013). Porn industry in decline: Insiders adapt to piracy, waning DVD sales (NSFW). Huffington Post, January 19, 2013. http://www.huffingtonpost.com/2013/01/19/porn-industry-in-decline_n_2460799.html.

MRO, Migrant Rights Organization. (2009). Three months after the sponsorship system in Bahrain was "scrapped", what really changed? Migrant Rights Organization. Nov. 11, 2009. http://www.migrant-rights.org/research/three-months-after-the-sponsorship-system-in-bahrain-was-scrapped-what-really-changed/.

Navarro, M. (2008). To adopt, please press hold. New York Times, June 5, 2008. http://www.nytimes.com/2008/06/05/fashion/05adopt.html?pagewanted=all.

Ntozi, J.P., Najjumba, I.M., & Ahimbisibwe, F., et al. (2003). Has the HIV/AIDS epidemic changed sexual behavior of high risk groups in Uganda? Afr Health Sci, 3 (3): 107–116.

Nyamathi, A., Covington, C., & Mutere, M. (2007). Vulnerable populations in Thailand: Giving voice to women living with HIV/AIDS. Ann Rev Nurs Res, 25: 339–355.

Okeowo, A. (2013). How the Lord's Resistance Army forces captives to become couples. Financial Times, July 5, 2013. http://www.ft.com/intl/cms/s/2/17decc7c-e380-11e2-bd87-00144feabdc0.html#axzz34vjJghJB.

Olaniyi, R. (2003). No way out: The trafficking of women in Nigeria. Agenda No. 55, 45–52.

OPTN, Organ Procurement and Transplantation Network. (2014). Organ Procurement and Transplantation Network, Health Resources and Services Administration, U.S. Department of Health & Human Services. http://optn.transplant.hrsa.gov/latestData/rptData.asp.

Orchard, T.R. (2007). Girl, woman, lover, mother: Towards a new understanding of child prostitution among young Devadasis in rural Karnataka, India. Soc Sci Med, 64 (12): 2379–2390.

Organization for Security and Co-operating in Europe, Office of the Special Representative and Coordinator for Combating Trafficking in Human Beings. (2013). Occasional Paper Series, No. 6. http://www.OSCE.org/CTHb/103393.

OSCE (2013, July). Trafficking in human beings for the purpose of organ removal in the OSCE Region: Analysis and findings, Occasional Paper Series, No. 6. Organization for Security and Co-operating in Europe, Office of the Special Representative and Coordinator for Combating Trafficking in Human Beings, Vienna, Austria. ISBN: 978-92-9234-440-5. http://www.osce.org/CTHb/103393?download=true.

Orlinsky, K. (2013). Women, bought and sold in Nepal. New York Times, August 31, 2013. http://www.nytimes.com/2013/09/01/opinion/sunday/women-bought-and-sold-in-nepal.html?module=Search&mabReward=relbias%3Ar%2C[%22RI%3A8%22%2C%22RI%3A12%22].

PBS, Public Broadcasting System. (no date). Bride kidnapping. http://www.pbs.org/frontlineworld/stories/kyrgyzstan/thestory.html.

Penhaul, K. (2010, Feb. 8). Americans jailed in Haiti tried taking other kids, officer says. CNN.com.

Pham, P.N., Vinck, P., & Stover, E. (2009). Returning home: Forced conscription, reintegration, and mental health status of former abductees of the Lord's Resistance Army in northern Uganda. BMC Psychiatry, 9: 23.

Porter, E. (2006). Law on overseas brides is keeping couples apart. New York Times, October 17, 2006. http://www.nytimes.com/2006/10/17/us/17brides.html?pagewanted=..&module=Search%26mabReward=relbias%3Ar%2C[%22RI%3A5%22%2C%22RI%3A16%22].

Rasor, K.R., Russo, R.M., & Turner, E.A. (2010/2011). Imperfect remedies: The arsenal of criminal statutes available to prosecute international adoption fraud in the United States. N Y School Law Rev, 55 (3): 801–822.

Razack, S.H. (2004). Imperiled Muslim women, dangerous Muslim men and civilized Europeans: Legal and social responses to forced marriages. Feminist Legal Studies, 12: 129–174.

Requena, M. (2006). Council of Europe says human trafficking has reached 'epidemic proportions'. The Associated Press, December 5, 2006. https://groups.yahoo.com/neo/groups/LomitaHarborConnection/conversations/messages/2420.

Reuters. (2014). Children being lured into Syrian civil war, suicide missions. The Jerusalem Post, June 23, 2014. http://www.jpost.com/Middle-East/Children-being-lured-into-Syrian-civil-war-suicide-missions-360246.

Reynolds, L., & McKee, M. (2010). Organized crime and the efforts to combat it: A concern for public health. Global Health, 6: 21.

Ribando Seelke, C. (2011). Trafficking in persons in Latin America and the Caribbean. Washington, DC: Congressional Research Service. http://digitalcommons.ilr.cornell.edu/cgi/viewcontent.cgi?article=1865&context=key_workplace

Richtel, M. (2007, June). For pornographers, Internet's virtues turn to vices. The New York Times, June 2, 2007. http://www.nytimes.com/2007/06/02/technology/02porn.html?pagewanted=all&action=click&module=Search®ion=searchResults&mabReward=relbias%3Ar%2C[%22RI%3A11%22%2C%22RI%3A16%22]&url=http%3A%2F%2Fquery.nytimes.com%2Fsearch%2Fsitesearch%2F%3Faction%3Dclick%26region%3DMasthead%26pgtype%3DHomepage%26module%3DSearchSubmit%26contentCollection%3DHomepage%26t%3Dqry472%23%2Fporn%2520video%2520rental

Rubin, A.J. (2012, June). Afghan rape case turns focus on local police. New York Times, June 27, 2012. http://www.nytimes.com/2012/06/28/world/asia/afghan-rape-case-turns-focus-on-local-police.html?pagewanted=all&action=click&module=Search&region=searchResults&mabReward = relbias%3Aw%2C[%22RI%3A10%22%2C%22RI%3A17%22]&url=http%3A%2F%2Fquery.nytimes.com%2Fsearch%2Fsitesearch%2F%3Faction%3Dclick%26region%3DMasthead%26pgtype%3DHomepage%26module%3DSearchSubmit%26contentCollection%3DHomepage%26t%3Dqry826%23%2FForced%2520marriage%2520illegal.

Ryerson-Cruz, G., et al. (2008). Before she's ready: 15 places girls marry by 15. Document NMS07381_ 0808, World Vision US, Federal Way, WA. http://corestg.worldvision.org/sites/default/files/pdf/early-marriage.pdf **Johnston, W.R. (2012, May) Historical international adoption statistics, United States and world. Retrieved from: http://www.johnstonsarchive.net/policy/adoptionstatsintl.htm.

Sabella, D. (2011). The role of the nurse in combating human trafficking. Am J Nurs, 111 (2): 28–37.

Sarkar, S., Chakraborty, S., Tansuhaj, P.S., Mulder, M. & Dogerlioglu-Demir, K. (2013). The "mail-order-bride" (MOB) phenomenon in the cyberworld: An interpretive investigation. Journal ACM Transactions on Management Information Systems, Oct; 4(3).

Scheper-Hughes, N. (2004). Parts unknown. Undercover ethnography of the organs-trafficking underworld. Ethnography, 5 (1): 29–73.

Scholes, R.J. (1997). How many mail order brides? Immigration Review, Spring; No. 28. http://www.cis.org/sites/cis.org/files/articles/1997/IR28/IR28.pdf.

Scholes, R.J. (1999). International matchmaking organizations: A report to Congress (1999). Violence Against Women Office, Washington, D.C.: Department of Justice, U.S. Government.

Sherman, S.S., Plitt, S., & ul Hassan, S., et al. (2005). Drug use, street survival, and risk behaviors among street children in Lahore, Pakistan. J Urban Health, 82 (3 Suppl 4): iv113–124.

Silverman, J.G., Decker, M.R., & Gupta, J., et al. (2006). HIV prevalence and predictors among rescued sex-trafficked women and girls in Mumbai, India. J Acquir Immune Defic Syndr, 43 (5): 588–93.

Silverman, J.G., Decker, M.R., & Gupta, J., et al. (2007). Experiences of sex trafficking victims in Mumbai, India. Int J Gynaecol Obstet, 97 (3): 221–6.

Smartt, U. (2003). Human trafficking: Simply a European problem? Europ J Crim Law Crim Just, 11 (2): 164–177.

Smolin, D.M. (2010). Child laundering and the Hague Convention on Intercountry Adoption: The future and past of intercountry adoption. U Louisville Law Rev, 441.

Stolz, B.A. (2010). Human trafficking: Policy. Crim Public Policy, 9 (2): 267–274.

Stone, S.R. (2004). Mail order brides. Taking a look from a new perspective. http://www.popcenter.org/problems/trafficked_women/PDFs/Stone_2004.pdf.

Stone, B. (2008). Craigslist agrees to curb sex ads. New York Times, November 6, 2008. http://www.nytimes.com/2008/11/07/technology/internet/07craigslist.html?fta=y.

Studnicka, A.C.S. (2010). Corruption and human trafficking in Brazil: Findings from a multi-modal approach. Eur J Criminology, 7 (1): 29–43.

Swarns, R.L. (2012). A family a few days a year. New York Times, December 8, 2012. http://www.nytimes.com/2012/12/09/world/americas/stalled-adoption-program-in-guatemala-leaves-families-in-limbo.html?pagewanted=all.

Tahirih Justice Center. (2008). Frequently asked questions. International Marriage Broker Regulation Act of 2005 (IMBRA), Tahirih Justice Center. http://www.tahirih.org/site/wp-content/uploads/2009/03/frequentlyaskedquestionsaboutimbra.pdf.

Tambiah, Y. (2004). Sexuality and women's rights in armed conflict in Sri Lanka. Reprod Health Matters, 12 (23): 78–87.

Tatlow, D.K. (2014). Crackdown on baby trafficking zeros in on websites. New York Times, February 28, 2014. http://sinosphere.blogs.nytimes.com/2014/02/28/crackdown-on-baby-trafficking-zeros-in-on-websites/?_php=true&_type=blogs&module=Search&mabR Also: http://www.nytimes.com/2006/12/18/world/europe/18iht-babies.3939121.html?pagewanted=all&module=Search&mabReward=relbias%3Ar%2C.

Topping, A. (2014). London gangs using children as drug mules as they seek to expand markets. The Guardian, January 5, 2014. http://www.theguardian.com/society/2014/jan/05/drug-gangs-using-children-as-mules.

Tucker, E. (2014) FBI rescues 168 children in sex trafficking crackdown. Christian Science Monitor, June 24, 2014. http://www.csmonitor.com/USA/Latest-News-Wires/2014/0624/FBI-rescues-168-children-in-sex-trafficking-crackdown.

Tyldum, G., & Brunovskis, A. (2005). Describing the unobserved: Methodological challenges in empirical studies on human trafficking. Int Migration Rev, 43: 17–34.

UK-SOA. (2003). United Kingdom, The Sexual Offenses Act (SOA), 2003. http://www.legislation.gov.uk/ukpga/2003/42/pdfs/ukpga_20030042_en.pdf

UN, United Nations. (2008, February 6). UN-backed container exhibit spotlights plight of sex trafficking victims. http://www.un.org/apps/news/story.asp?NewsID=25524&Cr=trafficking&Cr1.

UNCRC, United Nations Convention on the Rights of the Child. (1989). United Nations, Office of the High Commissioner for Human Rights. http://www.ohchr.org/EN/ProfessionalInterest/Pages/CRC.aspx.

UNDOC, United Nations Office on Drugs and Crime. (2014a) Human trafficking. UN Office on Drugs and Crime. https://www.unodc.org/unodc/en/human-trafficking/what-is-human-trafficking.html?ref=menuside.

UNECE (2004, 14–15 December). Economic roots of trafficking in the UNECE region – regional prep meeting for the 10-year Review of Implementation of the Beijing Platform for Action. http://www.unece.org/press/pr2004/04gen_n03e.htm.

UNIAP, United Nations Inter-Agency Project. (2007). Targeting endemic vulnerability factors to human trafficking. Strategic Information Response Network, United Nations Inter-Agency Project on Human Trafficking, Bangkok, Thailand, December 21, 2007. Retrieved from: http://www.no-trafficking.org/reports_docs/siren/gms02_siren_methodology_vulnerability.pdf.

UNODC. (2007). UN highlights human trafficking, BBC News, March 26, 2007. http://news.bbc.co.uk/2/hi/6497799.stm.

UNODC. (2008). United Nations, Office on Drugs and Crime. UN.GIFT. human trafficking an overview. New York, NY: United Nations.
UNODC, United Nations Office on Drugs and Crime. (2012). Global report on human trafficking. United Nations Office on Drugs and Crime, Vienna, Austria. http://www.unodc.org/documents/data-and-analysis/glotip/Trafficking_in_Persons_2012_web.pdf.
UNODC. (2014). Human trafficking. UN Office on Drugs and Crime. Retrieved from: https://www.unodc.org/unodc/en/human-trafficking/what-is-human-trafficking.html?ref=menuside.
UNODC. (no date). Preventing human trafficking. http://www.unodc.org/unodc/en/human-trafficking/prevention.html?ref=menuside.
UNODC/UNGIFT. (2009, February) Global report on trafficking in persons. UN Global Initiative to Fight Human Trafficking, UN Office of Drugs and Crime. http://www.unodc.org/documents/human-trafficking/Global_Report_on_TIP.pdf.
United States Department of Justice. (2004a). Anti-trafficking news bulletin. Washington, DC: U. S. Department of Justice, Civil Rights Division.
United States Department of Justice. (2005). U.S. Attorney General's report to Congress and assessment of U.S. activities to combat trafficking in persons. Washington, DC: U.S. Department of Justice, Attorney General's Office.
United States Department of State. (2010). Trafficking in Persons Report 2010 Country Narratives – Countries A through F. http://www.state.gov/j/tip/rls/tiprpt/2010/142759.htm.
United States Department of State. (2011). Trafficking in Persons Report 2011. Washington, DC: United States of America Department of State.
USDS. (2011). Trafficking in persons report 2011. United States Department of State, Washington, DC. http://www.state.gov/j/tip/rls/tiprpt/2011/
USDS, United States Department of State. (2012b), Fact Sheet: State Department on Lord's Resistance Army. Office of the Spokesperson, U.S. Department of State, March 23, 2012. http://translations.state.gov/st/english/texttrans/2012/03/201203232705.html#axzz353UgHbR7.
USDS, United States Department of State. (2013a). U.S. Laws on trafficking in persons. United States Department of State. Washington, DC. http://www.state.gov/j/tip/laws/.
USDS, United States Department of State. (2013b). The 2013 Trafficking in persons (TIP) report, U.S. Department of State. http://www.state.gov/documents/organization/210737.pdf.
USDS, United States Department of State. (2014). Global law enforcement data, Trafficking in persons report 2014. United States Department of State. Washington, DC. http://www.state.gov/j/tip/rls/tiprpt/2014/226647.htm.
USHHS, United States Health and Human Services. (2012). Labor trafficking fact sheet, 2012. http://www.acf.hhs.gov/programs/orr/resource/fact-sheet-labor-trafficking-english.
USHHS, United States Health and Human Services. (2014a) Donate the gift of life. United States Health and Human Services. http://www.organdonor.gov/about/data.html.
USHHS. (no date) Labor trafficking fact sheet. United States Health and Human Services. http://www.acf.hhs.gov/sites/default/files/orr/fact_sheet_labor_trafficking_english.pdf
Van Hook, M.P., Gjermeni, E., & Haxhiymeri, E. (2006). Sexual trafficking of women: Tragic proportions and attempted solutions in Albania. Int Soc Work, 49 (1): 29–40.
Vijeyarasa, R. (2010). The state, the family and language of 'social evils': re-stigmatizing victims of trafficking in Vietnam. Cult Health Sex, 12 (Suppl 1): S89–S102.
Voigt, K., & Brown, S. (2013). International adoptions in decline as number of orphans grows. CNN, September 17, 2013. http://edition.cnn.com/2013/09/16/world/international-adoption-main-story-decline/index.html.
Wallace, S.R. (2003). Note, international adoption: The most logical solution to the disparity between the numbers of orphaned and abandoned children in some countries and families and individuals wishing to adopt in others? Ariz J Intl & Comp Law, 20: 689, 692.
WETA. (2005a). The Mann Act: Full-Text. http://www.pbs.org/unforgivableblackness/knockout/mannact_text.html.
WETA. (2005b). The Mann Act. http://www.pbs.org/unforgivableblackness/knockout/mann.html.
Wheaton, E.M., Schauer, E.J., & Galli, T.V. (2010). Economics of human trafficking. Int Migr, 48 (4): 114–41.

WHO, World Health Organization. (1991). Human organ transplantation: A report on developments under the auspices of WHO (1987–1991). World Health Organization, Geneva, 1991. http://whqlibdoc.who.int/publications/1991/9241693045.pdf.
WHO, World Health Organization. (2012). Human trafficking. World Health Organization. http://www.who.int/bitsream/10665/773941/WHO_RHR_12.42_eng.pdf.
Wikipedia. (2014a). United States v. Maksym Shynkarenko. http://en.wikipedia.org/wiki/United_States_v._Maksym_Shynkarenko.
Wikipedia. (2014b). Escort agency. http://en.wikipedia.org/wiki/Escort_agency.
Wikipedia. (2014c). Massage parlor. http://en.wikipedia.org/wiki/Massage_parlor.
Wikipedia. (2014d). Kafala system. http://en.wikipedia.org/wiki/Kafala_system.
Williams, T.P., Alpert, E.J., & Ahn, R., et al. (2010). Sex trafficking and health care in Metro Manila: Identifying social determinants to inform an effective health system response. Health Hum Rights, 12 (2): 135–147.
Woerner, A. (2014). Living organ donation: A solution to the organ shortage in the US? Fox News February 24, 2014. http://www.foxnews.com/health/2014/02/24/living-organ-donation-solution-to-organ-shortage-in-us/.
Wong, J.C., Hong, J., & Leung, P., et al. (2011). Human trafficking: An evaluation of Canadian medical students' awareness and attitudes. Educ Health (Abingdon), 24 (1): 501.
World Bank (2013). Gap between rich and poor: World income inequality. World Development Index 2013. http://www.infoplease.com/world/statistics/inequality-income-expenditure.html.
Yemm, L.M. (2010). International adoption and the 'best interests' of the child: Reality and reactionism in Romania and Guatemala. Wash U Global Stud Law Rev, 9 (3): 555–574.
Yoshimi, Y. (2002). Comfort women. Sexual slavery in the Japanese military during World War II. New York: Columbia University Press.
Yusuf, A. (2012). Snatched childhoods. New Age, September 28, 2012.
Zimmerman, C., Kiss, L., & Houssain, M., et al. (2009). Trafficking in persons: A health concern? Cien Saude Colet, 14 (4): 1029–1035.
Zimmerman, C., Hossain, M., & Yun, K., et al. (2008). The health of trafficked women: A survey of women entering posttrafficking services in Europe. Amer J Pub Hlth, 98 (1): 55–59.

Chapter 10
Ransom Kidnapping

One form of kidnapping, ransom kidnappings (RKs), has occurred throughout history (Marongiu and Clarke 1993; Akpan 2010; see Appendices E and F, Tables F.10–F.15; *Columbia Electronic Encyclopedia* 2010, July 1). Famous RK victims have included Joseph from the Bible, Julius Caesar, and Richard the Lionheart (Mohamed 2008). In ancient Rome, Emperor Constantine (AD 315) was so concerned by the high prevalence of abductions that he made abductions a capital offense (Turner 1998).

In Italy, especially on the island of Sardinia; abductions go back to the fifteenth century (Marongiu and Clarke 1993).

The term, "kidnapping", emerged in the seventeenth century in England and some experts noted that the term referred to children who were "caught in sleep" or "napped" (Tzanelli 2006; Turner 1998). Kidnap is a compound of "nap", which is related to the word, "nab" or "snatch" and "kid", which refer to indentured servants, including children and other persons, who were taken to the colonies in America to work on plantations in the American colonies (Diamond 1985–1986).

RK fees were standardized in 1800 in the Sulu archipelago, which is now part of the Philippines. In that area, RK fees ranged from 2000 pesos for a European friar to 30–50 pesos for a male Filipino.

In the U.S., famous kidnappings such as the kidnapping-murder of Bobby Franks by Nathan Leopold, Jr., and Richard Loeb in 1924, the abduction-murder of the son of Charles A. Lindbergh in 1932, and organized criminal gangs' participation in "snatch racket activities" were prominent (*Columbia Electronic Encyclopedia* 2010, July 1; Moorehead 1980). Two years after the famous Lindbergh kidnapping-murder, the first federal law on kidnapping in the U.S. was introduced in Congress.

Different theoretical approaches have been used to explain kidnappings (Marongiu and Clarke 1993). The subcultural approach asserts that abductions emerge from the transmission of cultural values and norms that promote violence. In this way, kidnappings reflect the subculture of violence and these values and norms are transmitted over time from one generation to the next. In contrast, the

S. Morewitz, *Kidnapping and Violence*,
https://doi.org/10.1007/978-1-4939-2117-1_10

rational choice framework assumes that offenders commit abductions based on rational motives and systematic decision-making.

Marongiu and Clarke (1993), in their analysis of 132 RKs in Sardinia, discovered that the subcultural approach could not be used to explain fluctuations in the rates of kidnappings in Sardinia. Instead, the rational choice model is better able to account for changes in the offenders' assessments of risks and rewards in carrying out abductions in response to changing political, financial, and social conditions.

The rational choice model is reflected in the fact that historically, gangs, tribes, families, and others in political-social conflicts have used abductions as a weapon against adversaries and to achieve financial resources (Bailliet 2010; Mohamed 2008). However, in recent times, individuals and groups often commit RKs as a routine occupational activity. As a result, some kidnappers have shifted their focus from abducting individuals associated with warring groups to selecting citizens based on their perceived financial resources. In this way, according to de Sousa Santos (2002), the human body is converted into "the ultimate commodity".

Marongiu and Clarke (1993) identified two types of RKs that were perpetrated on the island of Sardinia. In the internal RKs, both the offenders and victims were similar in terms of their residence, socioeconomic status (SES), and cultural background. These internal RKs tended to take place in the inner pastoral regions of the island. In contrast, the victims in the external RKs were outsiders, tourists, businessmen or wealthy people from Sardinia. Higher ransoms tended to be extorted from victims in the external RKs.

Offenders carry out RKs using a variety of methods and time frames. So-called "express kidnappings" have become prevalent in Mexico (*Associated Press*, December 20, 2005, December 20; Hathaway 2007, April 14). In express kidnappings, perpetrators kidnap people with money and coerce them into quickly turning over money from automatic teller machines, bank, and other financial accounts (Hathaway 2007). Perpetrators can carry out express kidnappings in different ways. In one scenario, individuals on the street may be abducted and taken by automobile to an automatic teller machine, where the victim is forced to withdraw their money. The victims may be released unharmed after giving the ransom kidnapper their funds.

Perpetrators may injure their captives and show images of them to ensure that the ransoms will be paid quickly and that the full ransom amount is paid. In some instances, the abductors will cut off a body part and send it with their demand for a ransom. In the Ransom Kidnappings Project (RKP), 2.17% of the RK victims reportedly lost a body part (see Table F.15).

In other instances, RKs may last days, months, and even years. For example, the *Fuerzas Armadas Revolucionarias de Colombia* (FARC) has held RK hostages for years (Bailliet 2010). The abduction of Ingrid Bentancourt represents this long-term approach to kidnappings.

Perpetrators often will abduct wealthy victims or victims who have wealthy or noteworthy relatives (Marongiu and Clarke 1993). Findings from the RKP demonstrated that 9.28% of the RK victims were considered wealthy (see Table F.10). Almost 21% of the RK victims reportedly had a noteworthy relative.

Prevalence of RKs

Criminologists and forensic sociologists acknowledge the weaknesses in official crime statistics related to kidnappings, including RKs (Mohamed 2008). The actual incidence of RKs is unknown because many go unreported. Many kidnappings go unreported because the victims want to keep their ordeals secret and not involve the criminal justice system. Methodological difficulties result from the criminal justice systems' problems in counting and collecting data on kidnapping crimes. In this context, the ways in which officials define and categorize the crime as kidnapping vary, leading to inconsistencies in crime statistics.

Despite these barriers, available data from the insurance carrier, AIG, in Philadelphia, revealed that 20,000 ransom abductions occur each year (Wilder and Lipton 2008. April 3). A 2004 report by the insurance broker, Willis Group, estimated that between 8,000 and 10,000 incidents of RK take place annually (Willis Group Holdings Limited Conference Call 2004, December 16).

Latin America has been considered one of the worst places for kidnapping. Forty-eight percent of RKs take place in Latin America. Colombia has had some of the highest rates of RKs. In 1999, the countries with the highest reported rates of RKs were: Colombia (972), Mexico (402), the former Soviet Union (105), and Brazil (51).

In 2005, Mexico overtook Colombia as the world leader in kidnappings. In the first six months of 2005, Mexico had 194 kidnappings, compared to 172 kidnappings in Colombia (*Associated Press*, December 20, 2005).

RKs are prevalent worldwide. According to a 2006 *Washington Post* article, more than 430 foreigners had been kidnapped in Iraq since the U.S. invasion of that country in 2003 (Slevin 2006, June 7). According to the RKP, Mexico had the highest percentage of RK cases (69.87%), followed by Afghanistan (8.45%), Colombia (5.46%), and the U.S. (5.09%) (see Table F.12).

The rates of RKs have fluctuated over time (Wilder and Lipton 2008, April 3). The Philippines' rate of RKs increased from 53 in 1992 to 78 in 1994. In 1996, the rate went up to 113 and went down to 39 in 1999. In Italy, more than 600 RKs took place between 1968 and 1989 (Marongiu and Clarke 1993).

Wilder and Lipton (2008, April 3) note that the actual number of cases ranges between five to six times the reported rate. They estimate that the incidence per year of RKs is up to 100,000.

A variety of conditions at the local community, national, and international level increase the risk of RKs. Below are some of these conditions.

Globalization

Globalization increases the expansion of transnational corporations, with large corporations sending their employees and their families to other countries. As a consequence of this globalization, these employees and their family members in different countries are at increased risk of becoming RK victims (Wilder and Lipton 2008).

Breakdown in the Social Order, Armed Political Conflict, and Instability

During periods of economic, political, and social crises, and armed political conflict, kidnappers seek to achieve their political goals and quick and large ransoms as a means to attain their goals (Tzanelli 2006; Moorehead 1980; Caramazza and Leone 1984; *Associated Press,* December 20, 2005; Hansen 2003; Semple 2001, June 3; Akpan 2010; Network54.com 2004, April 1; Slevin 2006, June 7).

Political terrorists and other groups may kidnap individuals because they are in conflict with a nation's government or other organizations and groups. In the 1970s and 1980s, many high-SES individuals were kidnapped and taken hostage in Sardinia and Italy (Moorehead 1980; Caramazza and Leone 1984). Caramazza and Leone (1984) found that the conflict between a Marxist–Leninist group, the Red Barbagia, and the state was associated with the high incidence of abductions in Sardinia. Similarly, in Colombia, abductions have been associated with armed conflicts (Rubio 2004).

Politically oriented abductors typically kidnap individuals who represent or symbolize a targeted political-social group, including political leaders and government officials or country (Castiglione 2005; Moorehead 1980). The Red Brigades abducted and killed the leader of the Italian Christian Democratic Party, Aldo Moro (Moorehead 1980). The Baader-Meinhof gang kidnapped Schleyer, the head of the West German Federation of Industries. Political abductions also have included kidnappings and hostage taking of diplomats. For example, in the 1970s in Brazil and Uruguay, diplomats were taken hostage by political groups. Political groups may abduct foreigners, construction workers, religious missionaries, and others and hold them for ransom (see Table F.11).

Kidnapping victims may be killed by their captors during these unstable periods. In Mexico, between 1994 and 2000, 115 victims of abductions died (*Associated Press*, December 20, 2005). During this period, Mexico underwent a significant economic crisis. According to a 2006 *Daily Telegraph* article, at least 40 foreigners in Iraq had been murdered since the U.S. invasion of Iraq in 2003 (Poole 2006, June 6). A 2006 *Times* article revealed that at least 5,000 Iraqis had been abducted since the beginning of the war (Loyd and Hamdani 2006, February 18).

A wave of RKs occurred in Argentina when the country's banking system was in crisis, which supports the notion that RKs increase in failed or failing nations (Network54.com 2004, April 1). As a result of the public loss of confidence in the banks, many people stashed away approximately 28 billion dollars in their homes, which apparently resulted in a significant increase in kidnappings and other crimes.

In Colombia, criminals have committed abductions for decades (Semple 2001, June 3). However, abductions emerged as an extensive criminal industry during the 1990s when leftist guerrilla organizations, right-wing paramilitary forces, and the government engaged in armed conflict. In the late 1990s and beginning years of the twenty-first century, FARC transformed abductions into a large-scale, highly organized, and lucrative business. The second-largest left-wing rebel army, the *Ejercito de Liberacion Nacional* (E.L.N.) also has a played a major role in carrying out widespread kidnappings. The government of Colombia indicated that in 2000, 60% of the abductions were carried by left-wing rebel armies.

Rebel, guerrilla, and terrorist organizations and groups as well as legitimate governments use abductions to achieve a variety of political goals (Bailliet 2010; Yang et al. 2007; Castiglione 2005). These politically oriented abductions occur worldwide and often are committed by insurgents who are waging wars against civilians and governments (Amnesty International 2001).

In the RKP, 6.44% of the RKs reportedly were motivated by political goals (see Table F.14). Closely related to political goals are ethnic- and religious-oriented goals. Findings from the RKP demonstrated that in 6.07% of the RKs, ethnic motives played a role, and religious motives were responsible for 5.49% of the RKs (see Table F.14).

Politically oriented offenders may try to coerce politicians to not run for election. Criminal gangs may abduct police officers to discourage them from interfering with their criminal activities or get their preferred legislation enacted.

Frequently, perpetrators commit RKs to raise money to support their own insurgent activities (Bailliet 2010). For example, the FARC in Colombia carry out abductions to pay for their mission-related activities. In other cases, individuals participate in armed conflict to fund their criminal enterprises.

In other regions of the world dominated by war and armed conflict, RKs are especially prevalent. For example, in war-torn Iraq and Afghanistan, RKs have become commonplace. Amid social and political unrest in Iraq, Iraqi gangs and insurgents/rebels have started to kidnap many foreigners and Iraqis, including women and children for ransom (Bailliet 2010; Prusher 2003, September 10).

In September 2004, two Italian aid workers were abducted, and the kidnappers threatened to behead the two captives. The Iraqi police estimate that at least 15,000 Iraqis have been kidnapped in Baghdad since the end of the Saddam Hussein regime.

Abductors may select children randomly based on how they dress (Prusher 2003, September 10). These children do not necessarily have to come from middle- and high- SES families. The victims of kidnappings often do not seek police assistance because they fear being kidnapped again and also do not believe that the police will be effective in rescuing their loved ones.

In mid-July 2003, the authorities established a new Iraqi police unit to combat kidnappings and homicides (Prusher 2003, September 10). By early September 2003, the Iraqi police unit had arrested three abduction gangs. In one of the arrests, the Iraqi police discovered two children who had been abducted.

In Afghanistan, RKs, which once had been rare, have become a major source of funding for the Afghan insurgents and is second to the heroin trade as a source of revenues (Yousafzai et al. 2008; Bailliet 2010). Most of the RK victims in Afghanistan are Afghans.

However, the Taliban may benefit the most from kidnapping foreigners because they pay the highest ransoms. Taliban fighters reportedly kidnapped 23 Christian missionaries from South Korea while they were traveling on a bus on the Kandahar-Kabul highway. A spokesperson for the Taliban stated that the kidnapping of women, as in the case of the 18 female South Korean missionaries, was justified because it supported the religious tenet of "an eye for an eye" (NPR 2007, August 5).

Insurgents in Afghanistan and other countries use abductions to attack national development efforts, such as road construction projects. By kidnapping workers and managers at these sites, the insurgents can stop or delay the rebuilding process and also add to their war chests with millions of dollars in ransoms (Wonacott 2009, August 18).

Akpan (2010) showed how RKs in Nigeria's Niger Delta were used sometimes to financially support and maintain the Movement for the Emancipation of Niger Delta (MEND).

Other groups began to engage in RKs. These groups committed RAs under the umbrella of the general liberation struggle of the Niger Delta (Akpan 2010; Akasike 2008). These criminal groups found it easy to target victims for RKs. Criminal groups would target and kidnap a victim and then contact the victim's family members to demand a ransom. The criminals would then negotiate a ransom.

Failed and Failing Nations

Countries with the highest kidnapping rates are often failed or failing states (Bailliet 2010; Hastings 2009). In these failed or failing nations, the rule of law has broken down, and the public tends to distrust the government. These failed or failing nations have lost what Max Weber referred to as the ability of legitimate governments to monopolize violence. As a result, these failed or failing countries are not able to protect their citizens from RKs and other crimes such as maritime piracy hijackings. They are especially inadequate in sanctioning RK perpetrators.

Failed and failing countries have weak and fragmented laws (Bailliet 2010). In these nations, the police and other government officials are often corrupt and may participate in criminal enterprises such as RKs. Failed and failing nations are unable to offer social and economic security for their citizens due to high levels of poverty, unemployment, stratified SES groups, and severe inequality in income among different SES groups. Thus, RKs occur due to the lack of social and economic justice in failed and failing states.

Poverty and Countries with the Greatest Income Inequality

RKs have been especially prevalent in poor countries and those with the greatest income equality. In 1999, Colombia and Mexico were ranked number and two in the top ten countries for kidnappings (Wilder and Lipton 2008, April 3). In 2002, these two countries were ranked number eight and 15 in the countries with the highest income inequality (Gini Index 57.1 and Gini Index 53.1, respectively; World Bank 2002). Other countries with high kidnapping rates and significant income inequality include Brazil, Russia, Nigeria, and Venezuela (Wilder and Lipton 2008, April 3; World Bank 2002).

Poverty is a motivating factor for individuals who see committing RKs as a way out of their debt and other financial problems (Yang et al. 2007). Akpan (2010) noted that these abductions for ransom reflect the increased poverty and unemployment among residents in a prosperous, oil-rich region.

Although RK victims are often targeted based on their perceived financial resources, perpetrators do not limit their targets to wealthy persons or those who have wealthy family members (Bailliet 2010; O'Neil 2009). Younger individuals who have fewer financial resources may be targeted because they do not use bodyguards and armored vehicles (Bailliet 2010; Oliver 2007).

Transnational Criminal Networks

Transnational criminal networks operate invisibly (Bailliet 2010). In July 2002, the UN Economic and Social Council expressed alarm about the ability of criminal groups to commit abductions. Criminal groups use RKs to expand their financial resources, allowing them to fund their criminal operations and activities. Various types of groups carry out RKs, including professional abductors who are also involved in drug trafficking and criminal gangs who participate in money-laundering, human trafficking (HT), and the illegal weapons trade (Bailliet 2010). Average criminals in Haiti, Mexico, Iraq, and other nations also use this form of abduction to pursue their criminal objectives.

Another type of group involved in RKs is rebels or insurgents, such as the FARC in Colombia and rebels or insurgents in Afghanistan and Iraq (Bailliet 2010). Rebels and insurgents rely on RKs to fund their activities, coerce and terrorize government officials, and advance their groups' religious, political, and social ideologies (Bailliet 2010). Likewise, terrorist groups in Russia, Peru, Philippines, and other countries also commit RKs to finance their activities and advance their terrorist goals, objectives, and ideologies.

In addition, in countries such as Kyrgyzstan, China, Ethiopia, and Uzbekistan, bride abductions are common. Security forces in different nations also commit RKs (Bailliet 2010).

Drug and Criminal Gangs and Organizations

The presence of drug cartels and criminal gangs and organizations increase the likelihood of RKs (Bailliet 2010; Hathaway 2007, April 14; Wyler 2011; Josephs 2010, June 8; Yang et al. 2007; Diamond 1985–1986). Organized crime increases the risk of RKs (Diamond 1985–1986). In the U.S., organized criminal activities during the prohibition period facilitated a high rate of RKs. In Mexico and other countries, middle- and upper-SES individuals are abducted by these gangs (solutionsabroad.com no date). Criminal groups may murder their captives even after extorting money from their families, relatives, and friends.

In certain countries, criminal gangs and organizations frequently carry out the initial abduction of the victims and then sell them to guerrilla and terrorist organizations (Gearon 2010, April). Gangs and criminal organizations will select not only targets but also locations, including transportation centers and routes, where they can carry out their crimes (Semple 2001, June 3).

After capturing the victims, the gang members often will blindfold them and terrorize them so that they do not resist their captors. Criminal gangs and criminal organizations frequently will use motor vehicles to quickly transport the captives to pre-arranged hideouts where they can easily hold them without detection while they negotiate with their family members to collect a suitable ransom.

In Yang et al.'s (2007) analysis of kidnapping in Taiwan, small numbers of individuals often formed RK gangs under the leadership of a ringleader. In larger and more complex gangs, a leadership system emerges with its own set of rules. For example, in Afghanistan, local Taliban chiefs reportedly have feuded over their control of the best roads to carry out RKs (Yousafzai et al. 2008).

The FARC passed "Law 002", which demands a payment, "the tax for peace" from individuals and corporations that have assets more than $1 million (Semple 2001, June 3).

Criminal gangs who kidnap individuals for ransom are motivated by a variety of factors, including financial and political (Tzanelli 2006; Bailliet 2010; Turner 1998; Mohamed 2008; Akpan 2010; Yang et al. 2007). Analysts note that the laws of demand and supply regulate abductions (Tzanelli 2006; Gerth and Mills 1948). In these instances, the perpetrators calculate the most efficient means to attain their desired goals.

Common criminal who carry out RKs are essentially business persons; they are just engaged in illegal activities (*The Nation*, 2002, May 10). If demand is eliminated, then the abductors will not have any supply. Financially oriented abductors frequently will not abduct a person if someone will not pay their ransom.

Drug cartels have different motivations for carrying out RKs (Malkin 2009, July 26). Drug cartels may commit RKs as a way of responding to threats to their criminal activities. Drug cartel-related RKs and associated violence were not prevalent in the northern state of Chihuahua, Mexico, until the Mexican government began to wage its war against the drug cartels.

International Borders, Transportation Routes, and RKs of Migrants and Immigrants

Drug cartels and other criminal organizations and gangs increasingly are kidnapping thousands of undocumented immigrants and demanding ransoms (Wyler 2011, April 11; Josephs 2010, June 8). In Mexico, the country's National Human Rights Commission reported that in 2010, from April through September, 11,333 migrants were abducted. A majority of these kidnap victims were from Central America. Forty-four percent came from Honduras, 16.2% El Salvador, 11.2% Guatemala, and 5% Cuba.

Undocumented immigrants are especially vulnerable. Faced with poverty and unemployment in their country of origin, they are crossing borders illegally to work so that they can support themselves and their families. Drug cartels and criminal gangs will exploit undocumented immigrants' vulnerabilities by abducting them, knowing that the captives and their families will probably not contact the police (Castillo 2011, February 22). In this way, these undocumented immigrants are like the children who are kidnapped and forced to fight in armed conflicts as child soldiers.

Undocumented immigrants may be at increased risk for kidnapping by the drug cartels and criminal gangs when these organizations and groups are warring with each other (Josephs 2010, June 8).

Porous international borders also increase the opportunity for drug cartels and criminal organizations to kidnap undocumented migrants. For example, Mexico's porous southern and northern borders make it difficult for immigration authorities and the police to respond to the kidnappings and murders of undocumented immigrants (Josephs 2010, June 8).

Official Corruption

As in the case of HT and other crimes, official corruption in different governmental agencies increases the risk of RKs (Bailliet 2010; *Associated Press*, December 20, 2005; Josephs 2010, June 8). For example, in Mexico, current or former police personnel reportedly have participated in abductions or offered protection to kidnapping gangs in many cases (*Associated Press*, December 20, 2005). In addition, officials from the Mexican government's National Migration Institute reportedly may be in collusion with organized crime members in cases of kidnappings, sexual offenses, and other crimes (Josephs 2010, June 8).

Police corruption reportedly was involved in the kidnapping of a contractor and 14 of his employees in Afghanistan (Wonacott 2009, August 18). According to the Faryab Province police chief, investigators discovered that the abductors had assistance from within the police unit. Based on this information, the police chief reported that the police arrested two suspects and some relatives of the abductors.

Official corruption limits the apprehension and conviction of kidnappers and other criminals. In addition to government corruption, law enforcement agencies may lack the financial and technical resources to handle RKs, especially when the law enforcement personnel are overwhelmed by an increased rate of crime. Individuals who believe that they can make a lot of money without getting caught will be encouraged to commit RKs.

Technology and RKs

Technological factors can increase or reduce the risks of RKs. The rise of the automobile in the U.S. may have led to higher rates of abductions (Alix 1978; Diamond 1985–1986). Criminals could use motor vehicles to quickly abduct their victims and demand ransom payments. Technological improvements in highways such as the development of the interstate highway system in the U.S. increased the ease at which offenders could transport RK victims within states and across state lines. The easy access to automated teller machines also can facilitate high rates of RKs. In addition, technological developments such as online banking can increase the risk of RKs.

Offender Characteristics

Researchers are beginning to investigate the social, demographic, and behavioral characteristics of the typical kidnapping perpetrators. Offenders often have a criminal history. Based on the analysis of 7,042 males and 545 females who had been convicted of a minimum of one abduction in the 1979–2001 period. Soothill et al. (2007) discovered that 3.9% of the males and 2.6% of the females had been convicted for kidnapping more than one time during this period. About 51% of the male and 33.6% of the female offenders had prior convictions for those convicted of kidnapping in 2001. In these cases, the perpetrators' prior convictions varied significantly but the most common ones were theft and violent crimes.

Based on a 20-year follow-up of perpetrators convicted between 1979 and 1981, Soothill et al. (2007) discovered that three in five male convicts and one three female convicts were subsequently convicted at least one more time. The investigators found that kidnappers with co-convictions related to theft-related offenses declined during the follow-up period. In contrast, kidnappers with co-convictions for sex- and violence-related offenses increased during the same time period.

In Yang et al.'s (2007) investigation of abductions in Taiwan, which were based on 31 court cases, offenders were frequently male, unemployed, and had a previous conviction for a major offense other than abduction. Their criminal offenses included burglary, weapons-associated crimes, drug-related offenses, and manslaughter.

Using another data source, a survey of 146 inmates, Yang et al. (2007) showed that 97.3% of the 196 inmates were male, 42.5% were in the 21–30 age group, and a little more 50% had just a ninth-grade education. In their survey, approximately three out of 10 did not have a job at the time of their offense and the other inmates were employed in the private sector or had low-level government jobs.

Yang et al.'s (2007) survey results revealed that in contrast to their court data, two out of three inmates did not have a criminal record. In addition, approximately nine out of 10 inmates did not have a history of crime in their family. More than 50% of the inmates surveyed were single and approximately 25% were married with a "cordial" relation with their spouses and other members of the family.

According to Yang et al. (2007), 70% of the offenders often acted as a group to carry out the kidnapping. Perpetrators typically worked in small groups with two to three members. The researchers, however, did not find that perpetrators worked as part of an organized network of kidnappers. Typically, the groups were formed when a ringleader who was under financial pressure recruited his friend to join in a kidnapping plot.

Relationship Between Perpetrators and Victims

Investigators have assessed the social relations between kidnappers and their targets. Yang et al. (2007) discovered that victims were not randomly selected. In fact, more than 50% of victims were known by the ringleaders or co-offenders. Perpetrators knew about the financial prosperity of their targets from the media and other indirect sources such as gossip. Victims included both close acquaintances, relatives, and business associates as well as casual acquaintances, strangers, and well-known people in the community. In their study, geographical proximity between the perpetrator and the target was the common link among all types of targets.

The Kidnapping Process

In Yang et al.'s (2007) analysis, the kidnapping act was typically an urgent situation because of the desperate financial troubles of the offenders and the unpredictable actions of their targets. Unanticipated events will make the kidnappers' goals more difficult to achieve.

Yang et al. (2007) discovered that most of the abductors did not carefully plan their crime. The researchers suggest that this lack of planning may have been due to the fact that the perpetrators did not have experience in carrying out abductions and were participating in a one-time criminal group. Moreover, a detailed plan with a division of labor may not have been necessary since the kidnapping rings often did not exceed three members.

Abductors may capture their victims in different ways. For example, the perpetrators may stalk their potential targets, lure victims to a site where they could commit the abduction, and randomly come into proximity with targets and abduct those who appear prosperous (Yang et al. 2007). The offenders' relationship with the victims predicted the type of strategy employed. For example, kidnappers who had developed trust with acquaintances could use this trust to lure them to an abduction location.

Kidnappers must find ways to control the target's behavior once she or he has been abducted. This process of control is unpredictable and may be affected by the nature of the crime scene, the route that the perpetrators used to escape from the crime scene, and the characteristics of the offenders' hideout (Yang et al. 2007). The abductors must find a way to control the victims' psychosocial well-being and may use drugs, death threats and other verbal threats, physical violence, and homicide to control their captives (Morewitz 2008).

Abductors also must achieve the difficult goal of gaining the cooperation of the victims' families and avoid law enforcement detection and apprehension (Yang et al. 2007). The perpetrators may not have a way of knowing if their victims are cooperating. To help avoid police detection and apprehension, the offenders frequently will change the ransom drop-off location or use electronic banking methods. Perpetrators also will select ransom drop-off sites such as railroad stations and freeways since they allow for more anonymity than other locations.

RK and the Law

In countries around the world, kidnapping is a violation of criminal law (Bailliet 2010). Bailliet (2010) reports that financial gain is the major motivating force underlying abductions. These crimes also have the consequence of fostering fear in the community. In criminal laws dealing with kidnappings, the offenses include taking or depriving persons of their liberty, making threats of violence, including death threats, and keeping individuals in a location where the victims could not be located (Bailliet 2010; Morewitz 2008).

Penalties for abductions throughout the world vary significantly. They typically range from 1 to 10 years (Bailliet 2010). In RK cases in which the perpetrators commit other crimes such as homicide, torture, and rape, enhanced penalties can range from 10 to 20 years. Individuals who are convicted of RK can receive the death penalty (Prince 2009; Yang et al. 2007).

In the U.S. kidnapping was originally a common law violation that has become codified in state criminal statutes (Prince 2009; Ram 2008; Diamond 1985–1986; Parker 1969–1970). These state criminal laws have been criticized for being unclear and too broad (Prince 2009; Diamond 1985–1986).

Initially, kidnapping in the U.S. was considered the forcible taking away of persons from their country and moving them into another country. It was a misdemeanor, and those convicted faced a fine, brief incarceration, and pillory. The crime evolved from a similar misdemeanor, false imprisonment, which refers to illegally confining an individual. Kidnapping is the "most aggravated form of false imprisonment" (Diamond 1985–1986).

Now, kidnapping is a felony and those found guilty of the crime can face life in prison (Diamond 1985–1986). The requirement that offenders must transport the individual across national borders has been dropped.

States vary in how they classify the severity of the crime. For example, in California, kidnapping has been classified as simple or aggravated offenses (Diamond 1985–1986). In California, violations of the aggravated kidnapping law can result in harsher penalties. However, the California aggravated kidnapping statute has required evidence that the victim was abducted for reasons such as ransom or extortion [Cal Penal Code 209 (West 1971 and Supp. 1985)]. In New York, kidnapping laws have been classified into first- and second-degree crimes.

In the U.S., states still define the crime with regard to the transportation of the victim (Diamond 1985–1986). However, state laws differ in how much movement of the victim is necessary for crimes to be considered as kidnapping. For example, states vary in whether they consider crimes such as assault accompanied by movement of the victim as constituting kidnapping. In different states, various appellate decisions regarding this question have not resolved the legal controversies in kidnapping laws.

In the state of California, the courts have tried to determine the extent of movement that is necessary for the crime to be classified as kidnapping (Diamond 1985–1986). Not much movement of the kidnapping victim is necessary for a crime to be classified as kidnapping in the state of California (Diamond 1985–1986).

However, the California Supreme Court in 1961 determined in *Cotton v. Superior Court* that Penal Code section 207 should not be followed when the alleged crime involves movement of the victim that is not a major part of the alleged crime [*Cotton v. Superior Court,* 56 Cal. 2d 459, 364 P.2d 241, 15 *Cal Rptr.* 65 (1961); Diamond 1985–1986]. The *Cotton* case involved a labor dispute in which a person was reportedly dragged from a toilet about 15 feet and thrown to the ground and kicked in the back and legs. The court in this case noted that if even a small movement of the victim was involved any defendant in an assault case could be charged with kidnapping. As a result, defendants could be subjected to double jeopardy in violation of the U.S. constitution (Prince 2009).

In 1969, the California Supreme Court in *People v. Daniels* ruled that section 209 of the Penal Code, the aggravated kidnapping statute, excluded cases involving "stand-still robberies" and cases involving the transportation or movement of the victims that were incidental to the perpetration of the robberies [*People v. Daniels*, 71 Cal. 2d 1119, 459 P.2d 225, 80 Cal. Rptr. 897 (1969); Diamond 1985–1986]. In addition, the California Supreme Court in *People v. Daniels* determined that the aggravated kidnapping statute excluded cases that consisted of movements of the victims that did not elevate the risk of harm to the victims beyond what already existed in the commission of the robbery.

Diamond (1985–1986) noted that despite the *People v. Daniels* decision, the concept of incidental asportation or movement of the victim was still perplexing. In *People v. Timmons*, the California Supreme Court in 1971 used the *People v. Daniels* standard in a case involving a defendant who forced two robbery victims to drive in their automobile about five blocks [*People v. Timmons*, 4 Cal. 3d 411, 482 P.2d 648, 93 Cal. Rptr. 736 (1971); Diamond 1985–1986]. The defendant threatened force but did not exhibit a weapon. The California Supreme Court in *People v. Timmons* found that the movement of the victims did not substantially elevate the victims' risk of harm. The victims were not exposed to substantial physical injuries beyond that inherent in robberies themselves. The Court found in *People v. Timmons* that the defendant did not have a weapon, the police were not in a high-speed chase of the defendant, and the case did not involve reckless driving.

Convictions for both simple and aggravated kidnapping were examined by the California Supreme Court in *People v. Stanworth*. In this case, the defendant allegedly dragged one of his victims about 25 feet from a road to a field, tied her hands, raped her, and robbed her of about $15 dollars [*People v. Stanworth*, 11 Cal. 3d 588, 522 P.2d 1058, 114 Cal. Rptr. 250 (1974); Diamond 1985–1986]. In determining if an aggravated kidnapping charge should be upheld, the California Supreme Court determined that the movement of the victim about 25 feet was only incidental to the offenses since the defendant moved the victim in order to rape and steal from the victim. Thus, the first prong of *Daniels* was not supported. In addition, the California Supreme Court did not uphold the second prong of *Daniels* by ruling that the defendant's moving of the victim did not significantly increase risk of physical harm to the victim more than the risks inherent in the offenses involved in the case.

With regard to the simple kidnapping convictions, the California Supreme Court upheld four simple kidnapping convictions in *People v. Stanworth* [*People v. Stanworth*, 11 Cal. 3d 588, 522 P.2d 1058, 114 Cal. Rptr. 250 (1974); Diamond 1985–1986]. However, the *Stanworth* court rejected the *Daniels* standard in applying to simple kidnapping statute under section 207 of the Penal Code. The *Stanworth* court ruled that simple kidnapping does not have to take place in association with an underlying offense. For the simple kidnapping statute to be upheld, the *Stanworth* court ruled that the movement of the victim should not be "slight" or "insubstantial." The court supported a previous lower appellate decision that moving the victim 700 yards was not insubstantial.

In a later case, *People v. Thornton*, using the *Daniels* standard, the California Supreme Court supported the aggravated kidnapping conviction for two separate crimes [*People v. Thornton*, 11 Cal. 3d 738, 523 P.2d 267, 114 Cal. Rptr. 467 (1974); Diamond 1985–1986]. In the first incident, the defendant reportedly used force to enter a female victim's automobile and drove her four blocks. The defendant used his arm to keep the victim pinned to her seat and kept his arm around her throat. The defendant then robbed the victim and sexually assaulted her after parking the vehicle. In a separate crime, the same defendant reportedly put a gun to a female victim's back while she was standing outside a bar and commanded her to walk a block to a park vehicle about one block away.

In *People v. Thornton*, the court interpreted the first *Daniels*' requirement regarding more than incidental movement of the victim to involve "substantial" movement of the victim [*People v. Thornton*, 11 Cal. 3d 738, 523 P.2d 267, 114 Cal. Rptr. 467 (1974); Diamond 1985–1986]. The facts in the case indicate that moving the victim a block would constitute "substantial" movement.

The *Thornton* court found the second element of the *Daniels* standard supported since any "substantial" movement of the victim consists of coercive control of the victim and subjects her to elevated risk of physical harm [*People v. Thornton*, 11 Cal. 3d 738, 523 P.2d 267, 114 Cal. Rptr. 467 (1974); Diamond 1985–1986]. This increased risk of physical harm would not have taken place if the robbery had occurred at the time of the defendant's first contact with the victim.

The *Thornton* decision seems to contradict the *Timmons* decision that had reversed a conviction for aggravated kidnapping that involved greater movement of the victim (five blocks) by the defendant [Diamond 1985–1986; *People v. Thornton*, 11 Cal. 3d 738, 523 P.2d 267, 114 Cal. Rptr. 467 (1974); *People v. Timmons*, 4 Cal. 3d 411, 482 P.2d 648, 93 Cal. Rptr. 736 (1971)].

The state of New York uses a merger doctrine, which restricts kidnapping to conventional cases of abductions (Diamond 1985–1986);

Michigan uses factors to assess asportation that is incidental to abductions (Diamond 1985–1986).

In Kansas, the courts do not use the above approaches. Instead, they evaluate the extent to which asportation in a major way makes possible another criminal act (Diamond 1985–1986).

The Model Penal Code seeks to determine the degree to which the abduction victim is kept significantly isolated from her or his regular settings (Diamond 1985–1986). The Model Penal Code considers two factors: significant asportation or time involved.

Persons who become outraged by RK epidemics may focus on either a communitarian or cosmopolitan approach to the problem (Bailliet 2010). Those who take the communitarian strategy attempt to rally support in their respective countries for reforming the criminal justice system and larger political system. These individuals seek to strengthen or reform existing laws against corruption, reform laws against abductions, and improve the SES of the population, which is an underlying cause of RKs. In contrast, individuals who take the cosmopolitan approach escape the terror facing RK victims and potential victims by seeking asylum in other countries.

However, other countries fearing that asylum seekers will open the floodgates of immigration may develop restrictive asylum policies and practices to deny protection for these asylum seekers and deport them back to their countries of origin (Bailliet 2010). One way that countries can significantly restrict asylum is to have an immigration policy that denies asylum based on the generalized risk of abductions. For example, in the case of a woman from Haiti who suffered an attempted abduction, threats by telephone, "intervention" of her residence and the homicide of her sister, the Canadian Immigration and Refugee Board denied her asylum because she was not exposed to a particular risk (Bailliet 2010). Instead, with the epidemic of abductions in Haiti, the woman confronts the same risk of abduction that other Haitians face.

Countries also restrict asylum seekers by following the internal flight alternative theory (Bailliet 2010). These nations will deny asylum to kidnapping victims who can reasonably seek protection by relocating to another part of their country of origin. However, in one case, the Canadian Immigration and Refugee Board granted asylum to a Mexican family since they had no internal flight alternative (Bailliet 2010). Mexico has a national documentation system, making it easy to identify and locate citizens who relocate to another part of the country.

Some countries may improve their responses to abductions that are perpetrated by professional abduction groups. Bailliet (2010) notes that, as a result, unprofessional criminals may move into this area of criminal activity. For example, unprofessional criminal groups are mainly responsible for RKs in Mexico and Italy. These unprofessional groups have reportedly engaged in more violence against their victims than the previous professional kidnapping rings.

In addition to considering RKs as criminal offenses in national states, abductions are viewed as major human rights, humanitarian, and international criminal law (Bailliet 2010). However, according to Schloenhardt, a majority of transnational organized crimes fall outside the International Criminal Court's jurisdiction (Bailliet 2010). When nations do not effectively respond to transnational organized crimes, Schloenhardt calls for the establishment of an international criminal justice organization to investigate, prosecute, and punish violators of these offenses.

The UN is an international body that deals with RKs and other crimes. Abductions violate Article 1 of the UN Charter since ransom kidnappers deprive the victims of their freedom and liberty, physical and personal integrity, threaten their lives and in cases of homicide, violate their right to life.

Various UN groups may consider complaints or reports about RKs, including the Human Rights Committee, the Committee Against Torture, the Committee on the Rights of the Child, and the Committee on the Elimination of Discrimination Against Women (Bailliet 2010). The UN committees are especially concerned about children, women, immigrants, and other groups that are targeted by ransom kidnappers. Bailliet (2010) notes that although these groups are targeted, individuals from a variety of SES, gender, and other social and demographic backgrounds are also RK victims.

Nonnationals may be especially at risk for RKs in countries characterized by SES disparities (Bailliet 2010). The UN Committee on the Elimination of Racial Discrimination stresses the need to tackle these SES causes of abductions. For example, the Committee is dealing with antagonism between Lesotho nationals and Asian and South African white factory owners, which had led to abductions and other violent incidents and the departure of 100 Asian nationals who fear attack by Lesotho nationals.

The UN focuses on the obligation of countries to protect persons from abductions and offer solutions (Bailliet 2010). For example, according to the UN Human Rights Committee General Comment 31, nations are obligated to prevent human rights violations, and if they occur, they must investigate the violations and punish the perpetrators.

Violations of kidnapping laws are also addressed at the regional level (Bailliet 2010). For example, in *Avsar v. Turkey*, the European Court of Human Rights ruled that Turkey violated Articles 2 and 13 for not conducting a proper investigation of a man who was abducted and killed by village guards with the national government's complicity. Similarly, the Inter-American Court of Human Rights in Mexico issued an order for the state to investigate the abduction and murder of man with the police's and paramilitary's complicity (Bailliet 2010).

Officials also may view RKs as war crimes and crimes against humanity (Bailliet 2010). During war and armed conflict, abductions, including RKs, are illegal and can be prosecuted as war crimes. Hostage-taking is illegal in all cases involving both domestic and international armed conflict. According to Hans-Peter Gasser, hostage-taking during warfare occurs when adversaries hold individuals in their power, whether by consent or involuntarily, in order to achieve some particular objectives such as terminating military activities or releasing prisoners. When abductions are committed by armed groups for ransom only, international law may not be applicable. Rather, in these instances, criminal law would be used.

In terms of viewing abductions as crimes against humanity, the Rome Statute of the ICC refers to hostage-taking only, not kidnapping per se (Bailliet 2010). The statute covers cases of enforced disappearance, which requires complicity by the national government. Hostage-taking, according to the statute must be part of a systematic or widespread attack against a population. According to Bailliet (2010), epidemics of abductions may fulfill the "widespread" element of the crime. Cryer points out that the "attack" requirement suggests a certain degree of scale and organization, and abductions carried out over time may constitute an attack on the population (Bailliet 2010). According to Cryer, a crime epidemic per se may not necessarily represent a crime against humanity since these crimes may not relate to each other. However, state involvement in RKs such as the participation of corrupt police and judges in carrying out RKs can fulfill the requirement of a systematic or widespread attack directed against a population.

Outcomes of RKs

Researchers have studied the effects of RKs on the victims and their families. Hostages, including prisoners of war, civilians in concentration camps, and torture victims, individuals in abusive relationships, and members of abusive cults can suffer severe trauma-related problems (Cantor and Price 2007; de Fabrique et al. 2007; Solomon et al. 2012; Shemesh et al. 2008; West and Martin 1994; Corrado and Tompkins 1989).

Corrado and Tompkins (1989) suggest that hostages, concentration camp captives, and tortured captives tend to suffer initial shock associated with intense fear and anxiety. These victims then tend to outwardly accept their captors' control while inwardly suffering severe fright.

Over time, the victims during a period of adaptation may cope with their captivity by suffering post traumatic stress disorder (PTSD), complex PTSD, which consists of more persistent and diffuse symptoms and personality changes than PTSD, and the Stockholm syndrome (SS) (the paradoxical development of positive emotions between kidnapping victims and their perpetrators) (Cantor and Price 2007; de Fabrique et al. 2007; West and Martin 1994; Corrado and Tompkins 1989).

Captives who suffer from complex PTSD are especially vulnerable to physical violence on a recurring basis that is both self-inflicted and perpetrated by other individuals (Cantor and Price 2007). Persons with complex PTSD may have difficulty regulating their anger, sexual behavior, and self-destructive tendencies. They may also develop symptoms of dissociation and somatization and suffer from chronic guilt and shame. Individuals with complex PTSD may idealize their abuser, have trouble trusting others, and are at increased risk for subsequent victimization.

In 1974, the term, Stockholm Syndrome (SS), was coined after SS symptoms reportedly emerged in hostages after a bank robbery in Sweden. Many years before this phenomenon was recognized, former captives reported having paradoxical sympathetic feelings for their captors (West and Martin 1994). RK victims who suffer from SS identify with their aggressors. These individuals view their abductors in favorable ways through the process of introjections. In this way, both the captor and the captives are united together in a hostage setting and both are protected against the outside world (Harnischmacher and Muther 1987).

Other trauma-related problems that can occur in kidnapped victims include anxiety and depression (Cantor and Price 2007; West and Martin 1994). One investigation of RK victims in Sardinia, Italy, discovered that RK victims may suffer from PTSD and major depression (Cantor and Price 2007; de Fabrique et al. 2007; Favaro et al. 2000).

Childhood sexual abuse and child physical abuse by parents, which are other forms of captivity, have been linked to a range of problems, including anxiety, depression, school problems, PTSD, and SS (Cantor and Price 2007; Julich 2005; Boney-McCoy and Finkelhor 1996). Abduction attempts have been associated with similar outcomes.

In addition, RK victims and other captives may suffer from dissociative symptoms that result in an altered personality or pseudo-identity (West and Martin 1994). Captives develop a pseudo identity to help them cope with the overwhelming trauma of captivity.

Various conditions can increase the risk of these trauma-related disorders (Cantor and Price 2007; Steel et al. 2009). Kidnappers have tremendous power over their captives and this imbalance of power increases the victims' risk of traumatic sequelae. The risk of PTSD may increase if the victims are unprepared for the hostage-taking and if they are tortured (Cantor and Price 2007; Silove et al. 2002; Basoglu et al. 1997). Torture victims who are also sexually assaulted are at increased risk of suffering PTSD (van Velsen et al. 1996). In addition, torture victims are at increased risk of engaging in suicidal behavior (Ferrada-Noli et al. 1998).

Several factors may increase the risk of SS in kidnapped victims (Cantor and Price 2007). Kidnappers who threaten to physically harm and murder their victims increase the probability of SS in these individuals. Abductors who appear somewhat kind to them increase the victims' chances of developing the syndrome. In addition, victims who are kept isolated from the viewpoints of others besides the abductors have a higher probability of suffering SS.

RKs can have a major impact on not only the primary victims but also on the victims' families and friends (Bailliet 2010). Families as well as the RK victims can suffer substantial psychosocial problems. In a study, Navia and Ossa (2003) evaluated the psychosocial impact of RKs on the families during captivity and on the abducted persons and their families after the release. Abducted persons and their family members were examined 2–4, 5–8, and 9–15 months after the release. Based on a sample of 55 abducted and released persons and 158 family members, the investigators discovered that captivity was the period with the highest psychosocial distress. Psychosocial distress or PTSD symptoms did not vary between the three time periods after the release of the RK victims.

In many cases, families are forced into bankruptcy in paying ransoms and may not even see their loved ones alive after paying ransoms.

RK victims and their families often want to deal with their kidnappings quietly (Semple 2001, June 3). They may be fearful of reporting the incidents because of their lives and the lives of their families and friends will be in jeopardy if they contact the police. The victims of RKs and their rescuers may not feel that the incident is worth reporting since law enforcement responses will do more harm than good. As noted earlier, in many cases, current and former police may be corrupt and actually be involved in the RKs.

Abductors may kill their RK victims to eliminate witnesses (*Associated Press*, December 20, 2005). According to the RKP, 41.18% of the RK victims were killed (see Table F.15). Kidnappers also may murder their victims during botched RKs. In addition, perpetrators may kill their victims by torturing them or using other violence against them. Abductors also may murder their captives for political purposes. The National Counterterrorism Center reported that in 2004, 33 U.S. citizens were abducted abroad and 13 were murdered (National Counterterrorism Center no date).

The next year, 12 U.S. citizens reportedly were abducted in different countries and 6 were killed.

Do kidnappers vary systematically in their use of violence against captives? Based on a study of 181 abductions, Phillips (2013) addressed this issue by analyzing different violent techniques, including the use of psychological terror, among common criminals, organized criminals, and terrorists. The researcher discovered that terrorists were more likely to employ psychological torture, while common criminals relied on a variety of physical violence against their captives. Regardless of these results, the investigator showed that particular types of violence such as inflicting pain increased the probability that they would kill their captives.

In Yang et al.'s (2007) investigation, homicide was not frequent since individual violence was not the offenders' objective. Murdering the abduction captive took place when the captive had a close relationship with the offender and recognized him. Homicide also occurred when the captive attempted to escape or resist. Having only one perpetrator involved increased the risk that the kidnapping victim would be killed. A lone offender, when confronted with the multiple tasks involved in successfully carrying out a kidnapping, may view homicide as the best way to achieve control.

The problem of murdering kidnap victims has increased in Mexico (*Associated Press*, December 20, 2005). According to a report in 2005, abductors in Mexico were three times more likely to murder their victims than abductors in Colombia. In 2005, approximately one out of every seven kidnap victims in Mexico was killed by their abductors. Thirty-two abduction victims were murdered in Mexico between 1970 and 1976. During this period, leftist terrorist groups in Mexico began to systematically abduct successful business executives. The number of business leaders murdered between 1994 and 2000 increased to 115. This period was characterized by economic difficulties. Between 2000 and 2005, the number of abduction victims murdered rose to 199. In 2005 alone, about 43 kidnapped victims were killed by their abductors.

In other instances, the RK victims are let go or rescued. Findings from the RKP showed that 18.98% of the RK victims were let go and 40.36% were rescued (see Table F.15). The probability of rescuing may depend on a variety of factors such as law enforcement resources, skills, and degree of official corruption.

Paying the ransom demands may increase the probability that the captives will be let go. In 61.95% of the RKP cases, a ransom was paid (see Table F.15). Payments made in RKs can be very substantial. Huge RK payments in the past have established a precedent for current-day RK offenders (Clendenin 2006). Sears paid over $1 million ransom to win the release of an executive who had been abducted for three months in Colombia. Multinational companies paid more than $1 billion in ransoms to rescue business executives from 1978 to 1998 (Prochnau 1998). According to an article in 2001, billions of dollars in RK payments have been made for abducted business executives since 1980 (Merkling and Davis 2001).

The amount of RK ransoms paid have fluctuated over the years, but overall, the average ransom paid per victim has increased since the early 1990s (Wilder and Lipton 2008). In 1993, the average ransom paid per victim based on 107 incidents and 179 victims was $36,324.45, compared to $62,071.83 based on 63 incidents and 82 victims in 2005. The exact amount of money spent on RKs is unknown because these incidents often are surrounded by secrecy (Merkling and Davis 2001).

Not all offenders receive ransoms that they initially demanded. For example, Yang et al. (2007) discovered in their survey of kidnappers that only 21 out of the 84 offenders surveyed reported that they had received ransom amounts that they had desired or somewhat desired. These results may have been partly due to the fact that the perpetrators had not determined their ransom amount before carrying out the kidnapping. In their study of kidnapping in Taiwan, the researchers discovered that the abductors were very concerned about completing the ransom negotiation and appeared to want to speed up the haggling process, which is a cultural practice in Taiwan. The authors suggest that the final ransom amount agreed on seemed to be determined by idiosyncratic factors rather than by a systematic calculation.

Families who pay large ransoms for their abducted loved ones may find themselves destitute (Bailliet 2010) and governments rarely offer them complete restitution of their financial losses (Bassiouni 2003; Bailliet 2010).

In response to the increased incidence and costs of RKs, insurance companies are selling kidnap and ransom (K & R) insurance policies to reimburse multinational companies and nongovernmental organizations (NGOs) for making ransom payments (Clendenin 2006). The high rate of RKs has led to the emergence of an extensive criminal industry in which the abductors get paid, potential targets have the protection of insurance, and the insurance companies are paid premiums. Sales of R & K policies increased 20% after the 2001 terrorist attacks (Wong 2004, March 15). According to a 2006 *Emory Law Journal* article, currently, all of the top insurance companies and several so-called boutique insurers provide K & R policies (Clendenin 2006; American International Underwriters, Crisis management no date). Standard K & R policies include coverage for direct loss, expenses incurred in winning the release of the RK victims, and management and crisis response services.

Clendenin (2006) argues that K & R policies undermine U.S. counterterrorism policy that prohibits concessions to hostage takers. According to the U.S. Department of State, making concessions to hostage takers increases the risks that terrorists will kidnap others for ransom. Clendenin (2006) believes that K & R policies should emphasize prevention of RKs instead of responding to incidents. However, Kenney (2008) points out that if payment reimbursement is taken out of K & R policies, RK victims would have more difficulty in safely coming home.

The increase rate of RKs has led to media coverage of the problem and the U.S. Congress has begun to address this problem (Black 2003). U.S. leaders responded to the security problems posed by RKs and kidnappings in general by passing the USA Patriot Act. The Act classifies the abduction of United States citizens abroad as an act of terrorism (Clendenin 2006).

In addition to the costs of the ransom payments, a costly security industry has emerged to deal with RKs (Semple 2001, June 3). Security consultants and RK negotiators are employed to assist companies in effectively resolving RK incidents and minimizing additional risks. Security consultants may be involved in more than 30 RK cases annually (Merkling and Davis 2001).

Companies can make use of RK prevention programs, which include employee training, rigorous guidelines for travel, and email risk alerts (AIG Private Client Group—Kidnap and Ransom no date; Clendenin 2006). Security firms advise potential RK targets to dress down, not to display expensive jewelry, and avoid driving flashy automobiles. Bodyguards and armored vehicles are also used to protect potential targets of RKs.

Prevention of RKs may be achieved by reducing the root causes for RKs such as high levels of poverty and income inequality in countries. In addition, reducing the incidence of war and armed conflict, undocumented immigration, and government corruption should reduce the likelihood of RKs.

References

Akasike, C. (2008). Kidnappers unleash terror in Akwa Ibom. Punch on the Web. The Punch Newspaper, October 26, 2008, Nigeria.

Akpan, N.S. (2010). Kidnapping in Nigeria's Niger Delta: An exploratory study. J Soc Sci, 24 (1): 33–42.

Alix, E.K. (1978). Ransom kidnapping in America, 1874–1974: The creation of a capital crime (Perspectives in sociology). Carbondale, IL: Southern Illinois University Press.

Amnesty International. (2001). Amnesty International annual report. London: Amnesty International.

American International Underwriters, Crisis Management. (no date). Retrieved from http://www.aiu.com/BusinessLine/aiuCDA_bizline_fprod/0,1618,10,00.html.

Associated Press. (2005, December 20). Mexico kidnappings deadliest in Latin America. http://www.msnbc.msn.com/id/10546934/ns/world_news-america/t/m.

Bailliet, C.M. (2010). Towards holistic transnational protection: An overview of international public law approaches to kidnapping. Denver J Internat Law & Policy, 38 (4): 581–622.

Basoglu, M., Mineka, S., & Paker, M., et al. (1997). Psychological preparedness for trauma as a protective factor in survivors of torture. Psychol Med, 27: 1421–1433.

Bassiouni, C. (2003). Introduction to international criminal law. Leiden, Netherlands: Martinus Nijhoff Publishers.

Black, H.J.C. (2003). Implications of power blackouts for the nation's cybersecurity and critical infrastructure protection: Joint hearing on the electrical grid, critical interdependencies, vulnerabilities, and readiness before the subcommittee on cyber security, science, and research and development and the subcommittee on infrastructure and border security. 108th Congress 4 (2003).

Boney-McCoy, S., & Finkelhor, D. (1996). Is youth victimization related to trauma symptoms and depression after controlling for prior symptoms and family relationships? A longitudinal, prospective study. J Consult Clin Psych, 64 (6): 1406–1416.

Cal Penal Code 209 (West 1971 & Supp. 1985).

Cantor, C., & Price, J. (2007). Traumatic entrapment, appeasement and complex post-traumatic stress disorder: Evolutionary perspectives of hostage reactions, domestic abuse and the Stockholm syndrome. Austral & New Zeal J Psychiatry, 41: 377–384.

Caramazza, I.F., & Leone, U. (1984). Phenomenology of kidnappings in Sardinia – Towards an international perspective of a local crime problem. Publication No. 23, Rockville, MD: National Institute of Justice, United Nations Interregional Crime and Justice Research Institute.

Castiglione, C. (2005). Extravagant pretensions: Aristocratic family conflicts, emotion, and "public sphere" in early eighteenth-century Rome. J Social Hist, 38: 685–703.

Castillo, E.E. (2011, February 22). More than 11,000 migrants kidnapped in Mexico. Associated Press. http://www.utsandiego.com/news/2011/Feb/22/more-than-11000-migrants-kidnapped-in-mexico/.

Cotton v. Superior Court, 56 Cal. 2d 459, 364 P.2d 241, 15 *Cal Rptr.* 65 (1961).

Columbia Electronic Encyclopedia. (2010, July 1). Kidnapping, 6th Edition. New York: Columbia University.

Clendenin, M. (2006). "No concessions" with no teeth: How kidnap and ransom insurers and insureds are undermining U.S. counterterrorism policy. Emory Law J, 56: 741–775.

Corrado, R.R., & Tompkins, E. (1989). A comparative model of the psychological effects on the victims of state and anti-state terrorism. Int J Law Psychiatry, 12 (4): 281–293.

de Fabrique, N., Van Hasselt, V.B., Vecchi, G.M., & Romano, S.J. (2007). Common variables associated with the development of Stockholm syndrome: Some case examples. Victims & Offenders, 2: 91–98.

De Sousa Santos, B. (2002). Toward a new legal common sense: Law, globalization, and emancipation. 9 (2d ed.).

Diamond, J.L. (1985–1986). Kidnapping: A modern definition. Am J Crim Law, 13: 1–36.

Favaro, A., Degortes, D., & Colombo, G., et al. (2000). The effects of trauma among kidnap victims in Sardinia, Italy. Psychol Med, 30 (4): 975–980.

Ferrada-Noli, M., Asberg, M., & Ormstad, K. (1998). Suicidal behavior after severe trauma. Part 2: The association between methods of torture and of suicidal ideation in posttraumatic stress disorder. J Trauma Stress, 11 (1): 113–124.

Gearon, E. (2010, April). Maghreb mayhem. Middle East, 410: 25–27.

Gerth, H.H., & Mills, C.W. (1948). From Max Weber: Essays in sociology. London: Routledge and Kegan Paul.

Hansen, S. (2003, April). High net worth families, kidnapping risk. Trusts & Estates, April 2003, 35.

Harnischmacher, R., & Muther, J. (1987). The Stockholm syndrome. On the psychological reaction of hostages and hostage-takers. Arch Kriminol, 180 (1–2): 1-12.

Hastings, J.V. (2009). Geographies of state failure and sophistication in maritime piracy hijackings. Political Geography, 30: 1–11.

Hathaway, A. (2007, April 14). Kidnapping in Latin America, the basics. http://www.articlesbase.com/travel-articles/kidnapping-in-latin-amer.

Josephs, L. (2010, June 8). Criminal groups in Mexico are kidnapping Central American migrants, activists say. http://www.longislandwins.com/index.php/Blog/post/criminal_organiza….

Julich, S. (2005). Stockholm syndrome and child sexual abuse. J Child Sexual Abuse, 14: 107–129.

Kenney, S. (2008). Regional shortcomings and global solutions: Kidnap, ransom, and Insurance in Latin America. Conn Insur Law J, 14 (2): 557–588.

Loyd, A., & Hamdani, A. (2006, February 18). Five bodyguards killed as Iraq bank chief kidnapped. Times (London), February 18, 49.

Malkin, E. (2009, July 26). Side effect of Mexico's drug war: Fear and death in a Mormon town. New York Times. http://proquest.umi.com.libaccess.sjlibrary.org/pqdweb?index=0&sid….

Marongiu, P., & Clarke, R.V. (1993). Ransom kidnapping in Sardinia. Subcultural theory and rational choice. In R.V. Clarke & M. Felson. Routine activity and rational choice. Advances in criminological theory. Vol. 5. New Brunswick, NJ: Transaction Publishers.

Merkling, S., & Davis, E. (2001). Kidnap & ransom insurance: A rapidly growing benefit. Compensation Benefits Rev, 33 (6): 40–45.

Mohamed, M.K.N. (2008). Kidnap for ransom in South East Asia: The case for a regional recording standard. Asian Criminology, 3: 61–73.

Moorehead, C. (1980). Hostages to fortune – A study of kidnapping in the world today. New York: Atheneum.

Morewitz, S.J. (2008). Death threats and violence. New York: Springer Science+Business Media, LLC.

Navia, C.E., & Ossa, M. (2003). Family functioning, coping, and psychological adjustment in victims and their families following kidnapping. J Trauma Stress, 16 (1): 107–112.

Network54.com. (2004, April 1). Argentina: Wave of kidnapping as law and order breaks down. http://www.network54.com/Forum/280807/thread/1080861783/last-1….

O'Neil, S. (2009). The real war in Mexico: How democracy can defeat the drug cartels. Foreign Aff, 88: 63, 68 ("The fear of kidnapping plagues the upper, middle, and working classes alike.").

Oliver, R.S. (2007). In the twelve years of NAFTA, the treaty gave to me… What exactly? An assessment of economic, social, and political developments in Mexico Since 1994 and their impact on Mexican immigration into the United States. 10 Harv Latino L Rev, 53.

Parker, F.J. (1969–1970). Aspects of merger in the law of kidnapping. Cornell Law Rev, 55: 527.

People v. Daniels, 71 Cal. 2d 1119, 459 P.2d 225, 80 Cal. Rptr. 897 (1969).

People v. Timmons, 4 Cal. 3d 411, 482 P.2d 648, 93 Cal. Rptr. 736 (1971).

People v. Stanworth, 11 Cal. 3d 588, 522 P.2d 1058, 114 Cal. Rptr. 250 (1974).

People v. Thornton, 11 Cal. 3d 738, 523 P.2d 267, 114 Cal. Rptr. 467 (1974).

Phillips, E.M. (2013). The social organization of violence toward hostages: Does violence in captivity indicate which kidnappers will kill? J Interpers Violence, 28 (6): 1314–1337.

Poole, O. (2006, June 6). Iraqi gets life for role of murder of British Aid woman. Daily Telegraph (London), June 6, 2006, 15.

Prince, M.A. (2009). Two crimes for the price of one: The problem with kidnapping statutes in Tennessee and beyond. Tenn Law Rev, 76 (3): 789–818.

Prochnau, W. (1998). Adventures in the ransom trade. Vanity Fair, May 1998, 136.

Prusher, I.R. (2003, September 10). Kidnapping in Iraq on the rise. Christian Sci Monitor. http://www.csmonitor.com/2003/0910/p05s02-woiq.html.

Ram, C.V. (2008). Regulating intrastate crime: How the Federal Kidnapping Act blurs the distinction between what is truly national and what is truly local. Wash & Lee Law Rev, 65, 767–806.

Rubio, M. (2004, August). Kidnapping and armed conflict in Colombia. Paper presented at the PRIO Workshop on "Techniques of Violence in Civil War." Oslo, Norway.

Semple, K. (2001, June 3). The kidnapping economy in Colombia. New York Times. http://www.nytimes.com/2001/06/03/magazine/03KIDNAPPING.html.

Shemesh, A.A., Kohn, R., & Radomislensky, I., et al. (2008). Emotional distress and other health-related dimensions among elderly survivors of the Shoa living in the community. Isr J Psychiatry Relat Sci, 45 (4): 230–238.

Silove, D.M., Steel, Z., & McGorry, P.D., et al. (2002). The impact of torture on post-traumatic stress symptoms in war-affected Tamil refugees and immigrants. Compr Psychiatry, 43: 49–55.

Slevin, P. (2006, June 7). We have your husband. Wash Post, June 7, 2006, A18.

Solomon, Z., Horesh, D., & Ein-Dor, T., et al. (2012). Predictors of PTSD trajectories following captivity: A 35-year longitudinal study. Psychiatry Res, 199 (3): 188–194.

Soothill, K., Francis, B., & Ackerley, E. (2007). Kidnapping: A criminal profile of persons convicted 1979–2001. Behav Sci & the Law, 25 (1): 69-84.

Steel, Z., Chey, T., & Silove, D., et al. (2009). Association of torture and other potentially traumatic events with mental health outcomes among populations exposed to mass conflict and displacement: A systematic review and meta-analysis. JAMA, 302 (5): 537–549.

The Nation. (2002, 10 May). Retrieved from www.accordplan.net/press/20050223.

Turner, M. (1998). Kidnapping and politics. Intl J Soc Law, 26: 145–160.

Tzanelli, R. (2006). Capitalizing on value: Towards a sociological understanding of kidnapping. Sociology, 40: 929–947. http://www.soc.sagepub.com.

Van Velsen, C., Gorst-Unsworth, C., & Turner, S.W. (1996). Survivors of torture and organized violence: Demography and diagnosis. J Trauma Stress, 9: 181–193.

West, L.J., & Martin, P.R. (1994). Pseudo-identity and the treatment of personality change in victims of captivity and cults. In: S.J. Lynn, J.W. Rhue (Eds.), Dissociation: Clinical and theoretical perspectives. New York: Guildford Press.

Wilder, T., & Lipton, B. (2008, April 3). Top 10 kidnap rated countries with ransom stats. http://www.castlerockinternational.com/news/casualty-insurance/kidnap-ransom-extortion/104-top-10-kidnap-rated-countries-with-ransom-stats?showall=1.

Willis Group Holdings Limited Conference Call. (2004, December 16). Special contingency risks and DBA coverage. Comments of Derek Rogers, Div. Dir., Special Contingency Risks, Willis Group.

Wonacott, P. (2009). News in depth: Afghan road project shows bump in drive for stability. The Wall Street J Asia. http://proquest.umi.com.libaccess.sjlibrary.org/pqdweb?index=0&sid….

World Bank. (2002). Gap between rich and poor: World income inequality in 2002. HighBeam Research, 2005. http://www.infoplease.com/ipa/A0908770.html.

Wong, A. (2004, March 15). Insurers meet rising demand for kidnap and ransom insurance. Colum News Serv, New York, NY. http://www.jrn.columbia.edu/studentwork/cns/2004-03-15/644.asp.

Wyler, G. (2011, April 11). At least one American among bus passengers kidnapped in Mexico. http://www.businessinsider.com/american-among-those-kidnapped-in-….

Yang, S., Wu, B., & Huang, S.-L. (2007). Kidnapping in Taiwan: The significance of geographic proximity, improvisation, and fluidity. Intl J Offend Ther Compar Criminology, 51 (3): 324–339.

Yousafzai, S., Moreau, R., & Pape, E., et al. (2008). For the Taliban, a crime that pays. Newsweek, 152 (11): 70–72.

Chapter 11
Kidnapping: Carjacking and Related Crimes

"Carjacking is defined as completed or attempted robbery of a motor vehicle by a stranger to the victim. It differs from other motor vehicle theft because the victim is present and the offender uses or threatens to use force" (Klaus 2004). Carjacking may include other offenses such as kidnapping, robbery, rape, and homicide. Other types of motor vehicles are also hijacked. For example, in Albuquerque, New Mexico, an ambulance was reportedly hijacked with a sleeping ambulance worker inside (*Associated Press* 2014, February 8).

At present, little is known about carjacking as a social process; the socioeconomic status (SES), demographic, and social characteristics of the perpetrators and of the victims, the variety of methods, and the social impact of these crimes. Investigators are only beginning to conduct research on crimes that combine carjacking and kidnapping. In addition, the statistics on carjacking are of very poor quality, since there has been very little uniform reporting of these crimes. As a result, much of the information on carjacking is an approximation. "At present, it is not possible to determine the incidence of carjacking with any degree of accuracy" (Young and Borzycki 2008).

Carjacking has become a social and economic problem both in the US, and around the world. As a result, a wide variety of counter measure have been and are being developed by motor vehicle manufacturers, car alarm companies, inventors, legislators, law enforcement agencies, security/safety experts, employers, and others.

This chapter analyzes carjacking and other related offenses and illustrates key findings with cases from the Carjacking and Kidnapping Project (CKP).

Emergence of Carjacking as a Crime

The first known carjacking incident occurred in March 1912, when the Bonnot Gang, a French anarchist gang, carjacked a Dion Bouton, a high-end vehicle, in the Forest of Senart, which is located 22 km south-east of Paris. During the carjacking,

S. Morewitz, *Kidnapping and Violence*,
https://doi.org/10.1007/978-1-4939-2117-1_11

an armed chauffeur and young secretary were killed (Wikipedia-Bonnot Gang. Retrieved from en.wikipedia.org/wiki/Bonnot_Gang).

The first use of the term, "carjacking," has been attributed to an article written by Scott Bowles and E.J. Mitchell in *The Detroit News* on August 28, 1991 (Pulitzer 1996). They reported the murder of 22-year-old Ruth Wahl, a drugstore cashier in Detroit, who refused to give up her Suzuki Sidekick to the carjackers. Many other carjacking incidents had been previously reported, but this was the first time that the term "carjacking" was used (Williams 1993).

Vehicle Theft and Carjackings

In major US cities at the start of the 1970s, thieves stole unoccupied motor vehicles and sold them to so-called "chop shops" where the vehicles were broken up and then sold as parts to consumers or to automobile dealerships. Stolen vehicle parts were also sold to repair shops for resale to customers (Finn 2000; Hill 1998, April). Incidents of carjackings increased in the 1980s and 1990s, when improved vehicle security measures reduced the success rate of traditional methods of unoccupied vehicle theft.

Prevalence of Carjackings

The prevalence of carjackings varies in different countries and fluctuates over time. Because of the relatively low annual incidence of carjackings, researchers had to combine the National Crime Victimization Survey (NCVS) time periods in order to obtain an adequate sample size (Karmen 2010). Klaus (2004) estimated that in the US, between 1993 and 2002, an annual average of approximately 34,000 carjacking incidents with 38,000 carjacking victimizations took place. (This equates to 93 carjackings per day.) Annual carjacking rates fell from 2.1 per 10,000 persons during the years 1993–1998 to 1.3 per 10,000 persons during the years 1997–2002 (Klaus 2004). (Additional NCVS reports on carjacking have not been issued since 2004.). Carjacking represented about 3% of all car thefts in the US during the period 1997–2002, (Young and Borzycki 2008; CIUS 2011). In contrast, it is estimated that, between 1998 and 2001, carjackings constituted only about 1% of vehicle thefts in the UK (Levesley et al. 2004; Young and Borzycki 2008).

In South Africa, 14,999 motor vehicles were "hijacked" between January 2000 and December 2000. This corresponds to 25 carjackings per day (Crime Information Analysis Centre 2000; Davis 2003). Carjackings increased in South Africa between the 2002/2003 and 2008/2009 periods (Davis 2003; Burger 2009).

Media Portrayal of Carjackings

In the US, the UK, Canada, and Australia the media use the term: "carjacking." The same crime is described in the Philippines as "carnapping," and in South Africa as "hijacking."

In movies, television, video games, and other media, individuals are portrayed carjacking vehicles (Karmen 2010). For example: in the 2011 movie *Carjacked,* a single mother and her child were carjacked by a bank robber. Also, in the 16th episode of the television series, *Hawaii Five-O*, police detective Danny William's ex-wife and daughter were carjacked. Critics have asserted that the media have glamorized carjackings, and this probably encouraged some individuals to commit similar crimes.

Once this phenomenon had a name, the news media began to use it to describe high-profile and sensational cases (Karmen 2010). The media coverage of these crimes is disproportional to their actual prevalence. Based on a review of 682 articles concerning 339 carjackings in Louisiana from January 1993 to the end of June 2002, Cherbonneau and Copes (2003) found that the media devoted greater attention to carjackings which involved a death or injury than to routine cases with less serious outcomes.

CKP Case 001A illustrates the extensive media coverage of the carjacking, kidnapping, rape, and murder of a young couple from Knoxville, Tennessee. Media coverage of these sensational crimes can lead to so-called "moral panics" in which the public believes erroneously that these crimes are epidemic and demands new laws and strong law enforcement responses to deal with them (Cherbonneau and Copes 2003).

Motivation of Carjackers

Carjackings are committed for diverse reasons (Jacobs 2012; Davis 2003). Carjackers may be motivated by financial rewards, especially in the theft of high-value vehicles. In a small, qualitative study of carjacking in South Africa, the thieves indicated that they had targeted expensive vehicles such as a new Mercedes Benz or BMW (Davis 2003). In CKP Case 002B, a Mercedes Benz was carjacked.

In addition to high-value vehicles, some motor vehicles of certain popular makes, models, and years may be more likely to be carjacked than others. Research by the New Jersey Department of Law and Public Safety (2000) showed that in 1999, Ford vehicles were the most frequently carjacked vehicles (14%) in New Jersey, with the 1995 model year most frequently being selected (11%).

Thieves who are desperate for immediate money may commit carjackings (Burke and O'Rear 1993). However, since crimes such as armed robbery result in more immediate financial gain, investigators are unsure as to which group is more financially desperate (Jacobs, Topalli, and Wright 2003).

Thieves may carjack vehicles to facilitate their escape from other crimes. In these instances, the make, model and year are less important, because the criminals' primary interest is to leave the crime scene. In 2012, the perpetrators of the Boston Marathon bombing, carjacked a motor vehicle and kidnapped the driver in order to escape (Moskowitz 2013).

In many combined carjacking and kidnapping cases, the victims were forced to drive to automated teller machines (ATMs) and banks where, after withdrawing their money, they were robbed. In *US v. Singleton*, 16 F.3d 1419 (5th Cir. 1994), the robbers forced the victim to slide to the passenger side of his vehicle and then they drove to an ATM, where they forced the victim to withdraw two hundred dollars. In CKP Case 004D, the victim was carjacked and then forced to drive the two robbers to an ATM where they withdrew the victim's money. In CKP Case 00E5, two thieves carjacked a young man and forced him to drive them to a residence to buy cocaine.

On some occasions, the carjacker may seize a vehicle without realizing that someone, usually a child, is asleep in the back seat (New Jersey Department of Law and Public Safety 2000). In CKP Case 003C the thief stole a vehicle with a seven-month-year old infant in the back seat.

Potential carjackers may be influenced by the values of their peer group on instrumental violence, spontaneity, hedonism, ostentatious displays of wealth on the street, and excessive spending (Jacobs, Topalli, and Wright 2003; Jacobs 2012; Miethe and Sousa 2009; Young and Borzycki 2008). According to Burke and O'Rear (1993), some perpetrators carry out carjackings because of their own arrogance and desire to start a fight.

The perpetrator's impulsiveness or desire for thrills also may be the motivation for a carjacking. For example, in CKP 007J, two adolescents went on a "reckless ride" after carjacking a vehicle and forcing the elderly female driver into the car trunk.

Thieves may decide to commit a carjacking based upon their belief that the potential victim will be easy to control (Burke and O'Rear 1993; Copes et al. 2012; Jacobs 2012; Davis 2003). In South Africa, many carjackers attempt to determine if their potential victim is armed and/or can be easily overpowered. Yet, in other instances, they seem to target any car that enters their field of vision (Davis 2003). For example, in *US v. Singleton*, 16 F.3d 1419 (5th Cir. 1994), the thieves reportedly just liked a red 1991 Nissan Sentra entering a supermarket parking lot and selected it as their target.

Vehicle Security Technology

Thieves needs to be aware of and able to circumvent continuing technological improvements in vehicle security. They may use fraud, robbery, or burglary to obtain motor vehicle keys; they may also rewire the ignition or "hotwire" certain vehicles (Copes and Cherbonneau 2006; McDonold 2011, July). Some criminals now use electronic devices that unlock car doors. In CKP Case 002B, two thieves found the keys to a vehicle and then carjacked it and abducted the male victim.

Continuing improvements in anti-theft vehicle security have made many traditional methods of auto theft obsolete. In the US, the auto theft victimization rate (per 1,000 households) peaked in 1993, and by 2010 had declined by 74% (Lauritsen and Rezey 2013). This decline in vehicle theft may inadvertently have increased the probability of carjacking (Davis 2003; Clarke and Harris 1992; Miethe and Sousa 2009; McDonold 2011, July). This shift from unoccupied vehicle theft to carjacking is called functional displacement (Davis 2003).

Some thieves may consider whether a potential target has an anti-carjacking device such as a satellite tracking and recovery system. However, their awareness of these devices is not always a factor in their target selection. In several cases, the perpetrators indicated that although they did not know if their target vehicles had these anti-carjacking systems, they proceeded with the carjacking anyway (Davis 2003).

Lifestyle, Routine Activities, and Hot Spots

Friday and Wellford (1997);reported that some lifestyle and routine activities increased the risks of being carjacked. The NCVS findings also showed similar results (Klaus 2004).

In the US and South Africa, carjacking incidents often occur in open areas such as streets or near public transportation (Klaus 2004; Jacobs 2012; Davis 2003). According to the NCVS report, 44% of the cases occurred on the street or other open area or near a bus, train, or other public transportation, and 24% of the incidents occurred in parking lots, garages, or in proximity to commercial establishments (Klaus 2004). In CKP 004D, the carjacking took place as the victim was driving into a gas station. The carjacking in CKP 003C happened outside a store.

In the US, between 1993 and 2002, 93% of the nonfatal carjackings took place in cities or suburban areas and the remainder took place in rural areas (Klaus 2004). Similarly, an investigation of carjackings in South Africa found that the crimes often took place in the inner city or in central business areas (Hennop, Potgieter, and Jefferson 2001). In the CKP, both urban and suburban areas were the sites of carjackings.

The NCVS report concluded that 63% of the nonfatal carjacking cases in the US occurred within five miles of the victim's residence, 17% of the carjackings took place near or at the victim's residence, whereas only 4% happened more than 50 miles away from their residence (Klaus 2004). In CKP Case 002B, the carjacking occurred in the victim's driveway; in CKP Case 00E5, the carjacking occurred at the victim's apartment.

In the US, carjackings were more likely to occur in frequent crime areas (Jacobs, Topalli, and Wright 2003). These areas can become "hot spots" during certain times of the day or night, especially between 6 PM and 6 AM (Klaus 2004; Jacobs, Topalli, and Wright 2003). Individuals, who because of their lifestyle, work patterns, or other daily activities, drive in these hot-spot areas during these hours are at increased risk of carjackings. For example, in Fort Worth, Texas, 75% of all carjackings took place in one district. Similarly, two areas in the District of Columbia were associated with 50% of the carjackings.

Specific roads and highways also present higher risks of carjacking. In South Africa, road signs posted in some "hot spots" warn drivers about hijacking.

In the US, 68% of the carjackings took place between 6 PM and 6 AM (Klaus 2004). Researchers in South Africa also found that carjacking incidents were more likely to take place at their use by carjackers (Klaus, 2004; Jacobs, 2012; Burke and O'Rear, 1993). In CKP Case 00E5, the carjackings occurred in the evening.

In *US v. Singleton*, 16 F.3d 1419 (5th Cir. 1994), one of the perpetrators had a 0.38 caliber pistol and while another one carried a 0.22 caliber pistol. In CKP Case 006F, the robber brandished a firearm, forced the victim out of his vehicle and then stole his money. The thief also jumped into the victim's vehicle and sped away for a short time, but then returned and demanded that the victim drive him to a specific location.

Carjackers often rely on firearms to make conditional death threats, e.g., "Give me your car or I'll kill you." In *Holloway v. US*, 526 US 1, a co-offender pointed a firearm at the victim and threatened to shoot him if he did not give up his automobile and keys.

Carjackers also may use firearms as blunt instruments as a means of gaining control over the victim. In CKP Case 001A, one of the carjackers hit the victim in the face with a handgun to prevent him from escaping.

Similarly, in South Africa, carjackers used firearms and other weapons to commit carjackings. Hennop, Potgieter, and Jefferson (2001) showed that in South Africa between 1995 and 1998, the number of carjackers who used firearms increased by more than 55%.

Socio-Economic Status (SES) Factors

Some researchers have suggested that SES factors such as high levels of poverty and unemployment may increase the probability of carjackings (Klaus 2004; Davis 2003; Burke and O'Rear 1993). In South Africa, the high rates of poverty and unemployment may be associated with the high rate of carjackings (Davis 2003). Similarly, in the US, such SES conditions may be linked to these crimes (Young and Borzycki 2008; Burke and O'Rear 1993). For example: in the US, the victims of carjackings were more likely to live and/or work in the neighborhood and to have household incomes below $50,000 (Klaus 2004).

Social and Demographic Characteristics of Carjackers

Studies have described the social and demographic characteristics of perpetrators and victims involved in carjackings (Klaus 2004; Jacobs 2012; New Jersey Department of Law and Public Safety 2000; Friday and Wellford 1997; Davis 2003). The NCVS results showed that 56% of the carjackings in the US involved more than one offender (Klaus 2004). Likewise, Jacobs (2012) notes that these crimes often are carried out by multiple thieves and that the perpetrators and victims do not know each other. In South Africa, carjacking is usually a group activity in which two to three males often participate (Davis 2003).

When carjackers operate in groups, they can better control the victims and thus achieve their goals. In CKP Case 001A, five carjackers were involved in the carjacking, robbery, rape, and murder of a young couple. In CKP Case 004D, two carjackers worked as a team to prevent the victim from escaping out the passenger-side door.

The NCVS study showed that between 1993 and 2002, 93% of the carjackers were male, 3% were female, and 3% involved a mixed group of males and females. Females alone perpetrated 3% of the incidents (Klaus 2004). In CKP Case 006F, a male carjacked a middle-age man and then stole money from him. In CKP Case 001A, three males and 1 female were arrested for carjacking and other offenses.

In the NCVS report 56% of the carjackers were identified by the victims as African-American, 21% were identified as white, 16% were identified as other racial/ethnic groups such as Asian or Native American, and 7% were identified as either mixed race or unknown race/ethnicity (Klaus 2004). In CKP Case 001A, all of the suspects were identified as African American. In CKP Case 004D, the two suspects were identified as African American. In CKP case 010A, a Hispanic was identified as the suspect.

The New Jersey Department of Law and Public Safety (2000) found that 94% of the known perpetrators were male and 81% were African American. Thirty-eight percent of the known perpetrators were between 20 and 24 years old.

Social and Demographic Characteristics of Victims

In the US, in 90% of the carjacking incidents involved a single victim (Klaus 2004). For example, CKP Case 002B had one carjacking victim.

In South Africa, the presence of more than one adult in a car seemed to inhibit some carjackers from targeting that vehicle (Davis 2003).

In the NCVS report on carjackings in the US, the rate of victimization by carjacking in each group was higher for males (2.3 per 10,000 persons) than for females (1.1 per 10,000 persons) (Klaus 2004). In the CKP cases, both females and males were carjacked.

The NCVS data revealed that African Americans had a higher rate of carjacking victimization (3.3 per 10,000 persons) than whites (1.5 per 10,000 persons) and Asian or Native Americans (1.0 per 10,000 persons). Persons of Hispanic origin had a higher rate of carjacking victimization (2.6 per 10,000 persons) than those of non-Hispanic origin (1.6 per 10,000 persons) (Klaus 2004).

In the New Jersey Department of Law and Public Safety (2000) investigation, 71% of the victims were male and 51% were white. 21% of the victims were between 20 and 24 years old.

Carjacking as a Transactional Process

Given the ability of motorists to drive away from attempted carjacking incidents, perpetrators are faced with the task of controlling their victims during this dangerous process. As in other types of robbery, carjackers use coercion in the form of threatened or actual violence to control their victims and achieve their objectives. Carjackers develop crime scripts, which they memorize and use as guides for their behavioral patterns. These scripts also include possible responses to situational contingencies. Carjackers may scan potential targets and select those who would be least likely to resist (Copes et al. 2012).

When perpetrators select a target, they use copresence, e.g., they must approach their victim in an unthreatening manner until they are close enough to act without their target escaping (Jacobs 2012). Perpetrators may create an illusion of normalcy by hiding the fact they are about to pounce, or they may "blitz" the target by using shock and force.

CKP Case 002B illustrates the use of the blitz method for establishing copresence. In this carjacking incident, the two suspects approached the victim and demanded his money. In CKP Case 004D, the suspects established copresence by creating an illusion of normalcy. The suspects reportedly knocked on the vehicle's window to get the driver's attention. The offender then allegedly brandished a weapon and demanded that the driver moves to the passenger seat.

Determining how to control the carjacking victims can be a problem for the perpetrators. In CKP Case 007J, five teenage suspects carjacked an elderly female victim's vehicle and locked her in the trunk. In CKP Case 004D, the two suspects reportedly put duct tape on the male victim's eyes and drove him around for a while before they stopped the vehicle and fled.

In carjacking incidents, the perpetrators may use firearms and/or other weapons to make death threats (Morewitz 2008). In CKP 00E5, the suspect allegedly forced one of the two victims into a house and threatened to kill him if he left the kitchen table. In CKP Case 007J, two adolescent girls reportedly threatened to kill their victim if she told anyone about the incident.

Carjacking Outcomes

In the NCVS report, Klaus (2004) analyzed both attempted and completed carjacking incidents and found that at night, 42% of the crimes were completed, while during the day, 50% of the crimes were completed. In approximately 67% of all of the cases, the victim resisted the perpetrator. Among those victims who resisted, 24% threatened, chased or attempted to capture the carjacker; while 33% fled the scene and called for assistance and/or attempted to obtain assistance from others.

The elderly victim in CKP Case 007J repeatedly banged on her vehicle trunk after being forced into the trunk of her car during the hijacking and kidnapping. In CKP Case 00E5, the two carjacking victims drove to a police station and gave law enforcement personnel a description of the suspect.

Although offenders frequently use firearms and other weapons to carry out carjackings, most victims do not sustain injuries that require hospitalization. According to the NCVS results, 24% of the victims of nonfatal carjackings were injured. Among victims of completed carjackings, 32% were injured, and among victims of attempted carjackings, 17% were injured. Between 1993 and 2002, only one percent of all the victims of carjacking in the US sustained injuries that necessitated hospitalization. Approximately 14% of carjacking victims received treatment in emergency rooms and were discharged (Klaus 2004).

Six percent of carjacking victims received treatment at the scene of the crime or in a physician's office. Among injured carjacking victims, about 4% did not obtain medical assistance. Nine percent of victims had serious injuries such as gunshot and knife injuries, fractures, and internal injuries. Fifteen percent of injuries were minor. In CKP Case 004D, the carjacking victim was hit the face with a handgun, but the status of his facial injuries was not reported. In CKP Case 009G, one of the carjacking victims was shot by the suspect and then rushed to the hospital for emergency treatment. However, in the CKP, most of the carjacking victims were not physically injured.

Although carjackings rarely result in the victims' death, the victims are traumatized by the event and can develop post-traumatic stress disorder and/or suffer from anxiety, depression, and other psychological problems (Jacobs 2012; Fisher 1995; Klaus 2004). In CKP Case 009G, the carjacking victims, a father, mother, and their children, were in an ordeal that involved abduction by an armed carjacker and the carjackers' shooting of the father. In CKP 0075, the carjacking victim was threatened with death by the suspects who locked her the trunk of her car for two days without food or her medication.

Although homicides resulting from auto theft, including carjackings, are rare, some carjacking victims have been murdered. For example, in *US v. Singleton*, 16 F.3d 1419 (5th Cir. 1994), the carjacking victim, William Mullers, was killed in Hammond, Louisiana on November 15, 1992. Statistics from the Uniform Crime Reports showed that annually there are approximately 27 auto thefts that result in homicide (Cherbonneau and Copes 2003). However, in a 1999 study of 391 carjacking incidents reported to law enforcement in New Jersey, no homicides were reported (New Jersey Department of Law and Public Safety 2000).

Political and Cultural Conditions

Political and cultural factors may influence the prevalence of carjackings. For example, Davis (2003) suggested that the long-term political system of apartheid in South Africa and its resulting culture of violence, may have contributed to the high rates of carjacking there.

Countries with a high prevalence of official corruption can facilitate carjackings. The police and other officials may be involved in carjackings either directly by planning and carrying out the crimes themselves, or indirectly by ensuring that the charges are dismissed, dropped, or reduced. Countries with large-scale illicit drug manufacturing, distribution, and use may have high rates of carjackings, homicide, and related offenses (Davis 2003).

International Crime Groups and Organizations

Crime groups, drug cartels, and other criminal organizations may carry out carjackings as a primary criminal goal or to facilitate their other activities such as kidnapping, homicide, and drug crimes (Davis 2003). Carjackings also increase during periods of anomie such as during natural disasters in which societal norms break down.

Ineffective Border Controls

Carjackings are facilitated in countries with ineffective border controls. Where geographic factors, such as the existence of large areas of desert and lengthy borders, there may be difficulty in controlling smuggling operations, chop shop activities, and other illegal border activities related to carjackings. In addition, corruption among border control officials, and inadequate training and supervision of border control personnel, enable carjackers to move the stolen vehicles and/or the vehicle parts across borders.

Anti-carjacking and Anti-vehicle Theft Legislation

Various countries have enacted anti-carjacking and anti-vehicle theft legislation. The US Congress enacted the Motor Vehicle Theft Law Enforcement Act, Pub. L. No. 98-547, 98 Stat. 2754 (1984) (Finn 2000). As a result, the US Department of Transportation (USDOT) created a vehicle theft standard that required automobile manufacturers to apply identifying numbers or symbols on selected parts of passenger vehicles that the USDOT considered high-risk vehicles.

In the US, the federal Anti-Car Theft Act of 1992 (H.R. 4542, 102nd Congress (1991–1992) included the prohibition of carjacking and imposed stiffer punishment for the offense (Anti-Car Theft Act of 1992 (H.R. 4542, 102nd Congress (1991–1992); Karmen, 2010). The Anti-Car Theft Act of 1992 required the USDOT to mandate that automobile manufacturers apply these identifying numbers or symbols to an additional 50% of their remaining vehicle models by December 1994 without regard to the vehicle model's theft rate. The act also mandated the US Department of Justice (USDOJ) to evaluate the effectiveness of implementing the new anti-theft labels standard by 1997. The USDOJ required that if the new standard reduced chop-shop activities and vehicle theft rates then the act would extend to all remaining vehicle models by December 1997. This 1992 law contributed to a major drop in the auto theft victimization rate (per 1,000 US households) which peaked in 1993 and declined by 74% by 2010 (Lauritsen and Rezey 2013).

States such as California, Delaware, and Indiana have specific statutes prohibiting carjacking. In other states, such as Alabama and Alaska, the crimes may be prosecuted under general robbery statutes. State statutes define the offense and describe the elements that must be proven in order for an individual to be convicted. For example, the California statute requires the following four elements: (1) an individual possessed a vehicle; (2) the carjacker took that vehicle from that individual's immediate presence or from the passenger's immediate presence; (3) the taking of the vehicle was against the victim's will by force or fear; and (4) the carjacker intended to deprive the individual of that vehicle temporarily or permanently. The California law also has several legal defenses to carjacking: the offender did not employ force or fear; had consent to take another individual's vehicle; and/or was wrongfully convicted based on mistaken identity.

State laws can determine punishment based on the severity of the offense and provide different prison sentences and penalties based on that classification. Florida has a carjacking statute that provides enhanced penalties for the use of a deadly weapon when committing the carjacking. In California, the carjacking statute has enhanced penalties if the offender injures a victim, uses a gun, perpetrates the carjacking to benefit a gang, or abducts a person during the carjacking. Carjacking in California is also a "strike" under California's three strikes law. Under this law, the offenders must serve at least 85% of their sentence before they are eligible for parole. In Georgia, the carjacking statute has felony penalties with a minimum of 10 years in prison and a fine of $10,000. In Louisiana, the carjacking statute calls for a prison term of two to 20 years with hard labor. The carjacking statute has felony penalties for up to 30 years in prison.

State laws in the US regarding carjacking can specify other conditions. For example, in Louisiana, the carjacking statute allows the victim to use lethal force against the perpetrator (Kane 1997, August 24). Similarly, Arizona allows a carjacking victim to use lethal force as part of its definition of justifiable homicide (CNN US, no date). In Florida, a state with a significant tourist industry, a law was passed in 1993 that prohibited company logos and license plates that made it obvious that a vehicle was a rental or leased vehicle. This law was enacted after an increasing number of mostly international tourists had been carjacked in Florida.

In the US, media coverage of high-profile and sensational cases led to public outrage over carjackings (Kane 1997, August 24). In one such case, Pamela Basu and her 2-year-old daughter were carjacked in Maryland in the fall of 1992. Two carjackers forced Basu from her vehicle. In a struggle to protect her daughter, Basu became entangled in the seatbelt outside the vehicle. Basu was dragged for almost two miles before she was separated from the seat belt. A short time later, Basu's daughter, who had remained in her car seat, was thrown from the vehicle. Basu died from her injuries, but her daughter was uninjured. Extensive media coverage of the Basu carjacking and other high-profile cases such as the carjacking death of Ruth Wahl in 1991 helped to support the need for the enactment of the Anti-Car Theft Act of 1992 (H.R. 4542, 102nd Congress (1991–1992).

Introduced by New York Representative Charles E. Schumer in the Spring 1992 session of Congress, the act making carjacking a federal offense was signed into law by President George Herbert Bush. This federal law was authorized under the commerce clause of the US Constitution, which allows Congress to regulate issues involving interstate commerce (Goldberg 1994). According to this federal law, if a person possessing a firearm (defined under Section 921 of this statute), takes a motor vehicle that has been transported, shipped, or received in interstate or foreign commerce from an individual or in the presence of another person by force, violence, coercion, or attempts to do so, shall be: (1) fined under the statute or incarcerated for not more than 15 years, or both. (2) fined under this statue or be imprisoned for not more than 25 years, or both, if serious bodily injury occurs, and (3) fined under this title or incarcerated for any number of years up to life, or both, if death occurs. Under the act, US Congress authorized the Federal Bureau of Investigation and the US Attorneys to work with local and state officials in investigating these offenses. Under this federal statute, some of the crimes would be prosecuted in federal court.

The first case that was prosecuted under the new law involved perpetrators who used a stolen firearm (originally purchased legally) to murder two young men in Osceola County, Florida (Curtis, 1994, January 30). The defendants consisted of four young men who were members of the "Jack Boys," a gang from the lowest SES area of Auburndale, Florida.

Some critics of the Anti-Car Theft Act of 1992 (H.R. 4542, 102nd Congress (1991–1992), have argued that the commerce clause should not be applied to carjacking (Goldberg 1994). Critics note that just because an auto manufacturer has transported a vehicle on an interstate basis should not mean that the federal government has the authority to prosecute crimes that occur within a state.

In *US v. Cortner*, the Middle District of Tennessee ruled that the act was unconstitutional. This court found that just because a vehicle traveled interstate one time does not mean that the commerce clause should apply (*US v. Cortner*, No. 3:93-00009, US D.Ct., M.D. Tenn, decided Oct. 19, 1993). The court noted that by following this incorrect reasoning, the US Congress would have the power to regulate any activity using a bicycle or even walking.

However, in *US v. Watson*, the District Court for the Eastern District of Pennsylvania upheld the constitutionality of the Anti-Car Theft Act of 1992 (H.R. 4542, 102nd Congress (1991–1992) (*US v. Watson*, 815 F. Supp. 827 (1993); Goldberg 1994). That court did not challenge the US Supreme Court's acceptance of the right of the US Congress to regulate travel involving interstate commerce. Likewise, in *US v. Eskridge*, the District Court for the Eastern District of Wisconsin, the court did not question the broadening power of Congress to regulate carjacking under the commerce clause (*US v. Eskridge*, 818 F. Supp. 259 (1993); Goldberg 1994).

The Double Jeopardy Clause of the US Constitution has also been used to question the constitutionality of the Anti-Car Theft Act of 1992 (H.R. 4542, 102nd Congress (1991–1992). Since both it and 18 USC.A. carry different punishments for the same offence, under the Double Jeopardy Clause, no person should be put in jeopardy of life or limb for the same offense. Double jeopardy could occur because an individual who used a firearm during a carjacking could face punishment under both the Anti-Car Theft Act of 1992 (H.R. 4542, 102nd Congress (1991–1992) and also mandatory punishment under 18 USC.A., 924 (c). This latter statute prohibits carrying or using a firearm in the commission of a violent offense.

However, in *US v. Singleton*, 16 F.3d 1419 (5th Cir. 1994), the Fifth Circuit Court of Appeals held that the US Congress intended to impose cumulative punishments on offenders who carried or used firearms in committing carjacking crimes.

After *US v. Singleton*, 16 F.3d 1419 (5th Cir. 1994), the House of Representatives and Senate debated amendments to the Anti-Car Theft Act of 1992, resulting in the Violent Crime Control and Law Enforcement Act of 1994, Pub. L. No. 103–322, 108 Stat. 2119, which was signed into law by President Bill Clinton (Pub. L. 103–322; 108 Stat. 1796). This law made a murder that occurred as a result of carjacking a capital offense (Karmen 2010). In addition, this statute omitted the phrase, "possessing a firearm, as defined under section 921 of the title" and replaced it with the phrase, "with the intent to cause death or serious bodily harm." This second change eliminated the double jeopardy issue.

Another question that has been litigated is whether the Anti-Car Theft Act of 1992 (H.R. 4542, 102nd Congress (1991–1992) should apply to carjacking crimes that involve conditional intent of harming the victim. In a 7–2 decision, the US Supreme Court, in *Holloway v. US*, 526 US 1, held that the federal anti-carjacking law does apply to suspects who make conditional threats of harming carjacking victims. The federal statute applies to cases involving conditional threats since the law has the element of *mens rea*, which refers to the defendant's state of mind when the suspect carjacks the vehicle. The US Supreme Court ruled that the federal law applies in these cases if the suspect had the intent to kill or severely harm the carjacking victim if this was necessary to carjack the vehicle. The high court determined a reasonable interpretation of the federal law is that it applies to cases involving both conditional and unconditional intent (*Holloway v. US*, 526 US 1, 1999; Norborg 2000).

Criminal Justice Responses and Outcomes in the US

In the early 1990s, police departments throughout the US began to keep records of carjacking episodes separate from the category, "robberies of all types" (Karmen 2010). [Law enforcement personnel were to investigate carjacking crimes based on standard procedures and apprehend and arrest suspects based on their investigations and cooperation of local community residents and others who have witnessed the crimes.] In CKP Case 006F, the police reportedly used several leads to apprehend and arrest the suspect about three hours after the initial offenses.

In some jurisdictions in the US, law enforcement personnel may develop task forces to deal with the increased rates of carjacking in their communities (Williams 1993; Burke and O'Rear 1993). Williams (1993) describes the ways in which a Detroit Police Department carjacking task force was designed to enhance law enforcement responses to carjacking. The task force was designed to provide a community education-based, comprehensive approach to carjacking prevention, enhance the patrol force, identify chronic perpetrators, and improve the arrest and prosecution of carjackers. The task force consisted of patrol officers and personnel from the commercial auto theft and robbery units.

Burke and O'Rear (1993) suggest that these specialized tasks forces can assist law enforcement in identifying and apprehending offenders. They also assert that departments that use a special carjacking *modus operandi* file can be successful in targeting carjackers.

Carjacking suspects are charged based on the evidence and the relevant laws. In CKP Case 006F, the suspect was charged with carjacking, first-degree kidnapping with a firearm, first-degree robbery, and larceny. Some of the adolescent suspects in CKP Case 007J, who reportedly carjacked an 89-year-old woman and locked her in the trunk for two days, were charged with robbery, carjacking, kidnapping, and conspiracy. Other teenage suspects were charged with kidnapping and receiving stolen property.

Researchers are evaluating the impact of statutes and the courts in influencing sentence length and other criminal justice outcomes. One area of research is determining the extent to which demographic factors such as age and race influence criminal sentencing outcomes. Corley and Hawkins (2006) analyzed sentencing outcomes after the implementation of the Michigan Firearms Statute. Based on the sentencing outcome data from 54 circuit courts in Michigan in 2001, the authors found that younger offenders who were convicted of carjacking were sentenced to 11.5 fewer months than older offenders convicted for the same offense. The investigators also found that individuals who had been convicted for carjacking and who had a prior jail experience had 94.9 months added to their sentence.

Carjacking and Civil Law

Carjacking victims have file lawsuits against companies for alleged breach of their duty to maintain safe premises. For example, a female victim of carjacking filed a lawsuit against a hotel in Landover, Maryland. After the plaintiff was assaulted and carjacked in the parking lot of the hotel, she alleged that the hotel had breached its duty to maintain safe premises for hotel guests (*Security Law Newsletter* 2012, May).

Preventing Carjackings and Related Crimes

With increased public concern over vehicle theft, especially carjackings, and the passage of laws against such crimes, individuals, and organizations such as the auto insurance industry continue to seek ways to avoid vehicle theft and carjackings. Individuals should avoid driving in dangerous areas and driving alone. It is important to be vigilant while driving; to lock the car doors; to drive with the windows up; only park in areas that have effective lighting; and be cautious when approaching or leaving the vehicles (LAPD 2014); McGoey 2013; *Traffic Safety* 2006, May).

Despite these safety tips, there are no definitive ways to prevent carjackings. Drivers must be aware of their surroundings upon starting and stopping their vehicle and when they park in unfamiliar locations. Regardless of the precautions taken by drivers, the unpredictability and low probability of a carjacking limit the driver's ability to anticipate such a crime. In addition, potential victims face difficulty in safely opposing carjackers (Karmen 2010).

Nevertheless, carjacking victims have been criticized for not being vigilant enough while driving, especially when multitasking, e.g., listening to music, texting, or talking on the phone, or unloading and loading packages from their vehicle. Drivers must also be aware of carjacking traps such as being "bumped" in a staged accident (LAPD 2014; McGoey 2013).

References

Associated Press. (2014c). Canadian police rescue 5 children from online porn. http://www.nytimes.com/aponline/2014/06/19/world/ap-cn-canada-online-child-porn-sweep.html?ref=news&_r=0.

Burger, J. (2009). Worrying trends. The official 2008/09 South African crime statistics. South Africa Crime Quarterly 30: 3–11.

Burke, T.W., & O'Rear, C.E. (1993). Armed carjacking: A violent problem in need of a solution. The Police Chief 60(1): 18–24.

Cherbonneau, M.G., & Copes, H. (2003). Media construction of carjacking: A content analysis of newspaper articles from 1993–2002. J Crime & Justice 26(2): 1–21.

CIUS.(2011). Crime in the United States 2011, US Dept. of Justice, FBI, Uniform Crime Reports, 1992–2011, Table 1. http://www.fbi.gov/about-us/cjis/ucr/crime-in-the-u.s/2011/crime-in-the-US-2011/tables/table-1.

Clarke, R.V., & Harris, P.M. (1992). Auto theft and its prevention. In M. Tonry (Ed.), Crime and Justice: A Review of Research. 16, 1–54.

Copes, H., & Cherbonneau, M. (2006). The key to auto theft. Emerging methods of auto theft from the offenders' perspective. Brit J Criminol 46: 917–934.

Copes, H., Hochstetler, & Cherbonneau, M. (2012). Getting the upper hands: Scripts for managing victim in carjackings. J Research Crime Delinq 49(2): 249–268.

Corley, C.J., & Hawkins, H.C. (2006). The Michigan Firearms Statute: Are there racial/ethnic implications? J Ethnicity in Crim Justice 4(3): 67–79.

Crime Information Analysis Centre, South African Police Service. (2000). The incidence of serious crime in South Africa: January—December 2000. Pretoria, South Africa: South African Police Service.

Curtis, H. P. (1994, January 30). Youths steal guns to steal youths' lives. The Orlando Sentinel. http://articles.orlandosentinel.com/1994–01-30/news/9401300447_1_p....

Davis, L. (2003). Carjacking—Insights from South Africa to a new crime problem. Austral & New Zealand J of Criminolology 36(2): 173–191.

Finn, P. (2000). Labeling automobile parts to combat theft. FBI Law Enforcement Bulletin, 10–14.

Fisher, R.L. (1995). Carjackers: A study of forcible motor vehicle thieves among new commitments, 1985–1993. Albany, NY: New York Department of Correctional Services.

Friday, S.D.C., & Wellford, C. (1997). Carjacking: A descriptive analysis of carjacking in four Sates, Preliminary Report. Rockville, MD: National Institute of Justice/NCJRS.

Goldberg, S.B. (1994). Carjacking and the commerce clause. ABA Journal 80(1): 1–3. http://web.ebscohost.com.proxylib.csueastbay.edu/ehost/detaill?vid=6&....

Hennop, E., Potgieter, J., & Jefferson, C. (2001). The role of firearms in crime in South Africa: A detailed analysis of police dockets. Monograph no. 55. Cape Town, South Africa: Institute for Security Studies. http://www.iss.co.za/Pubs/Monographs/No55/Chap12.html.

Hill, P. (1998, April). Preventing car theft in Australia: "Golden opportunity" for partnerships. Trends & Issues in Crime & Crim Just, 86, 1–6.

Jacobs, B. A. (2012). Carjacking and copresence. J of Res in Crime & Delinq 49(4): 471–488.

Jacobs, B.A., Topalli, V., & Wright, R. (2003). Carjacking, street life, and offender motivation. Brit J Criminology 43: 678–688.

Kane, G. (1997, August 24). Lousiana carjack law allows justice, not lynching. The Baltimore Sun. http://www.articles.baltimoresun.com/1997–08-24/news/1997236075_/_carjackers-pasu-louisiana.

Karmen, A. (2010). Crime victims. An introduction to victimology. Belmont, CA: Wadsworth Cengage Learning.

Klaus, P. (2004). Carjacking, 1993–2002. Washington, D.C.: US Bureau of Justice Statistics.

LAPD, Los Angeles Police Department. (2014). Carjacking. The Los Angeles Police Department official website. http://www.lapdonline.org/crime_prevention/content_basic_view/1368.

Lauritsen, J.L., & Rezey, M.L. (2013). Measuring the prevalence of crime with the National Crime Victimization Survey. Bureau of Justice Statistics, US Dept. of Justice, NCJ 241656 http://www.bjs.gov/content/pub/pdf/mpcncvs.pdf.

Levesley, T., Braun, G., Wilkinson, M., & Powell, C. (2004). Emerging methods of car theft–theft of keys. Home Office Findings 239. London: Home Office. http://www.homeoffice.gov.uk/rds/pdfs04/r239.pdf.

McDonold, C.T. (2011, July). The changing face of vehicle theft. Police Chief 78(7): 40–45.

McGoey, C.E. (2013). Carjacking facts—Robbery prevention advice. http://www.crimedoctor.com/carjacking.htm.

Miethe, T., & Sousa, W.H. (2009). Carjacking and it consequences: A situational analysis of risk risk factors for differential outcomes. Security Journal 23: 241–258.

Morewitz, S.J. (2008). Death threats and violence. New York: Springer Science + Business Media, LLC.

New Jersey Department of Law and Public Safety. (2000). Carjacking offenses report, 1999. West Trenton, NJ: New Jersey Department of Law and Public Safety.

Norborg, C. (2000). Conditional intent to kill is enough for federal carjacking conviction. J Crim Law & Criminol 90(3):985–1012.

Pulitzer, L.B. (1996). Crime on deadline. New York, NY: Boulevard Books.

Security Law Newsletter. (2012, May). Woman sues Marriott after carjacking in high-crime area. Security Law Newsletter, 32(5): 11.

Traffic Safety. (2006). Reduce the risk of carjacks. Traffic Safety 6(5): 4.

US v. Eskridge, 818 F. Supp. 259 (1993).

Williams, M. (1993). Carjacking—One department's response. FBI Law Enforcem Bull 62(10): 1–3. http://web.ebscohost.com.proxylib.csueastbay.edu/ehost/detail?vid=6&....

Young, L.J., & Borzycki, M. (2008). Carjacking in Australia: Recording issues and future directions. Trends & Issues in Crime & Justice, No. 351, Australian Government. http://www.aic.gov.au/documents/9/A/A/%7B9AA24697-7925-4726-847D-4951284F8D23%7Dtandi351.pdf.

Chapter 12
Aircraft Hijacking

Threats to aviation security, including aircraft hijackings (AHs) have become increasingly complex and difficult (Wikipedia. no date. Airport security. http://en.wikipedia.org/wiki/Airport_security; Rumerman no date; Barbash et al. 1986). In fact, aviation security is an on-going problem as technology is used to respond to AHs and other threats to aviation security (Smialek and Spitz 1976). This chapter reviews the literature and uses data from the Aircraft Hijackings Project (AHP) to assess AHs in terms of aviation security legislation, policies, and procedures, offender and victim characteristics, and the patterns and outcomes of AHs (see Appendices G and H, Tables H.16–H.26).

In AHs, also called skyjacking and air piracy, individuals and groups take over, blow up, or damage aircraft and kidnap, kill, or injure passengers, crew members, law enforcement personnel, and security forces. AH on the ground is particularly difficult to resolve without loss of life and damage to aircraft since hijackers can be armed with lethal weapons and explosives (Smialek and Spitz 1976). Hijackers can easily control the few exits, making it very problematic for the police or special security forces to peacefully resolve the hijacking.

History of AHs and Aviation Security

In Arequipa, Peru, the first documented AH took place on February 21, 1931 (Wikipedia. no date. Hijacking. http://en.wikipedia.org/wiki/Hijackings). This hijacking was politically motivated. While on the ground, revolutionaries with weapons tried to force the pilot, Byron Rickards, to fly a Ford TriMotor plane. The revolutionaries wanted to use the plane to drop propaganda leaflets over Lima, Peru (Rumerman no date).

The first fatal hijacking incident occurred in July 1947, when three Romanian hijackers murdered an aircrew member (Rumerman no date).

S. Morewitz, *Kidnapping and Violence*,
https://doi.org/10.1007/978-1-4939-2117-1_12

In another AH incident, a diplomat, who had been terminated, and his family successfully hijacked a Bulgarian commercial plane to Istanbul, Turkey on June 30, 1948 (Wikipedia. no date. Hijacking. http://en.wikipedia.org/wiki/Hijackings). In order to escape, the hijacker had to murder the co-pilot, who was the head of Bulgaria's civil aviation and the radio operator.

On July 16, 1948, hijackers were unsuccessful in seizing a seaplane of the Cathay Pacific subsidiary company, known as the Miss Macao (Wikipedia. no date. Hijacking. http://en.wikipedia.org/wiki/Hijackings). As a result of their failed attempt, the plane crashed into the sea off Macau.

Six students with pro-communist leanings successfully hijacked a Greek T.A.E. Airlines aircraft on September 12, 1948 (Wikipedia. no date. Hijacking. http://en.wikipedia.org/wiki/Hijackings). The hijackers wanted to fly to Yugoslavia. The plane was diverted to Skopje and later that evening returned to Thessaloniki.

Governments may sponsor air piracy to achieve their goals. For example, in 1954, the Israeli government reportedly sponsored the hijacking of a Syrian jet (Wikipedia. no date. Hijacking. http://en.wikipedia.org/wiki/Hijackings). The Israeli government's goal may have been to achieve the release of imprisoned Israelis in Damascus, who had been spying in Syria. The US Department of State referred to this state-sponsored hijacking as unprecedented in the history of international relations. However, the intentions of the Israeli government in hijacking the Syrian aircraft have been disputed (Wikipedia. no date. Hijacking. http://en.wikipedia.org/wiki/Hijackings).

On November 1, 1955, Jack Graham allegedly committed the first large-scale act of violence against a US airliner by blowing up a Denver-bound airliner and killing all 44 passengers and crew on board (Rumerman no date). He was apprehended and received the death penalty.

In 1959, Fidel Castro took over Cuba, and the prevalence of AP increased (Rumerman no date). Initially, hijackers seized planes in order to escape the country. The pattern changed in May 1961 when the first US airliner was diverted to Cuba. That summer other hijackings of US airliners occurred. In response to this problem, the US government started to use armed guards on commercial airliners. President John F. Kennedy passed legislation that authorized the death penalty or a minimum of 20-year sentence for AHs.

To deal with the threats of AH, the Convention on Offenses and Certain Other Acts Committed on Board Aircraft (also known as the Tokyo Convention) was enacted in 1963 (Wikipedia no date). The Tokyo Convention called for the quick return of hijacked planes and hostages.

On February 21, 1968, an individual who was fleeing authorities seized a DC-8 airliner and diverted the plane to Cuba (Rumerman no date). This incident triggered a number of AH incidents in the US through the end of 1972.

American airports had few security procedures to prevent AHs before the 1970s (Wikipedia. no date. Airport security. http://en.wikipedia.org/wiki/Airport_security). Widely publicized AHs in the latter part of the 1960s led to the initiation of anti-AH legislation and procedures.

The US and 49 other countries passed the Convention for the Suppression of Unlawful Seizure of Aircraft (also known as the Hague Convention) Convention for the Suppression of Unlawful Seizure of Aircraft [Hijacking Convention], 860 U.N. T.S. 105, *entered into force*, October 14, 1971 (Rumerman no date). The Hague Convention classified AH as a crime rather than a political act. The Montreal Convention in 1971 was designed to improve the earlier conventions and was implemented in 1973 (Montreal Convention 1971).

The Federal Aviation Administration (FAA) established the Task Force on the Deterrence of Air Piracy after eight airliners had been hijacked to Cuba in January 1969 (Rumerman no date). The Task Force created an offender profile that could be implemented with metal detectors to screen airline passengers. Eastern Airlines started to use these measures in October 1969. In 1970, four additional airlines implemented the system.

In September 1970, an AH incident perpetrated by members of the Popular Front for the Liberation of Palestine (PFLP) resulted in the destruction of three out of four hijacked planes after the terrorists released most of the hostages (Wikipedia. no date. Aircraft hijacking. http://en.wikipedia.org/wiki/Aircraft_hijacking; Rumerman no date). Two offenders tried to hijack the fourth aircraft, an El Al Airlines plane, but armed guard on board foiled their attempt. This crime led President Richard Nixon to authorize a hijacking prevention program that included the use of federal marshals.

In 1971, D.B. Cooper allegedly hijacked Northwest Orient Airlines Flight 305 and obtained a ransom of $200,000 for freeing the passengers (Wikipedia. No date. Aircraft hijacking. http://en.wikipedia.org/wiki/Aircraft_hijacking). Cooper reportedly parachuted from the rear of the aircraft, a Boeing 727, and was never located. As a result of this hijacking, aircraft manufacturers developed the "Cooper Vane" that prevented anyone from lowering the rear stairs during flight (Wu 2004).

President Nixon increased the speed at which the FAA made rules to improve airline security after bombs were discovered on three airliners in early March 1972 (Rumerman no date). Despite these measures, four air pirates who were bound for Cuba murdered a ticket agent in October 1972. In the following month, three criminals seriously injured a Southern Airways co-pilot and forced the plane to takeoff despite intervention by the FBI.

In response to these violent incidents, the FAA established an emergency rule making mandatory the inspection of carry-on baggage and scanning of all passengers at the start of 1973 (Rumerman no date). In August 1974, an anti-hijacking law was enacted that required universal screening.

The number of AHs in the US never returned to the highest levels prior to 1973 following the implementation of these new security measures (Rumerman no date). The next hijacking incident in the US did not take place until nationalists from Croatia seized an airliner in September 1976. However, perpetrators carried out bombings between 1974 and 1975. A bomb on an American plane headed from Tel Aviv to New York exploded and killed all passengers and crew aboard in September 1974. The following year, in December 1975, a bomb in a locker at

LaGuardia Airport in New York exploded and killed 11 people. As a result of this airport bombing, airport officials relocated lockers where they could be monitored.

Cubana Flight 455, on October 6, 1976, was the first attack by terrorists to indiscriminately murder individuals on board the flight (Wikipedia. no date. Airport security. http://en.wikipedia.org/wiki/Airport_security). Cubana Flight 455, from Barbados to Jamaica, was crashed by terrorists and 73 people died in this crash. According to forensic evidence, anti-Castro Cuban exiles with connections to the US Central Intelligence Agency and the Venezuelan secret police, DISIP, were involved in the terrorist attack.

Air India Flight 182 in 1985 was the most lethal airline event that was due to a breakdown in airport security (Wikipedia. no date. Airport security. http://en.wikipedia.org/wiki/Airport_security). A bomb on board this flight blew up the plane, killing 329 people.

The US government made federal air marshals a permanent part of FAA personnel under the International Security and Development Cooperation Act of 1985 in response to a hijacking of an Athens-to-Beirut TWA airliner and increase in terrorist activity in the Middle East (Rumerman no date). In this two-week hijacking, Lebanese terrorists hijacked an Athens-to-Beirut TWA airliner. The perpetrators killed one passenger and eventually released the remaining people on board after Israel freed 31 Lebanese prisoners (Rumerman no date; Wikipedia. no date. Aircraft hijacking. http://en.wikipedia.org/wiki/Aircraft_hijacking).

Pan American Flight 103 was blown up over Lockerbie, Scotland, by a bomb on December 21, 1988, resulting in the death of all 239 people on board and 11 individuals on the ground (Rumerman no date). A bomb was planted in a radio-cassette player that had been loaded on board Pan American Flight 103 in Frankfurt, Germany. Before this lethal bombing, the FAA had issued a bulletin in mid-November that warned about this type of bombing method. Again, in December 7, 1988, the FAA issued a bulletin that a possible bomb would be placed on a Pan American airliner in Frankfort. Scottish judges convicted a Libyan intelligence staff member for participating in this aircraft bombing.

After the Lockerbie terrorist bombing, new security procedures were implemented for US airlines at airports in Europe and the Middle East (Rumerman no date). For example, as a result of the Lockerbie terrorism, all checked baggage had to be x-rayed or searched, and passengers had to be matched with their baggage.

The FAA facilitated research beginning in the 1990s to test the effectiveness of bomb-detecting technology and upgraded the effectiveness of screening staff at airports (Rumerman no date). Two accidental crashes of airliners in 1996 triggered the attention of the FAA to the dangers of hazardous cargo. As a result, the FAA banned specific hazardous materials from passenger airliners. The US government in 1997 appropriated funds to the FAA to hire more airport security staff and make use of new equipment.

In the late 1990s, the media and the Department of Transportation's Office of the Inspector General (OIG) criticized airport security measures for being too lax (Rumerman no date). The OIG in 1999 was critical of the FAA for not being quick enough in forbidding unauthorized individuals to access secure areas in airports.

The OIG report showed that OIG investigators repeatedly were able to access secure areas. The OIG also criticized the FAA for issuing airport IDs to access secure airport areas without performing sufficient corroboration. Nevertheless, only one AH had occurred in the US for the ten-year period following February 1991 (Wikipedia. No date. Aircraft hijacking. http://en.wikipedia.org/wiki/Aircraft_hijacking).

Terrorists seized four US airliners (American Airlines Flight 11, American Airlines Flight 77, United Airlines Flight 93, and United Airlines Flight 175) and crashed three of them into buildings and one of them crashed into the ground, killing a total of 2,985 people (Rumerman no date; Wikipedia. No date. Aircraft hijacking. http://en.wikipedia.org/wiki/Aircraft_hijacking). The perpetrators used three of the four planes as missiles to cause loss of life and damage to infrastructure, resulting in the worst terrorist attack in US history. The terrorists crashed United Airlines Flight 175 and American Airlines Flight 11 into the World Trade Center towers, in New York City, and the entire complex was destroyed. Offenders used American Airlines Flight 77 in a similar way at the Pentagon, in Washington, D.C., which resulted in the destruction of a portion of that building. As a result of the attacks, 2,985 people were killed. At the World Trade Center, 2,752 people died, in Washington, D.C., 189 died, and in a field near Shanksville, PA, 44 people died.

These terrorist attacks led to immediate and a substantial tightening of air security (Rumerman no date). The Aviation and Transportation Security Act (ATSA) in November 2001 made the federal government directly responsible for airport screening, which previously had been under the authority of the airlines and their contractors. The ATSA also authorized the development of a new US Department of Transportation entity, the Transportation Security Agency (TSA), to manage airport security and other modes of travel. The TSA was later integrated into the Department of Homeland Security (Poole and Carafano 2006). As a result, a large government workforce of passenger and baggage screeners was created to replace the private contract screeners that were previously hired by the airlines.

As a part of this federalization of airport security, the US Congress required that all check bags be screened for explosives by December 31, 2002 (Poole and Carafano 2006). This deadline was later delayed another year.

The federalizing of airport security is based on the assumption that all passengers are equally suspicious and should get the same screening and the belief that airport security should keep dangerous objects and materials of flights (Poole and Carafano 2006). They assert that the establishment of the TSA has been very costly but has not significantly improved airport security in the US Poole and Carafano (2006) note that as of September 2004, a total of $2.5 billion was spent on checked-baggage screening equipment even though the expensive explosive detection system (EDS) machines had a low throughput and high error rate (Poole and Carafano 2006; US Government Accountability Office 2005). Poole and Carafano (2006) reported that airports had difficulty installing EDS machines to meet Congress' mandated deadlines.

The system required that passengers transport their luggage to baggage screeners who would hand-feed them into the EDS machines (Poole and Carafano 2006). The loading manually of luggage into the EDS machines unexpectedly increased the hiring of baggage screeners. The total workforce of baggage screeners was close to about 60,000, compared to the pre-9/11 force of less than 20,000 baggage screeners.

Poole and Carafano (2006) suggest that a better risk-based model would screen passengers in terms of whether they were low risks (much information is known about the passenger), ordinary passengers (infrequent and leisure flyers), and high-risk passengers (nothing is known about the passenger or negative information is known about the passenger.

In addition to trying to improve passenger and baggage screening, other air security measures have been implemented. On commercial airlines, the cockpit doors have been reinforced and are now bullet proof (Wikipedia. no date. Aircraft hijacking. http://en.wikipedia.org/wiki/Aircraft_hijacking). To deter and stop potential hijackers, air marshals are now employed on certain airliners in the US, the United Kingdom, Australia, and India.

Some experts have suggested that remote control systems be implemented so that no one on board the flight could control the plane's direction (Wikipedia. no date. Aircraft hijacking. http://en.wikipedia.org/wiki/Aircraft_hijacking).

Another suggestion is that a plane can be shot down in case the aircraft will be used as a missile (Wikipedia. no date. Aircraft hijacking. http://en.wikipedia.org/wiki/Aircraft_hijacking). This procedure could result in the death of all people on board the plane. The Federal Constitutional Court of Germany struck down *Luftsicherheitsgesetz* or Air Security Law," which permitted the shoot down of aircraft to prevent a terrorist attack (Wikipedia. no date. Aircraft hijacking. http://en.wikipedia.org/wiki/Aircraft_hijacking). The court did not want to authorize the killing of innocent hostages to avoid a terrorist attack. However, Poland and other countries have passed laws to permit the shooting down of hijacked planes.

Officials from several other countries have indicated that they would shoot down hijacked commercial planes if they can determine that the plane will be used as a missile even if it results in the death of innocent people on board (Wikipedia. no date. Aircraft hijacking. http://en.wikipedia.org/wiki/Aircraft_hijacking). US fight pilots reportedly have been receiving training to shoot down commercial planes.

As a different way to stop potential hijackers, pilots on board US commercial planes can carry a handgun on the flight deck (Wikipedia. no date. Aircraft hijacking. http://en.wikipedia.org/wiki/Aircraft_hijacking).

Another security concern is the possibility that unauthorized persons will enter secure areas of airports. For example, an older man was able to drive his automobile through two security gates to reach an active runway at John F. Kennedy International Airport in New York on March 6, 2006 (Wikipedia. no date. Airport security. http://en.wikipedia.org/wiki/Airport_security).

The same day, a man ran through a secure gate at Midway International Airport in Chicago and was able to reach the runway (Wikipedia. no date. Airport security. http://en.wikipedia.org/wiki/Airport_security). The intruder was able to enter one of three perimeter entrances that did not use a camera. As a result of the security breach, 222 security officers underwent retraining and all perimeter gates were re-designed (Wikipedia. no date. Airport security. http://en.wikipedia.org/wiki/Airport_security; United States Subcommittee on Federal Workforce and Agency Organization, 2006).

Airports, like other facilities, are open to terrorist and criminal attacks in non-secure areas of airports (Wikipedia. no date. Airport security. http://en.wikipedia.org/wiki/Airport_security). Terrorists tossed grenades and shot individuals at El Al ticket counters at the Rome and Vienna airports in December 1985. These attacks killed 20 people. At the El Al ticket counter at Los Angeles International Airport, a man shot and murdered two individuals and injured four others on July 5, 2002.

Technological and law enforcement efforts also can help to reduce injury risks to bystanders and aircraft damage during Ahs. Smialek and Spitz (1976) report the development of short-range ammunition that can be used in commercial airlines' enclosed areas during AHs. Experimental research demonstrates that short-range ammunition has effective capacity to wound the offenders and at the same time has a reduced likelihood of damaging the aircraft wall. Because of the projectile's structure, richochet can be avoided, limiting injury to passengers, crew, law enforcement personnel, and others.

Passenger responses to AHs may have changed since 9/11 (Wikipedia. no date. Aircraft hijacking. http://en.wikipedia.org/wiki/Aircraft_hijacking). Before 9/11, flight crews recommended that passengers remain quiet in order to increase their likelihood of surviving the hijacking. Government officials and members of the public felt that violence would be less likely if the hijackers attained their goals. This trend was particularly evident during the hijacking of US flights to Cuba.

Since the crash of United Airlines Flight 93 on 9/11, passengers must now balance the risk of cooperating with hijackers with the possibility that their airplane may be used by terrorists as a missile (Wikipedia. no date. Aircraft hijacking. http://en.wikipedia.org/wiki/Aircraft_hijacking). In future AHs, the perpetrators may face more opposition from passengers, potentially resulting in more injuries and loss of life, but reducing the success of the AH attempts.

Hijacker Motivation

Because AHs are infrequent, research on their causes and underlying social, psychological, and political patterns are limited (Evans 1973). Reports on incidents may have scarce information about what happened and the offenders' motivation. Researchers may also differ in their interpretation of what constitutes a "successful" hijacking. Moreover, not all attempts or threats may be counted in air piracy databases.

Another issue is that offenders hijack aircraft for a variety of reasons (Dugan, LaFree, and Piquero 2005). Dugan et al. (2005), in their investigation of 826 cases of AHs from 1931 to 1985, analyzed three major motivating factors for AHs: terrorism, extortion, and transportation to Cuba.

Data on the social, ethnic, religious, behavioral, and political attributes of some of these AH hijackers are limited. The motivation underlying some refugee escapes via AHs is under dispute. For example, one government witness characterized most hijackers as criminals, dissidents, and those with mental disorders.

Some studies show that a majority of perpetrators use hostages in order to either travel to a certain destination and/or achieve various political goals (Dugdale-Pointon 2005). This typology is limited because an AH categorized as transportation-oriented may actually be based on political, ethnic, and religious goals.

Results from the AHP revealed that the first aircraft hijacker involved in the incident between 1956 and 2009 appeared to be based on political, ethnic, cultural, and religious motivation in 81.2% of the incidents (see Table H.17). During this period, the most frequent political, ethnic/religious, or national identity of the perpetrators in the AHP was Cuban (104), Arab/Palestinian (7), PFLP (6), and Iranian (3) (see Table H.21). The political, ethnic, or national identity of other hijackers included East German (2), Pakistani (2), Turkish leftist militants (2), and Lebanese Shi'a (2).

In some AH cases, the hijacker's motivation may not be clear. For example, on February 13, 1977, Adnan Mintas, a police academy cadet, tried to hijack the Turkish plane, Trakya, which had departed from Istanbul en route to Izmir, and tried to divert the flight to Belgrad, Yugoslavia (Wikipedia-List of hijacking of Turkish airplanes. http://en.wikipedia.org/wiki/List_of_hijacking_of_Turkish_airplanes).

To achieve their social, ethnic/religious, political, or criminal goals, terrorists may hijack aircraft in the air and divert it to another location (Comay 1976). For example, in 1968, three PFLP members hijacked an El Al plane en route to Rome and diverted the aircraft to Algiers (Wikipedia. no date. Aircraft hijacking. http://en.wikipedia.org/wiki/Aircraft_hijacking).

Terrorists may hijack an aircraft and try to exchange the aircraft and hostages for some political, social, ethnic/religious, or criminal goals. They may seek publicity for their cause or to obtain release for their imprisoned comrades (Dugdale-Pointon 2005; Comay 1976).

In some AH incidents, political, ethnic/religious, and social extremists may not be able to successfully divert their hijacked plane. For example, on August 24, 1984, seven young persons of Sikh origin hijacked an Indian jet, which was flying from Delhi to Srinagar (Wikipedia. No date. Aircraft hijacking. http://en.wikipedia.org/wiki/Aircraft_hijacking). They tried to divert the flight to the US However, the aircraft was flown to the United Arab Emirate. The hijacking reportedly was related to the Sikh struggle for secession in the Indian state of Punjab.

In other instances, the suspects may not be able to force the plane to take off. They will blow up the plane while it is on the ground or threaten to do so. In some instances, the hijackers will destroy the hijacked planes after releasing their hostages. In other situations, the terrorists will try to use the hijacked aircraft as a missile against a specific target.

As noted earlier, some offenders may hijack the plane in order to extort money (Dugan et al. 2005; Holden 1986, January). Perpetrators may try to extort ransoms for the release of a plane's passengers, and the amount of these ransoms varies significantly. Findings from the AHP demonstrated that ransoms reportedly were extorted in 4.5% of the incidents.

In 1971, after hijacking Northwest Orient Airline Flight 305, the perpetrator, D. B. Cooper, obtained a $200,000 ransom for the release of passengers. Cooper parachuted from the plane and was never seen again (Wikipedia. no date. Hijacking. http://en.wikipedia.org/wiki/Hijackings).

On January 12, 1972, Billy Gene Hurst, Jr., hijacked Braniff Flight 28 as it departed Houston Texas bound for Dallas Texas (Wikipedia. no date. List of notable aircraft hijackings. http://en.wikipedia.org/wiki/List_of_notable_of_aircraft_hijackings). The perpetrator released all 94 passengers after the plane landed in Dallas but continued to hold 7 crew members as hostages. He demanded a ransom of $2 million, parachutes, jungle survival gear, and other materials after hijacking Braniff Flight 38. All crew members fled the plane secretly after a 6-hour standoff and law enforcement officials arrested Hurst.

Contagion theory has been used to explain AHs (Holden 1986, January; Rich 1972; Dugan et al. 2005). Media coverage of one incident may encourage copycat hijackings in a cyclical pattern (Holden 1986, January; US House Interstate and Foreign Commerce Committee 1969). The media essentially transmits a "skyjack virus" (Rich 1972). Likewise, other researchers note that AHs are a fad (Chauncey 1975; Minor 1975). Social contagion theory is also used to explain increase rates of violent offenses following well-publicized suicides, and murder-suicides (Bollen and Phillips 1982).

One difficulty in analyzing the social contagion effects of AHs is that the definition of successful AH can be ambiguous (Holden 1986, January). Persons may be more likely to commit an AH if they perceive that at prior AH was successful. However, those AHs considered initially successful may not result in successful outcomes for the hijackers. For example, the D.B. Cooper extortion-related AH was initially considered successful when Cooper reportedly parachuted out of his hijacked plane. However, about a decade after that D.B. Cooper AH, the ransom payment was located in Washington State. Thus, potential hijackers may only be influenced by the initial outcomes of the AH and not its final outcomes.

Based on an analysis of AH attempts between 1968 and 1971, Holden (1986, January) discovered that only successful AHs in the US had a social contagion impact in the US For AHs committed abroad, neither successful nor unsuccessful AHs demonstrated social contagion impact.

In Holden's (1986, January) investigation, offenders in the US were more likely to commit a transportation-related AH if the previous AH in the US was a successful transportation-associated AH. Similarly, if the prior AH was a successful extortion-related AH, perpetrators in the US were more to commit this same type of AH. Another social contagion hypothesis is that hijackers are likely to attempt to carry out a better AH than the previous one (Hamblin, Jacobsen, and Miller 1973).

The social contagion approach supports the view that AHs are goal oriented (Holden 1986, January). Publicized AHs serve as advertisements to individuals that they can achieve their goals through AHs (Holden 1986, January). Individuals who were exposed to media accounts of AHs may view them as a reasonable method for achieving goals, especially those that are not readily available.

Many hijackers were of Cuban ancestry and may have perceived AHs as a way to return to Cuba when that objective could not be achieved by legal methods (Holden 1986, January). Similarly, African Americans, who could not use conventional methods to travel to Cuba, committed transportation-related AHs to travel to this country, which they thought had a more conducive political environment than the US For example, one offender, Ira David Meeks, who hijacked an aircraft to Cuba in April 1970, told officials in Cuba that "he felt persecuted as a black man in America and had heard that things would be better in Cuba" (Wikipedia. no date. List of Cuba- United States aircraft hijackings. http://en.wikipedia.org/wiki/List_of_Cuba-US_aircraft_hijackings).

In other AHs, the perpetrators have other personal goals. For example, a 19-year-old deserter from the US Navy hijacked a Boeing 727 from Key West, Florida, to Cuba on January 24, 1969, because he "didn't want to go to Vietnam" (Wikipedia. no date. List of Cuba—United States aircraft hijackings. http://en.wikipedia.org/wiki/List_of_Cuba-US_aircraft_hijackings).

Perpetrators who carried out another type of goal-oriented AHs, extortion-related AHs, were mostly white. These hijackers appeared to desire wealth as their goal. These findings indicate that the type of AH perpetrated is associated with different motivations and social characteristics of the perpetrators.

Another social contagion approach suggests that individuals with mental disorders hijack aircraft to obtain publicity due to their psychosocial impairment or low self-esteem (Holden 1986, January).

Related to the social contagion approach is the rational choice model, which asserts that individuals interpret and weigh the chances of success, the benefits, and costs related to AHs (Dugan et al. 2005; Chauncey 1975; Minor 1975; Landes 1978). Benefits for hijackers include internal ones such as wealth and external benefits such as increased public awareness of the offenders' political goals (Dugan et al. 2005). Costs related to AHs include the chances of being caught and punishment severity.

Other explanations of AHs focus on the impairment of the hijackers. Persons with mental disorders may have other motivations for hijacking aircraft. For example, Ichimura et al. (2001) analyzed the case of an individual with chronic alternate-world disorder (CAWD) who hijacked a jumbo jet. A person with this condition is fanatically obsessed in a virtual reality to such a degree that she or he can no longer differentiate between reality and virtual reality (VR). In their case analysis, Ichimura et al. (2001) investigated a man who developed CAWD after using light simulator software. This man then hijacked a jet in order to fly the plane on his own. The authors believe that with the increase use of VR, the incidence of CAWD will increase.

Other AH offenders may have suffered from different mental problems. For example, on January 11, 1969, a man who hijacked a 727 airliner from Jacksonville, Florida, to Cuba, was considered to be temporary insane (Wikipedia.

no date. List of Cuba—United States aircraft hijackings. http://en.wikipedia.org/wiki/List_of_Cuba-US_aircraft_hijackings). Two days later, a man who failed to hijack a Convair 880 from Detroit to Cuba had a history of mental impairment (Wikipedia. no date. List of Cuba—United States aircraft hijackings. http://en.wikipedia.org/wiki/List_of_Cuba-US_aircraft_hijackings).

At the end of that same month, on January 31, 1969, Allan Sheffield carried out a hijacking of a DC-8 from San Francisco to Cuba. The hijacker indicated that he is "tired of TV dinners and tired of seeing people starve in the world" (Wikipedia. no date. List of Cuba—United States aircraft hijackings. http://en.wikipedia.org/wiki/List_of_Cuba-US_aircraft_hijackings).

On March 17, 1969, a man carried out a hijacking of a plane from Atlanta, Georgia, to Cuba. He was later sent to a mental facility (Wikipedia. no date. List of Cuba—United States aircraft hijackings. http://en.wikipedia.org/wiki/List_of_Cuba-US_aircraft_hijackings).

In August of the same year, a man who hijacked a DC-9 from Philadelphia to Cuba was thought to be suffering from mental illness (Wikipedia. no date. List of Cuba—United States aircraft hijackings. http://en.wikipedia.org/wiki/List_of_Cuba-US_aircraft_hijackings).

In 1966, four years before hijacking a plane to Cuba, Ira David Meeks was diagnosed with paranoid schizophrenia (Wikipedia no date. List of Cuba—United States aircraft hijackings. http://en.wikipedia.org/wiki/List_of_Cuba-US_aircraft_hijackings).

In the AHP, 5.7% of the perpetrators were thought to possibly have mental health problems (see Table H.17). However, the mental health status of most of the aircraft hijackers was not known.

AH perpetrators also may be impaired from alcohol and other drugs. For example, John Milo Reese stole a plane from an airport in the Florida Keys area intending to deliver pizza to Fidel Castro as a way of kidnapping the dictator. The suspect crashed the plane on a beach in Cuba. Reese later indicated that he was slightly intoxicated and had "lost his bearings' in the air (Wikipedia. no date. List of Cuba—United States aircraft hijackings. http://en.wikipedia.org/wiki/List_of_Cuba-US_aircraft_hijackings). Young, immature persons may also try to hijack planes. In addition, airline pilots can take control of an aircraft and fly it to a non-scheduled location (Schuler, 2010, January 24). In various AHs, the underlying motivation is not known.

The rate of AHs increased significantly in the 1968–1969 period (Dugan et al., 2005; Holden, 1986, January). Twenty-seven plane hijackings and attempted hijackings to Cuba occurred in 1968. Eighty-two documented hijack attempts took place around the world in 1969, which was more than two times the total attempts between 1947 and 1967. The rate of AHs has declined since the peak of 385 hijackings that occurred between 1967 and 1976. The total number of AHs went down to 300 between 1977 and 1986 and declined to 212 between 1987 and 1996.

The AHP results showed that for the study period, 1956–2009, the highest annual rates of AHs were between 1968 and 1972 (see Table H.23). In 1968, 17 AH incidents occurred, and the annual frequency peaked at 37 in 1969 and then went down to 10 in 1972. In the AHP, the incidents had taken place an average of 31.67 years ago (see Table H.16).

Aircraft Hijacker Social and Occupational Characteristics

Majority of the AH suspects are male. Results from the AHP between 1956 and 2009 revealed that 97% of the aircraft hijackers are male and 3% female (see Table H.17).

About 60% of the AHs since 1947 have involved escapes by refugees (Wikipedia. no date. Hijacking. http://en.wikipedia.org/wiki/Hijackings; US House Interstate and Foreign Commerce Committee, 1969; Wikipedia-Hijacking. http://en.wikipedia.org/wiki/Hijackings).

Several hijackers in the AHP were associated with the military. For example, on May 3, 2007, two army recruits try to hijack a plane at the Jose Marti International Airport in Havana, Cuba. They were arrested before takeoff after the offenders murder a hostage (Wikipedia. no date. List of Cuba—United States aircraft hijackings. http://en.wikipedia.org/wiki/List_of_Cuba-US_aircraft_hijackings).

Several of the suspects in the AHP had aviation experience including a combination of aviation and military background. For example, a former Cuban air force pilot, Eduardo Guerra Jimenez, hijacked Delta Air Lines flight 1061 on June 12, 1979 (Wikipedia. no date. List of Cuba—United States aircraft hijackings. http://en.wikipedia.org/wiki/List_of_Cuba-US_aircraft_hijackings). Ten years before, Jimenez had hijacked a MIG jet to the US

Government agents have been involved in AHs. One hijacker in the AHP was a government agent. In the AHP, four of the AH suspects were students.

Hijacker Methods

Armed perpetrators typically obtain access to the aircraft's crew compartment and coerce the pilot to divert the flight by threatening to kill the pilots, flight attendants, and passengers and destroy the plane. On 9/11, hijackers took flying lessons in preparation for the attacks and then flew the planes themselves (Wikipedia. no date. Hijacking. http://en.wikipedia.org/wiki/Hijackings; US House Interstate and Foreign Commerce Committee, 1969).

Suspects frequently work together in trying to hijack an aircraft. According to the AHP, an average of almost two perpetrators attempted to take over planes during incidents between 1956 and 2009 (see Table H.16).

During AH incidents, hijackers have used a variety of weapons, including knives, handguns, and explosives. For example, in Australia, on November 15, 1972, hijacker Miloslav Hrabinec hijacked an Ansett Airlines flight 232 from

Adelaide, to Alice Springs, using a.22 sawn-off rifle and a knife (Wikipedia. no date. Hijacking. http://en.wikipedia.org/wiki/Hijackings).

Findings from the AHP demonstrated that during the incidents, the suspects were most likely to threaten people with guns or actually shoot people with the guns (17 incidents), followed by threatening people with bomb/explosives or using the explosive (12 incidents) and threatening or using a knife (5 incidents) (see Table H.22). The perpetrators allegedly threatened people with a toy gun (2 incidents), scissors (1 incident), and a grenade (1 incident). In 107 aircraft incidents, the type of weapon used, if any, could not be determined.

AH incidents have involved both commercial and general-aviation aircraft. In many of these incidents, hijackers tried to divert the flights to Cuba. According to a 1969 report, 34 of 46 AHs or attempted hijackings were successful (US House Interstate and Foreign Commerce Committee, 1969). All but one of these hijackings ended in Cuba. Findings from the AHP between 1956 and 2009 also showed that Cuba was the most frequently used location of diverted aircrafts during the AH incidents. Cuba was used 77 times as the location of diverted aircrafts during hijackings (see Table H.20).

Law Enforcement Responses and AH Outcomes

Hijackers and government authorities often follow a pattern of negotiation. The police may rely on experts trained in hostage negotiation in assessing whether the hostage taker is suffering from a mental disorder and in determining the appropriate strategy for resolving the AH and hostage situation (Rueth 1993). Typical psychological assessments should be altered to meet the unique characteristics of a hostage crisis. Rueth (1993) suggests that hostage negotiation experts conduct an onsite psychological evaluation that includes a mental status assessment that is based on observation and a history of the suspect obtained from different sources.

If negotiation efforts fail, the police or special security forces typically will use force to rescue the hostages and arrest the hijackers. Hijackers, police/security forces, flight crew, and passengers face death and serious injuries during these dangerous hijackings. In the AHP, between 1956 and 2009, one or more hijackers were killed in 12.4% of the AHs. In 3.6% of the AH incidents, police or security forces were killed. One or more pilots were killed in 5.7% of the AH incidents.

In the AHP, one or more passengers were killed in 11.3% of the incidents (see Table H.24). The largest number of passengers has been killed at one time when planes crash or are blown up during hijackings. According to the AHP, 6.2% of the planes crashed during the incidents (see Table H.24). The average number of passengers on board the planes during the incidents was almost 20 and the range was from 0 to 400 passengers (see Table H.16).

Responses by law enforcement and security forces can influence the outcomes of AH. Diverting hijacked aircraft can reduce the likelihood of injuries and death. For example, data from the AHP revealed that passenger deaths were less likely to occur when the hijacked planes were diverted to an unplanned destination. Similarly, AHP results indicated that hijackers were less likely to be killed when hijacked planes were diverted to a different destination.

Airplanes were also damaged during some of the AH incidents. According to the AHP, aircrafts were reported to have been damaged in 6.7% of the incidents (see Table H.24).

AH suspects may escape police apprehension. Government officials in the countries where the hijacking concluded may not prosecute the perpetrators. In other instances, information is not available about whether the offenders were arrested. Findings from the AHP demonstrated that 41.7% of the perpetrators escaped (see Table H.24). However, in many of these cases definitive information is not available.

If the hijackers do not escape or are not killed, they are often immediately detained for some time period after they are taken into custody. Results from the AHP revealed that suspects were arrested in 38.2% of the AH incidents (see Table H.24). In 9.4% of the cases, the perpetrators were incarcerated.

The hijackers who return to the United States face criminal prosecution and severe sentences if convicted. According to the 1969 report, two hijackers received minimum sentences of 20 years in prison under federal piracy statute.

In various countries, individuals convicted of hijacking and murder face execution. Angel Betancourt Cueto allegedly used a pistol in trying to hijack a plane that was en route from Santiago de Cuba to Havana with 97 passengers on board, on March 27, 1966 (Wikipedia. no date. List of Cuba—United States aircraft hijacking. http://en.wikipedia.org/wiki/List_of_Cuba-US_aircraft_hijackings). The pilot, Fernando Alvarez Perez, reportedly opposed the hijacking and landed the plane in Havana. Cueto allegedly murdered the pilot and seriously wounded the co-pilot. Later, Cueto was captured and executed.

The courts may acquit a hijacker on the grounds of temporary insanity. The court acquitted the man who hijacked the 727 Airliner from Jacksonville, Florida, to Cuba, on January 11, 1969, on the grounds of temporary insanity (Wikipedia. no date. List of Cuba—United States aircraft hijackings. http://en.wikipedia.org/wiki/List_of_Cuba-US_aircraft_hijackings).

On September 10, 1969, a Puerto Rican man failed to hijack a DC-8 to Cuba. He was sent to a mental facility and later released (Wikipedia. no date. List of Cuba—United States aircraft hijackings. http://en.wikipedia.org/wiki/List_of_Cuba-US_aircraft_hijackings).

In other instances, hijackers with a diagnosis of mental illness are sent to prison. On February 21, 1968, Lawrence Rhodes hijacked a DC-8, which was on route from Tampa, Florida, to Cuba. On February 10, 1970, he turned himself into authorities. A January 4, 1971 hijacking charge against him was dismissed, and he was committed to a mental facility. However, he returned to prison on July 8, 1971, and on July 17, 1972 Rhodes was sentenced to 25 years in prison for robbery.

Effectiveness of Aviation Security on AHs

Policy leaders enact aviation-related policies that are designed to increase the probability of catching the offenders to prevent AHs and increase the severity of punishment for committing AHs (Dugan et al. 2005). In a large-scale investigation of AHs from 1931 to 1985, Dugan et al. (2005) showed that increasing the certainty of getting caught using metal detectors and law enforcement personnel at passenger checkpoints reduced the chances that AHs would be committed. The researchers also found that after Cuba passed a law that criminalized AHs, perpetrators were less likely to divert flights to that country.

Similarly, Chauncey (1975) and Minor (1975) found that metal detector screening and baggage inspection/screening were associated with a reduction in AH attempts. In a study of mostly AHs in the US between 1961 and 1976, Landes (1978) demonstrated that such factors as increasing the chances of apprehending the hijackers through mandatory screening procedures, the conditional probability of a prison sentence, and increasing the prison sentence reduced AHs.

References

Barbash, G.I., Yoeli, N., & Ruskin, S.M. (1986). Airport preparedness for mass disaster: a proposed schematic plan. Aviat Space Environ Med 57(1): 77–81.

Bollen, K.A., & Phillips, D.P. (1982). Imitative suicides: A national study of the effect of television news stories. Amer Sociol Rev 47: 802–809.

Chauncey, R. (1975). Deterrence: Certainty, severity, and skyjacking. Criminol 12: 447–473.

Comay, M. (1976). Political terrorism. Ment Health Soc 3(5–6): 249–261.

Dugan, L., LaFree, G., & Piquero, A.R. (2005). Testing a rational choice model of airline Hijackings. Criminology 43(4): 1031–1065.

Dugdale-Pointon, T. (14 June 2005). Hijacking. http://www.historyofwar.org/articles/concepts_hijacking.html.

Evans, A.E. (1973). Aircraft hijacking: What is being done? Amer J Intern Law 67(4): 641–671.

Hamblin, R.J., Jacobsen, R.B., & Miller, J.L.I. (1973). A mathematical theory of social change. New York: Wiley-Interscience.

Holden, R.T. (January 1986). The contagiousness of aircraft hijacking. AJS 91(4): 874–904 http://pegasus.cc.ucf.edu/~surette/hijacking.html, http://www.jstor.org/discover/10.2307/2779961?uid=3739560&uid=2&uid=4&uid=3739256&sid=21102884157273.

Ichimura, A., Nakajima, I., & Juzoji, H. (2001). Investigation and analysis of a reported incident resulting in an actual airline hijacking due to a fanatical and engrossed VR state. Cyberpsychol Behav 4(3): 355–363.

Landes, W.M. (1978). An economic study of US aircraft hijackings, 1961–1976. J Law Econo 21: 1–31.

Minor, W.W. (1975). Skyjacking crime control models. J Crim Law Criminol 66: 94–105.

Montreal Convention (1971). Also known as the Convention for the Suppression of Unlawful Acts against the Safety of Civil Aviation, signed at Montreal on 23 September 1971. www.mcgill.ca/files/iasl/montreal1971.pdf.

Poole, R., Jr., & Carafano, J. (2006). Time to rethink airport security. The Heritage Foundation. http://www.heritage.org/Research/Reports/2006/07/Time-to-Rethink—Airport Security.

Rich, E. (1972). Flying scared. New York: Stein & Day.Rigler, Hon. W.R., & Wieder, H.L. (no date). The epidemic of parental child-snatching: An overview. http://travel.state.gov/family/abduction/resources/resources_545.html.

Rueth, T.W. (1993). Onsite psychological evaluation of a hostage taker. Psychol Rep 73(2): 659–664.

Schuler, D. (2010, Jan. 24). A short history of air hijacking. http://theglitteringeye.com/?p=10016.

Smialek, J.E., & Spitz, W.U. (1976). Short-range ammunition—a possible anti-hijacking device. J Forensic Sci 21 (4): 856–861.

United States House Interstate and Foreign Commerce Committee. (1969). Aircraft piracy. Washington, DC: US Government Printing Office.

Wu, A. (2004). History of airport security. American Public Media Home. http://savytraveler.publicradio.org/show/features/2000/20000915/security.

Chapter 13
Maritime Piracy and Kidnapping

Maritime piracy (MP) refers to robbery, plundering, kidnapping, and related crimes that are perpetrated at sea or around coastal and territorial waters. Agents who do not have a commission from a sovereign country commit these crimes. MP is a controversial term. One problem has to do with the site of the crime. According to Article 101 of the United Nations Convention on the Law of the Sea, piracy is committed on the high seas (Mo 2002). However, 72% of MP attacks occur while the vessel is berthed or anchored in port (Dillon 2000, June 22).

In addition, MP has been confused with maritime terrorism (Hanson 2009. April 13; Dillon 2005, Winter-Spring; Mo 2002). Some experts debate the association between MP and maritime terrorism. Some experts believe that MP is different from maritime terrorism, while other specialists argue that MP overlaps with maritime terrorism.

According to Dillon (2005, Winter-Spring), maritime terrorists carry out their attacks to achieve three primary goals. First, they attack vessels to foster fear in society. Second, they use maritime terrorist attacks to smuggle contraband such as arms. Third, maritime terrorists carry out their activities to raise money to fund their terrorist undertakings.

Moreover, maritime terrorists may attack ships as a means to obtain political asylum (Roach 2004). For example, on December 25, 2002, four Cuban crewmembers armed with knives hijacked the *M/V Sabrax*, 178-foot Panamanian freighter, and tried to divert the vessel to Puerto Rico and seek asylum there (Roach 2004). The U.S. Coast Guard boarded the ship later while in international waters and took control of the ship away from the hijackers. The U.S. government eventually repatriated the Cuban offenders to Cuba.

Maritime terrorists also seek other political objectives. For example, In October 1985, Palestinian Liberation Organization (PLO) terrorists hijacked the Italian passenger ship, *Achille Lauro*, off the Egyptian coast and kidnapped the passengers and crew for political purposes (King 2005). The PLO hijackers demanded the release of PLO terrorists who were incarcerated in Israel. After the Israeli

S. Morewitz, *Kidnapping and Violence*,
https://doi.org/10.1007/978-1-4939-2117-1_13

government refused their demands, the PLO terrorists murdered Leon Klinghoffer, a disabled Jewish American passenger and dumped his body overboard.

Another example of maritime terrorism was the suicide bomb attack against the *USS Cole*, a warship, on October 12, 2000 (Dillon 2005, Winter-Spring; Sanchez 2014, May 26). Terrorists used a suicide bomb on a supply raft to murder 17 U.S. navy sailors while the ship was anchored in the port of Aden.

Off Aden, Yemen, terrorists reportedly attacked the *Limburg*, a French oil tanker on October 6, 2002 (Dillon 2005, Winter-Spring; Sanchez 2014, May 26). In this attack, terrorists used a dinghy filled with explosives to murder one seaman on board the vessel. The attack also caused the spilling of 90,000 barrels of oil.

According to Dillon (2005, Winter-Spring), the International Maritime Organization (IMO) and the International Maritime Bureau (IMB) did not alter their MP policies to deal with maritime terrorism following the widely known *USS Cole* and *Limburg* terrorist attacks. These two organizations did not change their policies or definition of attacks in considering the threats from maritime terrorism.

MP and maritime terrorism may overlap in different ways (Hanson 2009, April 13). Both MP and maritime terrorism involve non-state actors as perpetrators and both consist of bands of brigands that are separate from nations. Moreover, both MP and maritime terrorism uses violence against mariners, including homicide and destruction of property to achieve their goals.

Prevalence of MP Attacks

Pirate attacks are prevalent in the waters of Southeast Asia, Somalia, West Africa, especially Nigeria, the Far East, and India (Hanson 2009, April 13; Roach 2004; Barrios 2005). MP is especially prevalent in four major locations (Hanson 2009, April 13). They occur in the Gulf of Aden, in proximity to Somalia and the Red Sea's southern entrance. MP occurs widely in the Gulf of Guinea, in proximity to Nigeria and the Niger River delta. Between Indonesia and Malaysia in the Malacca Strait, MP transpires. The subcontinent of India, especially between India and Sri Lanka, is a frequent site of MP. In addition to these four areas, MP attacks take place in other areas such as in the ports of Brazil and Ecuador and in certain ports in West Africa (Roach 2004).

Experts suggest that like crimes perpetrated on land, 50% of all maritime crimes are not reported (Forsyth et al. 2009; Burnett 2002; Mueller and Adler 1985). A majority of shippers do not want to report piracy incidents because their reports will trigger investigations and costly delays. According to Chalk (1998), shipowners spend an average of US$25,000 daily to operate a merchant vessel, making investigations very costly. Moreover, reporting piracy incidents could lead to increases in the shipowners' insurance premiums.

In the mid-twentieth century, MP was almost nonexistent (Forsyth et al. 2009). However, during the 1960s, the prevalence of these crimes began to increase. In the 1980s, MP was a problem, and its prevalence increased substantially in 1990s. For example, in Southeast Asian waters, 102 MP attacks were reported in 1991 (Chalk 1998). A total of 197 acts of violence that took place in 34 assaults were reported to the Regional Piracy Centre (RPC) in the first three months of 1997.

In the next decade, pirate attacks against vessels remain a problem. In 2000, 469 piracy attacks around the world were reported (Mo 2002). A total of 2,129 worldwide attacks on vessels had been reported to the IMO by December 2000.

In 2002, 370 piracy cases around the world had been reported, which was an increase from 335 attacks in 2001 (Roach 2004). The number of vessels that were hijacked increased from 16 in 2001 to 25 in 2002. The IMB asserted that greater participation of organized crime networks was responsible for this increase in maritime hijackings.

In 2003, 445 worldwide incidents had been reported (King 2005). In 2003, 100 assaults using firearms had been reported and 359 individuals on board vessels had been kidnapped in the course of different piracy attacks.

Between 2006 and 2009, MP attacks increased. In 2009, 406 worldwide incidents occurred (Digby, no date). Of the 406 pirate attacks, 1 in 9 was a successful hijacking. Pirates fired on 120 ships, boarded 153, and hijacked 49. Of the 406 attacks, pirates kidnapped 1,052 members of the crew on these vessels. Pirates injured 68 crew members and murdered 8.

In 2008, Somali bandits were responsible for over 50% of the piracy incidents. Somali pirates committed 47 of the 49 successful hijackings (Digby, no date). Of the 406 attacks, approximately two-thirds took place in the Gulf of Aden or near Somalia.

In 2009, 20 pirate attacks were reported in Nigerian waters, and at least the same number were not reported (Digby, no date). In eight of the 20 attacks, pirates committed violent robberies against crew members on board ships in the port of Lagos. However, they did not hijack these eight vessels. Off the coast of Indonesia, 28 pirate attacks were reported. Fourteen occurred in Malaysian waters in the Straits of Malacca, 12 in Bangladesh, in the anchorage off the port of Chittagong, and nine in the South China Sea in Malaysian waters.

MP Costs

MP costs are substantial (Hanson 2009, April 13; Kraska 2010). For example, more than US$7 million was paid to release the oil tanker *Maran Centaurus*, a very large crude carrier (Kraska 2010). These costs were more than twice as much as the US $3.2 million required to release the *Sirius Star*.

The total cost of MP worldwide is unknown. Some experts estimate that MP costs are US$1 billion annually (Hanson 2009, April 13). Digby (no date) reported a much lower estimate of worldwide shipping company losses from MP in 2008: US$60 to $70 million. Others assert that MP costs are up to US$16 billion each year. One specialist, Martin N. Murphy, suggests that the costs of MP, even if US $16 billion annually, are small compared to worldwide maritime commerce revenues, which are trillions of dollars. In another report, Bowden (2010) estimates that international economy costs associated with MP range between $7 billion and $12 billion.

Estimates diverge significantly because experts disagree about the ways to measure MP losses. For example, experts disagree about whether MP losses should combine the costs of ransom payments with insurance premiums, freight rates, and rerouting costs. MP losses also include robbery of individual mariners and ship and property damage.

According to Kraska (2010), ransom payments frequently account for only a small component of international shipping costs associated with MP. Attacks against cargo ships result in second-order costs, such as the costs of taking a vessel off-line, the costs of negotiating with the bandits, and the delivery of the ransom costs. The charter rate for a vessel is typically US$50,000 each day; therefore, US $3.5 million in costs will result from a vessel being off-line for two months. Conducting negotiations with pirates to gain the release of a ship may cost as much as US$500,000. It may cost an additional US$300,000 to deliver the ransom costs.

Early Pirates

MP dates back to ancient times (Land 2007). In the 13th century, the Sea Peoples threatened the Aegean. The Tyrrhenians and Thracians committed seaborne piracy in the classical period. The population on the island of Lemnos, who had opposed the Greeks, was a sanctuary for Thracian pirates.

In medieval times, the Vikings from Scandinavia were the most significant pirates (Land 2007). They raided coastal and inland areas in Western Europe and attacked the coasts of North Africa, Italy, and the Baltic Sea. The Vikings even plundered populations on their way up the rivers of Eastern Europe and the Black Sea and Persia.

In East Asia, Chinese pirates during the mid-Qing dynasty had a significant impact on the Chinese economy by attacking the Chinese junk trade.

The Arabs raided the Adriatic coast circa 872, and in 937, Irish pirates joined the Scots, Vikings, Picts, and the Welsh in their attack on England.

In North Africa, the Barbary pirates and privateers (or corsairs who used similar techniques as pirates, but who had a commission or letter of marquee from a government or government leader who approved the attack of enemy merchant vessels) plundered the ports of Tunis, Tripoli, Algiers, Sale, and Morocco. Between the 16th and 19th centuries, Barbary pirates reportedly captured between 1 million and 1.25 million Europeans and sold them into slavery in North Africa and Ottoman Empire.

The U.S. Navy was formed to combat the Barbary pirates. For almost 20 years, these pirates had attacked ships and taken into captivity American seaman without punishment (Boland 2010). Almost 1/6th of the federal budget of the U.S. went to making tribute payments for captured Americans.

An American seaman, Betsey, was captured in 1784 and 16 years finally passed before Americans began to combat the Barbary pirates (Boland 2010). After fierce battles, Lieutenant Stephen Decatur in 1815 stopped the threat of Barbary pirates.

The period between the mid-1550s and mid-1760s was the classic era of piracy in Caribbean. From the 1640s to the 1680s, Caribbean pirates had their greatest success. MP in the Caribbean emerged from the tensions over trade and colonization among competing European countries during this period.

Pirates were viewed by many people as clever and successful individuals who acted outside the restrictions of conventional life. However, many of them were actually poor and died young. Pirate clans functioned as limited democracies; they had the right to elect and replace their leaders. The captain of a pirate ship was often a great warrior in whom the men could trust. Pirates often shared whatever they obtained from their plundering, and pirates injured during battle might get special compensation.

Modern MP

Modern maritime pirates may commit a variety of offenses when they attack vessels in ports, in the territorial waters of coastal nations, and at sea (Forsyth et al. 2009; Chalk 1998; Dillon 2000, June 22). They will seize items or the ship, kidnap those on board for ransom or to achieve another objective, rob and/or murder these individuals, and damage or destroy the ship (Digby, no date). No type of ship is immune to piracy (Forsyth et al. 2009). Maritime security is also jeopardized by illegal and unsafe migration by sea and drug smuggling at sea (Roach 2004).

The lone survivor of a piracy attack on the *MN3 Normina*, a Philippine fishing trawler, reported how pirates had rounded up his nine crew members and murdered them to steal their cargo that consisted of a small catch of fish (Chalk 1998). He survived after being shot in the back of the head.

Bandits may pose as customs agents to board and hijack a vessel. In 1998, in the South China Sea, pirates reportedly posing as customs agents boarded and hijacked the *Chang Sang*, a cargo ship. The perpetrators murdered all 23 crew members and threw their bodies overboard.

In Somali waters, heavily armed bandits hijacked the *M/V Faina*, a Ukrainian tanker, with heavy weapons, and threatened to destroy the vessel unless their ransom was paid (Forsyth et al. 2009). This hijacking drew international attention because of the vessel was transporting 33 tanks and other heavy weapons.

A Thai ship was hijacked off the Somali coast, and a ransom had to be paid to free the hijacked vessel (Forsyth et al. 2009).

Off the coast of Somalia, Bandits hijacked the 288-foot *Le Ponant*, a French yacht, and her crew of 30 members (Forsyth et al. 2009).

In 2001, bandits armed with guns and knives hijacked a cargo ship off the coast of Riau Island, Indonesia (Hawkes 2001). The hijackers left the crew on an uninhabited island. Crewmembers were eventually rescued; however, the vessel and her cargo worth US$2.1 million have not been located.

MP has increased after bandits use two fast skiffs to attack *The Seabourn Spirit*, a luxury cruise liner, off the coast of Somalia in late 2005 (Kraska 2010). The pirates attacked the vessel with machine gun fire and grenades that were rocket propelled. As a result of the attack, the luxury cruise liner's 151 passengers were diverted from the port of Mombassa to Victoria to undergo repairs. The U.S. Navy had to dispose of unexploded ordinance. In this attack, one crew member was injured by shrapnel.

The hijacking of the *M/V Chern Maan Shyang I*, a Taiwan vessel, by nine Chinese crewmembers was an example an internal labor dispute (Roach 2004). In this incident, the Taiwan engineer and Chinese hijacker were killed during an argument and the ship's master suffered major stab wounds.

Pirates may hijack ships and kidnap crewmembers for other purposes. For example, pirates reportedly hijacked the *Dewey Madrid*, a supertanker, in order to learn how to steer the ship. The suspects did not physically harm the crew. Instead, they escaped from the supertanker after stealing manuals and technical information.

Attacks on vessels not only can disrupt maritime trade, but they can lead to catastrophic environmental damage (Chalk 1998). Attacks on heavily laden petroleum tankers could lead to massive oil slicks that damage fertile coastlines and populations. One piracy incident that was a "near miss" occurred in September 1992 when the supertanker, *Nagasaki Spirit* collided with a rogue ship, the *Ocean Blessing*, a container ship.

A variety of conditions facilitate modern MP (Forsyth et al. 2009; Chalk 1998; Kraska 2009, Autumn; Kraska 2010). The downsizing of navies after the Cold War ended has led to a breakdown in social control. The increasing amount of cargo shipped on the high seas is another factor that may encourage piracy.

Since the Taliban and al Qaeda forces in Afghanistan were defeated, their remaining forces have spread out (Roach 2004). Some of the Taliban and al Qaeda personnel may have escaped by sea. Al Qaeda may control vessels that can be used to transport terrorists, weapons, explosives, money, and other items. These al Qaeda-controlled vessels can perpetrate attacks on vessels.

Some nations ship conventional weapons that can be sold to terrorists. Nations and nongovernmental groups and individuals could use these same techniques to ship weapons of mass destruction (Roach 2004).

The rise in crime networks and their access to capital to fund these criminal operations have been viewed as a major contributor to the increase in MP (Roach 2004; Forsyth et al. 2009). In addition, the crime networks' access to sophisticated and high-powered weaponry has facilitated the increase in pirate attacks (Forsyth et al. 2009; Chalk 1998; Digby, no date).

The decline in the worldwide economy and the increase in poverty in developing countries may facilitate the recent increase in MP (Forsyth et al. 2009; Kraska 2009, Autumn). Countries that are poor frequently have few viable educational and occupational opportunities and sea piracy offers people a chance to get out of poverty (Digby, no date; Kraska 2009, Autumn). In Somalia, a bandit can make

$10,000 for successfully carrying out an attack; this amount is more than many individuals in Somalia can earn in ten years (Kraska 2010). However, successful bandits in Somalia are not safe with large amounts of money so they try to get out of the country.

Successful MP attacks bring substantial wealth to local economies. For example, in Somalia, the Puntland shoreline has enjoyed an increase in construction (Kraska 2010). In addition, fishing stocks have increased due to the threat of MP in Somalia.

Countries that are experiencing political unrest, war, or other forms of conflict are vulnerable to sea piracy (Kraska 2009, Autumn; Kraska 2010). Nations with weak governments and inadequate systems of social control facilitate these crimes. Complicit and corrupt governmental and law enforcement personnel also promote these offenses.

Hastings (2009) analyzed failed and weak nations and discovered that in failed states, maritime bandits can engage in abductions to secure ransoms that involve considerable time since they do have to be concerned about getting caught. In contrast, in states that were only weak but not failed, pirates have access to markets and an infrastructure of transportation for seizing vessels and their cargo and selling them for profitable gains.

The characteristics of insurance and security companies can foster sea piracy (Digby, no date). Local military organizations, security organizations, attorneys, community leaders, financiers, and other individuals also are often involved in supporting or responding to MP, and social, cultural, and financial factors can facilitate their involvement (Digby, no date).

Exploitation of seamen by the shipping industry and poor economic conditions in general may motivate seaman to become maritime pirates (Forsyth et al. 2009). For example, in the Philippines, labor contractors reportedly engaged in exploitative practices, creating substantial resentment and hatred among seaman.

The geography of a country's coastline can foster MP by providing pirates with close proximity to shipping routes (Kraska 2009, Autumn). A country's geography also can make detection and apprehension of maritime pirates difficult.

Existing laws and a country's relationship with nearby countries also affect the social control of MP (Hanson 2009, April 13). Laws forbid maritime police forces from pursuing pirates in territorial waters. For example, in June 2007, after bandits hijacked the *Danica White*, a Danish bulk carrier, the *USS Carter Hall* fired several warning shots in order to rescue the hijacked crew but could not pursue the hijacked vessel into Somali waters.

Somalia illustrates a country with many of the above facilitating conditions (Digby, no date; Kraska 2009, Autumn; Kraska 2010). Somalia is one of the poorest countries in the world, making MP an attractive career. Life expectancy at birth (49.6 years) is one of the worst ten countries in the world. With such a short life expectancy, individuals may not be concerned about risking their lives, especially for lucrative rewards. Per vessel, a majority of ransoms average US$2 million.

Since 1991, Somalia's government became ineffective, resulting in internal conflict and associated atrocities and mass murder (Digby, no date; Kraska 2010).

The ineffectiveness of the Somalia government means that power is in the hands of local groups and individuals. These local groups and individuals have developed a financial interest in committing MP. Corruption and clan loyalty are major facilitators of MP (Kraska 2010). The police, security groups, and government authorities ignore MP because of their clan loyalty. Moreover, Somalia also has a coastline of 3,025 km long, making it difficult to monitor and respond to pirates.

Conditions in Southeast Asia also facilitate attacks on vessels (Chalk 1998). Corrupt individuals in the Chinese government may facilitate rings of maritime pirates in Southeast Asian waters. Accessibility to technologically sophisticated munitions also has contributed to the growth of piracy in this region. The lack of an international legal framework also has promoted MP in Southeast Asian waters.

Pirate Characteristics

Little global research has been done on the individual characteristics of maritime bandits. However, some information is available on the characteristics of Somali maritime bandits. Many individuals who attack vessels around Somalia come from the Somali area of Puntland. In this region, attacking ships has become a conventional and even desirable occupation (Digby, no date; Kraska 2010). Most of these maritime pirates are men between the ages of 20 and 35. Their primary motivation is money.

The British Broadcasting Corporation (BBC), in 2008, reported that three types of Somali maritime pirate gangs attacked vessels (BBC News 2008, www.news.bbc.co.uk; Digby, no date). One type consisted of Somali pirate gang comprises ex-fishermen who are the so-called "brains" of the operation since they know the waters where the attacks take place. These gang members had relied on traditional fishing techniques until the 1990s when they were replaced by illegal trawlers. Somalia's ineffective government made it possible for these illegal trawlers to fish in these waters.

A second type of Somali maritime bandit gang consisted of former militiamen who provided the muscle for pirate attacks (BBC News 2008, www.news.bbc.co.uk). These ex-militiamen had developed expertise in fighting because of their involvement in different Somali conflicts.

Gangs with technical expertise comprised the third type of Somali maritime pirate gangs (BBC News 2008, www.news.bbc.co.uk). Young men with technical training and skills are able to carry out attacks using sophisticated marine technology, satellite phones, global position system (GPS), and military equipment.

Besides the pirate gangs, hundreds of other persons are involved and benefit from maritime piracy. The BBC reported on how the spoils from MP are divided up among different individuals and groups (BBC News 2008, www.news.bbc.co.uk). Based on a US $2 million ransom, pirates receive 30% of the share, sponsors who advance the initial funds for the operation get 30%; financiers who arrange the finance obtain 20%; groups on shore which control the pirate-based territory get 10%; and local community elders and officials obtain 10%. Analysts speculate that major global crime syndicates are also involved in MP.

Methods Used by Sea Bandits

Offenders use a variety of techniques in carrying out their attacks on vessels. Chalk (1998) described three methods used in Southeast Asia. One type is harbor and anchorage attacks and theft in which pirates attack ships using high-speed boats with crews armed with knives. The IMB refers to this piracy as "low-level armed robbery" (LLAR). Perpetrators obtain cash high-value personal items, with an average theft ranging from US$5,000 to US$15,000. Lax security methods facilitate these LLAR crimes and have been prevalent in Indonesian waters.

A second form of MP is the plundering and robbery of ships in territorial waters and on the high seas, which the IMB refers to as medium-level armed assault and robbery (MLAAR) (Chalk 1998). MLAAR offenses involve violent robbery that results in serious injuries or homicide. Organized and heavily armed gangs perpetrate these crimes using speedboats with outboard motors that frequently come from a mother ship (Digby, no date). The offenders frequently are equipped with rocket-propelled grenades and AK-47 s. This type of piracy occurs more often and can substantially impair maritime trade if perpetrated in narrow sea-lanes (Chalk 1998).

The third type of piracy involves hijacking vessels and converting them into phantom ships to carry out illegal trade (Chalk 1998). Known as major criminal hijack (MCHJ), perpetrators usually hijack ships and off-load their cargoes into lighters on the high sea. Pirates will either keep these shipments or sell them in a private market. Offenders then falsely reregister the ships with fraudulent documents so that they can transport new cargoes illegally. The pirates never deliver the shipments to the designated port. Instead, the hijacked ships sail to a different port where a predetermined individual buys the shipment. Pirates can also use these hijacked vessels to transport illicit drugs or other contraband (Forsyth et al. 2009). Large, well-trained and heavily armed gangs are used to carry out MCHJ offenses and the pirates are prepared to use their weapons.

The MCHJ/phantom ship crimes can be very costly to shipowners. Chalk (1998) noted that stolen cargoes cost more than US$200 million annually. In addition, these types of offenses have come increasingly more violent with pirates showing no hesitation in resorting to violence to achieve their criminal goals.

With sophisticated weapons left over from wars, such as the wars in Afghanistan and Cambodia, maritime pirates are able to obtain these high-technology weapons at inexpensive prices, and this trend contributes to MCHJ offenses (Chalk 1998). Perpetrators are able to attack vessels using weapons ranging from handguns and machine guns to Strella surface-to-air missiles (SAMs), anti-ship mines, and rocket-propelled grenades (RPGs).

Responding to MP

Shipping associations, shipowners, and international maritime bodies have developed mechanisms to fight MP in different parts of the world (Hanson 2009, April 13; Dillon 2005, Winter-Spring; Chalk 1998). A majority of the strategies are mainly defensive-oriented; they do not focus on correcting the instability of nation states, which plays an instrumental role in fostering MP (Hanson 2009, April 13).

Analysts have analyzed the anti-MP measures available or implemented in different regions where MP is prevalent. Hanson (2009, April 13) describes the tactics available or used to combat MP in the Gulf of Aden. Onboard deterrents are used and include basic tactics such as fire hoses, deck patrols, and carpet tacks.

Another onboard deterrent is arming the crew (Hanson 2009, April 13). However, most crews are not armed primarily because they are not skilled and do not wish to be armed. Crews are concerned that if they are armed the pirates will go attack them.

Ships also will use private security guards as an onboard deterrent (Hanson 2009, April 13). However, these guards have had an uneven record in deterring MP. One private security contractor, Blackwater, had provided a ship to escort ships sailing through the Gulf of Aden. Hanson (2009, April 13) notes that as of January 2009, no shipping organization had relied on this escort ship.

The shipping industry would like to have more anti-MP efforts from navies around the globe (Hanson 2009, April 13). However, there is concern that the shipping industry is not relying on primary deterrents against MP.

In addition to onboard deterrents, naval deployments are relied on to deter MP (Hanson 2009, April 13). For example, in the Gulf of Aden by 2009, countries, including the United States, Russia, China, and the United Kingdom, had deployed warships to combat MP. The EU NAVFOR, a European Union military operation, and Combined Task Force 150, a multinational group, also have been deployed as anti-MP patrols in the Gulf of Aden. In January 2009, the U.S. established CTF-151, a task force. This task force may enable the U.S. to collaborate with Eastern navies in order to fight MP.

Hanson (2009, April 13) reported that these naval deployments in the Gulf of Aden have had some positive outcomes. The percentage of successful MP attacks went down from 53% in August 2008 to 31% in October 2008. Unfortunately, in November 2008, none of the naval operations in the Gulf of Aden were able to deter the hijacking of an oil supertanker.

A big problem is that these naval deployments may have to be permanent in order to deter MP (Hanson 2009, April 13). Pirate activity may increase significantly in the Gulf of Aden if the naval deployments are removed and if political unrest remains in Somalia.

Regional anti-MP patrols are another tactic to deter piracy (Hanson 2009, April 13). One possibility is that countries in the region such as East African and Middle Eastern nations collaborate in regional patrols of the Gulf of Aden and Somalia coast. To facilitate these regional patrols, western navies could offer ships and technical consultations. A regional anti-MP center could be formed to coordinate anti-piracy activities by improving the sharing of information on MP actions.

The establishment of a coast guard is another strategy for combating MP. One suggestion is that to deter piracy in Somalia and the Gulf of Aden, a Somali coast guard be set up (Hanson 2009, April 13). The African Union or the United Nations could oversee an international coast guard, which is funded by the shipping industry. This coast guard could be effective, especially since Somalia has lacked a viable police force. However, this type of coast guard would be very difficult to implement because of the scarcity of qualified persons in Somalia to participate in the coast guard and the problems in transferring authority to government authorities in Somalia.

In Southeast Asia, similar strategies are employed. The Singapore National Shipowners Association (SNSA) offers both proactive and reactive techniques. The SNSA recommends installing concealed video cameras to record piracy incidents and place all valuable belongings in locked boxes. The SNSA also recommends using water hoses and other equipment to keep pirates from boarding a vessel.

The IMO recommends providing the highest degree of safety for the passengers and crew on board, having the crew maintain control of the ship's navigation, and getting the pirates to leave the vessel as soon as possible. The IMO suggests that "ship masters barricade the crew in secure areas" (Chalk 1998).

The RPC recommends that shipmasters provide a continuous anti-piracy watch (Chalk 1998). In case the ship is approached by pirates, evasive techniques should be implemented. For example, the shipmaster should increase the vessel's speed and begin to erratically alter course. The targeted vessel should approach any military vessels in the area and send a Mayday signal. If the evasive measures do not work, the shipmaster and crew should surrender to the pirates.

In Southeast Asia, unilateral actions have involved increasing coastal patrols and enhancing surveillance technology (Chalk 1998). These efforts have helped to effectively control piracy in the territorial waters of Singapore because of the small area that needs to be monitored and patrolled.

In Malaysia, four new anti-maritime pirate commando units were established to patrol the country's territorial sea-lanes (Chalk 1998). In the waters of the Sulu Sea, the nation also developed a special Sabah Police Field Force Brigade to deal with both pirates and illegal immigrants.

Indonesia has been accused of not making much effort to combat piracy (Chalk 1998). However, even this country has engaged in unilateral action to fight pirates. For example, naval personnel infiltrated pirate gangs and made thirty arrests in July 1992. The Indonesian government's Western Fleet has been successful in arresting pirates in the Malacca Strait and adjacent sea-lanes.

In regard to bilateral efforts, nations have participated in a number of activities (Chalk 1998). In Southeast Asia, Indonesia and Malaysia formed the Maritime Operation Planning (MOP) Team to conduct coordinated patrols in the Strait of Malacca, along their common borders. The governments of Malaysia and the Philippines signed a memorandum of understanding in 1994 to enable both nations to implement coordinated anti-piracy patrols along their shared sea boundary and share information obtained from these activities.

Various multilateral efforts have been launched to combat MP. One example of this multilateral initiative was the establishment of the Southeast Asian RPC (Chalk 1998). The RPC aids maritime officials in obtaining reports of suspicious vessel activity, issues status reports of piracy. The RPC also offers information on anti-piracy strategies and prepares reports on a regular basis.

Since MP can threaten U.S. shipping, the U.S. Navy, the Maritime Administration (MARAD), and other agencies participate in anti-MP efforts (Chalk 1998). The Defense Mapping Agency (DMA) uses its Navigation Information Network (NAVINFONET) to collect data on pirate attacks. On request, the DMA provides Anti-Shipping Activity Messages (ASAM) to any shipowner or operator. In addition, MARAD provides advisories about piracy incidents to all merchant ships under the U.S. flag.

Australia has focused its anti-MP activities in enhancing cooperative anti-piracy efforts to protect Australian national security interests (Chalk 1998). In 1997, the Australian government signed a bilateral maritime treaty with Indonesia to initiate shared action against "soft"/unconventional security problems such as MP. Their treaty could lead to similar treaties with other nations such as Singapore and Malaysia.

Dillon (2005, Winter-Spring) suggests that the IMB and IMO can more effectively respond to MP activities by focusing on four areas. First, the IMO should speed up its efforts to reduce corruption and extortion among port personnel. The IMO should increase inspection and reporting practices in ports. They should publish reports identifying ports that slow down vessels or that have evidence of corruption and organized crime.

Second, the IMO and IMB should report sea robbery differently than MP (Hanson 2009, April 13). At ports, police patrolling and investigation of sea robbery should be strengthened.

A third measure is that the IMO and IMB should widen the definition of MP to include pirate activities in both territorial waters and on the high seas (Hanson 2009, April 13).

Finally, Hanson (2009, April 13) suggests that the IMO and IMB should classify and report maritime terrorism differently than MP. In this way, the shipping industry and policy officials can formulate anti-maritime terrorism policies and procedures.

Problems in Fighting MP

Fighting MP presents many difficulties (Mo 2002). Pirates are very mobile and have technology and sophisticated weapons. Depending on the location, pirates can easily go between territorial waters, making it problematic for one nation to respond to pirates. Maritime bandits may not be easily identifiable because they are unemployed fishermen or seamen. The harsh poverty that many of these pirates experience is a major obstacle to fighting piracy. Conflicting interests also limit the effectiveness of anti-piracy efforts. For example, conflicts between public and private interests and conflicts between international demands and domestic concerns can limit the ability to control MP.

Ultimately, the success in deterring MP lies in improving the political stability and economy of nation states over time (Hanson 2009, April 13). For example, in 2006 in Somalia, MP came to a halt for a period of time when the Islamic Courts Union controlled Somalia.

Piracy and International Law

Two documents, the Geneva' Convention on the High Seas (April 29, 1958) (Also known as the Convention on the High Seas, April 29, 1958. U.N. Conference on the Law of the Sea {UNCLOS1}. Entered into force 30 September 1962) and the United Nations Convention on the Law of the Sea (LOSC) (10 December, 1982) can be used to fight piracy incidents (UN, United Nations, Convention on the Law of the Sea of 10 December 1982 (LOSC). (Chalk 1998; http://www.un.org/depts/los/convention_agreements/convention_overview_convention.htm). Each document has provisions against piracy and requires signatories to initiate anti-piracy activities. However, both laws restrict their jurisdiction to dealing with MP attacks on the high seas, and most piracy incidents take place in the territorial waters of countries. In addition, the LOSC's provision for extending coastal sovereignty to 12 miles and another 200 miles as Exclusive Economic Zones (EEZs) has weakened the effectiveness of international law to fight pirates.

Anti-MP activities are also limited by laws and policies related to sovereignty that until recent times prohibited outside nations from pursuing pirates inland and destroying their inland structures (Hanson 2009, April 13). The United Nations on December 2, 2008 passed a resolution that permits outside countries to go into the territorial waters of Somalia to pursue pirates. On December 16, 2008, another United Nations resolution gives implicit authorization for outside states to pursue pirates on land.

Outside nations face other legal obstacles in responding to MP in the Gulf of Aden and elsewhere (Hanson 2009, April 13). A variety of countries have vested interest after a vessel is attacked by pirates. Unfortunately, deciding which country should prosecute the pirates is not clear. For example, which country should prosecute pirates in a case in which a ship is built in the U.S., is owned by Greeks, managed by Italians, crewed by Cypriots, financed by Germans, has cargo that is owned by a multinational company, is attacked by pirates in international waters, and is arrested in Indonesia?

From a legal perspective, the best practice is to prosecute pirates in the area where they are arrested (Hanson 2009, April 13). However, countries in these locations may not have the justice system capacity to prosecute MP. For example, countries in eastern Africa do not have effective justice systems to prosecute MP attacks that take place in the Gulf of Aden.

United Nations resolutions in 2008 were passed to assist in the prosecution of offenders in MP attacks (Hanson 2009, April 13). In their 2008 resolutions, the United Nations does not require nations to accept MP suspects for prosecution. However, a clause in the December 2, 2008, United Nations resolution follows the 1988 United Nations Convention for the Suppression of Unlawful Acts against the Safety of Maritime Navigation by obligating states in coastal areas to prosecute MP cases unless they can demonstrate why the United Nations Convention is not applicable.

Critics suggest that the United Nations resolution is insufficient for prosecuting pirates (Hanson 2009, April 13). Experts recommend that nations involved in shipping and regional governments should establish agreements that coordinate the detention of MP suspects and determine where they will be jailed and prosecuted. The U.S. has developed such agreements, such as the maritime agreements to respond to drug trafficking in the Caribbean.

Nations also can enter into bilateral agreements for prosecuting MP (Hanson 2009, April 13). However, James Kraska notes that even if countries have an agreement, countries do not want to receive difficult MP cases (Hanson 2009, April 13). Because of this reluctance, some captured MP suspects have remained onboard warships for months.

Legal Issues Affecting Shipping Companies' MP-Related Losses

Shipping companies that face MP-associated losses face a number of legal and insurance issues (Lennox-Gentle 2010). Hawkes (2001) described some of these issues using the case of *New York Marine & General Insurance Company v. M/V Rauten* (U.S District Court for the Southern District 1999). While transporting cargo, the *M/V Rauten* was attacked by pirates and her cargo was stolen. The company that owned the goods used its insurance policy to recoup its losses. However, the insurance company filed a lawsuit against the shipowner for the cargo losses.

The shipowner filed a motion for summary judgment, arguing that the cargo losses resulted from a pirate attack and under the US Carriage of Goods by Sea Act of 1936, pirates were defined as "public enemies" (*New York Marine & General Insurance Company v. M/V Rauten,* U.S District Court for the Southern District 1999; Hawkes 2001). According to this Act, shipowners are not liable for actions caused by these public enemies.

The court denied the shipowner's motion for summary judgment, determining that the case must go to trial because the issues raised questions of fact (*New York Marine & General Insurance Company v. M/V Rauten,* U.S District Court for the

Southern District 1999; Hawkes 2001). The court ruled that the location of the ship when the pirate attack took place needed to be determined. If the attack on the vessel occurred immediately offshore, then the thieves would not be classified as pirates under the law. Another question that needed to be answered is whether pirates and so-called public enemies are the same. Another question of fact, according to the court, is whether the shipowners were negligent in regard to the incident. Hawkes (2001) points out that these three issues determine the shipowner's liability in a case of theft on a vessel.

The definitions of the terms, "piracy" and "high seas", have been clearly delineated (Hawkes 2001). For example, in a 1969 decision, the U.S. Supreme Court defined the "high seas" as "the international waters not subject to the dominion of any single nation." The definition of piracy originated in the law promulgated by King James I of England. King James I determined that piracy was "robbery on the high seas" that were perpetrated by persons of a "certain lewd and ill-disposed" character. According to the U.S. criminal code, individuals who commit crimes of piracy on the high seas as defined by the "law of nations" and who are "brought into or found in the U.S., shall be imprisoned for life."

The 1982 United Nations Convention on the Law of the Sea (UNCLOS) reaffirmed the same definition of piracy on the high seas (Hawkes 2001). In its Merchant Shipping and Maritime Security Act of 1997, the United Kingdom used the UNCLOS language (http://www.unesco.org/culture/natlaws/media/pdf/gb/gb_merchantships&maritsecu1997_engorof.pdf).

An international organization known as Comite Maritime International (CMI), which includes Interpol, the IMO, and the IMB, drafted the Model National Law on Acts of Piracy and Maritime Piracy (CMI, Comite Maritime International, no date; Hawkes 2001; themaritimeadvocate.com, no date). Their law extends the definition of piracy to encompass acts that take place on the high seas or in territorial waters of a specific country. In addition, the law defines a pirate as any person committing an act that constitutes piracy, and this law would define public enemies, thieves, and other assailants as pirates.

Even if the attackers in the *M/V Rauten* case could be considered pirates, were the crew negligent (*New York Marine & General Insurance Company v. M/V Rauten,* U.S District Court for the Southern District 1999; Hawkes 2001)? If the crew members of the *M/V Rauten* were negligent, would the shipowner remain liable? An important question is whether the piracy incident was foreseeable. If the incident was foreseeable, did the *M/V Rauten* crew use adequate precautions?

Case law dictates that shipowners must take reasonable precautions to protect for their crew and cargo (Hawkes 2001). If their vessel is attacked by pirates, an important question is whether the shipowners used reasonable procedures and practices against these threats. Reasonable procedures can be determined in light of the cost of implementing security procedures, how do these practices compare to those in the industry, and the type and degree of the threat. Reasonableness of security practices also can be evaluated in terms of the vessel's type of cargo, sailing routes, and ports of call.

MP can result in personal injury litigation (Hawkes 2001). The Jones Act of 1920 (also known as The Merchant Marine Act of 1920, P.L. 66–261) established a new cause of action for seamen who were injured on boarding a ship. Prior to the Jones Act of 1920 (also known as The Merchant Marine Act of 1920, P.L. 66–261), a seaman could only sue the shipowners for unseaworthiness. The seamen had to prove that the ship's particular unseaworthiness caused his or her injury.

Under the Jones Act of 1920 (also known as The Merchant Marine Act of 1920, P. L. 66–261), a seaman can sue the shipowners for being negligent in the way that they planned or failed to plan for MP attacks (Hawkes 2001). The number of these lawsuits is unknown. However, the cases are often settled before the time of the trial verdict.

With regard to the seaworthiness, a ship may be found unseaworthy if she is ready for her intended use or is not outfitted adequately or safe for a sea voyage (Hawkes 2001). A vessel that is not equipped or outfitted properly to protect against pirates may be considered unseaworthy if the ship takes routes into known pirate waters. If a vessel is deemed unseaworthy at the outset of the voyage, the shipowners may be liable for personal injuries resulting from the MP and cargo losses, and other losses.

Individuals may even be held criminally negligent for pirate attacks. According to the U.S. criminal code, a person "shall be fined not more than $1,000, imprisoned for not more than 5 years, or both" for knowingly sending or trying to send a U.S. ship to sea that is unseaworthy (Hawkes 2001).

In *United States of America v. Pedro Rivera* (United States Court of Appeals for the First Circuit 1997, http://www.leagle.com/decision/1997353131F3d222_1331), the court ruled on the issue of criminal liability. The original case arose from an accident and oil spill that did not result in injuries or death. In 1994, off the coast of San Juan, Puerto Rico, the tow wire that connected the tugboat, *Emily S*, to the barge, *Morris J. German*, parted, and the barge then ran aground, spilling her cargo. The general manager of the company that managed the tugboat, Pedro Rivera, was found guilty of violating the law because he failed to replace a towing wire that had deteriorated.

The case was then appealed to the U.S. Court of Appeals for the First Circuit to determine if the criminal conviction was legal and whether the conviction was justified based on the facts (United States Court of Appeals for the First Circuit 1997; Hawkes 2001). The appellate court determined that an individual can be found criminally negligent if the person actually sends a ship to sea knowing that the vessel is unseaworthy and that the unseaworthiness likely will put human life at risk. The appellate court held that the government only proved that the parting of the tow wire could endanger life and a significantly higher order of test was needed.

According to Hawkes (2001), *United States of America v. Pedro Rivera* (United States Court of Appeals for the First Circuit 1997. http://www.leagle.com/decision/1997353131F3d222_1331) established a precedent for the maritime industry. Future courts may hold that failure to provide effective security measures when sending a ship to waters where pirate attacks are likely could be the same as sending an unseaworthy vessel to sea (United States Court of Appeals for the First Circuit 1997, http://www.leagle.com/decision/1997353131F3d222_1331).

References

Barrios, E. (2005). Casting wider nets. Addressing the maritime piracy problem in Southeast Asia. Boston Coll Intl & Comp Law Rev, 28, 149.

BBC News (2008). Piracy. http://www.news.bbc.co.uk.

Boland, B. (2010). Piracy can and must be suppressed. U.S. Naval Institute Proceedings. 0041798X, 136 (7). Retrieved from http://web.ebscohost.com.proxylib.csueastbay.edu/ehost/detail?vid=4&….

Bowden, A. (2010). The economic costs of maritime piracy. One Earth Future Foundation Working Paper. Oceansbeyondpiracy.org. www.steamshipmutual.com/Downloads/Piracy/EconomicCostPiracyOEFReport.pdf.

Burnett, J.S. (2002). Dangerous waters: Modern piracy and terror on the high seas. New York: Dutton.

Chalk, P. (1998). Contemporary maritime piracy in Southeast Asia. Stud Conflict & Terrorism, 21: 87–112.

CMI, Comite Maritime International. (no date). Acts of piracy and maritime violence. www.comitemaritime.org/Uploads/pdf/Acts_PiracyWP.pdf.

Digby, B. (n.d.). The new pirates. Warringal Publications.

Dillon, D.R. (2000, June 22). Piracy in Asia: A growing barrier to maritime trade. Backgrounder #1379 on Homeland Security. The Heritage Foundation. http://www.heritage.org/research/reports/2000/06/piracy-in-asia-a-growing-barrier-to-maritime-trade.

Dillon, D.R. (2005, Winter-Spring). Maritime piracy: Defining the problem. SAIS Review of Intl Affairs, 25 (1): 155–165.

Forsyth, C.J., Gisclair, K.H., & Forsyth, Y.A. (2009). Waterborne crime: examining contemporary piracy. Deviant Behav, 30: 669–679.

Hanson, S. (2009, April 13). Combating maritime piracy. Backgrounder. Council on Foreign Relations. http://www.cfr.org/piracy/combating-maritime-piracy/p18376.

Hastings, J.V. (2009). Geographies of state failure and sophistication in maritime piracy hijackings. Political Geography, 30: 1–11.

Hawkes, K.G. (2001). Don't give up the ship. Security Management, 45 (9): 81–85.

King, J. (2005). The security of merchant shipping. Marine Policy, 29: 235–245.

Kraska, J. (2009, Autumn). Fresh thinking for an old problem. Report of the Naval War College Workshop on Countering Maritime Piracy. Navale War Coll Rev, 62 (4): 141–154.

Kraska, J. (2010). Freakonomics of maritime piracy. Brown J of World Affairs, 16 (2): 109–119.

Land, C. (2007). Flying the black flag: Revolt, revolution and the social organization of piracy in the 'golden age.' Managem Organiz History, 2 (2): 169–192.

Lennox-Gentle, T. (2010). Piracy, sea robbery, and terrorism: Enforcing laws to deter ransom payments and hijacking. Transp Law J, 37, 199.

Mo, J. (2002). Options to combat maritime piracy in Southeast Asia. Ocean Develop Int Law, 33: 343–358.

Mueller, G.O.W., & Adler, F. (1985). Outlaws of the ocean. New York: Hearst Marine Books.

New York Marine & General Insurance Company v. M/V Rauten (U.S District Court for the Southern District, 1999).

Roach, J.A. (2004). Initiatives to enhance maritime security at sea. Marine Pol, 28: 41–66.

Sanchez, R. (2014, May 26). Memorial Day marks ties between USS Cole attack and 911. http://www.cnn.com/2014/05/25/us/uss-cole-memorialday/index.html?iref=allsearch.

United States of America v. Pedro Rivera (United States Court of Appeals for the First Circuit, 1997). http://www.leagle.com/decision/1997353131F3d222_1331.

Chapter 14
Kidnapping Hoaxes

Hoaxes have occurred throughout history (Farquhar 2005). Individuals may falsely report that they were raped, kidnapped, or victimized in other ways (Lonsway 2010; Osava 2007). The media has reported a number of kidnapping hoaxes (KHs) over the years. They occur in the U.S. and other countries (Osava 2007, February 27; Holstege 2008, September 12; Huffpost World 2010, December 28). However, researchers know little about this phenomenon. This chapter reports on cases from the Kidnapping Hoaxes Project (KHP) to assess the social patterns of faked abductions and the impact of these hoaxes on local communities and law enforcement (see Appendix I).

Individuals participate in fake abductions for a variety of rational and nonrational reasons. Criminals use KHs to extort ransoms from unsuspecting victims. Individuals may fabricate a kidnapping as a publicity stunt or in response to the breakup of a relationship. Individuals may concoct a kidnapping story to cover up a homicide or other crimes that they have committed (Canning et al. 2011). In other instances, groups and governments may stage kidnappings or exaggerate the number of actual kidnappings to achieve political purposes.

Ransom KH, also known as "virtual kidnapping" is popular in certain countries such as Brazil, Mexico, Argentine, and the U.S. (Holstege 2008, September 12). According to the newspaper, *O Estado de Sao Paula*, the military police centre in Sao Paulo received 3,150 reports of fabricated kidnapping attempts in the first 45 days of 2007 (Osava 2007, February 27). These reports constitute a small percentage of the actual cases of fake kidnapping attempts since a majority of victims never report them. Many calls come from the country's prisons and are collect calls. Law enforcement advises individuals not to accept these calls unless know the person who is calling.

Persons who carry out fake kidnappings may use a variety of methods and resources. They may harm themselves to prove to the police that they were true victims of a kidnapping and assault and battery. They may also victimize their target. In Dewsbury, U.K., a 33-year-old mother, reportedly drugged her 9-year-old

S. Morewitz, *Kidnapping and Violence*,
https://doi.org/10.1007/978-1-4939-2117-1_14

daughter and tied to her to a roof beam as part of a ransom KH to make 50,000 lb (Wainwright 2008, November 13; KHP Case 32).

Offenders may act alone or enlist the help of friends and others in carrying out their KHs (KHP Case 48; Stolz 2009, March 26; KHP Case 55; ibnlive.in.com 2011, April 25).

KHs as Publicity Stunts

Individuals may fabricate a kidnapping as a publicity stunt. In 1950, a 22-year-old French actress reportedly staged a kidnapping and rape as a publicity stunt for her play, *No Orchids for Miss Blandish*, which is based on James Hadley Chase's mystery novel about an heiress who is abducted and raped by a gangster (museumofhoaxes.com no date; KHP Case 49).

Current and Past Relationships

Individuals in relationships and those who have been in relationships may fabricate kidnappings. The desire for autonomy and intimacy in dating relationships during adolescence may lead teenagers to stage kidnappings. In some cases, a teen couple may stage a kidnapping in order to stay together overnight (Bergreen 2011, May 24; KHP Case 11).

Persons may stage kidnappings to help them deal with the strains and tensions within relationships and the breakup of relationships. A person may stage a kidnapping to test her or his partner's true love and devotion. In Spain, in 2010, a woman reportedly staged her own abduction to test whether her husband would pay the ransom (Huffpost World 2010, December 28; KHP Case 15).

Other people may concoct a kidnapping story because they develop significant anxiety over getting married or other changes in roles. For example, the so-called "runaway bride" allegedly staged a kidnapping days before her lavish wedding in Georgia (KHP Case 37).

Domestic violence (DV) victims may stage a kidnapping/assault hoax to cover up the DV incidents and related injuries (Lavelle 2010, March 29; KHP Case 3).

Individuals may fabricate a story about their partner abducting their children in order to get custody of the children. The persons may feel that their partners are abusing the children and making up a story about them kidnapping their children is a viable way to gain sole custody of their children.

The police often have difficulty investigating cases of children who are falsely reported as kidnapped or missing (Canning et al. 2011). Law enforcement investigators often have trouble determining if the child has been actually kidnapped or if the parent has actually killed the child and made a false child abduction report. The lack of witnesses and a clear crime scene hamper their investigations into kidnapped or missing children.

In the Caylee Anthony homicide investigation, the mother, initially claimed that her daughter had been abducted (KHP Case 38). The mother later recanted her story and then claimed that her daughter had drowned in the family's swimming pool.

In an investigation of 61 adjudicated false reports, Canning et al. (2011) discovered that the mean age of the victim was 5 years of age. The victims had lived in high-risk families and were murdered by their biological parents. The victims were often killed because they were unwanted or considered an obstacle to some goal. In other instances, the children were murdered as part of a pattern of child abuse and maltreatment.

In other cases, a person may be in conflict with a partner or friend and may commit a KH in order to meet some unfulfilled need.

School- or Work-Motivated KHs

Persons may apply to college and fail to get admitted. On these occasions, the failed applicant may fabricate a kidnapping to avoid the embarrassment, humiliation, and stigma of telling her or his family and friends. Students may be experiencing humiliating poor school performance, the stresses of school, work, or other problems and drop out of school. Instead of telling their parents and friends, they fabricate their own kidnapping (Linthicum and Vives 2010, May 14; KHP Case 30). Children may use KHs to cover up the fact they ran away from home to avoid upsetting their parents (Fitzgerald and People 2006, July).

Some individuals may stage a kidnapping in order to avoid going to work (Pelton 1994a, June 8; Pelton 1994b, June 9; KHP Case 17).

Sometimes, persons who lose their jobs may fabricate a kidnapping to avoid telling their family members and friends that they lost their job. In other incidents, the offenders may use a KH to cover up their absence from work.

Alcohol and Drugs

Alcohol and drug use can affect KHs in different ways. The use of alcohol and other drugs can impair individuals' state of consciousness and judgment, which can lead them to stage a kidnapping. Intoxicated individuals also may make false allegations (Fitzgerald and People 2006, July).

Perpetrators also can use alcohol and other drugs to render their victims unconscious so that they are unable to resist a staged kidnapping or they are unaware of the incident (Wainwright 2008, November 13; KHP Case 32).

Persons who use and sell illicit drugs may be more likely to stage kidnappings than those who are not involved in illicit drugs (Hasch 2010; KHP Case 10).

Individuals who deal in illicit drugs may become in debt for substantial sums of money and stage ransom kidnappings or commit other crimes to pay their large debts.

Mental Health Problem-Related KHs

People who panic or suffer severe psychosocial difficulties may stage a kidnapping. In response to severe acute and chronic psychosocial problems, persons may experience an inability to cope and stage a kidnapping to deal with their difficulties. Some people may be paranoid, delusional, or suffer other mental problems that increase their risk of fabricating a kidnapping.

Other Stigmatizing and Humiliating Situations

Individuals may stage a kidnapping to avoid other stigmatizing and humiliating situations. Persons may fabricate a kidnapping because they are having difficulties coping with a health problem.

Racial Hoaxes

Persons may fabricate a kidnapping that involves alleged perpetrators of a different race. As a result of the national and international media focus, this incident and other racial hoaxes (RHs) may revive old racist fears and stereotypes (Russell 1995–1996).

Susan Smith became infamous in 1994 when she fabricated a 9-day kidnapping of her two sons. Smith reported that African-American men had perpetrated the kidnappings when in fact she had drowned her two sons.

In KHP Case 45, a 28-year-old African-American female entertainer reportedly accused white male members of the Duke University Lacrosse team of raping her and holding her against her will in a bathroom at a Duke University Lacrosse Team party (*Associated Press* 2006, December 22, KHP Case 45).

Hate Crime KHs

Persons also may commit hate crime hoaxes (HCHs) (Taibbi and Simms-Phillips 1989). These offenders fabricate abductions that depict hatred based on race, religion, race, ethnicity, and other social categories. HCHs can worsen tensions between social groups and may reinforce prejudice and stereotypes toward these groups. For example, in November 1987, an African-American adolescent in upstate New York reported that she had been raped and sodomized by a gang of white men (Taibbi and Simms-Phillips 1989).

HCHs can trigger community and national responses, especially from civil rights leaders. In the November 1987 case, African-American civil rights advocates took up the Brawley case and argued that the case illustrated the failure of the civil rights movement (Taibbi and Simms-Phillips 1989). The discovery of the hate crime as a hoax may have diminished the criticisms and credibility of the civil rights leaders.

Kidnapping and Sexual Assault Hoaxes

People will concoct stories of being both kidnapped and raped or sexually assaulted. In these instances, the person may claim that they were raped or sexually assaulted one time or numerous times.

False Rumors of Kidnappings at Stores and Malls

Some false rumors have been spread about children who are abducted in a large store or shopping mall (HelpFindMyChild 2009, July 17). One false rumor involved a young girl who was kidnapped in a large store. This young victim's hair was cut and dyed and her clothing was changed to disguise her as a boy before the child was secretly taken out of the store with detection by the police and store security. Similar false rumors of bizarre child abductions have been circulated in the U.K. In some of the rumors, the victim is either a boy or girl.

KHs Involving Automobiles

Individuals will fake kidnappings involving automobiles and other vehicles. In some cases, the person alleges that he or she is kidnapped and then stuffed into the trunk of a vehicle. In 1999, a woman reportedly concocted a story about being abducted and forced into the trunk of her automobile and driven to the Upper Peninsula of Michigan (Coen 1999, August 12; KHP Case 24). The suspect was discovered safe on a road near Norway, MI.

Offenders may make up a story about being kidnapped after having mechanical trouble or after a minor automobile accident, as in the Bonnie Sweeten hoax (Johnson 2009, May 27; KHP Case 26). The persons may claim that they were not only kidnapped but that their vehicle was also carjacked. In the Bonnie Sweeten hoax, the suspect claimed that she and her daughter were kidnapped, and the suspect's automobile was also carjacked. Individuals also will claim that others in the vehicle are kidnapped and stuffed in the vehicle's trunk.

Faked Abductions and Ransom Demands

The need for money is a significant factor in some KHs; individuals will fabricate a kidnapping to obtain ransoms from unsuspecting victims. In 2010, in Pittsburgh, PA, three men allegedly concocted a kidnapping story because they needed money (Hasch 2010).

Criminals use ransom KHs to extort money from the families of human trafficking (HT) victims and other vulnerable persons. In Mexico, a country plagued by kidnappings and HT, extortion gangs obtain ransom money in two ways without abducting them (Holstege 2008, September 12). In these so-called "virtual kidnappings", the offenders discover when people in the U.S. are traveling to Mexico and then demand a ransom from the travelers' family members. Abductors rely on the fact that the family members cannot communicate easily with the traveler, especially in remote areas where cell phone service is not available. The kidnappers hope that their threats to torture and kill their loved ones will prompt them to pay the ransoms before they discover that their loved ones have not been kidnapped.

A more frequently used technique is for the virtual kidnappers to obtain smugglers' lists of undocumented immigrants and contact their families in the U.S. (Holstege 2008, September 12; KHP Case 81). The virtual abductors pose as coyotes and demand ransoms. The perpetrators often demand ransoms at the time that the undocumented immigrants are waiting to cross the border or are on their route to a Phoenix drop-house.

The Phoenix division of the U.S. Immigration and Customs Enforcement (ICE) reportedly receive a report about smugglers holding a hostage on a weekly basis (Holstege 2008, September 12). According to the Assistant Special Agent-in-Charge Armando Garcia, about 25% of the abductions are fake. Families from different parts of the country are reporting ransom kidnappings and report that the kidnapper calls from a Phoenix-area cell phone. The abductors typically are demanding ransoms between $2,000 and $4,000, which is twice the average smuggling fee (*Associated Press* 2008, September 28; KHP Case 53).

Local and state law enforcement agencies in the U.S. are also receiving calls about virtual kidnappings of U.S. travelers in Mexico (Holstege 2008, September 12; KHP Case 82). The Phoenix Police Department reportedly investigated a possible kidnapping that was actually a fake kidnapping. In that case, parents received a ransom demand for $2,500 from someone who alleged that their 16-year-old daughter was kidnapped and being held hostage (Holstege 2008, September 12; KHP Case 82). The Federal Bureau of Investigation (FBI) initiated an international search for the girl and discovered that she was actually safe with relatives in Mexico. The parents did not pay the ransom.

As noted previously, in Brazil, individuals inside the country's prisons have made thousands of KHs in order to demand ransoms from unsuspecting persons (Osava 2007, February 27).

Elderly persons are vulnerable to scams about KHs. For example, in 2010, in Delaware County, a scam artist allegedly called an elderly couple and claimed that he had abducted their son (Shimell 2010; KHP Case 8). The perpetrator demanded money for his return. However, the police used a wiretap and determined that the call was a KH. Law enforcement concluded that the offender was trying to target senior citizens.

Faked Kidnappings for Political Gain

KHs can be used to aggravate ethnic tensions among rival ethnic groups who are vying for political power. For example, in Iraq in 2005, Iraqi security troops, who were supported by U.S. forces, surrounded the town of Madain after reports of Sunni militant abductions of up to 100 Shiites residents (Mohammed 2005, April 18). However, apparently these reports of numerous Sunni militant kidnappings were greatly exaggerated, possibly due to a dispute among tribes or as a political strategy.

Technology and False Kidnappings

Technology can speed up the transmission of false stories about kidnappings. As previously described, the spread of false rumors of child kidnappings at stores in the U.K. originated on the Internet and quickly spread to various towns (HelpFind MyChild 2009, July 17). Individuals can use cell phones to send text messages and photographs to facilitate the rapid transmission of false reports as in the case involving the woman in Spain who allegedly sent a text message and photograph from a mobile phone (Huffpost World 2010, December 28; KHP Case 15).

Moreover, technology can enable persons to make false police reports without being detected. In one incident, a girl used an emergency-only cell phone to report that a family member had abducted her in Indiana and that she was being held against her will in a house in Aurora, IL (Roth 2005, January 1; KHP Case 39). The telephone call could not be traced. Nevertheless, law enforcement arrested her and charged her with making a fake kidnapping report.

Technology also can be used to investigate alleged incidents and apprehend the suspects (KHP Case 10; Hasch 2010). Authorities in KHP Case 10 used a pen register, an electronic device that records dialed numbers, to ascertain the location of one of the suspects in the ransom KH. Law enforcement also placed a tracking device in the bag containing the $10,000 ransom that they delivered to the alleged kidnappers. Despite using the tracking device, the Pittsburgh Police Department reported that it lost the $10,000 ransom (Hasch 2010; Ove 2011).

Forensic audio analysis can be employed to solve KHs. Hanson (2004) analyzed a case study to illustrate the ways in which forensic audio techniques can be used to solve KHs.

Law Enforcement Responses to KHs

The police vary in their responses to alleged abduction reports depending on their perception of the credibility of the claims. In some countries such as Brazil and Mexico, the sheer volume of KH can drain the resources of law enforcement agencies (Osava 2007, February 27).

Police departments report spending considerable time and money to resolve KH cases (KHP Case 30; Linthicum and Vives 2010, May 14; KHP Case 28; Gottesman, February 2, 1994, p. 1; KHP Case 14; *Associated Press*, December 11, 2007). Authorities may investigate abduction claims using a variety of resources, including Special Weapons and Tactics (SWAT) teams and technology to assist in these cases (KHP Case 10; Hasch 2010; KHP Case 21; Yates 2004, February 21; KHP Case 28; Gottesman 1994, February 2). In these cases, the police are taken off of important cases to investigate fake abductions.

In KHP Case 32, the police in West Yorkshire, U.K., employed 200 officers to search for a 9-year-old girl, after her mother allegedly fabricated her abduction (KHP Case 32; Wainwright 2008, November 13). To carry out the search, authorities reportedly searched 1,800 properties, checked every park in Dewsbury, stopped up 1,760 automobiles and passersby, and used 75% of all of the law enforcement dogs. The police work involved 1,800 h. The huge police search reportedly cost almost pounds 3.2 million.

In some cases, the police report on the costs associated with investigating KHs. In KHP Case 5, Sgt. William Palmer stated that taxpayers, insurance companies, the three suspects' families and other individuals will have to pay thousands of dollars to cover the costs of the fake abduction case (*Associated Press*, March 14, 2011). The police reported that the police work alone in KHP Case 5 will cost more than $1,200. In this case, a homicide investigator was taken off of normal duties to work on the case and four other officers investigated the fake abduction.

In KHP Case 26, almost 28 h of multiple law enforcement agencies searched for a 38-year-old mother and her 9-year-old daughter before law enforcement discovered that it was a hoax (Johnson 2009, May 27).

In KHP Case 3, law enforcement in Chula Vista, CA, searched for two adult men who allegedly grabbed and beat a woman jogger on March 3 2010 (Lavelle 2010, March 29). Their investigation involved emailing 8,000 households to warn parents who children attending schools in the area. During the following week, the Chula Vista, CA, police organized a community meeting that attracted 200 people.

AMBER alerts may be issued for individuals who claim that a child has been abducted (KHP Case 12; Welch 2011, January 28; KHP Case 13; Anonymous, May

21, 2011, ktvu.com.) Authorities then will cancel the AMBER alert when they discover that the abduction was a hoax.

At some point in the investigations, the suspects confess, or the police realize that the kidnapping claim is fake. The hoaxers may then be charged with filing a false police report, disorderly conduct, or other crime (KHP Case 22; *Associated Press*, April 24, 2009).

Once the police discover that the kidnapping incident is a hoax, they may try to squash false rumors about the incident, especially when the rumors involve commercial establishments such as stores and shopping malls (Grzegorek 2010, December 15, KHP Case 41; helpfindmychild.net 2009, July 17).

Health and Social Services Professional Respond to Kidnapping and Sexual Assault Hoaxes

Not only are law enforcement agencies involved in investigating KHs, health and social services professionals, including hospital and emergency room staff, often respond to KHs that also involve injuries related to assault hoaxes (KHP Case 5; *Associated Press*, March 14, 2011; KHP Case 9; KHP Case 28; Gottesman 1994, February 2). Hoaxers may claim that they were sexually assaulted or were the victims of assault and battery.

In KHP 5, the suspects, three girls, reportedly were taken on ambulance rides to Hennepin County Medical Center (*Associated Press*, March 14, 2011). The suspects also had sexual assault examinations.

Suspects in fake abduction cases may have self-inflicted injuries to support their stories, and these injuries may lead to medical assessment and treatment in hospitals and other settings. For example, the suspect in KHP Case 9 may have intentionally hit her head, which she claimed resulted from being attacked from behind (Reynolds 2009).

In some cases, the alleged hoaxers may appear to be suffering from mental health problems, and they may receive mental health evaluation and treatment (KHP Case 4; Anonymous, September 30, 2009, ksat.com; KHP Case 26). In some fake kidnapping incidents, the suspects' attorneys will mention their clients' psychosocial status. In one KH, the attorney for the suspect reported that his client had received mental health therapy and was now spending time with her children (KHP Case 26; myfoxphilly.com no date).

Court Responses to KHs

The courts respond to KHs based on a number of factors, such as the type of charges filed, the seriousness of the charges, and publicity about the case. The suspects may face significant punishment, especially if the investigation of the staged abduction has been very costly.

Families may be broken up as a result of KHs. Child protection services (CPS) agencies will investigate these incidents and remove children from families if they believe that their safety and well-being is jeopardized.

If the suspects confess early in the investigation, they may receive a lighter sentence. Defendants may seek leniency by asserting that mental illness, age, or some other factor should lessen their punishment.

In KHP Case 35, the attorney for the suspect argued that his client suffered from severe mental illness and alcohol abuse (Inbar 2009, November 3). The attorney reported that about 4 months before the KH, his client had entered a rehabilitation clinic to obtain treatment. However, after his client had completed treatment, he characterized her as a "mental powder keg."

Defendants who are convicted may be fined for the offense and required to pay costs. For example, in KHP Case 48, the court fined the suspect $5,000 for the hoax and ordered her to pay $18,500 in costs (Stolz 2009, March 26).

Impact of Fake Kidnappings

Victims, including the family members of the suspects may become extremely embarrassed and humiliated by the incident and develop stress-related symptoms. They may become less trustful of people as a result of being victimized. Persons who are scammed in KHs may lose thousands of dollars or more if they pay a ransom.

The residents of local communities where abduction hoaxes occur can become angry and demoralized when they find out that the kidnapping was actually a hoax. Individuals who participate for hours or days in search parties can feel especially angry when they discover that the abduction was fabricated. The police and community leaders may become particularly concerned that highly publicized KHs create a "cry wolf" syndrome, inhibiting law enforcement and community residents from responding to real kidnappings in the future.

KHs involving stores and other commercial establishments can turn away customers who are fearful for the safety of themselves and their family members. The epidemic of KHs in certain countries can halt or limit tourism in those countries and can jeopardize economic investments and development in those nations.

Famous RHs can adversely impact nations because they can worsen existing race relations and resurrect old racist fears and stereotypes. In addition, highly publicized KHs involving relationships can affect gender relations and public views about marriage. For example, in KHP Case 23, the story of the so-called "runaway bride", may trigger changes in public expectations and beliefs about brides and grooms who are preparing for a wedding.

Policy and Organizational Responses to KHs

Pelligrini (2008) recommends further research to assess the underlying risk factors for criminal hoaxes. Security specialists offer advice on how to respond to KHs and other crimes such as extortion, hostage-taking, and kidnapping (Godfrey 1982). Security consultants provide strategies for determining if ransom abductions are real and ways to prevent these incidents.

References

Farquhar, M. (2005). Treasury of deception: Liars, misleaders, hoodwinkers, and the extraordinary true stories of history's great hoaxes, fakes, and frauds. London: Penguin Books.

Holstege, S. (2008, September 12). Fake kidnappers demanding real ransoms, ICE agents say. azcentral.com. http://www.azcentral.com/news/articles/2008/09/12/200080912virtualk….

Lonsway, K.A. (2010). Trying to move the elephant in the living room: Responding to the challenge of false rape reports. Viol Against Women, 16 (12): 1356–71, 1372–1374.

Osava, M. (2007, February 27). Epidemic of fake kidnappings. IPS ipsnews.net. Retrieved from http://ipsnews.net/news.asp?idnews=36751.

Huffpost World. (2010, December 28). Spanish woman fakes kidnapping to manipulate husband: Report. Huffingtonpost.com. http://www.huffingtonpost.com/2010/12/28/wife-fakes-kidnapping_n_….

Anonymous. (2009, September 30). ksat.com. Woman arrested in kidnapping hoax. She claimed twin sister was abducted. http://www.ksat.com/news/21157743/detail.html.

Anonymous. (2011, May 21). ktvu.com. Amber alert canceled in possible kidnapping hoax. http://ktvu.com/news/27979837/detail.html.

Associated Press. (2006, December 22). Duke District Attorney drops rape charges against 3 lacrosse players. Foxnews. http://www.foxnews.com/story/0,2933,238307,00.html.

Associated Press. (2007, December 11). Pregnant attorney admits kidnap tale was a lie. CNN.com. http://www.cnn.com/2007/US/law/12/11/lawyer.missing.ap/index.html.

Associated Press. (2008, September 28). Fake kidnapping scheme hits illegal immigrants in Arizona. http://proquest.umi.com.libaccess.sjlibrary.org/pdqweb?index=0&sid….

Associated Press. (2009, April 24). California mother accused of murdering baby daughter after kidnap hoax. Foxnews.com. http://www.foxnews.com/story/0,2933,517746,00.html.

Associated Press. (2011, March 14). Minneapolis kidnapping hoax. Wdio.com. http://www.wdio.com/article/stories/S2016248.shtml?cat=10349.

Bergreen, J. (2011, May 24). Kidnapping hoax may land teen couple in hot water. The Salt Lake Tribune. http://www.sltrib.com/sltrib/news/51874874-78/police-girlfriend-lake-….

Canning, K.E., Hilts, M.A., & Muirhead, Y.E. (2011). False allegations of child abduction. J Forensic Sci, 56 (3): 794–802.

Coen, J. (1999, August 12). Woman faked her abduction, Cops say Naperville resident charged in Michigan. Chicago Tribune. http://pqasb.pqarchiver.com/chicagotribune/access/43870580.html?F….

Fitzgerald, J., & People, J. (2006, July). Victims of abduction: Patterns and case studies. Crime & Justice Bull, 94, 1–14

Godfrey, D. (1982). Terrorism and banking. Studies in Conflict & Terrorism, 5 (4): 353–361.

Gottesman, A. (1994, February 2). Teen faked kidnap after breakup with girl. Chicago Tribune. http://pqasb.pqarchiver.com/chicagotribune/access/7974364.html?FM….

Grzegorek, V. (2010, December 15). Morning brew: Ugly Christmas sweaters, kidnapping Hoax goes viral, Russo to be sentenced, and Census confirms we're getting poorer. clevescene.com. http://www.clevescene.com/scene-and-heard/archives/2010/12/15/mor....

Hanson, D. (2004). Sound of crime: Forensic audio analysis can lead law enforcement to a criminal by hearing more than a mere voice on the phone. Law Enforcement Tech, 31 (9): 96, 98–101.

Hasch, M. (2010). Two men in Pittsburgh kidnapping hoax surrenders to police. *Pittsburgh Tribune Review*. http://www.pittsburghlive.com/x/pittsburghtrib/news/breaking/s_67235....

HelpFindMyChild. (2009, July 17). North Wales abduction story 'just an urban myth.' http://www.helpfindmychild.net/missing-child-hoax/store-child-abducti....

Ibnlive.com (2011, April 25).Fake kidnapping drama; NRI, friend booked. http://ibnlive.in.com/news/fake-kidnapping-drama-nri-friend-booked/1....

Inbar, M. (2009, November 3). Police: Florida wife faked her own abduction. Today.com. http://today.msnbc.msn.com/id/33600013/ns/today-today_people/t/polic....

Johnson, J. (2009, May 27). Kidnapping hoax: Philly mom, daughter found in Fla. Newser.com. http://www.newser.com/story/60277/kidnapping-hoax-philly-mom-dau....

Lavelle, J. (2010, March 29). Kidnapping hoax highlights the burden of false reports. Claim was given top priority. SignsonSandiego.com. http://www.signsanddiego.com/news/2010/mar/29/false-reports-a-bu....

Linthicum, K., & Vives, R. (2010, May 14). Woman invented kidnap hoax to avoid telling parents she would not graduate UCLA, police say. Los Angeles Times. L.A. Now. http://latimesblogs.latimes.com/lanow/2010/05/woman-invented-kidna....

Mohammed, K. (2005, April 18). Hints of hoax in kidnap reports. Chicago Tribune. http://pqasb.pqarchiver.com/chicagotribune/access/823335831.html?....

museumofhoaxes.com (no date). The kidnapping of Nicole Riche. http://www.museumofhoaxes.com/hoax/archive/permalink/the_kidnapp....

myfoxphilly.com (no date). Hoax not first based on racial stereotype. http://www.myfoxphilly.com/dpp/news/local_news/052909_Sweeten....

Ove, T. (2011). Man in kidnapping hoax now faces drug charges. post-gazette.com. http://www.post-gazette.com/pg/111081140200-100.stm.

Pellegrini, L.A. (2008). An argument for the criminal hoax. Ph.D. Dissertation, University of Southern California. ProQuest Publication Number 3341785.

Pelton, T. (1994a, June 8). Naperville hoax a real puzzler. Chicago Tribune. http://pqasb.pqarchiver.com/chicagotribune/access/7986166.html?FM....

Pelton, T. (1994b, June 9). Day-off scheme will mean day in court. Chicago Tribune. http://pqasb.pqarchiver.com/chicagotribune/access/7986232.html?FM.

Reynolds, T. (2009).Woman accused of killing daughter and faking kidnapping. badbreeders.net. http://badbreeders.net/tag/kidnapping-hoax/.

Roth, A.F. (2005, January 1). Girl charged in fake kidnap report: Aurora cops track teen by 911 calls. Chicago Tribune. http://pqasb.pqarchiver.com/chicagotribune/access/772774881.html?....

Russell, K. K. (1995–1996). Racial hoax as crime: The law as affirmation. Ind L J, 71, 593.

Shimell, D. (2010). Cruel kidnapping hoax targets senior citizens. NBCPhiladelphia.com. http://www.nbcphiladelphia.com/news/local/Cruel_Kidnapping_Hoax....

Stolz, G. (2009, March 26). Gold Coast – A sunny place for the shady. Courier Mail. http://www.couriermail.com.au/news/features/sunny-place-for-the-shad....

Taibbi, M., & Simms-Phillips, A. (1989). Unholy alliances: Working the Tawana Brawley story. Gardena, CA: Harcourt Brace Jovanovich Legal and Professional Publications.

Wainwright, M. (2008, November 13). Shannon Matthews drugged and tied up in mother's fake kidnap plot, court told. Guardian.co.uk. http://guardian.co.uk/uk/2008/nov/13/Shannon-matthews-kidanpp....

Welch, C. (2011, January 28). Woman arrested after Dallas kidnapping hoax prompts Amber Alert. Star-Telegram. http://www.star.telegram.com/2011/01/28/2804578/dallas-police-sear….

Yates, J. (2004, February 21). Banker charged with lying about kidnapping; FBI says he made up story of bomb on plane. Chicago Tribune. http://pqasb.pqarchiver.com/chicagotribune/access/548041971.html?….

Appendix A
Stalking and Violence Project (SVP) Research Methods

Domestic violence (DV) victims in some domestic courts are now given an opportunity to formally complain about different types of partner abuse and request court protection against these forms of abuse. As part of the Stalking and Violence Project (SVP), a new interpersonal domestic violence and stalking protocol was constructed to code self-report data on different forms of DV based on newly filed domestic orders of protection.

Sample

A random sample of 519 newly filed orders of protection (also known as restraining orders or protective orders) was drawn from new domestic court case listings that were published in legal newspapers in two cities (Midwest and West regions) between 1997 and 1999. The sample of orders of protection consisted of 519 self-reported victims and 519 accused persons.

Measures

An interpersonal stalking and DV protocol was constructed to code self-report data obtained from a content analysis of the newly filed domestic orders of protection. The protocol was pre-tested using 25 randomly selected new domestic orders of protection. The final protocol consisted of 154 variables.

One section of the protocol consisted of 29 residential, demographic, and family variables and 20 census tract measures of socioeconomic status (SES) for both the self-reported victims and accused individuals. The self-reported victims are the persons who are filing orders of protection to bar the accused persons from contacting them. SES variables for both victims and accused persons could be coded

S. Morewitz, *Kidnapping and Violence*,
https://doi.org/10.1007/978-1-4939-2117-1

directly from the orders of protection. Therefore, 20 census tract measures of SES for both victims and accused individuals were obtained by matching known residential addresses of victims and accused persons with the 1990 U.S. Census Bureau Census Tract database.

Information about the incidents or problems that led the alleged victims to file orders of protection against the accused persons is contained in the second part of the protocol. This section contains 89 variables concerning the type of relationship between the victims and the accused individuals, the victims' self-report narrative of what reportedly transpired, and the victims' reasons for filing the orders of protection. Three to four research assistants coded the self-report narratives independently, and their findings were compared to each other in order to maximize inter-rater reliability.

One dichotomous attempted/completed family kidnapping variable (Yes/No) was constructed from the victims' self-report narratives. If the victims reported that the respondents had threatened to kidnap their children or actually kidnapped their children for any period of time, the response was coded: Yes.

Other variables were coded in a similar manner. For example, one dichotomous death threat variable (Yes/No) was constructed from the victims' self-report narratives. If the victims reported that the respondents had threatened them with death, e.g., "I am going to kill you," the responses were coded: Yes.

Three stalking variables were constructed from the victims' self-report narratives. If the victims' narratives contained allegations that the accused individuals followed or stalked them, kept them under surveillance, or lay in wait for them, then these behaviors were coded as positive for the first stalking variable, "stalking." Before filing the orders of protection, victims were notified that stalking is illegal. The first stalking variable under-reports stalking since it may not include other behaviors such as receiving unwanted telephone calls and letters at home and at work that also are considered part of the stalking phenomenon. Thus, this variable only measures the victims' perception of stalking as a following or surveillance phenomenon.

The second stalking variable, "multiple acts of stalking," was constructed to be as comprehensive as possible. If the victims' narratives contained allegations about any type of repeated and unwanted communication and intrusion, e.g., threatening the victims in their homes or at work and making threatening calls to the victims at work, then the data were coded on a scale from 1 (one form of stalking) to 7 (seven forms of stalking).

The third stalking variable, "stalking distance," was constructed based on data from the multiple acts of stalking variable. The stalking distance variable measures the proximity of stalkers to the victims. Alleged perpetrators who stalked victims were ranked on a scale from 1 (sending a letter—least close) to 7 (being followed—most close). The stalking distance variable, like the multiple acts of stalking variable, does not rely on the victims' perception of stalking.

The last section of the protocol consists of 16 variables related to the self-reported victims' request for domestic court protection and the courts' approval or disapproval of their requests. Victims indicated whether they sought court protection for a variety of complaints, including physical abuse, stalking, and intimidation of dependents. This section also contains information on whether the court approved the victims' request for court protection in these specific problem areas.

Appendix B
SVP Results

See Tables B.1, B.2, B.3, B.4, B.5, B.6, B.7, B.8, and B.9.

Table B.1 Sample characteristicsof the victims of domestic violence (N = 519)

Variable	Classification	%	*p* value*
Gender	Female	83	
	Male	17	
			0.000
Racial/Ethnic background	White	21	
	African–American	56	
	Hispanic	20	
	Asian and others	3	
			0.000
Age (unknown)			
Marital status	Married	67	0.000
	Dating/Engaged	26	0.000
Parental status	Parents of at least one child	53	0.000
Income	% Living in census tracts with a median income:		
	< $20,000	40	
	$20,000–$39,999	50	
	$40,000–$59,999	9	
	$60,000–$79,999	1	
			0.000

*Note: Pearson Chi-Square tests of significance

S. Morewitz, *Kidnapping and Violence*,
https://doi.org/10.1007/978-1-4939-2117-1

Table B.2 Sample characteristics of the individuals accused of domestic violence (N = 519)

Variable	Classification	%	*p* value*
Gender	Female	20	
	Male	80	
			0.000
Racial/Ethnic background	White	22	
	African–American	54	
	Hispanic	21	
	Asian and others	3	
			N.S.
Age (years)	18–25	17	
	26–40	57	
	41–60	24	
	61 and older	2	
			N.S.
Marital status	Married	67	0.000
	Dating/Engaged	26	0.000
Income	% Living in census tracts with a median income:		
	< $20,000	40	
	$20,000–$39,999	52	
	$40,000–$59,999	7	
	$60,000–$79,999	1	
			0.000

*Note: Pearson Chi-Square tests of significance
N.S. = Not Statistically Significant

Table B.3 Characteristics of domestic violence victims of threatened or completed family kidnapping (N = 57) and domestic violence victims who were not the Victims of threatened or completed family kidnapping (N = 462)

Variable/Classification	Victims of threatened or completed family kidnapping	Those who were not the victims of threatened or completed family kidnapping	*p* value*
	%	%	
Gender (female)	89.5	81.7	N.S.
Racial/Ethnic background			
White	14.0	21.6	
African–American	44.0	57.0	
Hispanic	40.0	18.0	
Asian and Others	2.0	2.4	
			0.008

(continued)

Table B.3 (continued)

Variable/Classification	Victims of threatened or completed family kidnapping	Those who were not the victims of threatened or completed family kidnapping	*p* value*
	%	%	
Age (unknown)			
Marital/Relation status			
Married	38.6	26.5	N.S.
Dating/Engaged	8.8	28.5	0.001
Parents of at least 1 child	98.3	60.8	0.000
% Living in census tracts with a median income:			
<$20,000	32.4	39.8	
$20,000–$39,999	59.0	49.7	
$40,000–$59,999	7.9	9.4	
$60,000–$79,999	0.72	1.1	
			N.S.

*Note: Pearson Chi-Square tests of significance
N.S. = Not Statistically Significant

Table B.4 Characteristics of the domestic violence offenders accused of threateningor completing family kidnapping (N = 57) and domestic violence not accused of threatening or completing family kidnapping (N = 462)

Variable/Classification	Offenders accused of threatening or completing family kidnapping	Offenders not accused of threatening or completing family kidnapping	*p* value*
	%	%	
Gender (male)	87.7	79.2	N.S.
Racial/Ethnic background			
White	12.5	22.7	
African–American	39.3	56.3	
Hispanic	46.4	17.4	
Asian and others	1.8	2.7	
			0.000
Age (years)			
18–25	16.1	17.1	
26–40	71.4	54.6	
41–60	12.5	25.7	
61 and older	0	2.6	
			N.S.

(continued)

Table B.4 (continued)

Variable/Classification	Offenders accused of threatening or completing family kidnapping	Offenders not accused of threatening or completing family kidnapping	*p* value*
	%	%	
Marital/Relation status			
Married	38.6	26.5	N.S.
Dating/Engaged	8.8	28.5	0.001
Parents of at least 1 child	98.3	60.8	0.000
% Living in census tracts with a median income			
<$20,000	34.2	40.8	
$20,000–$39,999	57.5	51.0	
$40,000–$59,999	8.3	7.7	
$60,000–$79,999	0.40	0.51	
			N.S.

*Note: Pearson Chi-Square tests of significance
N.S. = Not Statistically Significant

Table B.5 Types of abuse committed against victims of threatened or completed family kidnapping (N = 57) and those not the victims of threatened or completed family kidnapping (N = 462)

Variable/Classification	Victims of threatened or completed family kidnapping	Those not the victims of threatened or completed family kidnapping	*p* value*
Types of abuse	%	%	
Threatened with physical harm	52.6	48.5	N.S.
Offender came to my job	10.5	10.2	N.S.
Victim stalked	22.8	29.2	N.S.
Victim hit by offender	64.9	67.1	N.S.
Victim pushed by offender	22.8	32.9	N.S.
Victim thrown down	17.5	16.5	N.S.
Victim choked	15.8	14.1	
Victim threatened with a weapon	10.5	8.9	N.S.
Weapon used against victim	17.5	16.9	N.S.
Objects thrown at victim	7.0	7.8	N.S.
Offender raped victim	12.5	6.5	N.S.

(continued)

Table B.5 (continued)

Variable/Classification	Victims of threatened or completed family kidnapping	Those not the victims of threatened or completed family kidnapping	*p* value*
Types of abuse	%	%	
Victim's property vandalized by offender	14.0	26.0	0.049
Offender stole victim's property	14.0	17.5	N.S.

*Note: Pearson Chi-Square tests of significance
N.S. = Not Statistically Significant

Table B.6 Causes for the domestic violence committed against victims of threatened or completed family kidnapping (N = 57) and those who are not the victims of threatened or completed family kidnapping (N = 462)

Variable/Classification	Victims of threatened or completed family kidnapping	Those not the victims of threatened or completed family kidnapping	*p* value*
Causes for the partner violence	%	%	
Jealousy	10.7	8.2	N.S.
Relationship ended	16.1	25.4	N.S.
Alcohol/Illicit drugs	23.2	19.5	N.S.
Child custody	80.4	5.6	0.000
Divorce	7.1	1.9	0.029

*Note: Pearson Chi-Square tests of significance
N.S. = Not Statistically Significant

Table B.7 Use of the emergency departments, shelters, counseling and other responses of the victims of threatened or completed family kidnapping (N = 57) and those who are not victims of threatened or completed family kidnapping (N = 462)

Variable/Classification	Victims of threatened or completed family kidnapping	Those who are not the Victims of threatened or completed family kidnapping	*p* value*
Nonlegal responses and outcomes	%	%	
Went to the ER	3.6	11.4	N.S.
Went to a shelter	10.7	4.5	N.S.
Went into counseling	5.5	5.6	N.S.
Told offender to go away	7.1	5.5	N.S.

(continued)

Table B.7 (continued)

Variable/Classification	Victims of threatened or completed family kidnapping	Those who are not the Victims of threatened or completed family kidnapping	*p* value*
Nonlegal responses and outcomes	%	%	
Took safety/security precautions	10.7	6.6	N.S.
Victim left home	12.5	8.5	N.S.
Remained in same residence with offender	14.0	17.2	N.S.

*Note: Pearson Chi-Square tests of significance
N.S. = Not Statistically Significant

Table B.8 Request for protective order (P.O.) and court approval for type of P.O. for the victims of threatened or completed family kidnapping (N = 57) and those not the victims of threatened or completed family kidnapping (N = 462)

Variable/Classification	Victims of threatened or completed family kidnapping	Those who are not	*p* value*
Type of P.O. requested/court approved P.O.	%	%	
Requested protection against physical harm	79.0	81.4	N.S.
Court approved P.O. re: physical harm	80.4	91.8	0.013
Requested protection against harassment	96.4	93.9	N.S.
Court approved P.O. re: harassment	93.5	96.8	N.S.
Requested protection against loss of liberty	61.8	60.0	N.S.
Court approved P.O. re: loss of liberty	80.4	81.4	N.S.
Requested protection of dependents	72.7	40.7	0.000
Court approved P.O. re: protection of dependents	65.2	42.9	0.004
Requested protection against deprivation	10.9	13.4	N.S.
Court approved P.O. re: deprivation	10.9	13.6	N.S.

(continued)

Table B.8 (continued)

Variable/Classification	Victims of threatened or completed family kidnapping	Those who are not	*p* value*
Type of P.O. requested/court approved P.O.	%	%	
Requested protection against neglect	14.6	12.9	N.S.
Court approved P.O. re: neglect	8.7	10.4	N.S.
Requested protection against exploitation	16.7	17.7	N.S.
Court approved P.O. re: exploitation	10.9	14.6	N.S.
Requested protection against stalking	50.0	66.8	0.015
Court approved P.O. re: stalking	52.2	70.2	0.013

*Note: Pearson Chi-Square tests of significance
N.S. = Not Statistically Significant

Table B.9 Other criminal justice responses and outcomes for offenders who threatened or committed family kidnapping (N = 57) and offenders who did not threaten or commit family kidnapping (N = 462)

Variable/Classification	Offenders who threatened or committed family kidnapping	Offenders who did not threaten or commit family kidnapping	*p* value*
Other Criminal Justice Responses and Outcomes	%	%	
Police contacted	35.7	29.8	N.S.
Offender arrested	20.0	9.3	0.020
Offender went to jail/prison	12.5	7.5	N.S.

*Note: Pearson Chi-Square tests of significance
N.S. = Not Statistically Significant

Appendix C
Cases

Duration of Partner Abductions

In Stalking and Violence Project (SVP) Case 2010A, Mr. A, the suspect, a 32-year-old man, reportedly kidnapped and falsely imprisoned Ms. B., his current or former girlfriend, at his friend's apartment for four days (see Appendix A-SVP Research Methods and Appendix B-SVP Results, Tables B.1, B.2, B.3, B.4, B.5, B.6, B.7, B.8, and B.9).

Children Taken Hostage

Individuals who take children hostages may also be friends of the children's parents. For example, in the Stalking and Violence Project (SVP) Case 00219 C, Mr. A, a 34-year-old man, allegedly did not permit his current or former girlfriend, Ms. B, and her children to leave home except for school (see Appendix A-SVP Research Methods and Appendix B-SVP Results, Tables B.1, B.2, B.3, B.4, B.5, B.6, B.7, B.8 and B.9).

Offenders and Third Parties

In one incident, a woman feared for her mother's safety after her mother told the suspect that he would not be allowed to go inside the residence (Salazar 2010). The suspect reportedly displayed a firearm and attempted to force his way into the home.

In another kidnapping and hostage-taking episode, the suspect reportedly pushed the kidnapping victim's female friend to the ground while the victim ran to the

S. Morewitz, *Kidnapping and Violence*,
https://doi.org/10.1007/978-1-4939-2117-1

basement of her home to try to get away from the suspect (Gorner 2010). The victim's friend was able to escape and call 911.

Partners Commit Violence During

Partner Abductions

During one kidnapping and hostage-taking siege, the suspect, a 31-year-old male suspect, reportedly physically assaulted a 42-year-old woman. The suspect also fired several shots at the woman, hitting her as she fled the apartment (Gorner 2010).

In another incident, the suspect, a male, age 46, reportedly sexually assaulted his estranged wife while he held her hostage at her workplace for six hours (abclocal.go.com no date).

In another case, a 28-year-old male suspect is accused of kidnapping his ex-girlfriend from her Clifton, New Jersey apartment and sexually assaulting her in Jersey City, New Jersey (*The Star-Ledger* Continuous News Desk 2010).

In several media reports, the kidnapper and hostage-takers were former boyfriends of the victim (*The Star-Ledger* Continuous News Desk 2010; Glod 2010; Fujimoto 2009). In one media report, the victim was a current girlfriend (Piazza 2010). The kidnappers and hostage-takers were married to the victims in other media reports (Owens 2008; Sangiacomo 2009).

Offenders' Use of Weapons in Partner Kidnappings

According to one report, the suspect, a male, age 44, allegedly abducted his girlfriend, age 41, at gunpoint. Her family stated that she had been in a dating relationship with the suspect, but they were not sure if they were still in a dating relationship (Fairhope police report kidnapping no date, http://blog.al.com/live).

In another case, a 23-year-old man reportedly kidnapped his ex-girlfriend at knifepoint while going to work at the Olive Garden in Green Oak Township (Scared Monkeys Missing Persons Site no date, http://missingexploited.com).

Break up of Relationships

A suspect reportedly beat up his former girlfriend until she was almost unconscious and abducted her using his truck after she notified him that "their relationship was over" (Fujimoto 2009).

In other captive-taking sieges, the suspects kidnapped and took their ex-girlfriends as hostages. For example, a former police officer, Joseph Alan Ciruti,

Jr., age 26, reportedly abducted his girlfriend using a firearm and then used handcuffs and shackles to restrain her (Adelson 2008). The suspect had been in a lengthy on-again, off-again relationship with her.

Individuals who idolize their partner and depend on them heavily to carry out their life plans and who have isolated themselves from others may kidnap their partners and hold them as hostages in retaliation against them for terminating the relationship.

Suspects' Use of Death Threats and Attempted Murder

One suspect reportedly kidnapped and falsely imprisoned his estranged wife and threatened to kill her by putting a handgun to her head. However, she was able to escape (Stage 6 Cases of Obsessive Ex Syndrome, http://www.obsessive-ex.com/oex/violence.html).

In SVP Case 2010 A, Mr. A, who reportedly kidnapped Ms. B, his current or former girlfriend, and threatened to set her on fire if she tried to escape (see Appendix A-SVP Research Methods and Appendix B-SVP Results, Tables B.1, B.2, B.3, B.4, B.5, B.6, B.7, B.8 and B.9; see Appendix C-Reported Cases of Partner Abduction).

In another captive-taking crisis involving the suspect and the victim, his 26-year-old former girlfriend, the judge in the case noted that the suspect had told his former girlfriend that "she was going to die that day, and she believed you" (Fujimoto 2009).

Commenting on a domestic violence (DV)-related kidnapping court case in Farmington, New Mexico, Chief Deputy District Attorney Dustin O'Brien stated that making someone fear for her life and threatening her if she leaves can be considered kidnapping (Piazza 2010). In this court case, the suspect, age 40, allegedly kidnapped his girlfriend and threatened her numerous times.

In another case, the suspect in a Geneseo, IL, standoff, allegedly had attempted to pull the victim out of a vehicle, pushing her down, choking her, and scratching her arms and back (Wellner et al. 2009). The victim also accused the suspect of grabbing her and her daughter each by the throat and saying, "You guys better never leave me."

Suspects may have a history of making suicide threats before kidnapping their partners and family members and taking them as hostages. In one incident, the suspect who reportedly kidnapped his former girlfriend and took her hostage, had threatened to kill himself one year earlier (Wellner et al. 2009). The suspect allegedly had told the victim that she and her family members would find him with a knife in his heart under the Christmas tree on Christmas Day.

Homicide and Suicide

In one hostage crisis, the suspect reportedly murdered his wife after abducting her and their 4-year-old son and holding them as hostages during a 7-hour siege (Sangiacomo 2009).

Kidnappers and hostage-takers may be at risk for committing suicide after they abduct their partners and take them as hostages. For example, authorities report that one suspect shot himself fatally after reportedly abducting his former girlfriend from her residence (Foxman 2010). Authorities reported that the suspect may have been very upset over the breakup of his dating relationship. The suspect's girlfriend had taken his gun away from him at one point during the kidnapping. The girlfriend reportedly escaped and was treated for nonlife-threatening injuries at a hospital in the area.

Offenders may attempt to commit suicide by police action during a hostage siege. For example, one suspect risked being shot and killed by the police. During a 10-hour siege in an apartment, the suspect reportedly shot the police a several times (Wellner et al. 2009).

In one case, the suspect reportedly kidnapped and murdered his former girlfriend after kidnapping her from the parking lot of a mall one evening (Stage 6 Cases of Obsessive Ex Syndrome, http://www.obsessive-ex.com/oex/violence.html). The perpetrator drove his truck with the woman's body inside the vehicle and then he shot himself while the victim's father chased him. The victim reportedly had asked her ex-boyfriend to meet her there so she could ask him to stop contacting her.

Partners Escalate Their Violent Behaviors

In a kidnapping and hostage-taking siege at the victim's workplace, the suspect allegedly pointed a firearm at another worker and then locked that employee in the office (abclocalgo.com no date).

Partners Have Interpersonal and Mental Health Problems

Partners may become extremely jealous and violent and then abduct their partner. In one incident, the suspect reportedly became jealous and enraged over a message that was left on his 23-year-old girlfriend's Facebook age, and then kidnapped, imprisoned, and tortured her for four days (FOXNews.com 2010). The suspect is accused of grabbing the victim's hair, dragging her, and making a death threat before choking her with a rope and a towel.

In one kidnapping and hostage-taking siege that ended in the husband reportedly killing his wife, the suspect was thought to have had mental problems (Sangiacomo 2009).

Offenders' Criminal History

In one kidnapping and hostage-taking crisis in which the suspect reportedly murdered his wife, the suspect had two previous DV charges against him, and the police knew him (Sangiacomo 2009).

Another kidnapping and hostage-taking suspect, the suspect was on probation in a prior DV case at the time of the incident and had a long arrest record that dated back to 1995 (Gorner 2010). In recent years, he had been found guilty in two DV cases. In 2008, the suspect was charged with misdemeanor domestic battery again and was also charged with resisting a police officer and assault. In addition, an order of protection against Wilson was issued in that DV case.

In one kidnapping and hostage-taking crisis, the suspect had a long criminal record, including three previous convictions for DV that involved three different women (Pritchard 2010). In another abduction and hostage-taking incident, the suspect had a history of DV against his former girlfriend. In 2006, he had been convicted of misdemeanor battery in an attack against his former girlfriend and, in 2005 he was sentenced to 60 days in jail for attacking her (Wellner et al. 2009).

In one kidnapping and hostage-taking crisis, the suspect reportedly had links to a gang (Pritchard 2009). The suspect was an alleged member of a gang and had three prior convictions for domestic violence against three different women.

In another incident, a reported gang member was wanted by the police for allegedly abducting his 23-year-old ex-girlfriend (Salazar 2010). The suspect reportedly came to his ex-girlfriend's parents' home. He banged on their door, asking to see her. His ex-girlfriend's mother came to the door and told the suspect that he was not permitted to go inside. The woman came to the door because she feared for her mother's safety. The suspect allegedly pushed his ex-girlfriend down the street and screamed: "Go, before the cops get here!"

Partners' Stalking Behaviors

In one case, the suspect in a 9-hour standoff, reportedly had called the victim repeatedly and had driven by her workplace a number of times (Wellner et al. 2009). The suspect also allegedly had chased after her in his vehicle after she had attempted to leave town after a fight.

Another suspect allegedly stalked and harassed his 21-year-old ex-girlfriend before dragging her by the hair at her home, forcing her into his sport-utility vehicle, and driving her against her wishes to his residence more than 45 miles away (Gorner 2010). Prior to the kidnapping, the suspect reportedly had made 40 calls to his ex-girlfriends and sent many threatening text messages.

In SVP Case Y2, Mr. V, a 28-year-old man, reportedly followed Ms. A, his estranged wife, to her workplace, a school, and waited for her outside her classroom (see Appendix A-SVP Research Methods and Appendix B-SVP Results,

Tables B.1, B.2, B.3, B.4, B.5, B.6, B.7, B.8 and B.9). Mr. V became very upset when Ms. A refused to get back together with him. Mr. V followed his estranged wife to her automobile and tried to take her automobile ignition keys away from her. Mr. V then tried not to let Ms. A close her automobile door. Mrs. A's friend arrived and her estranged husband finally left the scene. Four months later, Mr. V tried to take away Ms. A's automobile ignition keys and prevent her from driving away.

Offenders May Commit Arson

Gorner et al. (2010) reported on a kidnapping and hostage-taking siege in which the suspect allegedly broke into a second-floor apartment and started a fire there after fleeing from another apartment.

Partner Vandalism

In SVP Case Y2, Mr. V reportedly broke the automobile's front windshield with his fists during the second incident (see Appendix A-SVP Research Methods and Appendix B-SVP Results, Tables B.1, B.2, B.3, B.4, B.5, B.6, B.7, B.8 and B.9). The kidnappers and hostage-takers may also commit arson in these highly emotional incidents.

Pregnant Victims

In one incident, one suspect, a kidnapping and hostage-taking suspect reportedly kicked his nine-month pregnant girlfriend repeatedly in her stomach during an 11-hour siege (Pritchard 2009).

In SVP Case B5, Mr. L, a 27-year-old man, allegedly imprisoned Ms. M, his current or former girlfriend, who was pregnant at the time of the abduction (see Appendix A-SVP Research Methods and Appendix B-SVP Results, Tables Tables B.1, B.2, B.3, B.4, B.5, B.6, B.7, B.8 and B.9). Ms. M reported that when she was at his home, he would not let her out of the house.

Offenders' Substance Abuse History

Heavy alcohol may precede the abduction and hostage-taking incident. In a violent kidnapping and hostage-taking incident in Canada, the suspect reportedly had been drinking alcohol for several hours before assaulting his 25-year-old pregnant girlfriend repeatedly at 6 a.m. and then kidnapping her and taking her as a hostage (Pritchard 2009).

In another incident, a man was charged with kidnapping his former girlfriend, an 18-year-old woman, possessing drug paraphernalia, attempted unlawful flight, and misconduct involving weapons (*Associated Press* 2010, Southern Arizona man arrested in former girlfriend's kidnapping). A woman called the police, stating that her daughter had just been abducted from a residence and forced into an automobile at gunpoint.

A male suspect in one incident was charged with abducting his ex-girlfriend across state lines and unlawfully imprisoning her. The suspect's family stated that he is severely addicted to drugs and was hospitalized recently because of his drug addiction (Agar 2009).

In another case, a suspect in a kidnapping, hostage-taking incident and extra alarm fire had an extensive criminal history, including a 1996 drug-possession and distribution arrest (Gorner et al. 2010). After the offender had violated probation in the case, he was sentenced to two years in prison.

Duration of Partner Kidnappings

Partner kidnappings vary in their duration depending on the responses of the suspects, police, and other factors. An abduction and hostage-taking incident in an apartment lasted nine hours until the suspect surrendered to the police (Wellner et al. 2009). One hour earlier, his hostage, a former girlfriend, was able to leave the apartment.

Other kidnappings and hostage-taking situations are of short duration. In one incident, the suspect was arrested after kidnapping his wife and child and taking them hostage in their home for approximately 90 min in the evening (Owens 2008).

Law Enforcement Tactics

In one captive-taking crisis, the police established a command post at a telephone company (Wellner et al. 2009). Using a bullhorn, authorities reportedly attempted to convince the suspect that he would not be harmed if he came out peacefully.

In another case involving a 2½-hour standoff with one suspect, SWAT team members were called to the scene when the police tried to enter the apartment where a woman was being held hostage, but the suspect blocked their entry (Gorner 2010).

The police and other law enforcement personnel may use special tactics to resolve partner abductions and hostage crises. For example, in one case, hostage standoff, police used a bucket truck to get snipers on a rooftop near where the suspect reportedly was holding his former girlfriend hostage (Wellner et al. 2009).

In one captive-taking crisis in Ottawa Hills, OH, snipers manned nearby rooftops in case that this tactical strategy would be necessary to rescue the hostage (abclocal.go.com).

Criminal Justice System Responses

The suspect in one kidnapping case was charged with two counts of first-degree felony kidnapping, two counts of third-degree felony aggravated battery with a deadly weapon against a household member, second-degree felony retaliation against a witness, three counts of misdemeanor battery against a household member and interference with communications for two separate incidents involving his girlfriend (Piazza 2010).

In another kidnapping case, the suspect was charged with second-degree kidnapping, assault, and communicating threats (Owens 2008).

References

abclocal.go.com (no date). Hostage situation in Ottawa Hills. http://abclocal.go.com/wtvd/video?id=6787743

Adelson, J. (2008). Former Pearl River police officer booked with kidnapping. *The Times-Picayune*, May 9, 2008. http://blog.nola.com/tpnorthshore/2008/05/former_pearl_river_police_offi.html.

Agar, J. (2009). Former girlfriends testify about Jenison man's alleged abuse, kidnapping. *The Grand Rapids Press*. October 14, 2009. http://www.mlive.com/news/grand-rapids/index.ssf/2009/10/former_girlfriends_testify_abo.html.

Associated Press. (2010). Southern Arizona man arrested in former girlfriend's kidnapping. http://www.abc15.com/dpp/news/region_central_southern_az/yuma/southern-arizona-man-arrested-in-former-girlfriend%27s-kidnapping.

Fairhope police report kidnapping, retrieved from http://blog.al.com/live.

FOXNews.com (2010). California man accused of torturing, kidnapping girlfriend in rage over Facebook message. August 31, 2010. http://www.foxnews.com/us/201008/31/California-man-accused-torturing.

Foxman, A. (2010). County kidnapping suspect committed suicide, police say. http://www.vcstar.com/news/2010/apr/19/santa-rosa-valley-kidnapping-suspect-committed/?print=1.

Fujimoto, L. (2009). Man gets 10 years in kidnapping of girlfriend. *The Maui News*, Jun 27, 2009. http://www.mauinews.com/page/content.detail/id/520293/Man-gets-10-years-in-kidnapping-of-girlfriend.html.

Glod, M. (2010). Md. Man accused of kidnapping ex-girlfriend arrested, woman found. washingtonpost.com. April 20, 2010. http://voices.washingtonpost.com/crime-scene/montgomery/montgomery-police-search-for-k.html.

Gorner, J. (2010). Carpentersville man charged with kidnapping ex-girlfriend. http://articles.chicagobreakingnews.com/2010-04-06/news/28508442_1_carpentersville-man-girlfriend-cell-phone.

Gorner, J., Hoffman, H., & Ford, L. (2010). Hostage, cop hurt in shootings before West Side fire. http://articles.chicagobreakingnews.com/2010-01-10/news/28528019_1_hostage-situation-swat-officers-chicago-police-officer.

Owens, A. (2008). Durham man arrested after taking his wife, child hostage. Capitol Broadcasting Co. http://www.wral.com/news/local/story/4186837/.

Piazza, E. (2010). Judge decides evidence will stand in kidnapping case. The Daily Times, September 16, 2010. http://www.daily-times.com/ci_16089025?source=most_emailed.

Pritchard, D. (2009). Man jailed for violent hostage-taking. Sun Media, The Winnipeg Sun. http://cnews.canoe.ca/CNEWS/Crime/2009/11/02/11602671-sun.html.

Salazar, D. (2010). Gangster wanted in ex-girlfriend's kidnapping. April 7, 2010. http://www.ocregister.com.

Sangiacomo, M. (2009). Police shoot man, end hostage crisis in Lakemore. The Plain Dealer. http://blog.cleveland.com/metro/2009/01/police_shoot_man_end_hostage_c.html.

Scared Monkeys Missing Persons Site. (n.d.) Retrieved from http://missingexploited.com.

The Star-Ledger Continuous News Desk (2010). Jersey City man is accused of kidnapping, sexual assault of ex-girlfriend. September 16, 2010. http://www.nj.com/news.

Wellner, B., Lemmon, D., & Brown, C., et al. (2009). Geneseo standoff suspect has history of domestic violence, authorities say. http://qctimes.com/news/local/articles_5e45d6c-e6d5-11de-b96b-001cc4c002e0.html.

Appendix D
Missing Persons Project (MPP) Research Methods

The present investigation uses data from the Missing Persons Project (MPP), which is based on a random sample of 1,000 missing-persons reports that were filed between 1991 and 2013 and published on the North American Missing Persons Network (NAMPN) and the National Center for Missing and Exploited Children (NCMEC) websites. Each missing-person report was coded using a protocol that contains 291 variables. The coded data were entered into a data file and Chi-Square, correlational, and regression analyses were then performed using Systat 9 for Windows program (1999).

Reference

Systat 9 for Windows program (1999). www.systat.com.

S. Morewitz, *Kidnapping and Violence*,
https://doi.org/10.1007/978-1-4939-2117-1

Appendix E
Ransom Kidnappings Project (RKP) Research Methods

The present investigation uses data from the Ransom Kidnappings Project (RKP), which is based on a random sample of 534 ransom kidnappings (RKs) that occurred between 1874 and 2011 and were published in newspaper articles and as summaries of the incidents in the Wikipedia website. Each RK article or summary of the incident was coded using a protocol that contains 171 variables. The coded data were entered into a data file and Chi-Square, correlational, and regression analyses were then performed using Systat 9 for Windows program (1999).

Reference

Systat 9 for Windows program (1999). www.systat.com.

S. Morewitz, *Kidnapping and Violence*,
https://doi.org/10.1007/978-1-4939-2117-1

Appendix F
RKP Results

See Tables F.10, F.11, F.12, F.13, F.14 and F.15

Table F.10 Sample characteristics of the ransom kidnapping (RK) victims and their relatives (N = 534)

Variable	Classification	%	*p* value*
Gender	Female	19.67	
	Male	80.33	
			0.000
Racial/Ethnic background	White	28.03	
	African–American	3.79	
	Hispanic	57.58	
	Asian and Others	10.60	0.000
RK victim	No	90.72	
Considered wealthy	Yes	9.28	0.000
RK victim	No	79.33	
Has noteworthy	Yes	20.67	0.000
Relative			

*Note: Pearson Chi-Square tests of significance

S. Morewitz, *Kidnapping and Violence*,
https://doi.org/10.1007/978-1-4939-2117-1

Table F.11 Occupations of the ransom kidnapping (RK) Victims (N = 128)

Variable/Classification	Frequency	%	*p* value*
Occupations of the			0.000
RK Victims			
Oil workers	36	28.13	
Christian missionaries	23	17.97	
Construction workers	19	14.84	
Business executives	9	7.03	
Engineering/Construct	9	7.03	
Journalists	8	6.25	
Students	4	3.13	
Farmers/Cattlemen	3	2.34	
Politicians	3	2.34	
Drivers	2	1.56	
Editors	1	0.78	
Medical aid workers	1	0.78	
Attorneys	1	0.78	
Wives/Spouses	1	0.78	
Entertainers/Celebrities	1	0.78	
Physicians/Veterinarians	1	0.78	
Guides	1	0.78	
Contractors	1	0.78	
Business wholesalers	1	0.78	
Auto parts dealers	1	0.78	
Customs brokers	1	0.78	

*Note: Pearson Chi-Square tests of significance

Table F.12 Nations where the ransom kidnappings (RKs) occurred (N = 531)

Variable/Classification	Frequency	%	*p* value*
Nations where the RKs occurred			0.000
Mexico	371	69.87	
Afghanistan	45	8.45	
Colombia	38	7.16	
U.S.	29	5.46	
Nigeria	27	5.09	
Somalia	5	0.94	
Iraq	2	0.38	
Haiti	2	0.38	
Italy	1	0.19	
Belgium	1	0.19	

(continued)

Table F.12 (continued)

Variable/Classification	Frequency	%	*p* value*
Chechnya	1	0.19	
Costa Rica	1	0.19	
Netherlands	1	0.19	
China	1	0.19	
Australia	1	0.19	
Puerto Rico	1	0.19	
France	1	0.19	
Hong Kong	1	0.19	
Greece	1	0.19	
India	1	0.19	

*Note: Pearson Chi-Square tests of significance

Table F.13 Year when the ransom kidnappings (RKs) occurred (N = 339)

Variable/Classification	Frequency	%	*p* value*
Year when the RKs occurred			0.000
1874	1	0.30	
1924	1	0.30	
1927	1	0.30	
1932	1	0.30	
1933	3	0.89	
1934	2	0.59	
1935	1	0.38	
1936	1	0.30	
1953	1	0.30	
1956	1	0.30	
1957	1	0.30	
1960	2	0.59	
1963	1	0.30	
1968	1	0.30	
1973	1	0.30	
1974	4	1.18	
1984	1	0.30	
1987	1	0.30	
1989	1	0.30	
1991	1	0.30	
1992	1	0.30	
1995	1	0.30	
1996	1	0.30	
2002	1	0.30	

(continued)

Table F.13 (continued)

Variable/Classification	Frequency	%	*p* value*
2004	2	0.59	
2005	1	0.30	
2006	18	5.31	
2007	33	9.74	
2008	39	11.50	
2009	15	4.43	
2010	5	1.48	
2011	194	57.23	

*Note: Pearson Chi-Square tests of significance

Table F.14 Possible motives of ransom kidnappers (N = 534)

Variable	Classification	%	*p* value*
Ethnic motives	No	93.93	
	Yes	6.07	
			0.000
Religious motives	No	94.51	
	Yes	5.49	
			0.000
Political motives	No	93.56	
	Yes	6.44	0.000

*Note: Pearson Chi-Square tests of significance

Table F.15 Outcomes the ransom kidnappings (RKs) (N = 534)

Variable	Classification	%	*p* value*
RK victims injured	No	80.65	
	Yes	19.35	
			0.000
RK victims lost body	No	97.83	
Part	Yes	2.17	
			0.000
RK victims killed	No	58.82	
	Yes	41.18	0.000
RK victims	No	59.64	
Rescued	Yes	40.36	0.000
RK victims	No	81.02	
Let go	Yes	18.98	0.000
Ransom paid	No	38.05	
	Yes	61.95	0.000

*Note: Pearson Chi-Square tests of significance

Appendix G
Aircraft Hijackings Project (AHP) Research Methods

The present investigation uses data from the Aircraft Hijackings Project (AHP), which is based on a random sample of 202 aircraft hijackings (AHs) that took place between 1956 and 2009 and were published as summaries of the incidents in the Wikipedia website. Each AH summary was coded using a protocol that contains 171 variables. The coded data were entered into a data file and Chi-Square, correlational, and regression analyses were then performed using Systat 9 for Windows program (1999).

Reference

Systat 9 for Windows program (1999). www.systat.com.

S. Morewitz, *Kidnapping and Violence*,
https://doi.org/10.1007/978-1-4939-2117-1

Appendix H
Aircraft Hijacking Project (AHP) Results

See Tables H.16, H.17, H.18, H.19, H.20, H.21, H.22, H.23, H.24, H.25 and H.26

Table H.16 Sample characteristics of Aircraft Hijacking (AH) incidents (N = 202)

Variable	Mean ± S.D.	Range
# of Yrs ago that AH occurred	31.67 ±1 2.84	1–54
# of AH suspects	1.72 ± 2.06	1–19
# of Passengers on board	19.85 ± 53.15	0–400

Table H.17 Sample characteristics of the first Aircraft Hijacking (AH) suspects (N = 202)

Variable	Classification	%	*p* value*
1st AH suspect	Female	3	
Gender	Male	97	
			0.000
Politically-Motivated			
1st AH suspect	Yes	81.2	
	No	18.8	
			0.000
1st AH suspect may have mental disorders			
	Yes	5.7	
	No	94.3	
			0.000

*Note: Pearson Chi-Square tests of significance

S. Morewitz, *Kidnapping and Violence*,
https://doi.org/10.1007/978-1-4939-2117-1

Table H.18 Most frequent first Aircraft Hijacking (AH) suspects' countries of origin or ethnic origin (N = 202)

Variable/Classification	Frequency of suspects	% of suspects	*p* value*
Most frequent AH suspects' countries of origin			0.000
U.S.	30	14.85	
Cuba	29	14.36	
Palestine/Arab	14	6.93	
Turkey	8	3.96	
Iran	3	1.49	
India/South Asia	3	1.49	
Hungary	2	0.99	
Puerto Rico	2	0.99	
Philippines	2	0.99	
Japan	2	0.99	
East Germany	2	0.99	
Pakistan	2	0.99	
Lebanon	2	0.99	
Afghanistan	2	0.99	
Russia	2	0.99	
Sikh	2	0.99	
Croatia	2	0.99	
Cyprus-Turkey	2	0.99	

*Note: Pearson Chi-Square tests of significance

Table H.19 Most frequent departure locations of Hijacked Aircraft N = 202)

Variable/Classification	Frequency of Hijacked Aircraft	% of Hijacked Aircraft	*p* value*
Most frequent departure locations of Hijacked Aircraft			0.000
New York, NY	13	6.44	
Cuba	6	2.97	
Chicago, IL	5	2.48	
Los Angeles, CA		2.48	
Key West, FL	5	2.48	
Istanbul, Turkey	5	2.48	
Miami, FL	5	2.48	
Newark, NJ	5	2.48	
Atlanta, GA	4	1.98	

*Note: Pearson Chi-Square tests of significance

Table H.20 Most frequent locations of diverted aircraft during the Hijackings (N = 202)

Variable/Classification	Frequency of location	% of Locations	*p* value*
Most frequent locations of diverted Aircraft during the Hijackings			0.000
Cuba	77	38.31	
Miami, FL	4	1.99	
Jordan	3	1.49	
Algiers	2	0.99	.
Sofia, Bulgaria	2	0.99	
West Berlin	2	0.99	
New York, NY	2	0.99	
Kandahar, Afghanistan	2	0.99	
Diyarbakir, Turkey	2	0.99	
Israel	2	0.99	
Key West, FL	2	0.99	
Canada	2	0.99	

*Note: Pearson Chi-Square tests of significance

Table H.21 Aircraft Hijacking (AH) suspects' political/national/ethnic affiliation/type

Variable/Classification	Frequency	%	*p* value*
AH suspects' Political/National/Ethnic affiliation			0.000
None	38	18.81	
Cuban	104	51.49	
Arab/Palestinian	7	3.47	
PFLP	6	2.97	
Iranian	3	1.49	
East German	2	0.99	
Pakistani	2	0.99	
Turkish Leftist Militants	2	0.99	
Lebanese Shi'a	2	0.99	
Anti-President Nixon	2	0.99	
Sikh	2	0.99	
Amritsar, Punjab, India	2	0.99	
Sikh secessionist struggle			
Croatian terrorists	2	0.99	
Japanese red army	2	0.99	

*Note: Pearson Chi-Square tests of significance

Table H.22 Aircraft Hijacking (AH) suspects' weapon(s) type (N = 145)

Variable/Classification	Frequency of weapon(s)	% of Weapons	*p* value*
AH Suspects' weapons(s) type			0.000
None/Not known	107	73.79	
Gun	17	11.72	
Bomb explosive	12	8.28	
Knife	5	3.45	
Toy Gun	2	1.38	
Scissors	1	0.69	
Grenade	1	0.69	

*Note: Pearson Chi-Square tests of significance

Table H.23 Year that Aircraft Hijacking (AH) occurred (N = 202)

Variable/Classification	Frequency of AHs	% of AHs	*p* value*
Year that AH occurred			0.000
1956	1	0.50	
1958	2	0.99	
1959	2	0.99	
1961	2	0.99	
1966	1	0.50	
1967	1	0.50	
1968	17	8.42	
1969	37	18.32	
1970	22	10.89	
1971	17	8.42	
1972	10	4.95	
1973	4	1.98	
1974	2	0.99	
1976	3	1.49	
1977	4	1.98	
1978	4	1.98	
1979	3	1.49	
1980	2	0.99	
1981	5	2.48	
1982	2	0.99	
1983	2	0.99	
1984	3	1.49	
1985	4	1.98	
1986	2	0.99	
1987	1	0.50	

(continued)

Table H.23 (continued)

Variable/Classification	Frequency of AHs	% of AHs	*p* value*
1988	2	0.99	
1989	1	0.50	
1990	1	0.50	
1991	1	0.50	
1992	1	0.50	
1993	5	2.48	
1994	2	0.99	
1995	2	0.99	
1996	6	2.97	
1997	1	0.50	
1998	3	1.49	
1999	2	0.99	
2000	4	1.98	
2001	4	1.98	
2002	1	0.50	
2003	4	1.98	
2006	1	0.50	
2007	6	2.97	
2008	1	0.50	
2009	1	0.50	

Table H.24 Outcomes of the Aircraft Hijacking (AH) incidents (N = 202)

Variable	Classification	%	*p* value*
Hijacker arrested	Yes	38.2	
	No	61.8	0.001
Aircraft crashed	Yes	6.2	
	No	93.8	
			0.000
Aircraft landed	Yes	87.6	
	No	12.4	
			0.000
Passengers killed	Yes	11.3	
	No	88.7	
			0.000
Police/Security Forces killed	Yes	3.6	
	No	96.4	
			0.000

(continued)

Table H.24 (continued)

Variable	Classification	%	*p* value*
Pilots killed	Yes	5.7	
		94.3	
			0.000
Hijackers killed	Yes	12.4	
	No	87.6	
			0.000
Hijackers escaped	Yes	41.7	
	No	58.3	
			0.023
Aircraft damaged	Yes	6.7	
	No	93.3	
			0.000

*Note: Chi-Square Tests of Significance

Table H.25 Additional measures of Aircraft Hijacking (AH) outcomes (N = 202)

Variable/Classification	Mean ± S.D.	Range
# of Passengers killed	3.62 ± 18.19	0–128
# of Passengers injured	0.58 ± 5.39	0–50
# of Pilots killed	0.33 ± 0.70	0–2
# of Police/Security forces killed	0.14 ± 1.29	0–15
# of Hijackers killed	0.41 ± 1.86	0–19

Table H.26 Additional outcomes–type of Aircrafts most frequently Hijacked (N = 202)

Variable	# of Aircrafts Hijacked	% of Aircrafts Hijacked	*p* value*
Type of Aircrafts			
Most frequently Hijacked			0.000
Boeing 727	29	14.36	
DC-8	22	10.89	
DC-9	9	4.46	
Boeing 737	8	3.96	
Aeroflot Tu-104	4	1.96	
SE-210 caravelle VI R	3	1.49	
AN-2	3	1.49	
DC-10	3	1.49	

*Note: Chi-Square Tests of Significance

Appendix I
Kidnapping Hoaxes Project (KHP) Research Methods

The present investigation uses data from the Kidnapping Hoaxes Project (KHP), which is based on a random sample of 82 kidnapping hoaxes (KHs) that occurred between 1993 and 2011 and were published in newspaper articles and as summaries of the incidents in the Wikipedia website. To date, twenty-nine of the 82 KH articles or incident summaries have been coded using a protocol that contains 169 variables. The coded data were entered into a data file and Chi-Square, correlational, and regression analyses were then performed using Systat 9 for Windows program (1999).

Reference

Systat 9 for Windows program (1999). www.systat.com.

S. Morewitz, *Kidnapping and Violence*,
https://doi.org/10.1007/978-1-4939-2117-1

Bibliography

108 Stat. 1796. Anti-Corruption Act of 1993 Retrieved from http://www.gpo.gov/fdsys/granule/STATUTE-108/STATUTE-108-Pg1796/content-detail.html
Adepoju, A. (2005). Review of research and data on human trafficking in sub-Saharan Africa. Intl Migration, 43 (1/2): 75–98.
Afghanistan News Center. (2007, August 6). http://www.afghanistannewscenter.com/news/2007/august/aug62007.html
Agopian, M.W. (1981). Parental-child stealing. Lexington, MA: Lexington Books.
Agopian, M.W. (1984). The impact on children of abduction by parents. Child Welfare, 63 (6): 511–519.
Agopian, M.W., & Anderson, G.L. (1981). Characteristics of parental child stealing. J Family Issues, 2 (4): 471–483.
AIG Private Client Group. (no date). Kidnap and ransom. http://www.aigpcg.com/kidnap_ransom.htm
Albrecht, H.-J. (2007). Trafficking in humans and human rights. In S. Parmentier & E. Weitekamp (Eds.), Crime and human rights, 39–71. Series in sociology of crime, law and deviance, vol. 9. Amsterdam: Elsevier/JAI Press.
American International Underwriters, Crisis Management. (no date). Retrieved from http://www.aiu.com/BusinessLine/aiuCDA_bizline_fprod/0,1618,10,00.html
Americans for UNFPA (2007). http://www.americansforunfpa.org/NetCommunity/Page.aspx?pid=292.
Ankrom, L.G., & Lent, C.J. (1995). Cradle robbers. FBI Law Enforcement Bull, 64 (9): 1–7. Retrieved from http://web.ebscohost.comproxylib.csueastbay.edu/ehost/detail?vid=3&
Anonymous. (2012). Forced marriage– A consultation, summary of responses. Home Office, U.K., June 2012. https://www.gov.uk/government/uploads/system/uploads/attachment_data/file/157829/forced-marriage-response.pdf
Anonymous. (2014, May). Guidance forced marriage. Foreign & Commonwealth Office and Home Office, U K. https://www.gov.uk/forced-marriage
Anonymous. (2012). The crisis of child sexual exploitation in Brazil. LibertadLatina.org http://www.libertadlatina.org/LA_Brazils_Child_Prostitution_Crisis.htm
Anti-Car Theft Act of 1992 (H.R. 4542, 102nd Congress (991–1992)
Appel, A.E., & Holden, G.W. (1998). The co-occurrence of spouse and physical child abuse: A Review and appraisal. J Fam Psychology, 12: 578–599.
Arizona (2013). Presumptions; defense of a residential structure or occupied vehicle; exceptions; definitions. Arizona Fifty-First State Legislature—First Regular Session 13–419. http://www.azleg.state.az.us/FormatDocument.asp?inDoc=/ars/13/00419.htm&Title=13&DocType=ARS

S. Morewitz, *Kidnapping and Violence*,
https://doi.org/10.1007/978-1-4939-2117-1

Asbury, J. (1987). African–American women in violent relationships: An exploration of cultural differences. In R. Hampton (Ed.), Violence in the Black family. Lexington, MA: Lexington Books.

Asdigian, N.L., Finkelhor, D., & Hotaling, G. (1995). Varieties of nonfamily abduction of children and adolescents. Crim Justice Behaviour, 22: 215–232.

Associated Press. (2014, February 8). NM ambulance hijacked with sleeping worker inside. http://www.foxnews.com/us/2014/02/08/new-mexico-ambulance-hijacked-with-sleeping-worker-inside/

Athanasaw v. United States, 227 U.S. 326. (1913). http://supreme.justia.com/cases/federal/us/227/326/case.html

Aunapu, G., Epperson, S., & Kramer, S. (1993, December 27). Robbing the innocents. Time, 31.

Bajrektarevic, A. (2000). Trafficking in and smuggling of human beings: Linkages to organized crime: International legal measures: Statement digest. Vienna, Austria: International Centre for Migration Policy Development.

Belair, K. (2006). Unearthing the customary law foundations of "forced marriages" during Sierra Leone's civil war: the possible impact of international criminal law on customary marriage and women's rights in post-conflict Sierra Leone. Colum J Gender & Law, 15: 551.

Bell, J. L. (1995). Traumatic event debriefing: Service delivery designs and the role of social work. Soc Work, 40 (1): 36–43.

Bertone, A.M. (2000). Sexual trafficking in women: International political economy and the politics of sex. Gend Issues, 18 (1): 4–22.

Bonnar-Kidd, K.K. (2010). Sexual offender laws and prevention of sexual violence or recidivism. Am J Pubic Health, 100 (3): 412–419.

Book of Judges in the *Bible*. http://www.usccb.org/nab/bible/judges/judges21.htm.

Bryan Dos Santos Gomez Missing (2006). http://www.charleyproject.org/cases/d/dossantos-gomes_bryan.html

Butler, W.M., & Wrightsman, L.S. (1995). Child hostages. J Interpersonal Viol, 10 (3): 378–382.

Caffo, E., & Belaise, C. (2003). Psychological aspects of traumatic injury in children and adolescents. Child Adolesc Psychiatr Clin N Amer, 12 (3): 493–535.

California 2006 Election results. (no date). Proposition 83. http://igs.berkeley.edu/library/elections/proposition-83

Capron, A.M. & Danovitch, G. (2014). Kidneys aren't commodities. Los Angeles Times, June 30, 2014. http://www.latimes.com/opinion/op-ed/la-oe-0630-danovitch-and-20140630-story.html

Carmody, D.C., & Plass, P.S. (2000). Family abductions: An examination of the role of offender gender. Gend Issues, 18 (2): 58–73.

Carroll-Rowan, L., & Miltenberger, R.G. (1994). A comparison of procedures for teaching abduction prevention to preschoolers. Educ & Treatment of Children, 17: 113–129.

CBN. (1981). Annual reports. Central Bank of Nigeria.

Characteristics of suspected human trafficking incidents, 2007–2008. (no date). http://content.news14.com/human_trafficking.pdf.

Chiancone, J. (no date). Parental abduction: A review of the literature. Washington, DC: U.S. Department of Justice, Office of Justice Programs, Office of Juvenile Justice and Delinquency Prevention.

Chiancone, J., & Girdner, L. (2000). Issues in resolving cases of international child abduction. Final Report to the Office of Juvenile Justice and Delinquency Prevention. Washington, DC: American Bar Association Center on Children and the Law.

CNN U.S. (no date). Expanded self-defense laws. http://www.cnn.com/interactive/2012/04/us/table.selfdefense.laws/

COE, Council of Europe Convention. (2005). Council of Europe Convention on Action against Trafficking in Human Beings (CETS No. 197). http://conventions.coe.int/Treaties/Html/197.htm

Cohen, J.A., Deblinger, E., & Mannarino, A. (2004). Trauma-focused cognitive-behavioral therapy for sexually abused children. Psychiatr Times, 21 (10): 1–5.

Cohen, S. (1972). Folk devils and moral panics. New York: St. Martin's.

Convention for the Suppression of Unlawful Seizure of Aircraft (also known as the Hague Convention) Convention for the Suppression of Unlawful Seizure of Aircraft [Hijacking Convention], 860 U.N.T.S. 105,entered into force, Oct. 14, 1971

Copes, H., Hochstetler, & Cherbonneau, M. (2012). Getting the upper hands: Scripts for managing victim in carjackings. J Research Crime Delinq, 49 (2): 249–268.

Craun, S.W., & Theriot, M.T. (2009). Misperceptions of sex offender perpetration: Considering the impact of sex offender registration. J Interpers Violence, 24 (12): 2057–2072.

Cree, V.E. (2008). Confronting sex trafficking: Lessons from history. Int Soc Work, 51 (6): 763–776.

Wikipedia. (no date). Cuba – United States aircraft hijackings – Wikipedia. http://en.wikipedia.org/wiki/List_of_Cuba-US_aircraft_hijackings).

Dalley, M.L. (no date). Infant abduction from Canadian hospitals. National Missing Children Services, Royal Canadian Mounted Police. http://www.rcmp-grc.gc.ca/pubs/omc-ned/iach-rnnhc-eng.htm

Davidson, H. (1986, July-August). Missing children: A close look at the issue. Children Today, 26–30.

d'Orban, P.T. (1972). Baby stealing. Brit Med J, 2: 635–639.

d'Orban, P.T. (1976). Child stealing: A typology of female offenders. Brit J Criminol, 16: 275-281.

Duke, A. (2003, November 3). Bulgarian woman claims she's Maria's mom: 'We gifted her' to Roma family. www.cnn.com/2013/10/24/world/europe/europe-mystery-girls/

Dumont, M., Yzerbyt, V., & Wigboldus, D., et al. (2003). Social categorization and fear reactions to the September 11th terrorist attacks. Pers Soc Psychol Bull, 29 (12): 1509–1520.

D'Zurilla, T.J., & Goldfried, M.R. (1971). Problem solving and behavior modification. J Abn Psych, 78: 102–126.

Easton, J.A., & Turner, S.W. (1991). Detention of British citizens as hostages in the Gulf – Health, psychological, and family consequences. Brit Med J, 303: 1231–1234.

Ergas, Y. (2013). Babies without borders: Human rights, human dignity, and the regulation of international commercial surrogacy. Emory Intl Law Rev, 27: 117.

Eurasianet.org (January 27, 2000). International human rights law and bride kidnapping in Kyrgyzstan. Retrieved from http://www.eurasianet.org/departments/insight/articles/eav012400.shtml

Everett, E. (1997). Women's rights, the family, and organizational culture: a Lesotho case study. Gend Dev, 5 (1): 54–59.

Farrell, A., & Fahy, S. (2009). The problem of human trafficking in the U.S.: Public frames and policy responses. J Crim Justice, 37: 617–626.

Fass, P.S. (1993, December). Making and remaking an event: The Leopold and Loeb case in American culture. J Amer History, 80 (3): 919–951.

Fasting, U., Christensen, J., & Glending, S. (1998). Children sold for transplants: Medical and Legal aspects. Amnesty International—Danish Working Group for Children. Nurs Ethics, 5 (6): 518–526.

Feeney, F. (1986). Robbers as decision-makers. In D. Cornish & R. Clarke (Eds.), The Reasoning criminal: Rational choice perspectives on offending. New York: Springer- Verlag.

Feingold, D.A. (2010). Trafficking in numbers. In P. Andreas, K.M. Greenhill (Eds.), Sex, drugs, and body counts. London: Cornell University Press.

Feldmann, T.B., & Johnson, P.W. (1995). The application of psychotherapeutic and self psychology principles to hostage negotiations. J Am Acad Psychoanal, 23 (2): 207–221.

Finkelhor, D., & Dziuba-Leatherman, J. (1994). Children as victims of violence: A national survey. Pediatrics, 94: 413–420.

Finkelhor, D., Hotaling, G.T., & Sedlak, A. (1991). Children abducted by family members: National household survey of incidence and episode characteristics. J Marr Family, 53, 805–817.

Finkelhor, D., Ormrod, R., Turner, H., & Hamby, S.L. (2005). The victimization of children and youth: A comprehensive, national survey. Child Mistreat, 10: 5–25.

Finley, R.C. (1939–1940). The Lindbergh law. Geo Law J, 28, 908.

Fisher, H.A., & McGuire, M.F. (1934–1935). Kidnapping and the so-called Lindbergh Law. NYU Law Q Rev, 12, 646, 653.

Fisher, R., Ury, W., & Patton, B. (1991). Getting to yes. Negotiating agreement without giving in. (2nd ed.). New York: Penguin.

Fletcher, K. (1996). The management of released hostages. Adv in Psychiatr Treatment, 2: 232–240.

Forced Marriage – Wipedia. (no date). http://en.wikipedia.org/wiki/Forced_marriage

Forehand, R., Long, N., Zogg, C., & Parrish, E. (1989). Child abduction: Parent and child functioning following return. Clin Peds, 28 (7): 311–316.

Fowler, K. (2001). Medieval mercenaries: The Great Companies, Vol. 1. Oxford: Blackwell Publishers.

Fuselier, D., Zandt, C., & Lanceley, F. (1991). Hostage/barricade incidents. FBI Law Enforce Bull, Jan., 6–12.

Geneva' Convention on the High Seas. (April 29, 1958). (Also known as the Convention on the High Seas (April 29, 1958). U.N. Conference on the Law of the Sea (UNCLOS1). Entered into force 30 September 1962.

Gentleman, A. (2012). India nurtures business of surrogate motherhood. New York Times, March 10, 2008. http://www.nytimes.com/2008/03/10/world/asia/10surrogate.html?pagewanted=all&module=Search&mabReward=relbias%3Ar

Goldfried, M.R., & Davison, G.C. (1994). Clinical behavior therapy. New York: Wiley.

Government Accounting Office. (2006). Human trafficking: Better data, strategy, and reporting needed to enhance U.S. anti-trafficking efforts abroad. Washington, DC: Government Accounting Office.

Gray, J., Monday, M., & Stubblefield, G. (1999). Maritime terror. Boulder, CO: Vantage.

Greif, G.L., & Hegar, R.L. (1992). Impact on children of abduction by a parent. A review of the literature. Am J Orthopsychiat, 62 (4): 599–604.

Greves, H.M., Lozano, P. & Liu, L., et al. (2007). Immigrant families' perceptions on walking to school and school breakfast: A focus group study. Int J Behav Nutr Phys Act, 4: 64.

Gysels, M., Pool, R., & Nnalusiba, B. (2002). Women who sell sex in a Ugandan trading town: Life histories, survival strategies and risk. Soc Sci Med, 54 (2): 179–192.

Hammadi, S. (2011). Bangladesh arrest uncovers evidence of children forced into begging. http://www.guardian.co.uk/world/2011/jan/09/bangladesh-arrest-forced-begging.

Hashima, P.Y., & Finkelhor, D. (1999). Violent victimization of youth versus adults in the National Crime Victimization Survey. J Interpers Viol, 14: 799–820.

Hatcher, C., Barton, C., & Brooks, L. (1992). Families of missing children. Final report to Office of Juvenile Justice and Delinquency Prevention. San Francisco, CA: Center for the Study of Trauma. University of California, San Francisco.

Hatcher, C., Mohandie, K., & Turner, J., et al. (1998). The role of the psychologist in crisis/hostage negotiations. Behav Sci Law, 16 (4): 455–472.

Hegar, R.L., & Greif, G.L. (1991). Abduction of children by their parents: A survey of the problem. Social Work, 36 (5): 421–426.

Henrion, R. (2003). Female genital mutilations, forced marriages, and early pregnancies. Bull Acad Natl Med, 187 (6): 1051–66 [in French].

Hillman, R.G. (1981). The psychopathology of being held hostage. Amer J Psychiatr, 138: 1193-1197.

Hochstetler, A., Copes, H. & Williams, J.P. (2010). "That's not who I am:" How offenders commit violent acts and reject authentically violent selves. Justice Quarterly, 27 (4): 496- 516.

Hoke v. United States, 227 U.S. 308. http://supreme.justia.com/us227/308/case. html (1913).

Holloway v. U.S., 526 U.S. 1. https://supreme.justia.com/us/526/1/case.html.

Howell, J. (1989). Selected state legislation: A guide for effective state laws to protect children (2nd ed.). Washington, DC: National Center for Missing and Exploited Children.

Human Rights Watch. (2006). Reconciled to violence: State failure to stop domestic abuse and abduction of women in Kazakhstan. 8 (9): 117, Sept. 2006. http:// www.hrw.org/en/reports/2006/09/26/reconciled-violence.

Iaccino, L. (2014). Bolivia allows 10-year-olds to work legally to reduce poverty. International Business Times, July 4, 2014. http://www.ibtimes.co.uk/bolivia-allows-10-year-olds-work-legally-reduce-poverty-1455380

Ibnlive.com (2011, April 25). Fake kidnapping drama; NRI, friend booked. http://ibnlive.in.com/news/fake-kidnapping-drama-nri-friend-booked/1..

ILO, International Labour Organization. (2012a). 21 million people are now victims of forced labour, ILO says, International Labour Organization, Geneva. http://www.ilo.org/global/about-the-ilo/newsroom/news/WCMS_181961/lang–en/index.htm

ILO, International Labour Organization. (May 11, 2005). A global alliance against forced labour. ILO, May 11, 2005.

ILO, International Labour Organization. (2006). Forced labor statistics, Declaration of fundamental principles and rights at work, International Labour Office. http://digitalcommons.ilr.cornell.edu/cgi/viewcontent.cgi?article=1019&context=forcedlabor

ILO, International Labour Organization, International Programme on the Education of Child Labor (IPEC). (February 2002). Investigating the worst forms of child labour No. 20. Brazil. Children in drug trafficking: A rapid assessment.

ILO, International Labour Organization. (2013). Marking progress against child labour: Global estimates and trends 2000 – 2012. International Programme on the Elimination of Child Labour, International Labour Office, Geneva, Switzerland. http://www.ilo.org/wcmsp5/groups/public/—ed_norm/—ipec/documents/publication/wcms_221513.pdf

ILO, International Labour Organization, Minimum Age Convention, 1973 (No. 138). http://www.ilo.org/ilolex/cgi-lex/convde.pl?C138).

International Herald Tribune. (2006, December 5). Council of Europe says human trafficking has reached 'epidemic proportions' – Europe. http://www.iht.com/ articles/ap/2006/12/05/Europe/EU_GEN_Greece_Trafficking.php.

James, R.K., & Gilliland, B.E. (2001). Crisis intervention strategies (4th ed.). Stamford, CT: Brooks/Cole.

Johnston, J.R., Campbell, L.E., & Mayes, S.S. (1985). Latency children in post-separation and divorce disputes. J Amer Acad Child Psychiatry, 24: 563–574.

Jones Act of 1920 (also known as The Merchant Marine Act of 1920 (P.L. 66-261).

JUSTIA. (no date, a). *Hoke v. United States*-227U.S. 38 (1913). http://supreme.justia.com/cases/federal/us/227/308/case.html

JUSTIA, (no date, b). *Athanasaw & Sampson v. United States* – 227 U.S. 326 (1913). http://supreme.justia.com/cases/federal/us/227/326/case.html

Kaldor, M. (1998). Reconceptualizing organized violence. In Daniele Archibugi, David Held & Martin Köhler (Eds.). Re-imagining political cmty: Studies in cosmopolitan democracy, 91- 92.

Karolia, I. (2009). Father lashes out at negligent daycare. Eyewitness News, October 2, 2009. http://www.eyewitnessnews.co.za/articleprog.aspx?id=23077

Keen, M.H. (1965). The laws of war in the Late Middle Ages. Toronto: University of Toronto Press.

Kleinman, S. (1987). Trauma and its ramifications in Vietnamese victims of piracy. Jefferson J of Psychiatry, 5 (2): 3–15.

Kramer, D.N., & Landolt, M.A. (2011). Characteristics and efficacy of early psychological interventions in children and adolescents after single trauma: a meta-analysis. Eur J Psychotraumatol, 2 (10): 3402.

Kristof, N.D. (2014). He was supposed to take a photo. New York Times, March 22, 2014. http://www.nytimes.com/2014/03/23/opinion/sunday/kristof-he-was-supposed-to-take-a-photo.html

Kristof, N.D. (2012, January 25). How pimps use the Web to sell girls. New York Times, January 25, 2012. http://www.nytimes.com/2012/01/26/opinion/how-pimps-use-the-web-to-sell-girls.html?action=click&module=Search&region=searchResults&mabReward=relbias%3Ar%2C[%22RI%3A11%22%2C%22RI%3A16%22]&url=http%3A%2F%2Fquery.nytimes.com%2Fsearch%2Fsitesearch%2F%3Faction%3Dclick%26region%3DMasthead%26pgtype%3DHomepage%26module%3DSearchSubmit%26contentCollection%3DHomepage%26t%3Dqry546%23%2FPimps%2520use%2520the%2520web

Kristof, N.D. (2012, April 18). Not quite a teen, yet sold for sex. The New York Times, April 18, 2012. http://www.nytimes.com/2012/04/19/opinion/kristof-not-quite-a-teen-yet-sold-for-sex.html?action=click&module=Search&region=searchResults&mabReward=relbias%3Ar%2C[%22RI%3A10%22%2C%22RI%3A15%22]&url=http%3A%2F%2Fquery.nytimes.com%2Fsearch%2Fsitesearch%2F%3Faction%3Dclick%26region%3DMasthead%26pgtype%3DSectionFront%26module%3DSearchSubmit%26contentCollection%3Daponline%26t%3Dqry48%23%2FWhere%2520Pimps%2520Peddle

Kristof, N.D. (2014, February 12). When Emily was sold for sex. The New York Times, February 12, 2012. http://www.nytimes.com/2014/02/13/opinion/kristof-when-emily-was-sold-for-sex.html?action=click&module=Search&region=searchResults&mabReward=relbias%3Ar%2C[%22RI%3A10%22%2C%22RI%3A15%22]&url=http%3A%2F%2Fquery.nytimes.com%2Fsearch%2Fsitesearch%2F%3Faction%3Dclick%26region%3DMasthead%26pgtype%3DSectionFront%26module%3DSearchSubmit%26contentCollection%3Daponline%26t%3Dqry48%23%2FWhere%2520Pimps%2520Peddle

Kristof, N.D. (2012, March 17). Where pimps peddle their goods. The New York Times, March 17, 2012. http://www.nytimes.com/2012/03/18/opinion/sunday/kristof-where-pimps-peddle-their-goods.html?action=click&module=Search&region=searchResults&mabReward=relbias%3Ar%2C[%22RI%3A10%22%2C%22RI%3A15%22]&url=http%3A%2F%2Fquery.nytimes.-com%2Fsearch%2Fsitesearch%2F%3Faction%3Dclick%26region%3DMasthead%26pgtype%3DSectionFront%26module%3DSearchSubmit%26contentCollection%3Daponline%26t%3Dqry48%23%2FWhere%2520Pimps%2520Peddle

Kyckelhahn, T., Beck, A., & Cohen, T. (2008). Characteristics of suspected human trafficking incidents, 2007–2008. Washington, DC: Bureau of Justice Statistics, U.S. Department of Justice.

Lanceley, F.J. (1999). On-scene guide for crisis negotiators. Boca Raton, FL: CRC Press.

Lanning, K.V. (1995). Investigative analysis and summary of teaching points. In K.V. Lanning & A.W. Burgess (Eds.), Child molesters who abduct: Summary of the case in point series. 17–36. Alexander, VA: National Center for Missing and exploited Children.

LAPD, Los Angeles Police Department (2013). The LAPD official website: Carjacking (2013). http://www.lapdonline.or/crime_prevention/content_basic_view/1368

Lerner, J.S., Gonzalez, R.M., & Small, D.A., et al. (2003). Effects of fear and anger on perceived risks of terrorism: a national field experiment. Psychol Sci, 14 (2): 144–150.

Lefkowitz, M.R., & Fant, M.B. (2005). Women's life in Greece and Rome: A sourcebook in translation. JHU Press.

Levernier, J., & Cohen, H. (1977). (Eds.), The Indians and their captives. Westport, CT: Greenwood Publishers.

Libertadlatina.org (no date). LatAm – Brazil –Child prostitution crisis. Retrieved from http://www.libertadlatina.org

LII, Legal Information Institute. (no date). 18 U.S.Code 2421 – Transportation generally. Legal Information Institute, Cornell University Law School. http://www.law.cornell.edu/uscode/text/18/2421

Lotchin, R.W. (1974). San Francisco, 1846–1856: From hamlet to city. NY: Oxford University Press.

Louisiana law allows force on carjackers. August 17, 1997. http://www.nytimes.com/1997/08/17/us/louisiana-law-allows-force-on-carjackers.html
Luckenbill, D. (1981). Generating compliance: The case of robbery. Urban Life, 10: 25–46.
Luh, S.S. (2000). A mom's anguish. Baby abducted from hospital found dead. Chicago Sun-Times, May 3, 2000.
Lyons, J.A. (1987). Posttraumatic stress disorder in children and adolescents. A review of the literature. Develop & Behav Ped, 9 (6): 349.
Mack, J.E. (1994). Abduction: Human encounters with aliens. London: Simon and Schuster.
Mallett, M. (1974). Mercenaries and their masters: Warfare in Renaissance Italy. Lanham, MD: Rowman & Littlefield Publishers, Inc.
McDermott, R. (1992). Prospect theory in international relations: The Iranian hostage rescue mission. Polit Psychol, 13 (2), 237–263.
McGeorge, H.J. (1983). Plan carefully, rehearse thoroughly, execute violently: The tactical response to hostage situations. World Affairs, 146: 59–68.
McGuire, J. (1994). Re-painting the Golden Gate Bridge: Coordination of services for abducted children reunited with their families. Child Adolesc Soc Work J, 11: 149–164.
McNally, R.J., Lasko, N. B., & Clancy, S.A., et al. (2004). Psychophysiological responding during script-driven imagery in people reporting abduction by space aliens. Psycholog Sci, 15 (7): 493–497.
Meng, E. (1994–1995). Mail-order brides: Gilded prostitution and the legal response. U Mich J Law Reform, 28: 197.
Meltzer, M. (1994). Cheap raw material: How our youngest workers are exploited and abused. New York: Viking.
Merchant Shipping and Maritime Security Act 1997. http://www.unesco.org/culture/natlaws/media/pdf/gb/gb_merchantships&maritsecu1997_engorof.pdf
Minnesota Department of Public Safety. (2004). Interagency task force on domestic violence and sexual assault prevention report to the legislature. St. Paul, MN: Minnesota Department of Public Safety.
Misra, G., Mahal, A., & Shah, R. (2000). Protecting the rights of sex workers: The Indian experience. Health Hum Rights, 5 (1): 88–115.
Mitchell, J.M., Kurlycheck, M., & Hansen, J.A., et al. (2008). Examining child abduction by offender type patterns. Justice Q, 25 (3): 523–543.
Mohapatra, S. (2012). Achieving reproductive justice in the international surrogacy market. Annals of Health Law, 21(18): 191
Moore, S. (2009, August 14). In San Diego, jury indicts 17 in killings. New York Times. http://proquest.umi.com.libaccess.sjlibrary.org/pdqweb?index=0&sid..
Motor Vehicle Theft Law Enforcement Act, Pub.L. No. 98-547, 98 Stat. 2754 (1984).
Nader, K. (no date). Guilt following traumatic events. http://www.GeorgiaDisaster.info/MentalHealth/MH04DMHTraining/Guilt.ppf
Nahirny, C. (2005). Trends in infant abductions (2005). J Healthc Prot Manage, 21 (2): 95–99.
Namias, J. (1993). White captives: Gender and ethnicity in the American frontier. Chapel Hill, NC: University of North Carolina Press.
National Center for Health Statistics (1995). Vital statistics of the United States, 1991. 1, Natality. Washington, DC: Public Health Service.
National Center for Missing and Exploited Children (NCMEC). (1987). Accomplishing great things. Washington, DC: National Center for Missing and Exploited Children. www.missingkids.com
National Center for Missing and Exploited Children (NCMEC). (2002). NCME Annual Report 2002. Alexandria, VA: National Center for Missing and Exploited Children. www.missingkids.com
National Child Safety Council (NCSC) (no date). www.nationalchildsafetycouncil.org.
National Counterterrorism Center (no date). Worldwide incidents tracking system. Retrieved from http://wits.nctc.gov/Incidents.do

NHTRC, National Human Trafficking Resource Center. (2014). 2013 Statistical overview 1/1/2013 – 12/31/2013, Overview of incoming signals. National Human Trafficking Resource Center.

Noble, D.N., & Palmer, C.E. (1984). The painful phenomenon of child snatching. Soc Casework, 65 (6): 330–336.

Noesner, G.W. (1999). Negotiation concepts for commanders. FBI Law Enforcement Bull, 68: 6–14.

Noesner, G.W., & Webster, M. (1997). Crisis intervention: Using active listening skills in negotiations. FBI Law Enforcement Bull, 66: 13–19.

Parks, J.A. (2010). Care ethics and the global practice of commercial surrogacy. Bioethics, 24 (7): 333–340.

Penchaszadeh, V.B. (1997). Genetic identification of children of the disappeared in Argentina. J Am Med Womens Assoc, 52 (1): 16–21, 27.

Poche, C., Brouwer, R., & Swearingen, M. (1981). Teaching self-protection to young children. J Appl Behav Analysis, 14: 169–176.

Poche, C., Yoder, P., & Miltenberger, R. (1988). Teaching self-protection to children using television techniques. J Appl Behav Analysis, 21: 253–261.

Portland State University (no date). Multicultural topics in communication sciences & disorders: International adoption.

Pritchard, D. (2009). Man jailed for violent hostage-taking. Sun Media, The Winnipeg Sun. http://cnews.canoe.ca/CNEWS/Crime/2009/11/02/11602671-sun.html.

Projectjason.org (1987, August 4). Missing Girl: Carlina Renae White—NY—08/04/1987. Retrieved from http://projectjason.org.

Pub.L. 103-322. Retrieved from http://law.cornell.edu/jureeka/index.php?doc=USPubLaws&cong=103&no=322.

Pursurmankulova, B. (2004). Bride kidnapping: Benign custom or savage tradition? June 15, 2004. Voice of Freedom Initiative of the Human Rights Working Group.

Research based on case studies of victims of trafficking in human beings in 3 EU member states, i.e. Belgium, Italy, and The Netherlands. http://web.archive.org/web20080626234542/http://www.prostitute.nl/studie/documenten/mensenhandel/researchcasestraffick.pdf).

Ribando, C. (2005). Trafficking in persons in Latin America and the Caribbean. CRS Report for Congress.

Roberts, A.R. (Ed.). (2000). Crisis intervention handbook (2nd ed.). New York: Oxford University Press.

Rodrigues, J.J., Mehendale, S.M., & Shepherd, M.E., et al. (1995). Risk factors for HIV infection in people attending clinics for sexually transmitted diseases in India. BMJ, 311 (7000): 283–286.

Rogan, R.G., Hammer, M.R., & Van Zandt, C.R. (Eds.). (1997). Dynamic processes of crisis negotiation: Theory, research, and practice. Westport, CT: Praeger.

Romano, S.J., & McMann, M.F. (Eds.). (1997). Crisis negotiations: A compendium. Crisis Negotiation Unit, Critical Incident Response Group. Quantico, VA: FBI Academy.

Rumerman, J. (no date). Aviation security. U.S. Centennial of Flight Commissions. http://www.centennialofflight.gov/essay/Government_Role/

Sagan, C., & Druyan, A. (1997). The demon-haunted world. Science as a candle in the dark. New York, NY: Ballantine Books.

Salt, J. (2000). Trafficking and human smuggling: A European perspective. Intl Migration, Special Issue, 2000/1.

Sandler, T., & Scott, J.L. (1987). Terrorist success in hostage taking incidents: An empirical study. J Conflict Resolution, 31: 35–53.

Schetky, D.H., & Haller, L.H. (1983). Child psychiatry and law: Parental kidnapping. J Amer Acad Child Psychiatry, 22: 279–285.

Schiavone, S.K., & Jeglic, E.L. (2009). Public perception of sex offender social policies and the impact on sex offenders. Int J Offender Ther Comp Criminol, 53 (6): 679–695.

Sedlak, A.J., Finkelhor, D., & Hammer, H., et al. (2002). National incidence studies of missing, abducted, runaway, and thrownaway children. National estimates of missing children: An overview. Washington, DC: Department of Justice, Office of Juvenile Justice and Delinquency Prevention.

Senior, N., Gladstone, T., & Nurcombe, B. (1982). Child snatching: A case report. J Amer Acad Child Psychiatry, 21: 579–583.

Siegel, R.K. (1984). Hostage hallucinations. J Nervous & Mental Dis, 172: 264–272.

Skidmore, T.E. (2004). Brazil's persistent income inequality: Lessons from history. Latin Amer Politics Society, 46 (2): 133–150.

Skitka, L.J., Bauman, C.W., & Mullen, E. (2004). Political tolerance and coming to psychological closure following the September 11, 2001, terrorist attacks: an integrative approach. Pers Soc Psychol Bull, 30 (6): 743–756.

solutions.abroad.com. (no date). Kidnapping in Mexico. http://www.solutions abroad.com/en/security/security-category/kidnap…

Soothill, K., Francis, B., Ackerley, E., & Fligelstone, R. (2002). Murder and serious sexual assault: What criminal histories can reveal about future serious offending. Police Research Series Paper 144. London: Home office. http://www.Homeoffice.gov.uk/rds/prgpdfs/prs144.pdf

Soothill, K., Francis, B., & Liu, J. (2010). The importance of co-convictions in the prediction of dangerous recidivism: Blackmail and kidnapping as a demonstration study. Criminology & Crim Just, 10 (1): 23–36.

Spar, D.L. (2006). The baby business: How money, science, and politics drive the commerce of conception. Boston, MA: Harvard Business School Press.

Stage 6 Cases of Obsessive Ex Syndrome. http://www.obsessive-ex.com/oex/violence.html.

Sunder, M. (2204). Piercing the veil. Yale Law J, 112 (6): 1399–1472.

Taylot, J., Bolsvert, D., Sims, B., & Garver, C. (2013). An examination of gender and age in print media accounts of child abductions. Crim Just Stud: A Crit J Crime Law Soc, 26(2): 151–167.

Terr, L. (1983). Child snatching: A new epidemic of an ancient malady. J of Ped, 103: 151–156.

thefreelibrary.com. (no date). An ounce of prevention: Improving the preventative measures of

Thorne, C., Ferencic, N., & Malyuta, R., et al. (2010). Central Asia: Hotspot in the worldwide HIV epidemic. Lancet Infect Dis, 10 (7): 479–488.

Topalli, V., & Wright, R. (2004). Dubs, dees, beats, and rims: Carjacking and urban violence. In D. Dabney (Ed.), Criminal behaviors: A text reader. Belmont, CA: Wadsworth Publishing.

Tsutsumi, K., & Honda, S. (2005). OAS Rapid Assessment Report: Trafficking in persons from the Latin American and Caribbean (LAC) region to Japan. http://www.oas.org/atip/PDFs/Rapid%20Assessment%20(English).pdf.

Turner, J.T. (1985). Factors influencing the development of the hostage identification syndrome. Political Psychol, 6 (4): 705–711.

Uniform Child Custody Jurisdiction Act (UCCJA) (19 U.S.C. chapter 16) www.uniformlaws.org/shared/docs/child_custody_jurisdiction/uccja68.pdf

UN, United Nations. (2004, March 10) See Human Rights and Terrorism, G.A. Res. 58/174, 12, U.N. Doc. A/RES/58/174 (Mar. 10, 2004).

UN, United Nations, Convention on the Law of the Sea of 10 December 1982 (LOSC). http://www.un.org/depts/los/convention_agreements/convention_overview_convention.htm

UN, United Nations, Global Programme against Trafficking in Human Being. (no date). Coalition against Trafficking in Human Beings in the Philippines – Phase 1. Trafficking of Filipino women to Japan: Examining the experiences and perspectives of victims and government experts. http://www.unodc.org/pdf/crime/human_trafficking/Exec_summary_UNU.pdf

UN, United Nations, Office for the Coordination of Humanitarian Affairs (no date). Ethiopia: Surviving forced marriage. http://www.irinnews.org/Report.aspx?ReportID=69993

UN, United Nations, Office on Drugs and Crime. (no date). UN highlights human trafficking, BBC News, March 26, 2007. http://news.bbc.co.uk/2/hi6497799.stm).

UNCRC, United Nations Convention on the Rights of the Child. (1989). United Nations, Office of the High Commissioner for Human Rights. http://www.ohchr.org/EN/ProfessionalInterest/Pages/CRC.aspx

UNODC, United Nations Office on Drugs and Crime. (2004). Protocol to prevent, suppress and punish trafficking in persons, especially women and children, supplementing the United Nations Convention against Transnational Organized Crime. Annex II, Article 3, paragraph (a), p51 in U. N. Convention Against Transnational Organized Crime and the Protocols Thereto. United Nations Office on Drugs and Crime, Vienna, Austria. http://www.unodc.org/documents/treaties/UNTOC/Publications/TOC%20Convention/TOCebook-e.pdf

UN.GIFT. (no date). UN.GIFT_Kern_gesamt.pdf. http://ungift.org/docs/ungift/pdf/about/UNGIFT_progress_report09.pdf

UN.GIFT. (no date). UN.GIFT. http://ungift.org/ungift/index.html

Uniform Child Abduction Prevention Act, 2006 (cited in Miller et al. 2008)

Uniform Child Custody Jurisdiction Act (UCCJA) (19 U.S.C. chapter 16)

United States Bureau of the Census. (1989). Current population reports, Series P-20, no. 433 433. Marital status and living arrangements: March 1988. Washington, DC: U.S. Government Printing Office.

United States Department of Justice. (no date). Criminal section selected case summaries. Human trafficking. Washington, DC: U.S. Department of Justice, Civil Rights Division. http://www.justice.gov/crt/about/crm/selcases.php

United States Department of State. (2004).Victims of Trafficking and Violence Protection Act of 2000: Trafficking in persons report. http://www.state.gov/g/tip/rls/tiprpt/2004/

United States Federal Bureau of Investigation, The Dallas Division (no date). Swisher County, Texas man sentenced to 14 years in federal prison without parole for kidnapping former girlfriend. U.S. Department of Justice Press Release. http://dallas.fbi.gov/dojpressrel10/d1033110.htm

United States Subcommittee on Federal Workforce and Agency Organization. (2006, Nov. 6). Travel vs. terrorism. Washington, D.C.: United States Subcommittee on Federal Workforce and Agency Organization.

U.S. v. Cortner, No. 3:93-00009, U.S. D.Ct., M.D. Tenn, decided Oct. 19, 1993.

U.S. v. Singleton, 16 F.3d 1419 (5th Cir. 1994).

U.S. v. Watson, 815 F. Supp. 827 (1993).

Van Hasselt, V.B., Romano, S.J., & Vecchi, G.M. (2008). Role playing: Applications in hostage and crisis negotiation skills training. Behav Modif, 32 (2): 248–263.

Vila, G., Porche, L.-M., & Mouren-Simeoni, M.-C. (1999). An 18th month longitudinal study of posttraumatic disorders in children who were taken hostage in their school. Psychosom Med, 61 (6): 746–754.

Violent Crime Control and Law Enforcement Act of 1994, Pub. L. No. 103-322, 108 Stat. 2119.

Weiner, M.H. (2000). International child abduction and the escape from domestic violence. Fordham Law Rev, 69: 593.

Wellner, B., Lemmon, D., Brown, C., et al. (2009). Geneseo standoff suspect has history of domestic violence, authorities say. http://qctimes.com/news/local/articles_5e45d6c-e6d5-11de-b96b-001cc4c002e0.html.

Weschler, L. (1990). A miracle, a universe: Settling accounts with torturers. Pp. 146–147. New York: Pantheon Books.

Wheeler, J.G., George, W.H., & Marlatt, G.A. (2006). Relapse prevention for sexual offenders: Considerations for the "abstinence violation effect." Sex Abuse, 18 (3): 233–248.

Widgren, J. (1994). Multilateral co-operation to combat trafficking in migrants and the role of international organizations. Paper presented at the Seminar of the IOM on International Response to Trafficking in Migrants and Safeguarding of Migrant Rights. Geneva, Switzerland, October.

Wikipedia. (no date). Aircraft hijacking. http://en.wikipedia.org/wiki/Aircraft_hijacking.
Wikipedia. (no date). Airport security. http://en.wikipedia.org/ wiki/Airport _security.
Wikipedia. (no date).Bonnot Gang. http://en.wikipedia.org/wiki/Bonnot_Gang.
Wikipedia. (no date). Hijacking. http://en.wikipedia.org/wiki/Hijackings.
Wikipedia. (no date). Impressment. http://en.wikipedia/wiki/Impressment.
Wikipedia. (no date). Kidnapping. http://en.wikipedia.org/wiki/Kidnapping.
Wikipedia. (no date). List of hijacking of Indian eroplanes. http://en.wikipedia.org/wiki/List_of_hijacking_of_Indian_aeroplanes
Wikipedia (no date). List of hijacking of Turkish airplanes. http://en.wikipedia.org/wiki/List_of_hijacking_of_Turkish_airplanes
Wikipedia (no date). List of notable aircraft hijackings. http://en.wikipedia.org/wiki/List_of_notable_of_aircraft_hijackings
Wikipedia (no date). List of Cuba – United States aircraft hijackings. http://en.wikipedia.org/wiki/List_of_Cuba-US_aircraft_hijackings).
Wikipedia (no date). Tokyo Convention. Also known as the Convention on offences and Certain Other Acts Committed on Board Aircraft. http://en.wikipedia.org/wiki/Tokyo_Convention.
Williams, R. (2008, July 3). British-born teenagers being trafficked for sexual exploitation within UK, police say. http://www.guardian.co.uk/society/2008/jul/03/childprotection.internationalcrime.
Wilson, C. (1994). Freedom at risk: The kidnapping of free blacks in America, 1780–1865. Lexington, KY: The University Press of Kentucky.
Winch, J. (1987). Philadelphia and the other underground railroad. The Pennsylvania Magazine, 111 (1): 3–25.
Wright, R. (2009). Kidnap for ransom: Resolving the unthinkable. Boca Raton, FL: CRC Press, Taylor & Francis Group.
Wurtele, S.K. (1990). Teaching personal safety skills to four-year-old children: A behavioral approach. Behav Ther, 21: 25–32.

Index

S. Morewitz, *Kidnapping and Violence*,
https://doi.org/10.1007/978-1-4939-2117-1

MIX
Papier aus verantwortungsvollen Quellen
Paper from responsible sources
FSC® C105338

If you have any concerns about our products,
you can contact us on
ProductSafety@springernature.com

In case Publisher is established outside the EU,
the EU authorized representative is:
Springer Nature Customer Service Center GmbH
Europaplatz 3, 69115 Heidelberg, Germany

Printed by Libri Plureos GmbH
in Hamburg, Germany